More Peoples of Las Vegas
One City, Many Faces

EDITED BY Jerry L. Simich AND Thomas C. Wright

UNIVERSITY OF NEVADA PRESS ▲▲ RENO & LAS VEGAS

Wilbur S. Shepperson Series in Nevada History
Series Editor: Michael Green

University of Nevada Press, Reno, Nevada 89557 USA
Copyright © 2010 by University of Nevada Press
All rights reserved
Manufactured in the United States of America

Library of Congress Cataloging-in-Publication Data
More peoples of Las Vegas : one city, many faces /
edited by Jerry L. Simich and Thomas C. Wright.
p. cm. — (Wilbur S. Shepperson series in Nevada history)
Includes bibliographical references and index.
ISBN 978-0-87417-817-3 (pbk. : alk. paper)
1. Immigrants—Nevada—Las Vegas. 2. Minorities—
Nevada—Las Vegas. 3. Ethnology—Nevada—Las Vegas.
4. Cultural pluralism—Nevada—Las Vegas. 5. Las Vegas
(Nev.)—Emigration and immigration. 6. Las Vegas
(Nev.)—Ethnic relations. 7. Las Vegas (Nev.)—Social
conditions. I. Simich, Jerry L. II. Wright, Thomas. C.
F849.L35M67   2010
308.8009793'135—dc22   2009039099

The paper used in this book is a recycled stock made from
30 percent post-consumer waste materials, certified by
FSC, and meets the requirements of American National
Standard for Information Sciences—Permanence of Paper
for Printed Library Materials, ANSI/NISO Z39.48-1992
(R2002). Binding materials were selected for strength and
durability.

First Printing
19 18 17 16 15 14 13 12 11 10
5 4 3 2 1

WILBUR S. SHEPPERSON SERIES IN NEVADA HISTORY

MORE PEOPLES OF LAS VEGAS

CONTENTS

List of Illustrations   vii
Preface   ix
Introduction   xi

1: The Irish   1
   Michael Green

2: The Germans   29
   Carole Cosgrove Terry

3: The Japanese   52
   Andrew B. Russell and Fumiko Sasaki

4: The Cubans   76
   William Clayson

5: The Scandinavians   98
   Jonathan R. Strand and Melanie C. Young

6: The Muslims   114
   Aslam Abdullah

7: The Armenians   131
   Michelle Tusan

8: The Argentines   149
   Guillermo Monkman

9: The Koreans   165
   Kathleen Ja Sook Bergquist

10: The Thais   183
    Jiemin Bao

11: The Ethiopians   198
    Michelle Kuenzi

12: The Guatemalans 213
    John P. Tuman and Dawn Gearhart

13: The Colombians 231
    Timothy Pratt

    Contributors 241
    Index 245

ILLUSTRATIONS

(following page 130)
Five Foley brothers
Three Nevadans at Sons of Erin St. Patrick's Day parade
Tobel family observes their artesian well
Vagabonds German Karneval Club
Yonema "Bill" Tomiyasu
Japanese American Club at International Festival
Lujan family in 1964
Lujan family in 1967
Sons of Norway at Las Vegas Centennial Helldorado Days parade
Dr. Lonnie Hammargren
Students and teacher at Sunday Islamic school
Kirk Kerkorian
Jerry Tarkanian
Argentine Association of Las Vegas, Día de las Américas parade
Gaucho in Argentine Association float
Kim Sisters in casino
Sue Kim and the Kim Brothers
Buddhist monks at Thai Kathin festival
Thai women at Las Vegas Buddhist temple
Elizabeth and Fasil at Ethiopian Millennium Celebration
Members of EMAN leadership with Congresswoman Dina Titus
Huelga de Dolores celebration
Protest against FARC guerrillas

PREFACE

The University of Nevada Press published the first book on ethnicity of Las Vegas, *The Peoples of Las Vegas: One City, Many Faces,* in the city's centennial year, 2005. As long-term Las Vegans, we had observed the process of ethnic diversification for over three decades. As early as the 1970s, we noted new groups when they became visible in the Las Vegas Valley and sought out the ethnic restaurants and markets that they established. In 1976, we attended the first International Food Festival (today's International Food and Folklife Festival), and in the mid-1980s contemplated researching local ethnic groups in a more systematic way. By the turn of the twenty-first century, Las Vegas's ethnicity had evolved to the point that it begged for a study.

In the first book, we examined thirteen different ethnic groups: Southern Paiutes; African Americans; Jews; Mexicans, Salvadorans, and Chileans; Chinese, Filipinos, and peoples from the Indian subcontinent; and Greeks, Italians, Croats, and Poles. Some of those groups are prominent and long established, while others are virtually unknown and recently arrived.

Our purpose in this book is to build upon the findings of the first publication by examining thirteen additional ethnic groups that call Las Vegas home. We again follow the approach of probing both large and small, long-established and newly transplanted ethnic groups. From Asia, we include the Japanese, Koreans, and Thais; from Latin America, the Cubans, Guatemalans, Colombians, and Argentines; from Europe, the Irish, Germans, Armenians, and Scandinavians; from Africa, the Ethiopians; and we include a religiously rather than geographically defined group, the Muslims.

In the first book, we included a substantial amount of historical background to the contemporary scene in order to provide context for the case studies. To avoid duplication, that historical overview is not included in the present volume. Nonetheless, we believe that readers of this book would be well served to consult those historical sections—the introduction and chapters 1 and 2—in order to better appreciate the long-term transformation of a small railroad town into an ethnically diverse and vibrant metropolis.

We wish to thank the authors of the chapters that follow. Clearly, this book could not have been done without them. Most authors are members of the ethnic groups they researched, while some are not, but all donned ethnographers' hats and brought their subjects into the bright light of day. We especially salute the knowledge, energy, and versatility of Michael Green, who wrote about the Jews in the first book and the Irish in this one and cheerfully lent his extensive knowledge of Las Vegas history to both works.

We appreciate the University of Nevada Press for its interest in our topic and encouragement for us to undertake the current study. We are especially indebted to Press director Joanne O'Hare and to Charlotte Dihoff, Matt Becker, and Sara Vélez Mallea for their support along the way. We also value the copyediting performed by Sarah Nestor. Thanks go to Don Mirjanian for his skillful work with census data. And Mary Wammack again applied the admirable editorial and organizational talents that made the completion of the first volume possible.

INTRODUCTION

Historically, Las Vegas has not been known as an ethnic city. It is no New York, Chicago, or Los Angeles—cities whose identities are wrapped up in ethnic neighborhoods, churches, markets, restaurants, organizations, and festivals. Except for the traditional African American Westside, the Southern Paiute reservation, and the relatively recent Hispanic barrio in the northeast, Las Vegas lacks the ethnic neighborhoods that define the traditional American ethnic city. While Las Vegas hosts a plethora of ethnic restaurants, markets, clubs, and places of worship, these are not primarily organized within ethnic spatial boundaries; rather, they are scattered across the Las Vegas Valley, often housed in the omnipresent strip malls, where they are largely invisible to passersby. There are large numbers of ethnic festivals and other events throughout the year, but, perhaps because Las Vegas offers a great variety of competing entertainments, they do not seem to be widely known outside of the ethnic communities.

The present diversity of the peoples of Las Vegas is based on internal growth, migration, and immigration. From its founding through the 1970s, Las Vegas was essentially a community of European Americans; blacks; smaller minorities of Mexicans, Chinese, and Japanese; a small number of Southern Paiutes; and a sprinkling of other peoples. The most notable demographic change before the 1980s was the beginning of the growth of the Hispanic, primarily Mexican, population in the 1960s.[1] Then beginning in the 1980s, a sustained local economic boom created an almost insatiable demand for labor and opportunities for managers and entrepreneurs. That boom and the rise of Las Vegas as a retirement community quickened the pace of migration from within the United States. Las Vegas attracted increasing numbers of European Americans as well as African Americans and Native Americans from around the country, Mexican Americans from the Southwest, and Pacific Islanders.[2]

In 1980 Las Vegas's population was 82.5 percent white, 9.8 percent black, and 7.4 percent Hispanic; a few thousand Asians and American Indians rounded out the local demography. The ethnic diversification that became noticeable in the 1980s exploded in the 1990s. Las Vegas grew by 83.5 percent between 1990 and 2000—to 1,563,282 census-counted persons—led by increases of 260.6 percent among Asians and 262.0 percent among Hispanics. In 2000 Las Vegas was approximately 63.1 percent white, 20.6 percent Hispanic, 8.4 percent non-Hispanic black, 6.2 percent Asian, 0.7 percent American Indian, 0.2 percent North African, and 0.2 percent black African. Census Bureau estimates for 2006, the most recent available when the writing was finished, are not as detailed as decennial census data, but they reveal a continuation of previous trends. Las Vegas in 2006 was 53.0 percent white, 27.1 percent Hispanic, 9.4 percent non-Hispanic black, 6.9 percent Asian, and 0.6 percent American Indian, with the remaining 3 percent categorized as "other."[3]

These broad census categories merely scratch the surface of the changes in Las Vegas's ethnic makeup. People tend to think of the nearly one-quarter of Las Vegans who are classified as "Hispanic" as Mexicans or Mexican Americans, ignoring the growing presence of peoples from all the Latin American countries, most of which, in turn, are rich in ethnic diversity. Likewise, the "Asian" category tends, in the common sensibility, to homogenize peoples with profoundly different ethnicities and cultures. Similarly, if we did not probe beyond the category "American Indian," we would not discover that in addition to the native Southern Paiutes, Las Vegas is home to members of virtually every one of the dozens of tribes found in the United States and Canada as well as Indians from Latin America. And recent immigration from the Caribbean and Africa has greatly diversified Las Vegas's black population. Moreover, identifying immigrants by country of origin further blurs ethnic distinctions, as many countries—Mexico, the Philippines, India, and Nigeria, for example—host dozens or even hundreds of different ethnic groups within their borders.

It is immigration, above all, that has driven the ethnic diversification of Las Vegas in recent years. After declining under the impact of restrictive immigration laws, the Great Depression, and World War II, immigration to the United States has increased in each decade since the 1950s. To the traditional sources of immigrants—Europe, a few Asian countries, Mexico, and Canada—have been added virtually all the world's countries. In the 1990s, the greatest decade of immigration in American history, over thirteen million immigrants came to the United States. In 2000 over thirty-one million people, representing 11.1 percent of the U.S. population, were foreign born.[4]

Recent immigration has altered Las Vegas's demography even more profoundly than that of the country as a whole. The 2000 U.S. census indicated that 18.0 percent of Las Vegas's population was foreign born—over 50 percent above the national figure. Of the city's foreign born, 61.1 percent were from Latin America, 23.6 percent from Asia, 9.9 percent from Europe, 3.1 percent from "Northern America," 1.7 percent from Africa, and 0.4 percent from Oceania. Reflecting the impact of immigration, 26.0 percent of the population over five years of age spoke a language other than English at home, compared to the national figure of 17.9 percent. In 1990 Las Vegas ranked 44th among the 331 U.S. metropolitan regions for the proportion of its population comprised of "new" immigrants—those who had arrived in the last decade; in 2000, Las Vegas had risen to 26th. Estimates for 2006 confirm the presence of a growing immigrant population: 21.8 percent of Las Vegas's population was foreign born, compared with 12.5 percent nationally; 30.7 percent spoke a language other than English at home, compared with 19.7 percent nationally.[5]

Some immigrants have come directly to Las Vegas from their homelands around the globe, attracted by abundant jobs that do not require preexisting skills or proficiency in English: construction, landscaping and lawn maintenance, "back of the house" jobs in the casino resorts and restaurants, and other low-end occupations. Others came to southern Nevada after initially settling elsewhere in the United States, drawn by the prospect of jobs, cheaper living costs than in many metropolitan areas, or the opportunity for family reunification; the Los Angeles area has been a major source of secondary immigration to Las Vegas. Still others have arrived through refugee resettlement, a U.S. government program that places persons officially classified as refugees, and sometimes their families, in communities that can absorb them. While refugees have comprised a small fraction of Las Vegas's immigrants, some of them were undoubtedly the first person from their country to make the Las Vegas Valley their home. The first refugee from Uzbekistan, Togo, or Kosovo who resettled in Las Vegas normally started a stream of family members, fellow refugees from other U.S. locales, and in some cases undocumented compatriots. Thus refugee resettlement has had a multiplier effect in the process of ethnic diversification.[6]

There are many indications that ethnic diversification continues. In the first volume, two of our contributing authors identified restaurants serving forty-one ethnic communities, from the common Thai and Mexican to the more rare Honduran and Romanian, and markets catering to twenty-two ethnic groups in addition to numerous hybrid ethnic establishments.[7] Now we can add Malaysian, Indonesian, Serbian, Mongolian, Jamaican, and Himalayan (Tibetan, Nepalese, and Indian) to the list of restaurants and Laotian and Bulgarian to the markets; and since many of these ethnic institutions do not advertise in the Yellow Pages, we are confident that there are more to be discovered. There are more ethnic media and more, and more diverse, places of organized worship than existed just a few years ago, and one observes a growing number of languages on the commercial signs that dot the Valley.

There are other quantitative measures of the continuing diversification of Las Vegas's population. As recently as the 1970–71 school year, the student body of the Clark County School District was 82.6 percent white, 12.6 percent black, 3.4 percent Hispanic, 0.5 percent Asian, and 0.4 percent American Indian. By 2000–2001, whites, while still the largest group, had become a minority at 49.9 percent, while Hispanics had reached 28.8 percent, blacks 13.8 percent, Asians 6.6 percent, and American Indians 0.9 percent. Statistics for 2007–2008 reveal impressive growth of both the Hispanic (39.9 percent) and Asian (9.3 percent) populations, stability of the black (13.9 percent) and American Indian (0.8 percent) populations, and a significant decline of the white student body (36.1 percent); the Hispanic public-school population thus has passed the white. While there were 108 private schools in Clark County in 2007–2008, that number had not grown since 2003–2004 and the number of home-schooled students in 2007–2008 had dropped from the number in 2000–2001. Therefore, it appears that the Clark County School District enrollment figures are a reasonably accurate snapshot of the racial makeup of the Valley's youth.[8]

Data from the Clark County Court Interpreters Office shed further light on the growth of an immigrant population in the Valley. Six years after its establishment, during a twelve-month period in 1981–82, the office handled 1,655 court cases, or 138 per month, in 25 languages. In 1994 the load was 1,026 per month. By 2002 the monthly case load reached 2,953, and the office was charged with providing certified interpreters for 82 languages, 79 of which had been employed between 1994 and 2000. In 2007 the staff were providing service in 4,781 cases per month—a growth of 466 percent since 1994 and 162 percent in the 2002–2007 period. Even these impressive statistics fail to plumb the depth of Las Vegas's diversification. They do not reveal the number of Latin American countries whose natives were serviced, for example; and inversely, the growth of English-speaking populations from the Caribbean and parts of Africa is, of course, absent from these figures.[9]

Naturalization, or the granting of U.S. citizenship, provides yet another window on immigration. There were 3,578 immigrants naturalized in the 1970s in Nevada, a large majority of those in Las Vegas; in the 1990s, the number had risen to 24,736. During 2005–2006, 11,819 persons were naturalized in Las Vegas alone. A snapshot of naturalizations in Las Vegas in three recent periods reinforces our other observations. In 1985–87, people naturalized came from 79 countries; in 1999–2000, from 131 countries; in 2005–2006, from 138 countries. After constituting a majority in earlier years, persons from western Europe represented 8.9 percent of Las Vegas's new citizens in 1985–87, 2.9 percent in 1999–2000, and had rebounded to 3.1 percent in 2005–2006. The greatest suppliers of new citizens in 2005–2006 were, in order, Mexico, the Philippines, Cuba, El Salvador, and the People's Republic of China.[10]

A number of the book's chapters refer to Las Vegas's economic boom as a major, if not the major, pull factor fueling the Valley's rapid population growth and increasing its ethnic diversity. In several cases the authors refer to the boom as continuing, although it ended in 2008. That is because the boom collapsed shortly after the chapters were written. Since 2008, population growth in Las Vegas has slowed substantially. The number of immigrants arriving in Las Vegas also appears to have declined. The national press has reported that some Mexican and Central American immigrants have been returning home, despite bleak prospects there. Locally, a telling sign of the reduction of immigrant newcomers is enrollment in the Clark County School District's English-language learners program. After growing by 132 percent between 1998 and 2008, enrollment fell by nearly 2 percent between September 2008 and February 2009.[11] We cannot project the short-term effect of the economic recession on Las Vegas ethnicity, but we are confident that when prosperity returns, Las Vegas will once again be a magnet for both migrants and immigrants.

The findings of our initial study of Las Vegas ethnicity confirmed the notion that many local immigrants, particularly recent ones, live transnationally. Transnationalism is a complex phenomenon that derives from the recent surge in immigration, the revolution in telecommunications, globalization, and a host of other factors. At its most basic, transnationalism may be defined as "sustained ties of persons, networks, and organizations across nation-state borders."[12] Many immigrants today do not need to give up their identification with their home country, particularly those who comprise large communities. They have the ability to continue living their native cultures as fully as they choose _and_ are able to do so, while simultaneously integrating, to varying degrees, into U.S. society and culture. They may even have more than two locales that they call home. These dual or multiple ties are at the root of the concern expressed by those who argue that recent immigrants do not assimilate. This argument ignores the fact that, compared with the Europeans who arrived during the great wave of transatlantic immigration (1880–1914), today's immigrants possess far greater means of retaining their native cultures and ties to their home countries.[13]

The manifestations of transnationalism are readily visible in Las Vegas. Immigrants communicate with family and friends via the Internet, telephone, and fax. They receive news from the home country over the Internet and watch sports and entertainment on satellite television. Many can afford travel to the home country, where they have family and may retain a home, thanks to discounted air tickets or, in the case of Mexicans and Central Americans, to bus connections (Las Vegas has two companies offering direct service from Las Vegas to the Mexican border at El Paso). All these available tools make communication between Las Vegas and the rest of the world easier and faster than it was from coast to coast in the United States a generation ago.

Transnational living is not only facilitated by the ease of communication and travel. Local institutions play a fundamental role in sustaining ties with the home country. Ethnic restaurants reinforce identities through food and sometimes serve as the sites for weddings and other important life-cycle events. Ethnic markets are multipurpose institutions: they supply foods from home, both imported nonperishables and perishables grown in California for specific ethnic tastes. Markets also supply music, movies, and publications from the home country and often feature money-remitting services. They carry the locally published ethnic newspapers in the case of the larger groups, with the Los Angeles-published newspapers reaching out to the smaller groups still incapable of supporting a local publication. Local radio and television stations play an important role in reinforcing home cultures. Entertainers from the home country tour the United States and stop with increasing frequency in Las Vegas. Clubs, folkloric groups, and religious organizations work to preserve and disseminate national and even regional cultures of origin.[14]

Several of the groups examined in our first volume demonstrated transnationalism, the small colony of around one thousand Chileans providing a good example. Some Chileans came to the United States to escape the state terrorism of the Pinochet dictatorship (1973–90), and more have come for economic opportunity. In Las Vegas Chileans have a very active organization, the Chilean-American Association of Las Vegas. Their folkloric music and dance group, Ecos de Chile, performs locally and regionally. Too small to sustain a market, the Chilean community has had a restaurant off and on. Many local Chileans retain dual citizenship. Las Vegas Chileans have been active in the international "Encounters of Chileans Abroad," an organization dedicated to strengthening ties between the diaspora and the Chilean homeland. It lobbies for easing restrictions on the granting of Chilean nationality to immigrants' children and for the right to vote in national elections. In an interesting case of the country of origin's promoting transnationalism, the Chilean government in 2000 created the Directorate for Chilean Communities Abroad and officially designated the expatriates around the globe as "Region XIV"—an addition to the thirteen administrative regions into which the country is divided.[15]

A few words about definitions are in order. First, the concept of ethnicity, write the editors of the *Harvard Encyclopedia of American Ethnic Groups,* "is an immensely complex phenomenon."[16] Rather than adopt a strict definition, they list a series of components of ethnicity, some or all of which may describe any particular ethnic group. These are: common geographic origin; migratory status; race; language or dialect; religious faith or faiths; ties that transcend kinship, neighborhood, and community boundaries; shared traditions, values, and symbols; literature, folklore, and music; food preferences; settlement and employment patterns; special interests in regard to politics in the homeland and in the United States; institutions that serve specifically to maintain the group; an internal sense of distinctiveness; and an external perception of distinctiveness. The weight given to any of these characteristics depends, of course, on a cluster of factors, such as the size of the group, the length of its time in the United States, and its degree of assimilation.[17]

Second, we need to define the geographic parameters of our study. To most people, Las Vegas means the Las Vegas Valley, which includes the cities of Las Vegas, North Las Vegas, Henderson, and the contiguous urban core of unincorporated Clark County. The 2000 U.S. census defines Las Vegas as the city of Las Vegas, which includes only a portion of the urban area and excludes the Strip. Therefore, the statistics for 2000 found throughout the book refer either to Clark County or to the Las Vegas, Nevada-Arizona Metropolitan Statistical Area (MSA).

The urban core of the Las Vegas Valley contained 96.4 percent of Clark County's population in 2000; it contained 84.9 percent of the MSA, which adds Nye County, Nevada, and Mohave County, Arizona, to Clark County. Chapter authors cite both Clark County and MSA figures. Given the concentration of most non-European ethnic groups in the urban core, the figures for Clark County, and even more for the MSA, probably underreport the percentage of Las Vegas Valley residents who belong to Latin American, Asian, and African groups.[18] Ethnic diversity in the Las Vegas Valley, then, may be even more pronounced than our statistics suggest.

Third, since this book appears well after the 2000 census and prior to the release of the findings of the 2010 census, the chapter authors, where feasible, have incorporated some population estimates for 2006 from the Census Bureau's American Community Survey. These data are based on samples of the population rather than on the population as a whole. While they may be less reliable than regular census information, one must take into account the difficulties that census takers have in tracking down immigrants, in part because some of the newly arrived may be undocumented and others may view government officials with suspicion. This means that neither body of data should be treated as definitive, particularly in the case of immigrant populations. The Census Bureau maintains, however, that comparisons between the 2006 American Community Survey and the 2000 census in matters such as race and claimed ancestry are valid.[19]

The chapters that follow, we believe, strengthen the argument we made in the first volume that Las Vegas over the past three decades has become a city whose ethnicity is rich, varied, and worthy of study.

Notes

1. See Eugene P. Moehring, "Immigration, Ethnicity, and the Rise of Las Vegas," in *The Peoples of Las Vegas: One City, Many Faces,* ed. Jerry L. Simich and Thomas C. Wright (Reno and Las Vegas: University of Nevada Press, 2005), 1–17.

2. Studies of "old" immigration include Oscar Handlin, *The Uprooted: The Epic Story of the Great Immigration That Made the American People* (Boston: Little, Brown, 1951); John Bodnar, *The Transplanted: A History of Immigration in Urban America* (Bloomington: Indiana University Press, 1985). Roger Daniels, *Coming to America: A History of Immigration and Ethnicity in American Life* (New York: HarperCollins, 1990) covers both the traditional European and the beginnings of the "new" global immigration.

3. U.S. Department of Commerce, Bureau of the Census, *1980 Census of Population and Housing, Las Vegas, Nev. Standard Metropolitan Statistical Area* (Washington, D.C.: Government Printing Office, 1983), P-28; http://factfinder.census.gov/servlet/DDTable?ts=77728578655; http://factfinder.census.gov.servlet/QTTable?tx=77724691468; http://mumforddidyndns.org/cen2000/BlackWhite/DiversityBW DataPages/412msaBWCt.htm; U.S. Census Bureau, American Community Survey, "ACS Demographic and Housing Estimates—Las Vegas-Paradise, V=NV Metro Area," 2006; http://factfinder.census.gov/.

4. Studies of the newer currents of immigration include Alejandro Portes and Rubén G. Rumbaut, *Immigrant America: A Portrait,* 2nd ed. (Berkeley: University of California Press, 1996); Sanford J. Ungar, *Fresh Blood: The New American Immigrants* (New York: Simon and Schuster, 1995); David W. Haines and Carol A. Mortland, eds., *Manifest Destinies: Americanizing Immigrants and Internationalizing Americans* (Westport, Conn.: Praeger, 2001).

5. http://factfinder.census.gov/servletQTTable?_ts=78316446843 (accessed April 6, 2007); http://mumforddidyndns.org/cen2000/NewAme3ricans/NewAmerData/4120msaNuAmer.htm (accessed April 6, 2007); U.S. Census Bureau, American Community Survey, "ACS Selected Social Characteristics in the United States—Las Vegas-Paradise, NV Metro Area 2006," http://factfinder.census.gov/.

6. See Dina Titus and Thomas C. Wright, "The Ethnic Diversification of Las Vegas," in Simich and Wright, *Peoples of Las Vegas,* 28–31.

Introduction   xix

7. Ibid., 19–29.

8. Ibid., 22. Clark County School District data are courtesy of Tom Rodriguez, Executive Manager, Diversity and Affirmative Action Programs. On private schools and home-schooled students, see Nevada Department of Education, "Nevada Private Elementary and Secondary Non-Public Schools," at http://nde.doe.nv.gov/SDPrivateSchools.htm; Nevada Department of Education, "Research Bulletin, Student Enrollment and Licensed Personnel Information," at http://www.doe.nv.gov/Resources.htm#Bulletins.

9. Titus and Wright, "Ethnic Diversification," 22–23. Data are courtesy of former program administrator Mariteresa Rivera-Rogers and current (2008) program administrator Leland Page. Note that despite the large number of tourists who visit Las Vegas, both Rivera-Rogers and Page emphasize that the overwhelming proportion of cases they serve involve locals, not tourists.

10. http://www.dhs.gov/ximgtn/statistics/publications/YrBk05Na.shtm and http://www.dhs.gov/ximgtn/statistics/publications/YrBk06Na.shtm, courtesy of Marie Thérèse Sebrechts, Regional Media Manager—Southwest, U.S. Citizenship and Immigration Service.

11. *Las Vegas Review-Journal,* February 1, 2009.

12. Thomas Faist, *The Volume and Dynamics of International Migration and Transnational Social Spaces* (Oxford: Oxford University Press, 2000), 13.

13. There are dozens of books on transnationalism and related themes, among them: Michael Peter Smith and Luis Eduardo Guarnizo, eds., *Transnationalism from Below* (New Brunswick, N.J.: Transaction Publishers, 1998); Steven Vertovec and Robin Cohen, eds., *Migration, Diasporas, and Transnationalism* (Cheltenham, UK, and Northampton, Mass.: E. Elgar, 1999); Peter Hitchcock, *Imaginary States: Studies in Cultural Transnationalism* (Urbana: University of Illinois Press, 2003); Nyala Ali Khan, *The Fiction of Nationality in an Era of Transnationalism* (New York: Routledge, 2005). A well-known criticism of immigrants' retention of their native cultures is Patrick J. Buchanan, *State of Emergency: The Third World Invasion and Conquest of America* (New York: Thomas Dunne Books/St. Martin's Press, 2006).

14. Mexicans have established several clubs of immigrants from specific Mexican states, and Filipinos have several organizations of persons from specific islands.

15. Bernardo Arriaza, "The Chileans," in Simich and Wright, *Peoples of Las Vegas,* 289–302; Thomas C. Wright, "Chilean Diaspora," in *Encyclopedia of Diasporas: Immigrant and Refugee Cultures Around the World,* ed. Melvin Ember, Carol R. Ember, and Ian Skoggard (New York: Kluwer Academic/Plenum Publishers, 2004), 57–65.

16. Stephan Thernstrom, Ann Orlov, and Oscar Handlin, eds., *Harvard Encyclopedia of American Ethnic Groups* (Cambridge, Mass., and London: Belknap Press of Harvard University Press, 1980), iv.

17. William Petersen, "Concepts of Ethnicity," *Harvard Encyclopedia,* 234–42.

18. See Simich and Wright, *Peoples of Las Vegas,* xvi, n. 8.

19. For further clarification, see http://www.census.gov/acs/www/UseData/compACS.htm.

MORE PEOPLES OF LAS VEGAS

CHAPTER 1

The Irish

MICHAEL GREEN

The Irish have been integral to Nevada history, starting with the miners in the state's nineteenth- and twentieth-century mining booms. But as Nevada's population shifted south and turned to gaming and federal projects in the mid- and late twentieth century, Irish influence declined. That trend was especially evident in Las Vegas, where they have been less prominent than Italians and Jews, who dominated gaming; African Americans, whose struggle for civil rights helped shape the postwar era; and the burgeoning Latino population. Yet the Irish have played a significant role in Las Vegas from its beginnings, maintaining their heritage while blending into southern Nevada life and in larger numbers than many might suspect. According to the 2000 census, of 1,998,257 Nevadans, 220,488, or 11 percent, reported Irish or Celtic ancestry and 1.4 percent, or 28,962, were Scots-Irish, with more than 100,000 Irish among Clark County's 1.2 million-plus residents.[1]

But who is Irish? For some, the line runs through the mother; others accept any Irish ancestry. Last names make some obvious—but not all. Shifting borders have mingled English, Scottish, and Welsh with the Irish. Using the St. Patrick's Day motto—"There's a little bit of Irish in all of us"—makes the process no easier. As several Irish Las Vegans have said, those who are not Irish want to be. A pub owner said, "I don't know how many people have come to me and said, 'I'm Irish on my father's side or on my mother's side.' Irish is synonymous with fun and frivolity and we like to have fun. We cannot be accused of being staid"—nor of lacking influence. The Irish impact on Las Vegas has often been subtle, but never minor.[2]

Early History

The Irish made their presence felt from Las Vegas's beginnings. In 1855 the thirty Mormon missionaries sent to the area included Irish-born John Steele, designer of their fort, which later became the Las Vegas Ranch. Octavius Decatur Gass, its owner from 1865 to 1881, was Scotch-Irish, as was Senator William A. Clark, a Montana copper magnate who bought the ranch for the water rights he needed for a division point for his railroad and planned a townsite east of Main and Fremont that was auctioned off on May 15, 1905. Surveyor and engineer John T. McWilliams, an Ulster immigrant's son, platted a townsite west of the railroad tracks, but Clark overwhelmed him, and McWilliams's land became West Las Vegas, long a segregated area where blacks and some whites and Latinos lived.[3]

In Las Vegas's early years, most of the attention the Irish received consisted of St. Patrick's Day programs, but two businessmen showed their group's varied pursuits. In 1905 J. O. McIntosh, who also ran a wholesale liquor business, opened the Arizona Club in Block 16—First Street between Stewart and Ogden, where the railroad permitted liquor sales. With McIntosh moving to Utah and Al James in charge, the Arizona Club added prostitution, which lasted until 1942, when city officials closed Block 16 under pressure from federal officials. By contrast, Searchlight merchant James Cashman moved to Las Vegas in 1924 to run a garage and car dealership. He led the Elks Lodge in building the aptly named Cashman Field and starting the Helldorado parade and rodeo, pulled wires in the Democratic party, and persuaded Thomas Hull to build the El Rancho Vegas, which started the Las Vegas Strip. His family remained active in local affairs into the 2000s. James Jr. served in the legislature; he and sister Tona Cashman Siefert expanded their father's businesses; James III was active in the Chamber of Commerce until his death in 1995, and his brother Tim has held key posts in the Nevada Development Authority.[4]

The Irish made their presence felt early in the area's development in other ways. When legislators created Clark County in 1909, the first officials included sheriff Charles Corkhill, surveyor Charles McCarthy, assessor W. J. McBurney, and public administrator Charles Ireland. All four lost election bids in 1910, but McCarthy later became surveyor and assessor, Dan O'Leary recorder, and Ireland mayor. The Irish also belonged to key families. Active in mining and journalism in Goodsprings and Searchlight, recorder and auditor Frank Doherty wed longtime *Las Vegas Age* editor and local Republican leader Charles P. Squires's daughter, Florence. Leona McGovern, the daughter of C. N. McGovern, one of Las Vegas's first city commissioners in 1911, married Harley Harmon, later district attorney; their son Harley became a leading insurance executive and county commissioner, with his sons following him into business and politics.[5]

As with most local groups, the Irish populace mushroomed with Hoover Dam construction in the 1930s. The thousands of dam workers included Patrick McFadden. One son, John, began an insurance agency. Another, Leo, became a priest, rising to monsignor after a long tenure in Las Vegas that included starting the University of Nevada, Las Vegas's (UNLV's) Newman

Club. As Las Vegas grew during and after World War II, those in the military and involved in gambling seemed to wield the most influence: while wartime projects suggested a future in federal largesse, casino operators turned gaming into the engine that drove the Las Vegas economy. But opportunities existed, too, for the Irish, and they made the most of them, making contributions in a wide spectrum of occupations and endeavors. In Las Vegas they have been most visible in politics, gaming, the media, and religion.[6]

Politics

Politics long has provided Irish immigrants and their descendants with a way to help their people and gain support from other ethnic groups. What historian Kevin Kenny called "a tradition of subterranean politics, combined with a pervasive distrust of the law and conventional politics," led to successful and at times corrupt political machines in cities where the Irish settled in large numbers. Las Vegas put a different slant on this history. From its beginnings as a twenty-four-hour railroad stop, it had a reputation due to its downtown red-light district and its flouting of Prohibition. The casino industry's leaders were Italian and Jewish. As a newer community, Las Vegas lacked the entrenched establishment of many older cities and had no history of anti-Irish sentiment like that found in other cities. Thus, in Las Vegas, Irish politicians enjoyed more respect than their eastern counterparts—and proved capable of both honorable service and corruption.[7]

Several Nevada politicians had Irish roots. Though not from Las Vegas, they influenced the area as party leaders (William Woodburn, father and son, were Democratic national committeemen), state officials (Governors Emmet Boyle and E. P. Carville), and members of Congress (Barbara Vucanovich, Manhattan Project official Thomas Farrell's daughter, spent seven terms in the House and Maurice Sullivan one term there after four terms as lieutenant governor; George "Molly" Malone was a two-term U.S. senator). The dominant figure in twentieth-century Nevada politics, Pat McCarran, born in Reno in 1876 to immigrants from County Cork and County Londonderry, became a legislator, district attorney, and State Supreme Court justice. Elected to the U.S. Senate in 1932 after several tries, McCarran provided unparalleled constituent service and used patronage to help dozens of Nevadans earn law degrees in Washington, D.C., building a cadre of supporters. He never lived in Las Vegas and lamented its reliance on casinos, but aided its success. Like urban counterparts in Tammany Hall and Chicago's Daley machine, he grasped the value of delivering jobs and help. His legislation and lobbying helped southern Nevada obtain land for the airport named for him, the magnesium plant that began Henderson, the air base that boosted North Las Vegas, and the Nevada Test Site. Until dying in office in 1954, through committee chairmanships and seniority, he blocked federal efforts to interfere with gaming's development.[8]

Three governors with Irish and Las Vegas roots lacked McCarran's power but left their mark and outstripped his popularity. Mike O'Callaghan served in World War II and Korea as a teacher and coach in Henderson, a county juvenile services and state human resources director, and federal Job Corps and Office of Emergency Preparedness administrator. Beaten for lieutenant governor in 1966, he scored upsets in the 1970 primary and general elections for governor and rolled to reelection in 1974. Economically conservative and socially liberal, he pushed through fair housing laws and low-cost home loans, funding for the aged and for education, rehabilitation programs, and a consumer affairs office. On leaving office, he became an executive and a columnist with the *Las Vegas Sun* and published newspapers in Henderson and Boulder City until his death in 2004. His widow, Carolyn, died the following year, but their children remained active in community activities, befitting their parents: Michael as an attorney, Tim and Colleen as newspaper executives, Teresa as a hospital administrator.[9]

During O'Callaghan's first term, Bob Miller was a prosecutor and justice of the peace. The son of longtime Riviera executive Ross Miller and Coletta "The Irish Songbird" Doyle, Miller was district attorney (1979–87) and was elected lieutenant governor in 1986. When Richard Bryan resigned as governor in 1989 to become a U.S. senator, Miller finished his term and won two terms on his own, becoming Nevada's longest-serving governor (1989–99). Las Vegas boomed as never before during his tenure, but the state's tax structure, relying on biennial projections, led to frequent budget cuts. Forced to slash programs, Miller still pushed through a class-size reduction plan to improve elementary education and reforms in criminal justice. After ten years as governor, he declined overtures to seek higher office and joined a law firm before entering business and supporting another Miller in politics: his son, Ross, became secretary of state in 2006.[10]

Miller's successor, moderate Republican Kenny Guinn, came to Las Vegas in the 1960s to work for the local school district, rising to superintendent. After a decade in that post, he entered private business as an executive with Nevada Savings (now part of Wells Fargo) and Southwest Gas. Upon retiring, he took a dollar in pay to spend a year as UNLV's acting president. Long active in politics behind the scenes and long rumored to be eying high office, he easily won his first term as governor in 1998 and cruised to reelection in 2002. His effort to modify the state's tax structure in 2003 led to a battle with the legislature and irked many other Republicans, but Guinn left office still popular and enjoyed the chance to spend more time with his family and serve on various boards.[11]

No family, Irish or otherwise, influenced Las Vegas politics and law more than the Foleys. The son of one of the many Irish who immigrated during the potato blight of the 1840s, Chicago lawyer and fight promoter Thomas L. Foley relocated in 1906 to Goldfield. His son, Roger T., followed in 1910, became deputy district attorney, brought Helen Drummond to Goldfield to marry her, and moved his wife and five sons to Las Vegas in 1928. He became a district attorney and district judge. In 1945 Senators McCarran and James Scrugham named him to a federal judgeship, serving the whole state. Eventually, Foley and McCarran had a falling-out over the senator's use of patronage and Foley's independence. In 1953 Foley's evenhandedness enabled *Las Vegas Sun* publisher Hank Greenspun to win a settlement in a lawsuit against McCarran and local casino operators when they conspired to drive him out of business for criticizing the senator. Foley assumed senior status in 1957 but heard cases almost until his death at age eighty-eight in 1974.[12]

Foley's sons followed in his footsteps—in more ways than one. Also a district attorney (1951–55) and branded a "moral reformer"—by a politician who had just taken a bribe—his oldest son, Roger Drummond Foley, won ribbing for prosecuting Lili St. Cyr for performing her "bubble dance" at the El Rancho Vegas. In 1958 he cruised to victory in the attorney general's race and, on civil libertarian grounds, opposed Governor Grant Sawyer and gaming regulators when they created the List of Excluded Persons, known as the "Black Book," to ban reputed mobsters from casinos. In 1962 Foley became Nevada's newest federal judge and, like his father, heard cases almost until his death in 1996. His key rulings included a consent decree to improve conditions at the local jail; the Baneberry case, which forced the federal government to admit the health risks of nuclear testing; and protecting the endangered desert pupfish in Devil's Hole, in Nye County, prompting a bumper sticker by angry rural Nevadans: "Kill the pupfish and Foley too!"[13]

The family's importance goes beyond the two Roger Foleys. The younger judge had four younger brothers, all attorneys who practiced together in the 1950s and entered public service. Tom was a district judge from 1983 until his death in 1993, George a district attorney and behind-the-scenes Democratic force, Joe a two-term member of the University of Nevada Board of Regents, and John a state senator. And the brothers' twenty-six children uphold the tradition. Joe's daughter Helen served in the State Assembly and State Senate before becoming a consultant and lobbyist, and son Danny became an attorney active in community groups, especially the St. Rose hospitals. An executive for several nonprofit groups, Roger's daughter Mary Lou has been a Democratic activist—as has John's daughter, Liz, an attorney. George Jr. built a prominent law firm and eventually became a U.S. magistrate.

Another Irish Democratic family influenced politics and law: the Mowbrays. John Mowbray moved to Las Vegas in 1949 with wife Kathlyn "Kax" Hammes, whose father, Romy, built the Marycrest neighborhood, including plans for Bishop Gorman High School and St. Anne's Elementary School, near Maryland Parkway. A deputy district attorney for Roger D. Foley and a bankruptcy referee before governor Sawyer named him district judge in 1959, Mowbray began the public defender's office. In 1967 the Nevada Supreme Court expanded from three to five justices, and Republican Gov. Paul Laxalt appointed him. Mowbray remained on the court for twenty-five years, retiring in 1992 and dying in 1997. His sons reflected the Mowbray history: Romy developed housing tracts, while John became a prominent lawyer.[14]

While the Foleys and Mowbrays followed the tradition of Irish Democrats, the McNamees were among the area's top Republicans. Frank McNamee Sr. came to Eureka, Nevada, in 1883 and was a barber before passing the bar and moving to Lincoln County. His son Leo, born there in 1888, moved to Las Vegas in the early 1910s and opened a law firm that represented the Union Pacific, which dominated Las Vegas into the 1940s, among other clients. After the elder McNamee's death in 1933, Frank Jr. joined Leo's practice. Before Leo's death in 1958, his son John had joined the firm; so did another son, Joe, who served in the Assembly before leaving the law to invest in real estate and hotels—including the Marina, now part of the MGM Grand. Frank went on to be a district judge and state Supreme Court justice. Leo's daughter Fran married Julian Moore, a Basic Magnesium and gaming executive; another daughter, Marian, was a longtime nun.[15]

The Irish contribution to local politics and law extends beyond these prominent families. District judges Thomas O'Donnell, John McGroarty, and James Brennan were influential on the courts and beyond. John O'Reilly and Bill Curran chaired the state Gaming Commission, while Jon Collins was part of Nevada's largest law firm and served on the state Supreme Court. One of Las Vegas's first women attorneys, Nelle Price, was married to Roland Wiley, a district attorney. North Las Vegas Fire Department battalion chief John Oceguera rose to Assembly majority leader in 2007. William Byrne was an assemblyman and Henderson's mayor. Larry Brown migrated from sports to politics, serving on the Las Vegas City Council and then the Clark County Commission. Son of a five-term county assessor, Jim Bilbray became a regent, legislator, and four-term congressman; his daughter Erin is a party activist, Bridget is a school district administrator, and Shannon, completing the circle, works in the district office of a member of Congress, Dina Titus. Jim Joyce shaped laws and campaigns as Nevada's top political consultant and lobbyist in the 1970s and 1980s; with his death in 1993, son, Robin, took over his agency while daughter, Marilee, was active in the local and national media.[16]

Just as immigrants and their descendants found opportunities in local politics, forming the core of many urban machines, the Irish influenced local politics in Las Vegas. An insurance agency and movie theater owner before three terms as mayor (1931–35, 1943–51), Ernie Cragin was instrumental in expanding municipal services but also helped enforce local racial segregation. Successful in insurance and real estate, an assemblyman and a county commissioner, three-term mayor Bill Briare (1975–87) advocated downtown rebuilding and better transportation. Serving from 1991 to 1999 and running unsuccessfully for governor in 1994 and 1998, Jan Laverty Jones pushed to build the Fremont Street Experience canopy in downtown Las Vegas and for redevelopment, then became a Harrahs executive.[17]

While Irish names show up in offices from legislator to city official, others stayed behind the scenes. Colorado River Commissioner and water company owner Walt Casey was a key cog in the GOP. Democratic party stalwart Bill McGarry owned the Quorum Club, where politicians met to talk and quaff a few. Just as his father had held office early in the century, George Ullom was Nevada Resort Association (NRA) director, Las Vegas city manager, Public Service Commission and Tax Commission chair, and county registrar of voters. Robbins Cahill, once Nevada's top gaming regulator and NRA director, and Thom Reilly were county managers.[18]

Irish politicians across the country, especially local ones, have also faced charges of graft. Las Vegas has been no different from other cities in this respect. Labor organizer and county commissioner James "Sailor" Ryan was found guilty of taking bribes to back zoning changes. As a Las Vegas councilman (1995–2003), Michael McDonald enjoyed broad support in his district for his commitment to local issues and his constituents. In the 2000s four current and former county commissioners went to prison for "G-Sting," a scandal involving bribes they took from the owner of a topless club. Three of the four had Irish blood: ex-policeman Lance Malone; former assemblywoman Erin Kenny; and Mary Kincaid-Chauncey, previously a North Las Vegas city councilwoman.[19]

Gaming

While Italians and Jews dominated Las Vegas's gaming industry, the Irish also held important casino jobs as owners and executives. Most of the Strip's builders in the 1940s and 1950s were tied to the predominantly southern and eastern European "Great Migration" through Ellis Island and other points of entry during the late nineteenth and early twentieth centuries. By contrast, Irish casino operators coalesced mostly downtown on or near Fremont Street, eventually expanding local gaming and their influence beyond those properties. Unlike their Italian and Jewish counterparts, whose illegal activities led them to discourage their families from following their example, the Irish also welcomed their children into the business. The Irish also played a role in keeping the casino floor and its amenities running: a Culinary Union official said, "Immigrant Irish and Italians founded our union."[20]

Before and especially after the state legislature approved wide-open gambling in 1931, Las Vegas's most prominent casino operator was J. Kell Houssels. He operated the Las Vegas Club and El Cortez downtown and Tropicana on the Strip, as well as investing in numerous local businesses. His Showboat on Boulder Highway, with former El Cortez executive Joe Kelley in key posts for four decades, became the first locals' casino, with such innovations as bowling lanes, which became the home of a nationally televised championship each year.[21]

By Houssels's death in 1979, his legacy included J. K. "Ike" Houssels Jr., who made an important mark in the industry and community. While the elder Houssels was not Irish, he married Alice O'Shaughnessy of New Orleans, and the younger Houssels and his family are proud of their Irish heritage. A graduate of West Point and Stanford Law, J. K. Houssels Jr. served in the Assembly and practiced law. He negotiated the deal for the Tropicana to present the long-running Folies Bergere before succeeding his father in operating the Tropicana and the Showboat. He moved the Showboat into Atlantic City, Australia, and other jurisdictions before selling the company to Harrahs in 1998 for more than $1 billion. He joined several others in building and opening the Union Plaza in 1971. His wife, Nancy, cofounded the Nevada Ballet Theatre, which the family continues to support, and his sons, Jake, Josh, and Eric, have been active in gaming and an investment firm.[22]

The Houssels family enjoyed close connections with another Irish family of casino operators, the Gaughans. A Nebraska-born bookmaker, John D. "Jackie" Gaughan first visited Las Vegas in 1943, while stationed at the Tonopah Army Air Base. Returning after the war, he ran a race book and invested in the downtown Boulder Club and the Flamingo, joining his mentor from Omaha, Edward Barrick, who owned a percentage of the Fremont and the Horseshoe and whose widow, Marjorie, became a prominent donor to UNLV and other local causes. Gaughan invested with the Houssels in the Showboat and served on its board of directors. In the early 1960s, he bought the El Cortez and the Las Vegas Club, followed by other downtown casinos, building a reputation as a shrewd, hands-on operator whose innovations included paycheck-cashing wheels and giveaways. Part of the group that opened the Union Plaza in 1971, he bought out his partners. In 2004 he sold four downtown clubs, then he sold his last remaining property, the El Cortez, in 2008—but continued to live there and serve as a goodwill ambassador.[23]

Just as the Houssels' role in gaming has been multigenerational, Gaughan's sons have followed in their father's footsteps. Jackie Jr. held various executive posts until his death in 2002. Michael opened the Barbary Coast at the Strip and Flamingo in 1979. From that grew Coast Casinos, including the Gold Coast and the Orleans west of the Strip and the Suncoast in Summerlin. Gaughan operated the slot machines at McCarran International Airport and started NASCAR's South Point Racing, for which his son Brendan drives. In 2004 Gaughan sold Coast Casinos to Boyd Gaming for $1.3 billion, then bought what is now South Point from Boyd in 2006 while also expanding his role at the El Cortez as his father aged. Like his father, Gaughan also gave back to the community as a donor to local organizations, especially Bishop Gorman High School and UNLV.[24]

Another leading Las Vegas family, the Boyds, share Irish roots and ties to the Houssels and Gaughans. A Scot-Irish native of Oklahoma, Sam Boyd dealt on California coastal cruise ships and in Hawaii before coming to Las Vegas in 1941. Rising to shift boss and investor in the Sahara Hotel when it opened in 1952, he became general manager of the downtown Mint in 1957, using giveaways and country entertainment to draw customers. The first Boyd casino, Henderson's Eldorado, became his through odd circumstances. Mirroring the Houssels, Boyd's only son, Bill, went to law school, with his father saying, "If you get an education, no one can ever take it away from you, and you'll have some independence." When the Eldorado's builder offered Bill Boyd a percentage in lieu of a fee to represent him, Boyd took the deal and his family members bought the rest.[25]

Thus began one of the world's largest gaming corporations. After opening the Union Plaza with Houssels, Jackie Gaughan, and Frank Scott, Boyd sold out and opened the nearby California. In 1979, after Bill joined his father full-time, came the western-themed Sam's Town on Boulder Highway, south of the Showboat. In 1983 state officials asked the Boyds to run the Stardust and the Fremont to end the hotels' ties to Chicago organized crime interests. They agreed, then purchased the two hotels. They bought Main Street Station, part of a downtown redevelopment effort, after leasing its hotel tower. Besides acquiring Michael Gaughan's Coast Casinos, Boyd's company teamed with MGM Mirage in Atlantic City's Borgata. In 2007 Boyd imploded the Stardust and planned

Echelon Place, with 5,000 hotel rooms, 30 restaurants, 300,000 square feet of retail, 750,000 feet of convention space, and 140,000 square feet of casino space. The Boyds moved into other jurisdictions but remembered Las Vegas: UNLV's football team plays in Sam Boyd Stadium, honoring his contributions of time and money, and Bill Boyd provided $5 million to start, then another $25 million, to UNLV's law school, which is named for him.[26]

Another family of Irish descent played a major role in gaming downtown: the Binions. Born in Texas in 1904, Lester "Benny" Binion ran clubs in Dallas and ran afoul of the law until moving to Las Vegas in 1946. He joined the elder Houssels in the Las Vegas Club, then moved to the Westerner. Opening Binion's Horseshoe in 1951 at Second and Fremont, he became the first downtown operator to put in carpeting and send limousines to the airport to pick up gamblers, and he installed a horseshoe with a million dollars in it, a must-see for tourists. He explained his philosophy simply: "Make little people feel like big people."[27]

Jailed for tax evasion in 1953, Binion never regained his license. But his family won back the casino, with wife, Teddy Jane, and sons, Jack and Ted, as executives. In 1970 his sons persuaded him to add the World Series of Poker, which became a major attraction. They expanded the Horseshoe by buying the Mint next door and knocking out the wall. After Binion's death in 1989 and a legal fight, the Horseshoe went to his daughter Becky Behnen and properties in other states to Jack Binion. In 2004 Behnen sold the Horseshoe and Jack Binion sold his interests to Harrahs but remained active as a consultant. Ted Binion lost his license over drug use and mob ties and died in 1998. Convicted of his murder, his girlfriend, Sandy Murphy, and her boyfriend, Rick Tabish, were found not guilty at retrial, with Irish-born mining executive William Fuller financing much of their defense.[28]

Like Binion and other gaming figures, Guy McAfee lived on both sides of the law. A Los Angeles sheriff's department vice detective, he also ran illegal casinos. In the late 1930s, reforms drove several Southern California gambling veterans up Highway 91 to Las Vegas. McAfee stopped on the highway to Los Angeles—he named it for his old Southern California haunt, the Sunset "Strip"—and ran the 91 Club until selling it to the Last Frontier's builders, then ran the downtown Frontier Club. In 1946 he rounded up local investors to open the Golden Nugget. McAfee remained active in the industry until his death in 1960, and Steve Wynn later made the Nugget the foundation of a resort empire.[29]

Other Irish casino owners won distinction. Gary Mahoney's family owned the Silver Nugget and the Opera House in North Las Vegas until selling them in 2007 to Jeffrey Fine, whose grandmother, Barbara Greenspun, came from an Irish Jewish family.[30] After running North Las Vegas and West Las Vegas casinos, Don Laughlin moved south and created an eponymous town, now with 11,000-plus hotel rooms, and his innovations included space for recreational vehicles, child-care facilities, and a bridge that was built across Davis Dam to replace a dangerous road. The Irish also filled a variety of tourism jobs, from dealer to executive. Arriving in 1946, Herb McDonald changed Las Vegas as a publicist, an executive, a Chamber of Commerce director, and a cofounder of Las Vegas Events, for which he imported the National Finals Rodeo (with Binion's help) and other events. Emmett Sullivan owned a major slot-carousel business; John Redmond went from gaming agent to MGM Mirage president, and Bill Noonan from Las Vegas city manager to executive posts at the Fitzgeralds and Boyd Gaming; Thomas McCartney headed marketing at New York New York and the Luxor; and as Las Vegas Convention and Visitors Authority director, onetime performer Barney Rawlings led the effort to build the Convention Center's east wing and Sam Boyd Stadium.[31]

Yet, even while gaining top administrative posts, few Irish became prominent as Strip hotel owners. Dancer Michael Flatley reportedly tried to buy the Aladdin and planned an Irish-themed Shamrock hotel-casino on the Strip, but to no avail. Before moving to the Strip, the Houssels and Boyds made their names downtown and in locals casinos. Among those in key jobs or on boards of directors, Thomas McGinty aided the Desert Inn's success, but less prominently than Moe Dalitz and his Jewish partners, who also ran illegal casinos in Ohio and Kentucky. Tom Gallagher headed Park Place Entertainment and later ran for Congress, but Arthur Goldberg built Park Place into an Atlantic City giant, then combined it with other companies in Las Vegas. As in politics, Irish triumphs in gaming were more local—perhaps a reflection of their tradition of involvement in local affairs.[32]

Media

Nationally, journalism has been a major profession for the Irish, and Las Vegas has been no different. Charles "Corky" Corkhill was founding editor of the *Las Vegas Age,* the only survivor of the three weekly newspapers published at the time of the May 15, 1905, auction that gave birth to the town. After the *Age*'s sale in 1908, Corkhill stayed in Las Vegas, becoming sheriff and beginning the *Las Vegas Review* in 1909 by declaring its political loyalty, "provided the Democrats behave themselves and 'come across' occasionally." The *Review* changed owners several times before longtime mining camp editor Frank Garside bought it in 1926.[33]

Two of Las Vegas's leading journalists were Garside's editors, brothers Al and John Cahlan. In 1926 Al joined Garside as editor and part-owner; three years later, John arrived. They expanded the paper into the daily *Las Vegas Review-Journal* (*R-J*) and published it until 1960, when Donald Reynolds, who bought out Garside, forced out Al Cahlan; John left the next year. McCarran allies who made the *R-J* his local organ, the Cahlans were active in politics, Al in the Assembly and as a Democratic national committeeman and Colorado River commissioner, John as a university regent. After their departure from the *R-J*, Al Cahlan tended to investments and wrote a *Las Vegas Sun* column until his death in 1968; John Cahlan worked for the Southern Nevada Industrial Foundation and the Chamber of Commerce, cowrote a history of Las Vegas, and chaired the city's Diamond Jubilee celebration before his death in 1987.[34]

In the 1950s, the Cahlans feuded with *Sun* publisher Hank Greenspun, whose paper also had a strong Irish presence. A Jewish colleen he met in Ireland during the war, Barbara Greenspun worked with her husband at the *Sun* and in business and community affairs. Their children followed in their footsteps, with Brian investing in tourism and media, Danny involved in arts and technology, and Janie active in animal rights. Barbara's brothers Doug and Les Ritchie also were *Sun* executives. An entertainment columnist from 1967 until his death in 2002, former record producer and publicist Joe Delaney was active in local media, theater, and charities; taught UNLV classes on hotel entertainment; and produced and hosted documentaries about Ireland for the local public television affiliate. The Irish tradition continued with editor Michael Kelley, assistant managing editor Tom Gorman, and longtime reporter Mary Manning—and at the *R-J* with the married team of editorial page editor John Kerr and city editor Mary Hynes.[35]

Other journalists and broadcasters moved between outlets. Colin McKinlay was a reporter and editor for several papers and press officer for the Culinary Union and for Sen. Howard Cannon. Red McIlvaine was a popular broadcaster, *Sun* columnist, and publicist until his death in 1993. Jack Sheehan edited magazines and wrote a *Sun* column and several books about Las Vegas. Dave McCann was Channel 8 sports director until switching to morning anchor, doubling as UNLV's football and basketball broadcaster. Las Vegas's most popular print journalist in the 1990s and 2000s, John L. Smith, the grandson of an Irish Catholic with "formidable faith and the arm strength of [Dodger outfielder] Duke Snider," wrote a column for the *R-J*, appeared as a commentator on local television, and published several popular books about Las Vegas history.[36]

Religion

While the Irish have predominated in the Roman Catholic priesthood, they have been active in other denominations. Rev. Michael Garrison converted from Catholicism to become an Episcopal priest, serving several small parishes throughout southern Nevada before moving on to become the Episcopal bishop of western New York. Rev. Sandra McCarroll presided at St. Christopher's Episcopal Church in Boulder City. Irish-born priest Rev. Gerry McNulty was Veterans Administration and Hospital chaplain. But from the days of Father Patrick Manogue on the Comstock, the Irish have been associated with the Catholic priesthood in Nevada and have influenced Las Vegas's religious development. When the Irish joined other Catholics in 1908 to start St. Joan of Arc church on Second between Lewis and Bridger, the fund-raising committee included Mrs. D. D. Hickey, K. K. Horan, and Mrs. Charles Ireland.[37]

In 1931 Pope Pius XI finally created the Nevada Diocese, based in Reno, and named Thomas K. Gorman bishop. The first priest ordained in the diocese was his secretary and vice chancellor, Thomas Collins, from Tralee, County Kerry. With Gorman's support, Collins opened the Catholic Welfare Program in Reno and Las Vegas, providing soup kitchens and homeless shelters. He opened USO (United Service Organizations) facilities for servicemen, their families, African American wartime workers, and Boulder City residents. Named monsignor in 1947, he became pastor of St. Joan of Arc in 1953. In two years, he remodeled it and oversaw the opening of southern Nevada's first private high school, Bishop Gorman. Collins returned to St. Joan's in 1962, retired in 1977, and went home to Ireland, which he had tried to visit as often as possible, relying on his counterpart at St. Anne's, Father John McVeigh, to fill in for him.[38]

For most of its history, Las Vegas was part of the statewide Diocese of Reno. With Gorman's transfer to Dallas–Fort Worth in 1952, Bishop Robert J. Dwyer succeeded him. His tenure included construction of what became the Guardian Angel Cathedral on the Strip, with support from casino operators ranging from Binion to Dalitz. After Dwyer became archbishop of Portland, Oregon, in 1966, new bishop Joseph Green started the Catholic Services Appeal and instituted Vatican II reforms. Replacing Green in 1974, Norman McFarland succeeded in efforts to rename it the Diocese of Reno–Las Vegas before departing in 1987.[39]

McFarland's successor became the first Bishop of Las Vegas. Daniel Walsh celebrated his installation in Las Vegas and maintained a residence there. In 1995 Pope John Paul II divided the diocese, charging Walsh with Clark, Lincoln,

White Pine, Nye, and Esmeralda Counties. Given the Latino influx—acknowledged in the late 1980s with a Hispanic ministry—Walsh dealt with a rapidly expanding church as most American dioceses scaled back, then moved to Santa Rosa, California. By late 2007, the Roman Catholic Diocese of Las Vegas under Bishop Joseph Pepe included 94 priests, 26 parishes, and an estimated Catholic population of 700,000—many of them Latino but with a heavy Irish influence, including Catholic Charities executive director Monsignor Patrick Leary and longtime priests McVeigh, James Bevan, William Kenny, John McShane, Francis Timoney, and Kevin McAuliffe.[40]

Within the Catholic Diocese are several convents and nuns active in education, hospitals, social services, and other community endeavors—but none more prominently over the years than Sister Rosemary Lynch. A member of the Franciscan Order with a ministry in nonviolence, she continued working for Pace e Bene Nonviolence Service into her nineties while aiding immigrants as well. Also active in antiwar and antinuclear efforts, she founded Citizens Concerned About the Neutron Bomb and protested for many years at the Nevada Test Site as one of the founders of the Lenten Desert Experience, which attracted such antinuclear protesters as Daniel Ellsberg and Martin Sheen.[41]

The Stillpoint Spiritual Development Center reflected a different religious ideal: an interfaith retreat. Once a school principal in County Clare, Roisin O'Loughlin pursued graduate studies in Chicago, writing a dissertation on spiritual counseling. Moving to Las Vegas, she founded the center with fellow Catholics Delise Sartini and Alice Nielson. Located in an office park, Stillpoint featured offices for retreats or group meetings, a library, a meditation room, and private counseling offices.[42]

Community

While some ethnic groups have been associated, in the public mind or through stereotyping, with certain pursuits, the Irish have demonstrated adaptability and versatility in their involvement in local activities. The Irish made a name for themselves in sports. Fighting in 120 boxing matches from 1937 to 1949 and working in security for Binion's and Caesars Palace before starting a lawn-care business, Coleman "Coley" Welch was also the father of John Welch, a UNLV basketball player and assistant coach. In 1967 Bill Ireland became UNLV's first football coach, spent five years at that post, rose to the position of athletic director in 1973, and contributed to such key hires as that of basketball coach Jerry Tarkanian. Don Logan joined the AAA minor-league baseball team when it started in 1983, and a quarter of a century later he remained president and general manager after they became the 51s.[43]

As the Irish built communities around the United States, they literally helped build Las Vegas. John and Florence Murphy built the North Las Vegas Airport and helped start Bonanza Airlines. Harold Cunningham was president of Nevada Test Site operator Reynolds Electrical and Engineering Company, and his wife, Cynthia, was on the state board of education and was active in the cultural community. Los Angeles developer Carlton Adair, whose daughter Valerie became a district judge, helped finance the Hacienda and became general manager of the Dunes. In 1966 a federal land deal brought him 2,243 acres he was never able to develop; others realized his dream of Lake Las Vegas. After Hank Chism's arrival in the 1950s, Chism Homes became one of the area's leading builders—with Chism active in many local organizations to boot. Similarly, Al and Martin Collins moved to Las Vegas from Reno in the early 1950s and eventually built such residential projects as Spanish Oaks and Whitney Ranch in addition to commercial developments.[44]

Police work provided a road to respectability in many communities, and several of Las Vegas's top law-enforcement officers have had Irish roots. The first sheriff, Corkhill, had no police experience but also served as postmaster and assistant fire chief. John McCarthy joined the Las Vegas police in 1956 and ran the narcotics division before winning a term as sheriff in 1978. In 2006 Doug Gillespie won the election for sheriff. Whether in the police or sheriff's department or, since 1973, the Metropolitan Police Department, as well as in the suburban departments of North Las Vegas, Henderson, and Boulder City, Irish names have been prominent.[45]

The Irish also made a mark in education. Perusing school names suggests their impact. Among elementary schools, John Beatty long taught at Henderson's Basic High and Jack Dailey taught at several high schools; Fay Galloway rose from custodian to school district operations director; James Smalley taught at Henderson Junior High for twenty-nine years; teacher and administrator Estes McDoniel was Henderson's mayor; Margaret Bailey took her brother Robert's name on joining the Dominican Order of Sisters and taught at a local Catholic school. In the middle schools, Kathleen and Tim Harney and Jack and Terry Mannion were longtime educators. At the University of Nevada, Las Vegas, Irish faculty have included Eugene Moehring, historian of Las Vegas and UNLV; emeritus professor of political science Andrew Tuttle; Mark Twain scholar Joseph McCullough; Irish literature specialist Richard Harp; and cultural critic and MacArthur genius grant recipient Dave Hickey, while at the College of Southern Nevada (CSN), anthropologist Kevin Rafferty and English professor Robert Fuhrel have researched Irish topics.[46]

Entertainment, Food, and Drink

Irish-style entertainment has long been part of Las Vegas. Showrooms have catered to lovers of Irish entertainers, from Rosemary Clooney to onetime Last Frontier headliner Ronald Reagan. Some stars made Las Vegas home. Peter Lind Hayes and Mary Healy wanted to be near his mother, nightclub operator Grace Hayes, and were active in the community. Phyllis McGuire of the McGuire Sisters gave time and effort to numerous civic groups. Wayne Newton had an Irish grandmother and a long career, making thousands of showroom appearances and buying the Aladdin Hotel. A key figure in production shows, Margaret Kelly formed the Bluebell Girls dance team and worked with choreographer Donn Arden in the Stardust's Lido de Paris and MGM Grand's Hallelujah Hollywood. And the Irish made major contributions behind the scenes: Lucille Cunningham spent nearly thirty-five years handling Liberace's business affairs; Rocky Sennes was an entertainment director and managed the Las Vegas–based Irish Showband; and Dick Feeney has produced shows on the Strip and downtown for two decades.[47]

Las Vegas welcomed not only entertainers with an Irish background, but more traditional Irish entertainment as well. Popular Strip shows included "Riverdance" and "Lord of the Dance," which Michael Flatley began after Riverdance fired him in 1996 in a copyright dispute; his show spent four years at New York New York, followed by time at the Venetian. Brendan Boyer's Irish Showband performed at the Barbary Coast, Stardust, and Lady Luck starting in the early 1970s, when Boyer was a leading Elvis Presley impersonator. Downtown, the Golden Nugget briefly featured "Spirit of the Dance." Most pubs featured regular entertainment by such groups as the Wild Celts, Killian's Angels, and Finnegan's Wake. Dubliner Jimmy Conway and his Irish band played various venues and his wife, Carmel, served drinks at Paddy's Pub. Irish bands and cabaret nights have been popular at local hotel-casinos and community centers.[48]

Nor has Irish culture been neglected. Exhibits by Irish artists and performances by Irish singers and dancers have been popular—and not just around St. Patrick's Day. An early 1980s local festival honored James Joyce. Nobel laureate Seamus Heaney spoke at UNLV. Irish literature classes have been popular at UNLV and the College of Southern Nevada (CSN), and Irish music draws large crowds in community concert series and the UNLV performing arts. Legitimate theater included actor Brian Keith in "Letters of an Irish Parish Priest" at UNLV in 1993. The Celtic Storm Dance Company and the Sharon Lynn Academy of Irish Dance performed throughout the area. A long-running favorite on Nevada Public Radio was "The Thistle and Shamrock."[49]

Irish themes in tourist and local casinos are common. Las Vegas is known for themed resorts, and one major hotel-casino is Irish themed. Fitzgeralds downtown began as the Sundance in 1980 and changed its name in 1988 on (appropriately) St. Patrick's Day. Don Barden, the only African American corporate chief executive of a Las Vegas casino, bought it in 2001. On the second floor, part of the Blarney Stone may be rubbed for good luck. Evoking Ireland are its green, shamrock-filled signage and its leprechaun mascot, Mr. O'Lucky, joined by cousin Irish Chase (Leonard Chase, onetime Sundance owner Dalitz's nurse and leader of the local Sons of Erin, was the first leprechaun). For St. Patrick's Day, Fitzgeralds featured drum-and-pipe corps, green beer, corned beef and cabbage, and Irish stew.[50]

Other Irish-style properties were smaller than their themed counterparts. On the Strip, O'Shea's, first in the Hilton chain and later under Harrahs, operated next to the Flamingo. With its leprechaun mascot and Dublin' Up Lounge, it held events in conjunction with St. Patrick's Day and set a record when 220 customers joined the Great Guinness Toast, the largest simultaneous nationwide toast—more than 320,000 participating. The Pot O' Gold Casino closed and reopened as the Emerald Isle at 120 Market Street, amid downtown Henderson's redevelopment. It boasted a nine-foot, lighted "emerald" atop a sixty-foot tower, with an interior modeled on a seventeenth-century Irish village, including murals and building facades.[51]

More than hotels, Irish pubs became a hot ticket. According to then–Palace Station general manager Jonathan Swain, the 1994 World Cup soccer matches in the United States brought the Irish into local bars, "where soccer was being played, and the Irish theme took off from there," about the time "Riverdance" became popular. Some pubs failed—Carlos Murphy's and Moose McGillicuddy's by UNLV and Houlihan's in northwest Las Vegas, more typical bars than Irish pubs. But Las Vegas even housed an office for McNally Design Group USA, which built Irish bars around the world through its subsidiary, the Irish Pub Company—and, locally, at the J. W. Marriott in Summerlin and Green Valley Ranch Station.[52]

Some Irish pubs aimed at locals. At downtown Hennessey's Tavern, part of a chain, the Claddagh Room served private parties, with Finnegan's Wake and the Old Castle Knights in the lounge and management stressing "the traditional cozy or clubby feel indigenous to Irish or English pubs." Tom and Karen Lally ran Lally's of Las Vegas in the northwest. The Scopoulis family owned Finnegan's Pub on Eastern en route to Henderson and Craig Road in North Las Vegas. Paddy's Pub operated in Paradise Township. Brothers Fred and Bob Keck ran Skinny Dugan's on West Charleston for thirty-three years until its sale to Fred Gluckman and Margot Aiken, who renovated it with a retro look.[53]

Several newer pubs emphasized Irish ambience and decor, from Kavanaugh's Irish Pub and Grill in North Las Vegas to Molly Malone's in Southern Highlands. For Sean Patrick's Irish Pub on West Flamingo, owners Bob Trigero, Madison Graves, and Michael Morrissey (the pub was named for his son) hired Ireland's The Pub Dressing Company, which used Irish tile, wood, and slate floors and served Irish stew and Guinness-marinated steak. On Horizon Ridge in Henderson and moving to Boca Park across the Valley, Three Angry Wives included a coat of arms for owners Sean, Mike, and Kevin Higgins. They named the pub for their wives, who probably were not angry at their Irish names for bar food—Belfast and Killarney omelettes, Connemara quesadillas, and Irish nachos.[54]

While these locations catered to locals, resorts reminded tourists that just as the Strip gave them the chance to travel through time, they could get to Ireland via Las Vegas. The Desert Passage shops at the Aladdin, now Planet Hollywood, featured McGrail's of Erin, which offered Irish entertainment for St. Patrick's Day and Irish clothing. With Green Valley Ranch Station's Fadó's interior built in Ireland, general manager Dan Carroll said it would "reflect a Victorian pub in Dublin." Its "Irish fusion" cuisine included colcannon. In 2008 the pub was called Quinn's, with entertainers Darby O'Gill and the Little People; Fadó moved to the Park Place development on south Eastern, with an interior put together in Ireland. The Auld Dubliner Irish Pub, also in California and Illinois, opened at MonteLago Village Resort at Lake Las Vegas on St. Patrick's Day 2006.[55]

One of the Strip's themed hotels reminded visitors the Irish have been part of its inspiration's past and present. In 2003 New York New York announced plans for Nine Fine Irishmen, with artifacts and traditional drinks Murphy's Red, Guinness, and Beamish. It was a $14 million project to build and import the material, but co-owner Paul Nolan said, "If someone understands Ireland and its pub and the pub culture, then they'll get this." Jack's Irish Pub at Palace Station had Irish entertainment and a nightly Irish jig contest, with the winner getting a free pint of Guinness. Named for Orleans builder Michael Gaughan's son, Brendan's Irish Pub featured various Irish drinks and bands. Part of a national chain whose Las Vegas location marked its first foray west of the Mississippi and claiming to be the area's wildest Irish pub, McFadden's Irish Pub took over two bars at the Rio, the Scottish-Irish Tilted Kilt and the

Dragon Bar, to form a 7,000-square-foot facility with a 100-foot mahogany bar and plans for hardwood floors and private parties.[56]

Another resort for tourists and locals was among the first to appeal to the Irish in everyone. At Summerlin's J. W. Marriott, J. C. Wooloughan Irish Pub, managed by County Donegal's Declan McGettigan, offered a Spirit of Ireland Festival, an interior custom built in Ireland, and "snugs"—private rooms. "Every little piece you see in there, outside of the dry wall, came from Ireland—the wood, the tiles, the bric-a-brac. It gives a greater sense of authenticity"—as do traditional Irish music, a Sunday night jig contest, Irish sports on television, and bartenders from home. Its menu included Irish stews and pies, soda bread, sticky toffee pudding, and potato pancakes with meats wrapped inside.[57]

One pub combined the history of local and tourist pubs. President of McNally Design Group USA, Brian McMullen, opened McNally's Las Vegas operations and helped design and build Nine Fine Irishmen, Fadó, and J. C. Wooloughan. Then he and his wife opened McMullan's Irish Pub west of the Strip on Tropicana. Manager Neil Burns, of Enniskillen, County Fermanagh, said, "I've been to a lot of so-called Irish bars in America and they're not really Irish." The grandson of bar owners in Glenarm, County Antrim, McMullan defined an Irish pub as "where you have a christening, communion, marriage, and wake, and they're all the same person." Their pub featured family photos and Irish sayings painted on the walls.[58]

Organizations

The Irish have faced problems similar to those of other ethnic groups in Las Vegas. As the local population approached two million early in the twenty-first century, a sense of community became harder to generate. Much like Southern California, Las Vegas grew and sprawled. Growth, distance, travel time, and work schedules at variance with a nine to five, Monday to Friday existence discourage involvement in clubs and organizations. The Irish exemplify overcoming and suffering from these problems.

Born in 1978, the Irish American Club sought to preserve Irish culture, history, literature, and the arts and served corned beef, soda bread, and Irish cream cookies at its meetings. Up to fifty members by the late 1990s, it took part in the annual St. Patrick's Day parade and aided the St. Vincent Dining Room, Las Vegas Academy High School for the Performing Arts, and Nathan Adelson Hospice, but it dissolved in 2008, due largely to financial issues, with three charter members still in the area: Margaret Welch, Cyn Winzer, and Dona Brown. Active in the Irish American community, Brown has been the Nevada Arts Council's representative for Irish culture and executive director of the International Festival Association, formed in 1976 to hold an annual multicultural fair. An antique dealer "when I'm not volunteering—volunteering is my middle name," Brown also teaches Irish music and dancing to advanced students in the Gael Force Music Academy.[59]

Southern Nevada's oldest Irish group, the Sons of Erin, now numbers well over two hundred members. Its biggest event is the St. Patrick's Day celebration. As then-president Ron Hohenstein, the son of an Irish mother, put it in 2002, "We kind of further the Irish tradition. It's socializing with fellow Irishmen. It's an opportunity to raise funds for charities," including St. Jude's Ranch for Children, Catholic Charities of Southern Nevada, and Christmas dinner for four hundred seniors. The Sons of Erin meets monthly at McMullan's, has a full slate of officers—president, first and second vice presidents, treasurer, and secretary—and hosts an annual golfing fund-raiser, spring and fall picnics, and social events. It has built on tradition: many club presidents return for additional terms, and past presidents receive the "green jacket" from the incoming president. For many years, the Sons of Erin worked with the Daughters of Erin, an otherwise independent group that held an annual Christmas party and funded scholarships for women attending UNLV and the University of Nevada, Reno.[60]

According to longtime member Don Jaye, the Sons of Erin began at Skinny Dugan's in 1966, thanks to "a group of business guys of Irish descent who decided they needed a club for themselves," but not just for "raising hell on St. Patrick's Day." Charter member Joe Delaney, St. Patrick in more than twenty-five parades, said, "We felt we could do things during the year to raise money, particularly for seniors and disadvantaged children," with the parade, a golf tourney, and annual award dinners. In 1967 they began a St. Patrick's dance at the Elks Lodge, with Brendan Boyer and the Royal Irish Show Band performing, and added the Christmas dinner. The Sons of Erin attracted a variety of members: club president Ted Farrell was a Metropolitan Police administrator and civilian auditor, 2004 Son of the Year Steve Morrissey was a project superintendent for a development firm, and 2006 Son of the Year and club vice president Jim Ermi was a software engineer.[61]

Their first parade marched down West Charleston on St. Patrick's Day, 1967. Due to traffic and attendance concerns, it moved to the Saturday closest to March 17. In 1976 Cohen & Kelly's Irish Pub became the site of a postparade block party, and it remained so until 1987, when the party moved to Fitzgeralds, then to other hotels downtown and on the Strip. In 1985 the parade added a grand marshal, starting with then-Governor Richard Bryan. In 2005 the Sons of Erin moved the event to Henderson after thirty-eight years in Las Vegas. Parade entertainment director Bob Feeney said costs were too high in Las Vegas, and club president Dick Linton added, "We didn't have an argument or fight with the city of Las Vegas." The city had waived fees, but Henderson helped more financially.[62]

In Henderson the parade and its accompanying events grew. Singer Ashley Davis, formerly of "Lord of the Dance," and the Fearon O'Connor School of Irish Dance performed in 2007. The next parade grew more. It had a sponsor (thanks in part to realtor and Sons of Erin vice president Larry Abbott) and was known as the Coldwell Banker Wardleys St. Patrick's Day Parade and Festival, lasting three days on Water Street. Feeney reported 120 parade entrants and a variety of entertainers. The City of Henderson donated the site and police to provide security. The parade drew about 20,000 viewers in 2007 and did still better in 2008.[63]

The Sons of Erin and the Irish American Club were not alone in promoting Irish heritage and culture. Notre Dame alumni club members qualified as Fighting Irish or their fans; according to president Jeanne Langen, they hold a "universal Notre Dame night" each April, with a speaker from the campus, a "school sendoff picnic" for students and parents, student and alumni events, and efforts to aid the homeless led by club priest Father John McShane. In 2000, Metro Police sergeant Paul Page started a branch of the Police and Fire Emerald Society, begun in New York in the 1950s; members work with youth and families in need, especially those associated with the police and fire departments, and their annual "Golf for the Heroes" event raises money for their foundation to fund these efforts. The Sun City Summerlin Irish Club began in 1998 and grew to about eighty members who welcome dancers and performers with Irish connections and speakers on Irish-related topics.[64]

One of Ireland's most popular sports has gained popularity in Las Vegas. The Sin City Irish Rugby Club brought together Irish and non-Irish who enjoyed one of the Emerald Isle's favorite sports. In 1998 the group spun off from the Las Vegas Blackjacks. Both clubs played throughout the region, and in 2008 the Blackjacks added a rugby program for boys between ages fourteen and eighteen. Women literally got into the game with the Las Vegas Slots Women's Rugby Club. Together, they demonstrated the survival and vibrancy of the Irish in Las Vegas.[65]

Conclusion

Several members of the Irish community worried about their group early in 2008. Neither the first nor the last ethnic group with such concerns, they cited intermarriage, lack of interest among the young, and financial problems as issues that kept social organizations and cultural awareness from growing as they should. But southern Nevada's growth has meant more Irish moving to the Valley and seeking outlets to show their pride in their past and themselves—whether through pubs that transport them vicariously to the Emerald Isle or through groups that enable them to meet those of similar mind and background. And while the local economy was suffering the effects of a nationwide recession in 2008, continued tourism and construction meant probable continued success for such prominent members of the Irish community as the Gaughans and the Boyds, important figures who can be cited as examples to inspire organizing and activity.

On one March 17 in the 1970s, lunch at a local elementary school included cookies with green icing. The children threw them away. When a playground worker asked why, they said their parents told them to avoid moldy food. The students felt better upon learning why the cookies were green, then spent the day, without prompting, pinching anyone not wearing green. As long as the pinching goes on, and the area keeps growing, the Irish will remain a force in Las Vegas.[66]

Notes

1. Wilbur S. Shepperson, *Restless Strangers: Nevada's Immigrants and Their Interpreters* (Reno: University of Nevada Press, 1970); Ronald M. James, *The Roar and the Silence: A History of Virginia City and the Comstock Lode* (Reno: University of Nevada Press, 1998); Jerry L. Simich and Thomas C. Wright, eds., *The Peoples of Las Vegas: One City, Many Faces* (Reno and Las Vegas: University of Nevada Press, 2005); Kevin Rafferty, "Catholics in Nevada," in *Community in the American West*, ed. Stephen Tchudi (Reno: A Halcyon Imprint of the Nevada Humanities Committee, 2001), 201–30. See also Stephan Thernstrom, ed., *Harvard Encyclopedia of American Ethnic Groups* (Cambridge: Harvard University Press, 1980), 524–45; www.census.gov.

2. *Las Vegas Review-Journal*, March 15, 2007. These comments came up in numerous interviews and conversations.

3. Fred E. Woods, *A Gamble in the Desert: The Mormon Mission in Las Vegas (1855–1857)* (Salt Lake City: Mormon Historic Sites Foundation, 2005); Ralph J. Roske and Michael S. Green, "Octavius Decatur Gass: Pah-Ute County Pioneer," *Journal of Arizona History* 29, no. 4 (Winter 1988): 371–90; A. D. Hopkins and K. J. Evans, eds., *The First 100: Portraits of the Men and Women Who Shaped Las Vegas* (Las Vegas: Huntington Press, 1999), 5–32; David Hackett Fischer, *Albion's Seed: Four British Folkways in America* (New York: Oxford University Press, 1988); *Hurricane Valley Journal*, January 9, 2008; Florence Lee Jones and John F. Cahlan, *Water: A History of Las Vegas*, vol. 1 (Las Vegas: Las Vegas Valley Water District, 1975), 6–54; Eugene P.

Moehring and Michael S. Green, *Las Vegas: A Centennial History* (Reno: University of Nevada Press, 2005), 1–56.

4. *Las Vegas Age,* October 2, 1909, May 10, 1913; Moehring and Green, *Las Vegas,* 9–56; Ralph J. Roske, *Las Vegas: A Desert Paradise* (Tulsa: Continental Heritage Press, 1986); Hopkins and Evans, *First 100,* 54–56, 115–20; *Las Vegas Review-Journal,* February 3, 1995, December 8, 2005.

5. Hopkins and Evans, *First 100,* 36–39, 84–87; *Las Vegas Age,* October 29, 1910, February 24, 1917, March 3, 1917, October 15, 1921; James S. Olson, "Pioneer Catholicism in Eastern and Southern Nevada, 1864–1931," *Nevada Historical Society Quarterly* 26, no. 3 (Fall 1983): 159–71; Richard E. Lingenfelter and Karen Rix Gash, *The Newspapers of Nevada: A History and Bibliography, 1854–1979* (Reno: University of Nevada Press, 1984), 110. Clark County's Web site, www.accessclarkcounty.com, includes results of all county elections.

6. *Las Vegas Review-Journal,* January 6, 2007; Robert V. Nickel, "Dollars, Defense, and the Desert: Southern Nevada's Military Economy and World War II," *Nevada Historical Society Quarterly* 47, no. 4 (Winter 2004): 303–27; Moehring and Green, *Las Vegas,* 80–131.

7. Kevin Kenny, *The American Irish: A History* (New York: Longman, 2000), 163.

8. Russell R. Elliott and William D. Rowley, *History of Nevada,* 2nd ed. (Lincoln: University of Nebraska Press, 1987); *Political History of Nevada* (Carson City: State Printing Office, 1996); Jerome E. Edwards, *Pat McCarran: Political Boss of Nevada* (Reno: University of Nevada Press, 1982); Michael Ybarra, *Washington Gone Crazy: Senator Pat McCarran and the Great American Communist Hunt* (New York: Steerforth Press, 2004); Ralph L. Denton and Michael S. Green, *A Liberal Conscience: Ralph Denton, Nevadan* (Reno: University of Nevada Oral History Program, 2001), 61–116; Grant Sawyer, Gary E. Elliott, and R. T. King, *Hang Tough! Grant Sawyer: An Activist in the Governor's Mansion* (Reno: University of Nevada Oral History Program, 1993), 23–38.

9. *Las Vegas Review-Journal,* March 6–13, 2004; *Las Vegas Sun,* March 6–13, 2004; Hopkins and Evans, *First 100,* 311–14; Sawyer, Elliott, and King, *Hang Tough!* 159, 174–75; Denton and Green, *A Liberal Conscience,* 341–45; Joseph N. Crowley, "Race and Residence: The Politics of Open Housing in Nevada," in *Sagebrush and Neon: Studies in Nevada Politics,* ed. Eleanore Bushnell (Reno: University of Nevada, Reno, Bureau of Governmental Research, 1973), 55–74; Annelise Orleck, *Storming Caesars Palace: How Black Mothers Fought Their Own War on Poverty* (Boston: Beacon Press, 2005).

10. Bob Miller and Ross Miller have been the subject of ample media attention. Also, Governor Miller spoke with me extensively about his family.

11. Guinn received much news coverage throughout his career, which has roughly paralleled my residence in southern Nevada. See also Jon Ralston, *The Anointed One: An Inside Look at Nevada Politics* (Las Vegas: Huntington Press, 1999).

12. Hopkins and Evans, *First 100,* 235–40. On the Foleys, see Sawyer, Elliott, and King, *Hang Tough*; Denton and Green, *A Liberal Conscience*; Edwards, *McCarran*; and Hank Greenspun and Alex Pelle, *Where I Stand: The Record of a Reckless Man*

(New York: David McKay, 1966). Mary Lou Foley provided me with background on her family's history. The ensuing paragraphs on the Foleys are based on newspaper accounts and conversations over the years with the late Judge Roger D. Foley, George Foley Sr., Mary Lou Foley, and Helen Foley.

13. Ed Reid and Ovid DeMaris, *The Green Felt Jungle* (New York: Trident Press, 1963), 113; *Las Vegas Review-Journal,* January 12, 1996.

14. Hopkins and Evans, *First 100,* 252–54; Denton and Green, *A Liberal Conscience,* 123, 229–30, 259; *Las Vegas Review-Journal,* March 6, 1997; *Las Vegas Sun,* March 17, 1997.

15. *Las Vegas Review-Journal,* December 12, 2003; author's files (I wrote a history of the McNamee family for its private use).

16. www.accessclarkcounty.com; *Las Vegas Review-Journal,* December 5, 2005, January 22, 2007; *Las Vegas Sun,* June 30, 1998, April 25, 2003; Denton and Green, *A Liberal Conscience,* 177–78, 184, 303–304, 359; www.lionelsawyer.com; Hopkins and Evans, *First 100,* 315–17; Marilee Joyce, ed., *The Gentle Giant: How Jim Joyce Helped Shape Nevada Politics for a Generation* (Las Vegas: Nevada Publications, 1994); Dennis Ortwein, interview by author, April 23, 2008; Aileen Murphy, interview by author, April 25, 2008; Marilee Joyce, interview by author, April 20, 2008.

17. *Las Vegas Review-Journal,* September 3, 1997, November 7, 2003, December 9, 2006; *Las Vegas Sun,* October 25, 1998; Eugene Moehring, *Resort City in the Sunbelt: Las Vegas, 1930–2000,* 2nd ed. (Reno: University of Nevada Press, 2000), includes numerous references to Cragin; Hopkins and Evans, *First 100,* 111–14, 180–82.

18. *Las Vegas Review-Journal,* April 7, 1988, November 27, 1993, September 3, 1997, November 7, 2003, April 8, 2004, December 3, 2006, December 9, 2006; *Las Vegas Sun,* February 11, 1997, October 25, 1998; Moehring, *Resort City in the Sunbelt.* See also Hopkins and Evans, *First 100,* 111–14, 180–82; George L. Ullom, Jamie Coughtry, and R. T. King, *George Ullom: Politics and Development in Las Vegas, 1930s–1970s* (Reno: University of Nevada Oral History Program, 1989); Robbins Cahill, "Recollections of Work in State Politics, Government, Taxation, Gaming Control, Clark County administration and the Nevada Resort Association" (Reno: University of Nevada Oral History Program, 1977).

19. *Las Vegas Review-Journal,* November 7, 2003; *Las Vegas Sun,* April 19, 1996. The G-Sting scandal received extensive local news coverage.

20. *Las Vegas Sun,* May 1, 2006.

21. Ibid., February 2, 2004; Houssels Biography File, Department of Special Collections, Lied Library, UNLV; Stanley W. Paher, ed., *Nevada Towns & Tales: Volume II—The South* (Las Vegas: Nevada Publications, 1982), 419; Moehring and Green, *Las Vegas.* I have conducted extensive interviews with Houssels Jr. on his family's history, and he and his wife Nancy provided a great deal of useful information.

22. *Las Vegas Review-Journal,* July 30, 1992, April 29, 1998, January 12, 2006; www.nevadaballet.com.

23. Bill Moody and A. D. Hopkins, "Jackie Gaughan: Keeping the Faith on Fremont Street," in *The Players: The Men Who Made Las Vegas,* ed. Jack E. Sheehan

(Reno: University of Nevada Press, 1997), 120–32; *Las Vegas Review-Journal,* January 16, 1993, May 8, 2008; Reid and DeMaris, *Green Felt Jungle,* 222–23, 226.

24. Sheehan, *The Players,* 120–32; *Las Vegas Review-Journal,* December 18, 22, and 23, 2005, July 26, 2006, January 27, 2008.

25. Sheehan, "Sam Boyd's Quiet Legacy," in Sheehan, *The Players,* 104–19; *Las Vegas Review-Journal,* January 27, 2008. I am indebted to Gina Polovina, vice president of government and community affairs for Boyd Gaming, for information on the Boyds.

26. *Las Vegas Review-Journal,* October 5, 1993, December 11, 1993, May 13, 2005, February 14, 2006.

27. A. D. Hopkins, "Benny Binion: He Who Has the Gold Makes the Rules," in Sheehan, *The Players,* 48–67; Hopkins and Evans, *First 100,* 224–27. Lee Barnes's superb novel, *The Lucky* (Reno: University of Nevada Press, 2003), provides excellent insight into Binion and his family.

28. See also Jeff German, *Murder in Sin City: The Death of a Las Vegas Casino Boss* (New York: Avon Books, 2001).

29. *Los Angeles Times,* February 21, 1960; Tom Sitton, *Los Angeles Transformed: Fletcher Bowron's Urban Reform Revival, 1938–1953* (Albuquerque: University of New Mexico Press, 2005); Sergio Lalli, "Cliff Jones: 'The Big Juice,'" in Sheehan, *The Players,* 23–34.

30. Michael Wiesenberg, *The Ultimate Casino Guide: 1000 Great Casinos from America, Canada, and Around the World,* 218; *Las Vegas Review-Journal,* June 19, 1992, June 18, 1995, August 19, 1995, April 29, 1996, December 19, 1997, August 18, 2006; *Las Vegas Sun,* January 5, 2001; *Las Vegas Business Press,* January 16, 2006, August 21, 2006, February 14, 2007; http://library.nevada.edu/arch/casinosbytime.html.

31. Hopkins and Evans, *First 100,* 329–31; Richard B. Taylor, ed., *Laughlin, Nevada History,* 2 vols. (Wilbraham, Mass.: Van Volumes, 1988); *Las Vegas Review-Journal,* December 13, 1992, July 10, 2002, December 3, 2004, December 9, 2005, April 17, 2006; *Las Vegas Sun,* March 14, 2003, July 9, 2003, January 30, 2006. Harvey Diederich, a longtime Las Vegas publicist and friend of McDonald, and Excalibur executive Valerie Moon were helpful in tracking down his background. See also Dick Odessky, *Fly on the Wall: Las Vegas' Good Old, Bad Old Days* (Las Vegas: Huntington Press, 1999).

32. *Las Vegas Sun,* August 9, 2002, April 28, 2003, October 10, 2003.

33. Michael S. Green, "The Las Vegas Newspaper War of the 1950s," *Nevada Historical Society Quarterly* 31, no. 3 (Fall 1988): 155–57; *Las Vegas Review,* September 18, 1909.

34. Hopkins and Evans, *First 100,* 88–94; Green, "The Las Vegas Newspaper War of the 1950s," 155–82; John F. Cahlan, "Reminiscences of a Nevada Newspaperman, University Regent, and Public-Spirited Citizen" (Reno: University of Nevada Oral History Program, 1969); John F. Cahlan and Jamie Coughtry, "John F. Cahlan: Fifty Years in Journalism and Community Development" (Reno: University of

Nevada Oral History Program, 1987); Florence Lee Jones and John F. Cahlan, *Water: A History of Las Vegas,* 2 vols. (Las Vegas: Las Vegas Valley Water District, 1975).

35. *Las Vegas Review-Journal,* August 8, 2002; *Las Vegas Sun,* August 8, 2002; Greenspun and Pelle, *Where I Stand.*

36. *Las Vegas Review-Journal,* January 13, 1993, March 16, 1995, November 20, 1997, July 16, 2006; *Las Vegan: The City Magazine,* March 1980.

37. *Las Vegas Age,* March 21, 1908; *Las Vegas Review-Journal,* March 20, 1996; *Las Vegas Sun,* October 20, 1999; *Boulder City News,* March 16, 2006; John Bernard McGloin, SJ, "Patrick Manogue, Gold Miner and Bishop and His 'Cathedral on the Comstock,'" *Nevada Historical Society Quarterly* 14, no. 2 (Summer 1971): 24–31.

38. Hopkins and Evans, *First 100,* 190–92.

39. http://www.lasvegas-diocese.org.

40. Ibid.; *Las Vegas Review-Journal,* November 11, 1998, April 7, 2001; *Las Vegas Sun,* June 17, 1998.

41. *Las Vegas Review-Journal,* April 20, 1992, March 28, 2007, May 12, 2007; *Las Vegas Sun,* May 26, 2001, February 14, 2003, December 7, 2004.

42. *Las Vegas Sun,* June 3, 2006; www.stillpointcsd.org.

43. *Las Vegas Review-Journal,* June 29, 2002, August 1, 2007. *Las Vegas Sun,* March 17, 1998, December 7, 2000, June 21, 2001, March 26, 2002.

44. *Las Vegas Review-Journal,* June 21, 1992, September 9, 1993, January 13, 2001, October 24, 2002, October 25, 2004, January 9, 2008; *Las Vegas Sun,* February 11, 2000; Cynthia Cunningham ms., Department of Special Collections, Lied Library, UNLV; Hopkins and Evans, *First 100,* 156–58.

45. *Las Vegas Review-Journal,* June 23, 1998, June 26, 1998; Dennis N. Griffin, *Policing Las Vegas: A History of Law Enforcement in Southern Nevada* (Las Vegas: Huntington Press, 2005).

46. www.ccsd.net.

47. *Las Vegas Review-Journal,* January 31, 1992, April 19, 1992, August 29, 1996, April 22, 1998, April 10, 2008. See also Donn Knepp, *Las Vegas: The Entertainment Capital* (Menlo Park: Lane Publishing, 1987).

48. *Las Vegas Review-Journal,* March 13, 2002, August 6, 2002, March 14, 2004, June 24, 2008; *Las Vegas Sun,* June 6, 1997, December 11, 1998, March 30, 2000, August 4, 2000, March 15, 2001, July 12, 2001, November 16, 2001, September 13, 2002, September 5, 2003, February 10, 2004.

49. *Las Vegas Sun,* April 12, 1996, September 4, 1997, June 9, 1998, February 17, 1999, March 25, 1999, March 26, 1999, October 14, 1999, February 4, 2000, October 12, 2001, April 12, 2002, September 11, 2002, September 12, 2003, January 7, 2004, September 2, 2004.

50. www.fitzgeralds.com; *Las Vegas Review-Journal,* December 6, 2000, December 10, 2000, March 16, 2001, October 18, 2001; *Las Vegas Sun,* December 10, 2001, November 1, 2007.

51. *Las Vegas Review-Journal,* March 17, 1997, December 22, 2005; *Las Vegas Sun,* March 14, 2003, May 23, 2003, August 23, 2005; www.osheaslasvegas.com; www.emeraldislandcasino.com.

52. *Las Vegas Review-Journal,* March 18, 1996, March 16, 2001, November 9, 2005; *Las Vegas Sun,* January 31, 2001, September 14, 2001, July 3, 2003, January 30, 2007; *The Washington Post,* April 25, 2008; www.irishpubcompany.com. The author confesses to doing primary research across from UNLV during his undergraduate and graduate studies there.

53. *Las Vegas Review-Journal,* March 17, 1993, February 27, 1998, July 2, 2006; *Las Vegas Sun,* March 14, 1997, October 9, 2006; www.hennesseyslasvegas.com; www.alohavalley.com/directory/nightclub/lally-s-of-las-vegas/view-details.html.

54. *Las Vegas Review-Journal,* June 21, 2000, July 12, 2000, October 26, 2001, March 13, 2002; *Las Vegas Sun,* online, January 31, 2008; http://threeangrywives.com.

55. *Las Vegas Review-Journal,* March 16, 2001, March 13, 2002, March 17, 2006, December 22, 2006, March 16, 2007; *Las Vegas Sun,* April 18, 2000; *UNLV Rebel Yell,* March 13, 2008; www.aulddubliner.com.

56. *Las Vegas Review-Journal,* December 19, 2001, March 13, 2002, March 14, 2003, March 7, 2008; *Las Vegas Sun,* March 13, 2003, July 9, 2003, November 28, 2006, online edition, January 31, 2008; *Los Angeles Times,* March 4, 2008; *UNLV Rebel Yell,* March 13, 2008; *Las Vegas Weekly,* January 17, 2008; www.orleanscasino.com/entertainment/brendans-pub.

57. *Las Vegas Review-Journal,* March 13, 2002, March 14, 2003, March 15, 2007; *Las Vegas Sun,* August 25, 2000, October 10, 2000, December 5, 2003; www.rampartcasino.com/JCWooloughans.htm.

58. *Las Vegas Review-Journal,* March 14, 2003, March 15, 2007; *Las Vegas Sun,* January 31, 2001, December 4, 2002, August 18, 2004; *Los Angeles Times,* March 4, 2008; www.irishpubcompany.com; www.mcmullansirishpub.com.

59. *Las Vegas Review-Journal,* May 28, 1996; *Las Vegas Sun,* August 25, 2000; Dona Brown, interview by author, April 25, 2008; www.iffalv.org.

60. *Las Vegas Review-Journal,* March 17, 1998, March 17, 2002; www.lvsoe.net; *40th Anniversary Edition, Las Vegas Sons of Erin St. Patrick's Day Parade & Festival Program,* March 16–19, 2006.

61. *Las Vegas Review-Journal,* March 17, 1998, March 17, 2002; *Las Vegas Sun,* December 11, 2001; *38th Anniversary Edition, Las Vegas Sons of Erin St. Patrick's Day Parade & Festival Program,* March 13, 2004; *40th Anniversary Edition, Las Vegas Sons of Erin St. Patrick's Day Parade & Festival Program,* March 16–19, 2006.

62. *Las Vegas Review-Journal,* March 18, 2005, March 16, 2006; *Las Vegas Sun,* February 1, 2005; *40th Anniversary Edition, Las Vegas Sons of Erin St. Patrick's Day Parade & Festival Program,* March 16–19, 2006.

63. *Southeast View,* March 13, 2008; *Las Vegas Sun,* February 23, 2007; *Las Vegas Review-Journal,* March 16, 2007.

64. www.nvemeraldsociety.org; *Las Vegas Sun,* September 4, 1996, November 10, 1998, July 11, 2001; www.suncity-summerlin.com; Aileen Murphy, interview by

author, April 26, 2008; Regina Haucke, interview by author, April 26, 2008; Jeanne Langen, interview by author, April 28, 2008.

65. http://lasvegas.undclub.org; *Southeast View,* April 29, 2008; www.sincityirish.com; www.lasvegasblackjacksrugby.com.

66. The playground worker, my decidedly non-Irish mother, was shocked.

CHAPTER 2

The Germans

CAROLE COSGROVE TERRY

Since the early years of Las Vegas, Germans have constituted a small percentage of the city's population that never congealed into an ethnic enclave or community. In fact, it was not until the 1970s that German immigrants and German Americans in Las Vegas were able to form ethnic organizations. After peaking in the 1980s, these groups are finding their memberships either declining or stable but small. Further, unlike several European American groups, the Las Vegas Germans do not share the bond of a common religion. As a result, they are very diffused and maintain a relatively low visibility. Individual German newcomers today, regardless of their age, still cling to at least some form of their heritage and attend some German festivals, but they tend to acculturate with the passage of time. The study of Las Vegas's Germans helps one understand how a European immigrant population, once very prevalent and influential in America, is becoming absorbed into the mainstream culture.[1]

Immigrating from Germany

In 1986 approximately 44 million, or 18 percent, of the American population claimed some German ancestry. Most Americans who self-identify as "German stock" are descended from pre-World War I immigrants from Germany, Austria, and Switzerland. Germans immigrated in three "waves" separated by wars and periods of economic hardship in Europe. The first wave in the 1700s comprised mostly farmers, often families or entire communities, who fled religious persecution and settled largely in Pennsylvania. As a result of mispronouncing or misunderstanding the word for German, "Deutsch," their neighbors called them "Dutch," a label still used today. Many descendants of these early arrivals still practice customs and traditions brought by their forefathers. The second wave, arriving in the 1800s before the Civil War, included skilled craftsmen, farmers, and political refugees "pushed" by overpopulation, overdivided farms, periodic famine, and political persecution and "pulled" to Texas, California, and the Midwest by enthusiastic pamphlets and letters, adventurous plans for new German colonies, and the California gold rush. Before the 1850s, the less skilled remained in the larger cities, particularly New York, St. Louis, Cincinnati, and Milwaukee, creating ethnic enclaves such as Kleindeutschland (Little Germany) in New York. In these settlements, the German language, taverns and beer gardens, and formal Vereine (clubs) gave immigrants a sensation of living almost as they had in the "homeland."[2]

After the Civil War, a third wave of unskilled laborers looking for work in America's burgeoning industrial cities peaked in 1885 and subsided appreciably by 1912. Some found themselves without jobs or working long hours at menial tasks in unhealthful factories and living in overcrowded, miserable tenements. As a result, many joined the growing labor movement and participated in antimanagement strikes, fostering an anti-German sentiment among the native born. In addition, Americans interpreted Kaiser Wilhelm's highly militaristic policies after 1890 as a push for world dominance and a threat to the United States.[3]

This anti-German sentiment escalated with the unprovoked sinking of the passenger liner *Lusitania* in May 1915, and when the United States entered World War I in 1917, violence erupted across the country. Although there is only one recorded execution by mob violence, German Americans were flogged, their homes and schools vandalized, their newspapers attacked, and some of their towns renamed. Even foods were renamed: hamburger became "liberty steak," frankfurters, "hot dogs," and sauerkraut, "liberty cabbage." In Nevada the anti-German frenzy was not as violent as in some areas, but Edward von Tobel Sr. cautioned his children against speaking German outside their home, and he lamented the prejudice in letters to his parents in Germany. Articles in the *Las Vegas Age* changed from features about benevolent German generosity to articles on potential spying and descriptions of German atrocities. As a result, across the country and in Nevada, many German immigrants denied their roots and abandoned their birth language, culture, and heritage.[4]

After World War I, restrictive government policies caused the previously massive German immigration to slow to a trickle. During the interwar years and World War II, blatant anti-German hysteria did not surface largely because most of the immigrants and their descendants spoke English, had anglicized their names, and had assimilated to a large extent into the American mainstream culture. Las Vegas, however, had one incident. In 1938 Edward W. Scott "mowed down" and killed German-born Larry Saunders because Saunders symbolized the whole "Hun Army." Immediately after World War II, lenient policies allowed refugees and relatives of American servicemen to immigrate easily, but with the 1952 McCarran-Walter Act and subsequent 1965 Hart-Cellar Act, the United States resumed restrictive immigration policies, giving preference to newcomers from developing nations over those from industrialized ones. Unless associated with the government, a major institution, or a corporation, "ordinary" German immigrants still find obtaining green cards a long and tedious process.[5]

German Americans' deliberate abandonment of their ethnic identity under the pressures of World War I, combined with the subsequent reduction of immigration from Germany to a trickle, presents a methodological challenge to the study of Las Vegas Germans. Among European Americans, ethnic identity is voluntary, as the case of the Germans readily underscores. Since most of the numerous Hoffmans, Warners, and Schmidts, along with the many more German-descended people with anglicized surnames, do not recognize their German heritage—except once a decade in the census record—this study necessarily focuses on those relatively few who do self-identify as German. These are largely immigrants, although they also include second- and even third-generation people of at least partial German background who cultivate their ethnic identity in various ways.[6]

Early Settlers in Las Vegas

Basically a railroad town in its early days, Las Vegas attracted first- and second-generation Germans to skilled positions as engineers, carpenters, and ice-plant operators as well as to allied businesses. Some even came before the city's official founding on May 15, 1905. Frank and Martha Matzdorf, who arrived in a mule-drawn cart in 1905, for example, opened the first hotel and restaurant, The Meadows, and then operated The White House, an adobe brick hotel located on East Bridger Street. Mrs. Matzdorf lived there until her death in 1950. Winnie Westlake, another early settler, came before the 1905 land auction, and, until the 1920s, operated a rooming house adjacent to her home, the first wooden structure on South Second Street.[7]

Businessmen Peter Buol, Edward Von Tobel Sr., and Jake Beckley arrived in 1905, and Jake's brother, William, followed in 1908. All were sons of German Swiss immigrants, and all were well established by 1910. Edward's wife, Maria, was born in Germany. Buol, the first mayor of Las Vegas and a real-estate developer, was very instrumental in the early growth of Las Vegas. With German-born Peter Maurer as an employee, Von Tobel and Jake Beckley quickly opened a lumber business on south First Street that operated until 1965. Jake left that business in 1908 to join his brother in a clothing business at First Street and Fremont that operated until 1942. Von Tobel was an officer in the Elks, Masonic, and Eagles Lodges, and William Beckley was an early member of the Elks, Rotary Club, and Chamber of Commerce. The social activities of the ladies of all three families were often listed in the newspapers, indicating how assimilated they had become into the American culture. Sharon Schmidt, von Tobel's granddaughter, recalls that her grandmother followed German customs and cooked German cuisine, but there were no German-oriented organizations in town and her family did not purposely socialize with other Las Vegas Germans. Nor did a German spatial enclave develop—in contrast to several Eastern cities—owing to the small numbers of Germans and their ability to assimilate quickly.[8]

Newspapers provide information on the activities of other early German settlers. Joseph S. Smith, who listed Germany as his birthplace in the 1910 census, originally worked at the ice plant, but he also built many residences and became the first Ford Motor dealer and later the TWA agent in Las Vegas. Charles A. Wescher owned and operated the Nevada Shoe Store from 1917. In the 1920s and 1930s, Suzette Lampe was the proprietor of Suzette's Beauty Shop, and Samuel Gelber operated an electric shop until he retired in 1943. Richard Roschel operated an ice-cream parlor with William Beckley and frequently donated food for Christmas baskets for the needy. Taking in boarders supplemented the income of businessmen such as print-shop owner William Laubenhumer and entrepreneur William Beckley, who took in his brother, Jacob.[9]

German roots were common to other successful early arrivals. Ella Wengert's German husband, Frank, worked on the railroad. Her son, Cyril S. Wengert, became an influential banker and vice president of the original Southern Nevada Power and Telephone Company and of its successor, Nevada Power Company. He was active in numerous community organizations, including the Knights of Columbus, Chamber of Commerce, and Rotary Club. Ella's daughter married Harley A. Harmon, well-known businessman, community leader, chairman of the Nevada Public Service Commission, and one-time candidate for governor. Clarence Underhill, whose wife had German parents, owned the Economy Laundry and was one of the founders of the Coca-Cola bottling plant. As reported in the media, Germans were accepted by their American neighbors. It is not known if they adhered to specific German rituals or celebrations, but one might assume that all replicated the von Tobel family by practicing the traditions to some extent at home but rarely in public. Many of the original Las Vegas Germans survived into the 1950s and 1960s and many of their descendants still call Las Vegas home.[10]

Since the 1940s, Las Vegas's German born have included senior citizens, many from California, coming to take advantage of the warm weather and lower living costs. Younger immigrants are attracted by Las Vegas's many employment opportunities. Perhaps because of their small numbers and the cultural dictate of quick assimilation during and after World War I, the German newcomers in Las Vegas never congregated in ethnically defined neighborhoods. According to the 2000 U.S. census, of the 6,621 German born residing in Nevada, 4,665 lived in Las Vegas. In 2007, with the metropolitan Las Vegas population at around 2 million, retired honorary consul for Germany Sigrid Sommer estimated that 35,000 to 40,000 southern Nevadans claim German ancestry, but of those, according to the *Las Vegas Review-Journal*, in 2005 only 6,910 spoke German.[11]

Celebrating German Culture

All German customs, traditions, or rituals come under the cultural umbrella of Gemütlichkeit, a philosophy of life and way of living that emphasizes a balance between hard work and joyful celebration of Sundays and holidays. In Las Vegas, Gemütlichkeit is most evident among immigrants, but some second- and third-generation German Americans share in it. Whether Catholic, Lutheran, or nonprofessing, whether originally from northern or southern Germany, Austria, or Switzerland, they all share customs and celebrations.[12]

German newcomers in Las Vegas tend to celebrate their Christmas and Easter holidays and Karneval and Oktoberfest festivals with traditions they brought from their native home, with regional differences dictating some variation in rituals. On December 6 in northern Germany, children watch for the sinister Knecht Ruprecht aus dem Walde (the servant from the wood), as well as for gift-bearing St. Nicholas, whereas Knecht is absent in the South. Der Weihnachtsmann (Father Christmas) often brings gifts on Christmas Eve in the North, whereas das Christkind (the Christ Child) does so in the South. At Easter time only northern Germans create der Osterbaum (Easter tree), where eggs are blown out, decorated, and hung on yellow forsythia branches. These regional differences in celebratory rituals tend to blur by the second or third generation in the United States.[13]

At mid-nineteenth century, German immigrants brought the Christmas tree and gift-giving traditions to America, and magazines featured scenes of families encircling a tree with gifts. These practices were "Americanized" and commercialized by merchants in the late 1800s to promote seasonal purchases. Santa Claus himself evolved from St. Nicholas by layering onto the saintly, gift-bearing bishop the image of a German-style Yankee peddler to create the puckish, treasure-laden icon that merchants adopted to promote the season. Most German Las Vegans today celebrate Christmas on

December 24th, but where homes include members from two cultures, they may add Santa Claus and gift exchanges on Christmas morning.[14]

A German Christmastime ritual centers on St. Nicholas himself, the fourth-century patron saint of children. On the evening of December 5, children put their shoes or boots outside their door in hopes of receiving sweets, fruits, and nuts from him, rather than a stick for bad behavior. Dreaded Knecht Ruprecht accompanies St. Nicholas in northern Germany. Most of Las Vegas's Germans practice the tradition when children are in their homes, and a few still do so for their grandchildren. Two other widely practiced German Christmastime traditions in both religious and nonreligious homes are the Advent wreath and Advent calendar. The pine-branch wreath has four candles, one to be lit for each Sunday in Advent. The Advent calendar was invented in Munich in the late 1800s to help children anticipate Christmas. From December 1 through the 24th, both adults and children faithfully open a window in a Christmas scene looking for a chocolate or a sweet. Calendars with chocolates are now available in local stores; however, in the past, old-timers report, they had to be imported by friends from Germany.[15]

The Easter egg and the chocolate bunny are secular icons originating in Germany that were also exploited by late nineteenth-century American merchants. The word "Ostern" (Easter) comes from the Germanic goddess Ostara, the icon of springtime. The origin of the Easter bunny is the Osterhase (Easter rabbit), a pre-Christian sacred animal who would lay and decorate eggs and leave them and a life-sized version of himself for children to find. Originally simply hard boiled and colored, Easter eggs were later made of paper, wood, or sugar when they moved out of the folk into the commercial arena.[16]

German public festivals draw immigrants and their descendants closer to their roots. The celebration that Americans identify as quintessentially German is Oktoberfest. This festival originated in 1818 in Munich, Bavaria, and the original Hofbräuhaus, founded there in 1828, has operated continuously since except for wartime interruptions. Attendees in lederhosen, green jackets, and hats with brushes drink beer, sing songs, stomp their feet, and sway together to the "oom-pah-pah" brass-band music. In Las Vegas's past, Oktoberfest celebrations were held at the larger local German clubs, in tents at hotels, in lodges, and at the long-gone Alpine Village restaurant. The German-American Social Club of Nevada and the Deutsch American Society of Southern Nevada still hold celebrations with music by the Dummkopfs, dancing by the Schuhplattlers, imported beers, and German foods, and the local Hofbräuhaus—a replica of the Munich original—has added celebration venues since it opened in 2004.

Maifest is a comparable festival held in the spring but is not as widely known as Oktoberfest. In Las Vegas, the German-American Social Club and Deutsch American Society host evenings of drinking, dining, and watching the Schuhplattlers dance around a Maypole, and the Hofbräuhaus offers special beers and brass bands. Maifest attracts fewer celebrants to the clubs than Oktoberfest, but attendance is growing as more and more Americans become familiar with the festival.[17]

Karneval (also known as Fastnacht or Fasching) is a winter and early springtime festival originating in communities along the Rhine River. Although officially beginning on November 11 at 11:11 AM, the various German Vereine or clubs hold fancy-dress balls or "Galas" after the New Year and throughout the Lenten season. Mocking local authority or royalty, they each choose a Prinzenpaar, a "princely pair" or prince and princess, to reign over the activities of the season and to invite those in neighboring communities to join them at their events. In America clubs under the auspices of the German-American Mardi Gras Association organize Karneval galas nationwide during the winter.

In Las Vegas the Gala is currently held at the Union Plaza Hotel in early January. Participants include members from clubs across the country, a few people from Germany, and the general public. The festivities last two days: Friday evening is costume night, with the crowning of the Gala's Prinzenpaar, and each club performs a dance or skit for the audience. Saturday night is more traditional, as members wear their uniforms in bright colors and parade about the room honoring the Prinzenpaar of each club. Members wear Orden, medallions representing their membership that particular year and past years. German is the predominant language, although English is becoming more prevalent as the number of English-speaking members grows. Some Las Vegas Germans feel that some of the ritual is lost in translation, but Barbara Phillips, president of the Vagabonds Club, believes that the growing use of English will not alter the festival, because the music by German bands, the German food, and the nonstop dancing by performers and celebrants alike will never change.[18]

An integral part of any German festival is its brass band popular music, and Las Vegas has had several venues where it is played. As early as the 1970s, the four-man Bavarian Brass Band, featuring founder Franz Praxl on the traditional button-box accordion, Willie Brencher on tuba, Gerhard Kinzel on guitar, and Walter Buchner on drums played regularly for the German-American Social Club of Nevada and for local festivals. After the group disbanded in 1982, Praxl went on to join the Dummkopfs, a five-piece band specializing in German "omm-pah-pah" music that still entertains at many club-sponsored festivals today. The irony is that the current performers are not German born; the group evolved from an English comedy ten-piece group called the Nitwits featured at the Stardust hotel who later donned lederhosen and played German music but with the same slapstick format. Locals remember them playing at the Mount Charleston Lodge for over twenty-one years, and currently they play twice a week at the Skyline Casino on Boulder Highway as well as at festivals and private functions. Since it opened in 2004, the Hofbräuhaus restaurant has regularly imported brass bands directly from Bavaria.[19]

Herb and Nicki Albinus entertained at the German-American Social Club as the two-person "Autobahn" Las Vegas German band until December of 2006. Herb played the keyboard and accordion, and Nicki sang both German classical and folk songs. Both are fluent in German and well versed in the German band, Schlager (German pop hits), and folk repertoires.[20]

A small German dance group, the Bavarian Schuhplattlers (also known as the Volks Dance Group) regular appear at the Maifest, Oktoberfest and at the International Food and Folklife Festival held in April as well as at venues beyond Las Vegas. The group of sixteen performers, aged eighteen to eighty-two, began informally in the 1970s at the German-American Social Club. In 1991 Art Ruckle, born in America but extremely interested in German culture, assumed leadership of the group and enlisted other interested dancers to revitalize it.[21]

Germans do not have to leave their homes to enjoy ethnic entertainment. Over the years, three radio shows featuring German music and conversation have operated in Las Vegas. In 1972 Christine Stanley began the first German-language radio show, *Bells of Home*; she was joined by Gerhard Kinzel, who served as engineer and learned the technical side "from scratch." Because of funding problems, the show lasted only two years. In 1987 Kinzel, performing under his first name, Gerhard, started the second, very popular one-hour German language and music show on KLAV radio. Kinzel knew that many taped the show, because he could hear his program when driving around Las Vegas in his car. Lack of financial sponsorship forced him to leave KLAV, but within a week, KUNV radio, the University of Nevada, Las Vegas (UNLV) station, had recruited him. He occasionally conducted interviews but was careful to stay away from the politics. Kinzel continued at KUNV until 1992, when management changed the station's programming to an all-jazz format.[22]

The third show began on November 4, 2002, when Herb Albinus resuscitated a program that a German group, Dara Vela, had abandoned after only one performance. With the initial sponsorship from Cafe Heidelberg, he played German music CDs and provided entertainment for forty-eight weeks until he moved to New York. Rather than see the program cancelled, Sylvia Brunn, with the technical help of Frank Schleidt, took his place and still broadcasts The *Las Vegas German Show* on Sunday mornings on KLAV (AM1230). It features "the best German Musik on Las Vegas's only German Radio Show," according to their publicity. Although the conversation is mostly in German, particularly during interviews with guests from Germany, English and German are used for current-event announcements to reach as wide an audience as possible. Although Brunn and Schleidt currently have three corporate sponsors and a sponsorship club for monthly donations, they are always looking for more advertisers. The Sunday morning hour precludes those who regularly attend church, but many Germans listen, old-timers and newcomers alike.[23]

German Organizations in Las Vegas

With some European ethnic groups such as the Greeks and Serbians, religious affiliation bonds newcomers together, but such is not the case among German southern Nevadans. Approximately a third of those interviewed for this chapter attend various Catholic churches, a third Protestant, mainly Lutheran, and a third do not attend any church. Those who do go to church report that although there may be a few Germans in their congregation, they do not find any formal or informal groups.

German social clubs in Las Vegas are the only formal institutions available for immigrants to help combat homesickness and for interested German Americans to affirm their ethnic identity. After the first was founded in 1972, several others followed, each with a different flavor and emphasis reflecting the members' interests. The oldest, largest, and most visible club today, the German-American Social Club of Nevada, was founded by 40 to 50 Germans and German Americans. They advertised in the local newspapers to attract members and met and held festivals "just about anywhere that would give us a place" until, in 1981, they bought their current clubhouse on east Lake Mead Boulevard in North Las Vegas. Membership grew to a peak of 640 in the mid-1980s. The club sponsored a Karneval group, Rotweiß (Red and White), and a folk-dance group, and members danced to the Bavarian Brass Band and regularly held Oktoberfest and Maifest celebrations.[24]

Currently, German-American Social Club membership has fallen to the high 300s, as many of the early members have moved or passed away. The decor and ambience of its clubhouse in North Las Vegas remains true to its German roots, and one is immediately thrust into the atmosphere of a tavern in a German town. The only requirement for membership today is a strong interest in German culture and music. Since some members are second generation, English is the primary language, but those who wish to keep or improve their German language skills can easily find native speakers with whom to practice. The club still advertises in the newspapers, in the telephone book, on the Internet and on the Sunday morning German radio show, but many younger German immigrants are not interested in joining. The club also promotes itself at the annual International Food and Folklife Festival. The organization is nonprofit, and members of the club volunteer all the labor, including cooking and bar-tending. Its bar, offering a wide variety of German beers, is open six nights a week, and on Saturday nights volunteers cook dinner for 80 to 90 members and visitors can sample various cuisines, dance to live bands, and enjoy imported beers at a very reasonable price. Its yearly Oktoberfest, held over three days, attracts as many as 1,000 celebrants, and the two-day Maifest as many as 600. As an outreach to younger members, the club offers dinners and programs with an international flair, ranging from Irish to Hawaiian. Some older members dislike this international flavor and the growing substitution of the English language for German.[25]

Members of the German-American Social Club looking for a more intimate group formed the Deutsch American Society of Southern Nevada in 1982. Their goal is to keep German traditions alive, and they emphasize speaking in German over English in a smaller setting. In the 1980s membership was in the 100s, but as the older members died or moved away, its membership has shrunk to 34. In 1993 the club purchased a clubhouse on Blue Diamond Road, but due to the increasingly expensive upkeep costs, it recently sold the building. Currently, members meet monthly in each others' homes for a potluck Sunday brunch. They also have several members-only events: a summer picnic; a Weihnachten (Christmas) party to exchange gifts and sing German carols; and on St. Nicholas day, a tree-decorating party. Two of the officers recognize that since the majority of the members are in their sixties, the club's long-term future is cloudy.[26]

Others anxious to sustain German language and traditions can join the German Friendship Club. Because the club meets at The Trails, the community center of the Las Vegas suburb of Summerlin, membership is restricted to Summerlin residents, but associate members who live outside the area can attend special festivals. This limits the number of members to the mid-30s, but that level has remained constant over the six-year life of the club. Except for summer, the group meets monthly to converse in German, enjoy Kaffee und Kuchen (coffee and cake), watch German movies, and plan special picnics and holiday celebrations around Maifest and Christmas. For Oktoberfest, they visit the German-American Social Club. At the Hofbräuhaus, they organize a Stammtisch (regulars' table) where they gather to enjoy the cuisine and music. Although most members are retired, the president hopes that posting announcements at The Trails will attract younger German immigrants to the club.[27]

Not surprisingly, both UNLV and the College of Southern Nevada (CSN) sponsor German clubs. Founded by German-born Elfriede Manning in 1992, the CSN club is the older. As faculty advisor, she creates venues where students can familiarize themselves with German language and culture. Membership is limited to the first- and second-year students, and approximately 20 of 50 potential members are involved in the club's activities. Members gather monthly at a Stammtisch in the student union to watch subtitled German movies. Other events include meals at the Cafe Heidelberg and Hofbräuhaus restaurants, hiking at Mount Charleston, an end-of-the-semester party in May, and a Christmas party at the German-American Social Club.[28]

UNLV's Deutscher Klub was formed in 1999 by Dr. Daniel C. Villaneuva, assistant professor of German in the Foreign Language Department, who sought opportunities for students to practice their German by interacting with noncampus persons interested in Germany and its culture. Its 150 members include UNLV students and faculty, first- and second-generation Germans, and interested members of the community. Members are recruited not only through UNLV but by contact with retired honorary consul Sommer. Approximately 40 attend the many regularly scheduled events, including a weekly Stammtisch on campus to sharpen language skills, four off-campus dinners per year at local German restaurants, and a very popular hike at Mount Charleston. For Oktoberfest and Maifest, the group often goes to the German-American Social Club celebrations. Club membership also helps students seeking educational opportunities in Germany, and several have won prestigious scholarships, including a Fulbright. Members also support German-related community events such as helping Sommer entertain dignitaries from Germany. They act as judges for the Clark County School District Language Fair, where high-school students demonstrate their German verbal skills with spelling bees, speeches, and language projects. Currently, thirteen of the forty public high schools in Las Vegas offer German-language classes.[29]

Another local German organization is the American Historical Society of Germans from Russia (with national headquarters in Nebraska), which represents a specific element of German culture. Around thirty second- and third-generation German American southern Nevadans ranging in age from fifty to eighty meet to concentrate on preserving the history and heritage of the "Volga Germans," as they are commonly known. Beckoned from Prussia by Catherine the Great of Russia in 1763, the forebears of these Las Vegans steadfastly maintained their German language, culture, and religion—Roman Catholic or Evangelical Lutheran—existing as German "islands" in the Russian countryside. When forced from Russia by broken promises and World War I upheavals, as many as 240,000 immigrated to the United States by 1920. Today, club members speak both modern German and the eighteenth-century language used by their forefathers. They celebrate Oktoberfest at home or in public venues. At their meetings, members sing old German folksongs and share potluck dinners featuring old family German-Russian recipes they have collected in a cookbook. But like other second- and third-generation Germans, says Mary Mackett, the group's secretary, "we assimilated."[30]

Las Vegas Germans support two Karneval clubs, the Karnevalgruppe Las Vegas Piepen and the Vagabonds, both of which have their roots in the Rotweiß Club formed in 1972 by the German-American Social Club of Nevada. Their first Rotweiß celebration was in the basement of the Elks Lodge at 900 Las Vegas Boulevard North, and members adopted a standard red-and-white uniform and formed a dance group. In 1984 some members formed their own Karnevalgruppe Las Vegas Piepen, adopted green-and-white uniforms, and created their own dance group. Piepen members, mostly the German-born who belong to the Deutsch American Society, strictly adhere to German traditions, conduct many of their meetings in German, and have a small members-only celebration on November 11. As members grow older or move away, the club has become smaller and the dance group has disbanded. The members discontinued electing a Princenpaar, but they still choose an Orden each year, participate in the Gala at the Union Plaza, and attend some celebrations in other communities.[31]

Barbara Phillips formed the Vagabonds for younger members and interested Americans looking for flexibility in rituals while staying true to the spirit of Karneval. They adopted purple and white as their colors and design specific Orden for each year. Rather than a standard uniform, participants can wear any outfit in purple and white provided it replicates the costume's military tradition to some extent. Because some of their forty members also belong to the German-American Social Club, they often conduct meetings and have informal gatherings at that venue. The Vagabonds elect a Prinzenpaar to rule during the club's local festivities and represent the club in other cities' celebrations, and they ceremonally bury him the weekend before Ash Wednesday.[32]

Other small, informal groups speak to the diverse interests of Germans living in Las Vegas, demonstrating again how fractured the ethnic community is. The Las Vegas Schützen Club (shooting club) meets regularly at the American Shooters Supply and Gun Club to practice marksmanship, and its ten members travel to regional gatherings in Anaheim and San Jose, California.

Some Germans at UNLV formed an informal book club to review German-language literature, which meets eight to ten times per year and conducts its business mostly in German. Members are mostly in their mid-fifties and up, reflecting the generally older membership in Las Vegas's German clubs.[33]

The variety of clubs for German-born and German Americans, their differences in focus and purpose, and the declining membership of the larger groups reflect a diffused community. Without a recognized core institution, whether a church, school, neighborhood, specific restaurant, or inclusive association, it is difficult for Germans to identify with a broader community of fellow Germans and to strengthen their cultural ties.

German Immigrants in Las Vegas

German immigrants practice, at least to some extent, the rituals they learned in Germany and maintain close contact with friends and family left behind. They also agree about the differences between Las Vegas and "home." Many arrived with at least a minimal knowledge of English and professional training to ease their way into the job market. But there is little uniformity in the sample group of sixty-seven immigrants interviewed for this chapter regarding church attendance, festival or club activities, or concern about transmitting customs to future generations. Thus no stereotypical picture of a German immigrant emerges, but each has an interesting and unique history.

Seven of the sixty-seven interviewees are single or widowed female seniors who came to Las Vegas from other U.S. locations as retirees. Four immigrated with American husbands in the 1950s, one was sponsored as a governess, one joined her relocated family, and another had a German husband with a guaranteed job in Las Vegas. All remember that they emphasized assimilation and learning English at home and did not teach their children German. Today they declare they are mostly American in culture. None attends club events. As a group, they continue some German rituals and enjoy dining in German restaurants, especially the "cozy" Heidelberg Cafe, although Gerda Darmstadt says, "If you want to eat good German food, you have to make it yourself."[34]

Although friendship groups emphasizing German heritage generally do not exist within Las Vegas's churches, ten members of St. Andrew Lutheran Church in Sun City Summerlin are an exception. They visit with each other quite often, gathering to exchange greetings each Sunday. They are all retired couples with both the husband and wife from Germany; most came to the United States in the 1950s. All speak German at home and faithfully follow the traditional customs, with only a slight variation due to birthplace. They enjoy eating at German restaurants, and one attends the Karneval Gala in January. This grouping, however, may be coincidental and a function of residence and age as well as ethnic background.[35]

Of four other senior couples interviewed, three do not attend club activities, and the fourth couple attends only the German book-club meetings. Although all are retired, the similarity ends there. A dentist and a scientist with the Environmental Protection Agency have lived in Las Vegas over twenty-five years, and two others, a retired sheet-metal worker and a tool-and-dye maker, arrived in the 1990s. One couple identifies with the American culture, but the other three retain their German heritage and raised their children to be bilingual. All uphold some German customs, but only two frequent German restaurants. These four couples, plus the five living in Summerlin, represent members of a diffused German American community who do not relate to any central ethnic institution, real or imagined.[36]

On the other hand, the ethnically based clubs form the social center for other immigrant senior citizens, both single and married, and several hold offices in the clubs. The German-American Social Club still draws founding member Else Lappoehn, second president "Uncle Willy" Brencher, and Helene Syburra, who prefer supporting the club rather than dining in German restaurants or attending other groups' festivities. They remember the German community in the 1970s as small and spread throughout the city. The Deutsch American Society has three active senior members, including Helga Schneider, its secretary, who came to Las Vegas in the 1960s; Winifred "Winnie" Stone, treasurer, in the 1970s; and Irmgard Petrasek in the 1980s. All three prefer the more "pure," traditional rituals and the members' predominant use of the German language. They practice German customs, but, again reflecting regional differences, only Schneider creates der Osterbaum, and Der Weihnachtmann brings gifts to her home on Christmas Eve.[37]

Seniors may predominate at the clubs, but three younger women are extremely active in the larger clubs and represent the small corps of younger volunteers who help keep the clubs operating. At the German-American Club, fifty-five-year-old Sylvia Brunn is enthusiastic and keenly interested in preserving a place for Germans and German Americans in Las Vegas; she uses her weekly radio show to promote that cause, helps arrange events for visiting German groups, and regularly cooks German dinners for club members. She came to Las Vegas in 1969 and worked at the old Alpine Village restaurant, but she recalls that in the early days it really did not compete with the club. At age sixty-one, Greta Brizzoli energetically leads the German Friendship Club, and she is very faithful in celebrating holidays in "the German way." She wishes Germans were more open about their roots and believes that some are reluctant to practice the customs and culture for fear of prejudice. Barbara Phillips, at age thirty-three, has been the president of the Vagabonds Karneval since its founding. She arrived in Las Vegas in 1986, is fluent in German, dances with her father's Schuhplattlers group, and teaches her young children the German Easter and Christmas customs. Despite her American parentage, Phillips, unlike others in her age group, is keenly interested in German music, dancing, and Karneval, but acknowledges that fewer and fewer Las Vegans are interested in German traditions and that English-language and non-German events are slowly increasing at the German-American Social Club. Although these three women have a common interest in German culture, their different choices of club activities again reflect Las Vegas German community's diversity and relative lack of cohesion.[38]

In contrast, eight other immigrant women, all under sixty-five, do not belong to any of the German clubs, because they are either too busy working or raising families or are just not interested. They all practice German customs in their homes, some more than others, and generally attempt to pass the German language and traditions on to their children. Their occupations are wide ranging: a hand physical therapist, a teacher at CSN, a banker, a project manager for the Clark County School District, a real-estate agent, a secretary at the food-importing firm of Praml International, a nurse, and a former personal assistant to magicians Siegfried and Roy. Three have German husbands, two American, one Hawaiian, one Ethopian, and one is single. Those in bicultural families still attempt to create "German homes," but they include rituals of the second culture. Some miss Germany more than others and make more frequent contacts with family and friends and more trips "home" than others.[39]

Since the 1960s and 1970s, the expanding restaurant and hotel scene has attracted chefs, food-service entrepreneurs, and other culinary professionals. Hans Lackinger, who arrived in 1962 and worked at both the Dunes and Desert Inn, recalls that at one time the kitchen at the Desert Inn was "entirely German." Today, according to Bellagio's executive chef Wolfgang von Weiser, European-trained chefs, including Germans, work beside those trained in America. German-schooled Heinz Lauer helps train Americans as associate education managers for the new Cordon Bleu schools in North America, one of which is located in Las Vegas. Like others, he worked on a number of cruise ships before coming to America. As one would expect, five German-born chefs prepare the cuisine at the Hofbräuhaus. Although the restaurant courts tourists for most of its business, many residents, especially those from southern Germany, enjoy the authentic replica building, the cuisine and imported beer, and the bands that Munich-native entrepreneur

Stefan Gasteger has brought together. Heidi and Rudi Putzi have built a large food-importing business, Praml International, which supplies European items to restaurants and hotels. All these immigrants practice German traditions, those with more children more intensely, but none currently frequents the local German clubs; rather, they connect through groups related to their occupation.[40]

The UNLV and CSN academic communities have attracted several German born, and the stories of two at UNLV and one at CSN are illustrative. Dr. Ralph Buechler, associate professor of German and chair of UNLV's Foreign Language Department, came to Illinois with his parents in 1958. He never envisioned living in an urban, desert setting, as he preferred a smaller town with "forest, fog, and rain," but in 1989 UNLV offered him an opportunity unmatched elsewhere. He enjoys listening to the Sunday radio show, reading the German publications *Die Zeit* and *Der Spiegel*, visiting German restaurants and attending club-sponsored festivals, and serving as faculty advisor to the UNLV Deutscher Klub. Dr. Clemens Heske, associate professor in the Department of Chemistry, on the other hand, does not attend German-based festivals or regularly dine in German restaurants. He belongs to the UNLV Deutscher Klub, but he also oversees a German "minigroup" in the science departments. He immigrated with his family in 2004 and confirms that they speak German and celebrate the German holidays at home but acknowledges that their Christmas is split between Christmas Eve and morning. At UNLV, he explains, he and his team, three of whom are German, have unique opportunities to explore exciting projects looking for breakthroughs in the field of energy and alternative fuels "necessary for the technologies of tomorrow." He particularly enjoys teaching at UNLV because of the "give and take" in the classroom as compared to Germany, where the "professor is the god of the lecture hall." Elfriede Manning is the driving force behind the CSN German Club there. Besides German teachers and instructors, she includes chefs, restaurateurs, and professionals in the building industry in her friendship group. She practices German rituals at Christmas and Easter with her son, listens to the German radio program, is a member of the German-American Social Club, attends the Karneval and other German festivals, and keeps in close touch with friends and family in Germany.[41]

Patricia Mulroy, Klaus Kuerten, and Sigrid Sommer further demonstrate the diversity of the Germany community. Mulroy, born and educated in Germany, has lived in Las Vegas since coming in 1974 for studies at UNLV, subsequently rising to be general manager of the Southern Nevada Water Authority. Like many, she experienced culture shock when leaving "green, green Germany for the barren, brown desert." Mulroy observes that a cohesive

German ethnic community never developed in Las Vegas, and today's clubs, although attempting to unite German Americans, have instead contributed to the community's diffuseness and low visibility. In her family she has kept German traditions, blending them with those of her Irish husband, Robert, and she describes herself and her children as multicultural, with a more international than German American outlook.[42]

Klaus Kuerten does not fall into any of the previous categories. Although a senior citizen, he is not retired, working at Nevada's Department of Health and Human Services, where he helps fellow seniors through the state health-insurance program. Drawn to Las Vegas by a friend in 1996, he had to "start over," as his training did not help him find employment. Kuerten speaks German with his wife at home but is not interested in joining the clubs, does not listen to the radio program or read German newspapers, and rarely visits German restaurants. Like Mulroy, he misses the "green meadows of Bavaria," but he says, "America is my country now."[43]

Sigred Sommer is well respected in Las Vegas and, through her former position as honorary consul, has had a unique perspective on the German community. She agrees that it is inchoate, noting that of the Las Vegans who currently claim German ancestry, at least three-fourths are more American than German. Sommer adds that, as in other cities, the older generation in the clubs clings to traditions and does not offer younger members incentives to join; furthermore, they often disagree on how to attract a new generation. She confirms that immigration today is much more difficult than in the early post–World War II years. Sommer reports that the many German tourists she helped in her role of honorary consul enjoyed its climate and excitement but would hesitate to relocate to Las Vegas. Sommer and her husband religiously adhere to German rituals in their home, but she is saddened that the German culture seems to be disappearing perhaps, she feels, because the immigrants never organized as did the Serbians or the Greeks.[44]

The most internationally known and visible Germans living in Las Vegas are magicians and animal trainers Siegfried and Roy. Born in different parts of Germany, Siegfried Fischbacher in the south and Roy Horn in the north, they first performed in Las Vegas in 1974. Later they thrilled audiences at the New Frontier and, in 1990, moved to the Mirage, but their act, featuring trained tigers, was dramatically cut short by an attack on stage that severely injured Horn in October 2003. During their long residence here, they have visited the Cafe Heidelberg and the Swiss Cafe and have promoted Maifest and Oktoberfest at the Hofbräuhaus by tapping beer kegs to begin the festivities. At home the two observe German customs, read German newspapers and magazines, watch German television, converse in German, train their animals in both German and English, and frequently both entertain friends and family in Las Vegas and return visits back home. Like Kuerten and Sommer, Siegfried and Roy feel welcome and comfortable in Las Vegas, but they also miss the German green forests.[45]

Conclusion

By deliberately abandoning their culture during and after World War I and with the ever-decreasing number of immigrants, Germans have seen their influence and presence in America wane, and Las Vegas reflects that general pattern. In early Las Vegas, Germans never united into a cohesive, ethnically based community and, despite efforts in the 1970s and 1980s, such a community does not exist today. Religion has not provided any glue to pull the Germans together, and the clubs have splintered, leaving a vacuum where a central institution might have been a unifying influence. Because of their diversity and their tendency to assimilate quickly, immigrants have not contributed to the creation of a German community; although most practice German traditions to some extent in their homes, they do not consistently celebrate their heritage in public. There is a consensus among the immigrants that without a public, core organization, transmitting their heritage to succeeding generations will be difficult, and some believe that by the second or third generation, their descendants will be completely assimilated into the American mainstream. The history of the Germans in Las Vegas, then, demonstrates how a once-powerful immigrant group in America can almost disappear over time when there is no bond to hold it together.

Notes

1. In 1979, 66.8 percent of those claiming German heritage relate to old immigrant stock. Reed Ueda, *Postwar Immigrant America: A Social History* (Boston: Bedford Books of St. Martins Press, 1994), 105.

2. Because Germany did not exist as a political entity until 1871, "German" indicates those who resided in the central European Germanic States such as Bavaria, Prussia, and Württemburg that subsequently became that nation. Kathleen Neils Conzen, *Immigrant Milwaukee 1836–1860: Accommodation and Community in a Frontier City* (Cambridge: Harvard University Press, 1976), 4; Rachel Davis-DuBois and Emma Schwepp, *The Germans in American Life* (New York: Thomas Nelson and Sons, 1936), 36, 56, 169; Howard B. Furer, ed., *The Germans in America 1607–1970* (Dobbs Ferry, New York: Oceana Publications, 1973) 14–15; Ann Galicich, *The German Americans* (New York: Chelsea House, 1989), 13–15, 17, 19, 47, 57, 60–61; Stanley Nadel, *Little Germany: Ethnicity, Religion and Class in New York City, 1845–1880*

(Urbana: University of Illinois Press, 1990), 40; Walter Nugent, *Into the West: The Story of Its People* (New York: Vintage Books, 1999), 48, 105; Ueda, *Postwar Immigrant America,* 20, 107.

3. There was a brief resurgence in 1891 and 1892, but that was only temporary. Furer, *Germans,* 65; Kathleen Neils Conzen, "Germans in America," in *Harvard Encyclopedia of American Ethnic Groups,* ed. Stephan Thernstrom (Cambridge: Harvard University Press, 1980), 411; Furer, *Germans,* 56, 59, 65, 68; Galicich, *German Americans,* 13–15, 73–74, 76–79; Nadel, *New York,* 66, 70–71, 75, 123, 128; Ueda, *Postwar Immigrant America,* 83–84.

4. Conzen, *Encyclopedia,* 406; Furer, *Germans,* 72–73; Galicich, *German Americans,* 81–84, 87; *Las Vegas Age,* June 10, 1905, January 5, 1907, April 6, 1907, August 19, 1911, November 25, 1911, May 26, 1917, February 9, 1918, February 16, 1918; Carolyn Rose, *Never Discouraged: The Story of Ed and Mary Von Tobel and Early Day Las Vegas, 1905–1868* (privately published, August, 1997), 33; Sharon Schmidt, interview by author, October 26, 2006; Wilbur S. Shepperson, *Restless Strangers: Nevada's Immigrants and Their Interpreters* (Reno and Las Vegas: University of Nevada Press, 2005), 60–61, 132.

5. The lower numbers were a result of the Immigration Acts of 1917 and 1924, which reversed the previous open immigration. Legislation immediately after World War II included the Displaced Persons Act, the War Brides Act, and the Refugee Relief Act. Ernest Martens, for example, received his green card after ten years of processing and does not expect to receive his citizenship for another five years. Ernst Martens, interview by author, January 29, 2007. Conzen, *Encyclopedia,* 406, 411; Davis-Dubois, *Germans in American Life,* 19; Furer, *Germans,* 80–81; Galicich, *German Americans,* 89, 94–95; *Las Vegas Review Journal,* June 27, 1938; Eugene P. Moehring, "Immigration, Ethnicity and the Rise of Las Vegas," *The Peoples of Las Vegas: One City, Many Faces,* ed. Jerry L. Simich and Thomas C. Wright (Reno and Las Vegas: University of Nevada Press, 2005), 2; Nugent, *Into the West,* 296; Ueda, *Postwar Immigrant America,* 20, 37–38, 171.

6. Sixty-seven southern Nevadans responded to appeals in Roman Catholic and Lutheran church bulletins, German club newspapers, or referrals by friends. Sixty were born in Germany, and of the remaining seven, the four from neighboring countries consider themselves German and the three American born are closely affiliated with Las Vegas's German cultural organizations. Interviews were tape-recorded by the author, and most were donated to the Special Collections Department, University of Nevada, Las Vegas.

7. Minnie Westlake was Austrian born but German was her spoken language, according to the 1910 census. U.S. Department of Commerce, Bureau of the Census, *Thirteenth Census of the United States (1910),* vol. 1, Microfilm copy 45, Reel 1; U.S. Census Bureau, *Fourteenth Census of the United States (1920),* Microfilm copy 45, Reel 1; U.S. Census Bureau, *Fifteenth Census of the United States (1930)* (Washington, D.C.: Government Printing Office, 1933), 693–94; *Las Vegas Review-Journal,* December 16, 1930, June 22, 1956, June 7, 1964; Eugene P. Moehring, "Profile of a

Nevada Railroad Town: Las Vegas in 1910," *Nevada Historical Society Quarterly* 34, no. 4 (Winter, 1991): 466–87.

8. *1910 Census; Las Vegas Age,* May 30, 1914, October 25, 1922; Moehring, "Profile," 479; Eugene P. Moehring, *Resort City in the Sunbelt: Las Vegas 1930–1970* (Reno: University of Nevada Press, 1995), 7, 234; *Las Vegas Review-Journal,* May 26, 1933, March 14, 1936, January 12, 1942, March 15, 1947, February 1, 1965; Rose, *Von Tobel,* 3, 12, 39, 41.

9. *1920 Census; 1930 Census;* Moehring, "Profile," 466, 480, 482; *Las Vegas Review-Journal,* April 23, 1930, December 16, 1930, June 30, 1932, December 7, 1933, April 23, 1935, July 28, 1936, July 7, 1942, January 30, 1943, July 16, 1943, December 1, 1943.

10. *1920 Census; 1930 Census; Las Vegas Review-Journal,* November 6, 1930, April 12, 1934, April 17, 1937, July 3, 1937, September 5, 1938, April 10, 1945, January 7, 1948, June 7, 1964, March 1, 1965; Ueda, *Postwar Immigrant America,* 86.

11. http://fisher.lib.virginia.edu/collections/stats/histcensus/php/newlon. http://dmla.clan.lib.nv.us/docs/insla/socNevadaforeignborn; Juliet V. Casey, "LV a Linguistic Melting," *Las Vegas Review-Journal,* March 12, 2005, B1; Conzen, *Encyclopedia,* 406; Waltrud Bailey, interview by author, May 14, 2007; Gerta Darmstadt, interview by author, February 12, 2007; Ingrid and Gerhard Grimmick, interview by author, February 1, 2007; Erna and Helmut Haber, interview by author, February 6, 2007; Gerda Hanson, interview by author, February 12, 2007; Diether and Gisela Jodewischat, interview by author, May 2, 2007; Rudi Lorenz, interview by author, January 8, 2007; Irmgard Petrasek, interview by author, February 5, 2007; Luzie and Franz Schumaker, interview by author, February 14, 2007; Sigrid Sommer, interview by author, January 13, 2007; Gerta Spence, interview by author, March 26, 2007; Helene Syburra, interview by author, January 25, 2007; Angela Ugorak, interview by author, February 9, 2007; Sandy and Gunter Wrase, interview by author, January 29, 2007; Wolfgang von Wieser, interview by author, June 6, 2007.

12. Conzen, *Encyclopedia,* 424; Davis-DuBois, *Germans in American Life,* 63; Greta Brizzoli, interview by author, March 19, 2007; Ralph Buechler, interview by author, May 9, 2007; Stefan Gasteger, interview by author, March 28, 2007; Clemens Heske, interview by author, May 25, 2007; Barbara and Heinz Kiunte, interview by author, January 25, 2007; Else Lappoehn, interview by author, April 22, 2007; Annette Meyer, interview by author, February 19, 2007; Petrasek, interview; Elke Rogge, interview by author, February 20, 2007; Kristen Tefsay, interview by author, February 20, 2007; Angela Ugorak, interview by author, February 9, 2007; Jennifer M. Russ, *German Festivals and Customs* (London: Oswald Wolff, 1982), 136.

13. Conzen, *Encyclopedia,* 417; Davis-DuBois, *Germans in Ameican Life,* 63, 169; Albert B. Faust, *The German Element in the United States,* vol. 2 (Boston: Houghton, Mifflin, 1909), 250; Buechler, Heske, Elfriede Manning, interviews by author, May 22, 2007; Russ, *German Festivals,* 52.

14. Faust, *German Element,* 383; Bailey, Buechler, Manning, interviews; Leigh Eric Schmidt, *Consumer Rites: The Buying and Selling of American Holidays* (Princeton: Princeton University Press, 1995) 124, 130, 132–34.

15. Lappoehn, interview; Russ, *German Festivals,* 304, 8–10.

16. The company still making dyes and colored paraphernalia, Paas Dye Company, opened in 1879 in New Jersey. Schmidt, *Consumer Rights,* 224; Kathleen Neils Conzen, "Immigrants, Immigrant Neighborhoods, and Ethnic Identity: Historical Issues," *Journal of American History* 66, no. 3 (December 1979): 603–15; Davis-DuBois, *Germans in American Life,* 80, 170; Buechler, Gasteger, Manning, interviews; Russ, *German Festivals,* 45, 52.

17. A number of immigrants from the north do not celebrate Oktoberfest because it is a "southern thing." Heske, interview; Bailey, Sylvia Brunn, interviews by author, January 21, 2007, April 21, 2007; Gasteger, interview; Hans Lackinger, interview by author, May 10, 2007; Helga Schneider, Manning, interview by author, February 16, 2007; Winifred Stone, interview by author, February 19, 2007; Tefsay, interview; Daniel Villanueva, interview by author, April 27, 2007.

18. The German American Mardi Gras Association was formed in 1983 and currently includes twenty-one member clubs across the country. German American Mardi Gras Association, "Program," January 12–13, 2007. Some immigrants from northern Germany do not attend Karneval, as they feel it is only southern. Grimmick, Stone, Wrase, interviews; Lackinger, Barbara Phillips, interview with author, April 13, 2007.

19. Both Franz Praxl and German-born Suzy Firth have passed away, but Firth continues the same format. "Dummkopfs Publicity Release," Las Vegas, Nevada, January 21, 2007; Brunn, Brian Firth, interview by author, May 2, 2007; Gerhard Kinzel, interview by author, March 15, 2007; *Las Vegas Review-Journal,* October 2, 1971, June 25, 1994, B6, October 5, 2004, E2.

20. www.german-americanclubofnevada.com; Herb Albinus, interview by author, June 6, 2006; Kinzel, Brunn, interview by author, June 6, 2006.

21. *Las Vegas Review-Journal,* September 24, 2003, C1, September 15, 2004, E1; Art Ruckle, interview by author, April 21, 2007.

22. The Kiuntkes, who came in 1998, fondly remember the show. Kinzel, Kiuntke, interviews by author.

23. www.german-americanclubofnevada.com/autobahn.atm; Albinus, Bailey, Brizolli, Brunn, Buechler, Mimi Hollingsworth, interviews by author, February 2, 2007; Kinzel, Kiuntke, Petrasek, Phillips, Rogge, Ruckle, Syburra, interviews.

24. www.german-americanclubofnevada.com/history/info.htm; Conzen, "Immigrants," 603; Willy Brencher, interview by author, January 21, 2007; Brunn, Lappoehn interviews; Robert Laxalt, "The Melting Pot," *East of Eden, West of Zion: Essays on Nevada,* ed. Wilber S. Shepperson (Reno: University of Nevada Press, 1989), 37–38.

25. Brencher, Brunn, Lappoehn, Phillips, Wrase, interviews; Gerda Darmstadt, interview by author, February 2, 2007.

26. Kinzel, Petrasek, Schneider, Stone, interviews.

27. Brizzoli, Lackinger, interviews.

28. Manning, interview.

29. Although American born, Dr. Villaneuva has always had a strong interest in Germany. Two examples of community members are thirty-year-old Annette Meyer and fifty-four-year-old Waltrud Bailey, the self-proclaimed "mother of the club." Both have American husbands. Bailey "splits" her Christmas between German and American rituals. Meyer reports that club members helped her transition to the United States and Las Vegas. Bailey, Buechler, Meyer, Villanueva, interviews.

30. Galicich, *German Americans,* 73–75; Marilyn J. Mackett, interview by author by e-mail, May 17, 2007; Le Vern J. Rippley, *Encyclopedia,* 425–30.

31. Kinzel, Phillips, Stone, interviews.

32. Phillips, interview.

33. Ulla and Werner Beckert, interview by author, March 28, 2007; Ruckle, interview.

34. "Senior Citizen" is one over sixty-five years old. Willy Brencher is the lone single man, a staunch supporter of the German-American Social Club. Sieglinda Bartell, interview by author, March 28, 2007; Brencher, Darmstadt, Marianne Dembowski, interviews by author, February 20, 2007; Hanson, Hollingsworth, Spence, interviews.

35. Sandy Wrase immigrated in 1973. Grimmick, Jodewischat, Kiuntke, Wrase, interviews; Margret and Richard Kuzniarek, interview by author, January 26, 2007; Simich and Wright, *Peoples of Las Vegas,* 31, 134–36.

36. Werner and Ulla Beckert, interview by author, May 25, 2007; Haber, Lorenz, Schumacher, interviews.

37. Brencher, Lappoehn, Petrasek, Schneider, Stone, Syburra, interviews.

38. Brizzoli, Brunn, Phillips, Syburra, interviews.

39. Nurse Angela Stolte reports that at least three other Germans also work in that profession. Claudia Alexander, interview by author, February 9, 2007; Heide Coleman, interview by author, January 30, 2007; Sylvia Edmondson, interview by author, February 14, 2007; Iris Gassman, interview by author, January 23, 2007; Angela Stolte Rogge, interview by author, January 26, 2007; Tefsay, interview; Laxalt, " Melting Pot," 37–38.

40. German restaurants are in short supply in Las Vegas. Swiss Cafe, Cafe Heidelberg, and Hofbräuhaus are the only ones remaining today. Alpine Village, torn down in 1997, was a favorite as long ago as the 1960s. *Las Vegas Review-Journal,* March 7, 1993, AA9, March 26, 1007, E1. Heinz Lauer was a former officer at the German-American Social Club, but his current job-related duties keep him away. www.praml.com; Heinz Lauer, interview by author, January 20, 2007; Clemens Heske Gasteger, interview by author, May 25, 2007; Gerhard Ottinger Lackinger, interview by author, March 28, 2007; Rudi Putzi, interview by author, January 16, 2007; Sommer, interview.

41. Buechler, Heske, Manning, interviews.

42. Patricia Mulroy, interview by author, April 18, 2007.

43. Klaus Kuerton, interview by author, February 2, 2007.

44. The U.S. Census Department estimated that 230,451 reported German ancestry in the city of Las Vegas/Paradise area in 2006, but only 6,757 were actually born in Germany. http://factfinder.census/gov; *Las Vegas Review-Journal,* November 7, 2001, "City," 5A, February 11, 1999, E2, March 23, 2006, E3, March 30, 2006, E3; Sommer, interview.

45. http://www.rotten.com/library/bio/entergainers/magicians/siegfried-and-roy; Gasteger, Siegfried and Roy through Kala Peterson, interviews by author, April 19, 2007.

CHAPTER 3

The Japanese

ANDREW B. RUSSELL AND FUMIKO SASAKI

World War II radically disrupted and divided the history of the Japanese Americans, as roughly 90 percent of those living on the U.S. mainland were uprooted from their homes and exiled to concentration camps. For the Japanese of Las Vegas, the war years must also be viewed as the culmination of one phase of their history and the start of another. That said, the local Japanese community managed to avoid the wartime devastation typically experienced elsewhere in the region, giving their story more continuity. Unusual and somewhat fortuitous developments laid the foundation for those positive wartime experiences in Las Vegas, then an isolated corner of the Far West. "Luck," to be sure, played only a supporting role in the human drama. More than anything, hard work and a reputation for excellence explain why the Japanese became the premiere agricultural pioneers of the Valley and an integral component of the railroad's workforce in the early twentieth century, why the war caused limited damage, and why their good fortunes persisted thereafter. As Las Vegas experiences another incredible boom at the dawn of this century, accompanied by problems and possibilities surrounding diversity, we are encouraged to revisit the unique history of this ethnic community against larger backdrops.

The Issei and the Exclusionists

The Japanese who would eventually settle in southern Nevada were part of a brief and relatively modest wave of immigration that began around 1890, peaked just after the turn of the century, and quickly tapered off thereafter. Known as the Issei, or first generation, most of them migrated to Hawaii and the U.S. mainland due to dislocation and hardships associated with overcrowding, land reforms, and the rapid modernization of Japan. As with certain other groups such as the Chinese, Italians, and Greeks, the Issei viewed themselves as sojourners and planned to return home with riches from America. Most came from economically depressed agricultural regions, and like most of the "new immigrants" arriving from southern and eastern Europe at the time, the Japanese came expecting to make a better life for themselves and their families back home.

In other respects, however, the Issei were unusual among the new immigrants. As a distinct racial group in the West, their history became more closely intertwined with that of other Americans of color struggling against prejudice, most notably the Chinese, Mexicans, Native Americans, and African Americans. Anti-Japanese sentiment grew particularly fierce in the Far West, where the vast majority settled, in part because they "inherited" the strong anti-Chinese sentiment of earlier days. California emerged as the greatest hotbed of this brand of prejudice, but the rest of the West, to varying degrees, also exhibited strong animosity toward "Orientals." Like the Chinese before them, the Issei established an impressive legacy, but prejudice and institutionalized discrimination seriously obstructed their path to a better life in most places.[1]

On the one hand, the industrious Issei registered some very remarkable accomplishments, fueled by ambition, hard work, and a nationalistic pride that functioned as an antidote to Anglo-Saxonism. They practiced "social engineering" aimed at controlling anti-Orientalism, such as policing criminal activities in their communities and pushing their Americanized offspring, the Nisei, to excel. Since Japan had established public schools, the Issei enjoyed a literacy rate of well over 90 percent, and they devoured helpful travel guides, newspapers, and the other fruits of their vernacular press to advance in America. Economically, they helped fill a niche that opened as a result of Chinese exclusion. The Japanese, along with other new immigrants, played an instrumental role in the early 1900s, building and maintaining the western railroads, processing fish and harvesting produce and lumber, and helping to mine coal and copper. Soon they were making an even greater impact on the course of western agriculture, namely as independent truck farmers of vegetables and berry crops.

As it was with the Chinese, these advances came despite intense discrimination. The Japanese endured organized hate campaigns, legal restrictions, and extreme institutional racism that prevented the Issei from becoming U.S. citizens, curtailed and then halted Japanese immigration, and restricted their right to farm and engage in other economic enterprises.[2] The emergence of Japan as a competitive industrial and military world power shaped the unusual experience of the Nikkei, the Japanese people in America, as well. Diplomatic tensions contributed to concerns about Japanese aliens, who were denied U.S. citizenship until after 1952, and the American-born Nisei also faced irrational questions about their loyalty because Japanese law gave dual-citizenship status to many of them. The decades-long campaign against "the

Japs" grew out of racial prejudice, economic animosity, nationalistic passions, and a crowding of the Japanese Americans into California, where roughly 80 percent of the non-Hawaiian contingent resided by 1940. A steady supply of "Yellow-Peril" propaganda fueled the hatred, as the Issei and their offspring plowed ahead by forging a very strong subculture.[3]

Immigration restrictions and alien land laws were the most obvious signs of the overt prejudice in the prewar years. By 1907 President Theodore Roosevelt and Japanese diplomats began formulating a "Gentleman's Agreement" that greatly curtailed Issei immigration from Japan and migration from Hawaii to the U.S. mainland. Nonetheless, "cheap and docile" Japanese labor remained a favorite target of American unions, while Japanese farmers were labeled "unfair competitors" because husbands and wives both worked the fields. By 1913 California and Arizona had passed the first anti-alien land laws to prevent "aliens ineligible for citizenship" (code for the Japanese) from purchasing farmland, and they followed those laws by enacting land-leasing restrictions in the 1920s. As the rhetoric intensified, most other western states would pass similar measures. The exclusionists won a series of battles to curb the influx of Japanese men and women that culminated in the 1924 National Origins Act, which halted all further immigration from Japan. This finally stemmed much of the intense hostility. Nevertheless, another full-blown and violent campaign against the Japanese farmers of central Arizona erupted in the early 1930s, and the maturing Nisei generation continued to encounter major roadblocks to their pursuit of American dreams. In short, World War II exclusion fit into and completed a long pattern of intense, targeted abuse.

The Nevada Context

A more mixed reception greeted the sons of Nippon who passed through Nevada in these early years. Following California's lead, the first session of the Nevada Territorial Legislature (1861) passed laws that thoroughly privileged white males and restricted the rights of the Chinese, African Americans, and Native Americans. These restrictions carried over to statehood (1864), but school segregation proved impractical in the sparsely populated state, and most other forms of legal discrimination were declared unconstitutional in the 1880s. Other factors shaped a more hospitable climate for the Japanese newcomers, particularly those aspiring to become farmers and business owners. Immigrants comprised nearly one-third of the state's population by the time of statehood and 44 percent by 1870. Thus, Nevada's forefathers wrote safeguards protecting an alien's right to own property into the state's constitution.

When some Nevadans banded together in 1920 to try to restrict Japanese land-ownership rights, they learned that this would require a complex legislative process. In 1924 the people voted to remove the alien-property-rights protection from the constitution, paving the way for legislative action the following year. But passage of the National Origins Act and other factors brought the campaign to an abrupt end, and Nevada emerged as one of the only western states that never passed an alien land law.[4]

The earliest influx of Japanese into Nevada was quite small and mainly included "house boys" (as domestic workers here to study English were called), cooks, and a few mine workers. The peak influx came soon after 1900, as the construction of several new railroads and a boom in sugar-beet farming attracted hundreds of recent immigrants from Japan. At that point, Nevadans debated legislation that would have prevented the Japanese from working on railroads and publicly financed projects, but these restrictions failed to pass. Throughout the Progressive Period and into the 1920s, some northern Nevada newspapers and influential politicians, including Senators Tasker Oddie and Key Pittman, came to support exclusion at the national level. Still, Nevada politics was hardly characterized by rabid anti-Japanese sentiment. Nevada's strong political ties to California attenuated after the turn of the century; politicians became "more responsive to local institutions" and more "Nevada-oriented." Likewise, organized labor made few inroads politically during the era, and efforts to restrict Asians workers were "pretty much over" by 1914, according to historian Russell Elliott. Nevadans did amend their miscegenation law in 1911 to keep the race lines pure after some sensationalized cases in which Japanese-European American couples managed to obtain marriages licenses, and this revised ban against intermarriage remained on the books until 1959.[5] Conversely, powerful corporate enterprises fought to protect their valued Japanese workers and potential land investors in the early years. These included various railroads, the copper-mining companies of eastern Nevada, and entities involved in commercial sugar-beet farming and land development, particularly around Fallon and Las Vegas. On balance, all of this created an environment where the Nikkei enjoyed a more even playing field than in most western states.[6]

Settling in Southern Nevada

The Japanese played a significant role in Las Vegas's development from the very beginning. A fair estimate is that over a hundred recent immigrants from Japan helped to construct the San Pedro, Los Angeles and Salt Lake Railroad—the "Salt Lake Route," as it came to be called—marking the birth of modern Las Vegas. Japanese labor-contracting firms supplied these crews, and some of the men undoubtedly worked on other recently constructed rail lines in the state. In 1906 the *Las Vegas Age* newspaper offered a dramatic announcement of their presence when it reported on a "bloody riot" involving a Japanese railroad-construction crew working near Caliente, roughly 125 miles northeast of Las Vegas. Some of the Japanese were being housed or transported in a boxcar that became disconnected from one train, rolling downhill and crashing into the rear of another train. A massive fight broke out between (unspecified) other workers and the Japanese, who suspected that the "accident" was deliberately planned. Several people sustained critical injuries, and a deputy sheriff was killed in the melee. The paper reported estimates of two hundred Japanese in the area and rumors that Caliente had been turned into a fortified stronghold to repel any further attacks.[7]

As dramatic as that sounds, the *Age* actually offered a relatively unbiased report of the incident and assured its readers that the crisis had passed. Three years later, when some Japanese workers were jailed in Las Vegas for attempting to organize a union, the newspaper did accuse the "swarthy sons of Japan" of attempting to "create dissension." However, the newspaper ultimately made light of the situation, facetiously linking the release of the laborers from jail to the arrival of a Japanese warship in San Pedro Harbor, California. Because the laborers were released, the paper joked, "international peace was restored" and the warship did not have to steam up the Colorado River for a rescue attempt.[8]

The *Age* and its owner-operator, Charles "Pop" Squires, recognized how important the railroad was to the economy of the nascent community. This may help to explain why the paper never launched any campaigns against the vital Japanese component of the railroad's workforce in these formative years. A similar reception greeted the first contingent of Japanese farmers who arrived in Las Vegas around January 1914. That month, the *Age* announced that a "syndicate of Japanese capitalists" had purchased the Winterwood Ranch, consisting of five thousand acres in Paradise Valley. Featuring artesian water, this land was considered the best available for farm development in the blossoming community. "The most important feature of the deal so far as Las Vegas is concerned," the *Age* noted, was that "this land will be immediately brought under cultivation."[9]

A relatively tolerant local press, a paternalistic railroad company, isolation that created a frontier atmosphere, and a growing demand for fresh produce combined to smooth the way for Japanese settlement in Las Vegas. These positive factors seem fortunate, indeed, when viewed against that wider backdrop of the international, national, regional, and statewide developments bearing down on Japanese Americans in this supposedly "progressive" era. Clark County, carved out of Lincoln County in 1909, proved to be exceptionally hospitable to Japanese railroaders and farmers over the long run as well. While these two economic groups comprised one larger ethnic community, significant differences characterized their lives and experiences in Las Vegas. Thus each group's history will be profiled independently.

The Railroaders

Initially brought in as track workers, the Japanese came to fill more permanent craft jobs on the Salt Lake Route. Many came to work in the steam-train repair shops and roundhouse of Las Vegas. Only 14 Japanese, mainly common railroad "laborers," were identified by the 1910 census of the township, but roughly 40 more arrived following a railroad strike in 1912. The 1920 census registered 62 Japanese in and around Las Vegas, a town which then boasted a total population of roughly 2,300, and most were listed in the census manuscripts as skilled workers and semiskilled "helpers" in various shop crafts. The official tally was probably too low; witnesses estimate the size of the Japanese railroad community of the 1920s at upward of 150 men, women, and children, which would have ranked them among the largest minority groups of that period.[10]

In any case, this particular railroad earned a reputation for hiring and promoting Japanese workers. Corporate managers liked them for "their efficiency, ambition, long employment, and trustworthiness," according to a government report of the period. By 1913 the railroad employed about thirty Japanese section foremen, in charge of small crews that maintained sections of track in California, Nevada, and Utah, and it was more inclined than other companies to hire and promote Japanese as machinists, mechanics, boilermakers, painters, and the like—skilled shop jobs that other companies usually reserved for white workers.[11] Several of the railroaders captured in the 1920 census were already married and had children, which can be taken as another indication of economic advancement.

Most of these railroaders and their families lived on a section of railroad property just west of town that was known as the "Japanese Colony" or the Japanese Settlement. Their living quarters have been described as similar to duplex apartments. Some Italians, Mexicans, and other immigrant families also lived in railroad housing, but relatively few native whites lived among the Japanese. Thus, they were somewhat segregated and isolated from the larger community, but seemingly by choice, as some Japanese workers lived elsewhere in town in the 1920s and 1930s. According to a 1922 newspaper article, the Japanese residents of the colony paid the company only one dollar a month in rent and received free ice, water, and electricity—strong incentives, perhaps, to tolerate the drawbacks of residential segregation and proximity to the noisy rail yards.[12]

Although this contingent of the Japanese population did not integrate much into the larger community, it seems to have suffered relatively mild discrimination. The employees enjoyed an equitable pay scale, seniority rights, and praise and admiration from their supervisors. Because of their physical separation and the language barrier, residents of the Japanese Colony tended to keep to themselves to a great degree and, unfortunately, we still have little firsthand information about what life was like for this group. One can imagine that many of the flavors of the home country abounded. Favorite foods such as rice, soy sauce, and fresh fish were easily freighted in from the West Coast. They may have had family or community bathhouses, semiorganized Buddhist or Shinto religious services, or Japanese language classes for the children. Adults would likely have engaged in long conversations and debates about Nippon's role in world affairs, drawing evidence from the vernacular newspapers that were regularly delivered by rail to most families of the isolated interior. As disappointing as it is, in retrospect, to know so little about the mysterious world of the Japanese Colony, ignorance about these "peculiar habits" and isolation from the European American mainstream back in early Las Vegas probably helped to reduce local fears, animosity, and suspicions.

At the ethnic and cultural intersections, relations were seemingly very peaceful. While racism certainly existed, Japanese residents were not often denied access to local businesses, schools, hospital facilities, or theaters in the early days. By the 1920s, local Salvation Army volunteers had taken a special interest in the group, offering up frequent social and recreational events as well as prayers. The Baptist Church also ministered to the Japanese Colony, and on Christmas Eve in 1930, the newspaper announced special holiday preparations. The church planned to deliver services in Japanese and English and distribute gifts to the children, and the article promised that Santa Claus would appear. The following day's issue recounted the Christmas festivities celebrated at the park by a large cross section of the community. Participants included "Mexican girlies with bright dresses, Indian tots with jet black hair and Japanese kiddies with smiling oriental eyes and white teeth." The town, it said, was under the intoxicating spell of "Christmas cheer, that spirit which wipes out all distinction between class, color and creed."[13] And yet it helped, the year around, that many of the local Japanese were Christians, and that the Buddhist Church ministers based in other towns rode the "prairie circuit" and came only infrequently to Las Vegas.

Even as the Japanese railroad community thrived in the 1920s, various factors contributed to its decline in that decade, and only a few railroaders would remain by the mid- to late 1930s. Restrictive immigration laws insured a steady decrease of new immigrants, and the Issei propensity to gravitate from wage work toward farming and small-business proprietorship further reduced the railroaders' ranks. The biggest factor, however, was a major national railroad strike in 1922 that led to a general reduction of the shop operations and jobs in Las Vegas.

The paternalism of the San Pedro, Los Angeles, and Salt Lake evaporated once the Union Pacific Railroad assumed sole ownership of the Salt Lake Route in 1921. As a result, local workers eagerly joined the walkout called by the craft unions in July of 1922. It is unlikely that the Japanese shop men of Las Vegas belonged to the unions at the time, and a local newspaper report suggests that the Union Pacific expected that their loyal Japanese employees would maintain operations during the strike. But that was not to be. Forty Japanese workers joined the walkout, and in retaliation they and their families were evicted from company housing. According to this newspaper report, their spokesman, Tom Sakai, spoke "good English" and showed "a remarkable knowledge of the strike situation." In addition, he and his countrymen supposedly agreed that "the first Jap boy who scabs will get licked."[14]

The company made no concessions to striking workers, and the strike collapsed by September. Some Japanese workers may have scabbed during the strike, which would have caused resentment. Scholarly studies of the strike make no mention of Japanese, but one notes that "bitterness lingered for years afterwards" toward those who abandoned the strike and returned to work, as some Japanese workers eventually did. Perhaps this prompted an upstart newspaper, the *Las Vegas Review* (later called the *Las Vegas Review-Journal*), a self-declared "friend of labor," to publish what appears to be the first local anti-Japanese editorial a year later. It denounced the Japanese as not fit to become good Americans and for sending their American wages back to Japan. It also approved of California's efforts to restrict Japanese landownership rights and supported the ongoing efforts to exclude the "sons of Mikado." Still, this lone editorial hardly constituted an anti-Japanese crusade of the type brewing in other parts of Nevada and the West at the time. The writer made no reference to the local Japanese community, while he included Greeks and "Hindus" as unfit material for the making of Americans.[15] The racist outburst seemingly did not strike a chord.

The strike's negative impact on the local Japanese community was indirect and long term. In the wake of the strike, the Union Pacific began to dismantle its Las Vegas shop facilities, in part to "punish" its unruly workers. Some repair and service operations continued in Las Vegas, but most of those jobs moved to Caliente, Southern California, Utah, and elsewhere. By the late thirties, virtually all of Las Vegas's Japanese railroaders had been laid off, had relocated, or had retired, leaving very few in the area.[16] Elsewhere in the interior West, the war years would bring mass termination of Japanese industrial workers, expulsion from company-owned housing, and untold hardships for the Japanese Americans associated with the Union Pacific and most major railroads and mining operations in the region.[17] Las Vegas dodged this negative legacy largely by chance, owing to the gradual exodus that preceded the war.

The Farmers

Unlike the railroaders, the Japanese farm families who came to be scattered around Las Vegas and Clark County would have to face the challenges of World War II. However, their fundamental contributions to the county's development would not go unnoticed during the crisis. These Japanese Americans, more so than the bulk of the railroaders, had integrated to a remarkable degree over the preceding decades. Among the farm families, both generations built strong ties of friendship with members of the larger community that paid huge wartime dividends.

Agricultural development was a prime concern of Las Vegas residents in the 1900s "frontier days." Railroad washouts occurred frequently during the city's first decade and sometimes threatened local food supplies. At best, produce and provisions had to be shipped across hundreds of miles of desert on uncertain schedules. But producing crops locally involved major challenges. Despite artesian water in some places, the Las Vegas Valley was not, and is not, prime farmland. Weekend gardeners still complain about the alkaline soil, cutting desert winds, scorching summers, and seemingly unpredictable frosts. Not surprisingly, no one had made a serious attempt to farm in the Valley prior to 1914.[18]

Given the circumstances, it is little wonder that Pop Squires and his *Age* so heartily welcomed the syndicate of Japanese farmers that year—with no mention of the alien land laws just passed by California and Arizona. Regrettably, research has shed no more light on this transaction, but subsequent land records do list numerous Japanese individuals owning ten acres or more and probably farming. Others may have leased fields or undeveloped land. Neither the contemporaneous Japanese American press nor the scholarly literature offers much information about this particular frontier experiment. Fortunately, we have a detailed account of southern Nevada's most famous farmer and enough about other Japanese American families to illustrate the core points.

Yonema "Bill" Tomiyasu was among those who contemplated a move from hostile California to "friendly" Las Vegas in 1914, though he did not settle there until two years later. A friend, M. M. Riley, had invited him to assess the farming potential of the area. First impressions must have been discouraging, but he saw no future in California.

By 1917 Bill had married Toyono, a college-educated "picture bride." A handsome concert pianist, Toyono was extremely tall and the daughter of a noted Christian missionary. As such, she was a good candidate for a special type of arranged marriage: Bill and Toyono were wed in a ceremony performed in Japan, one centered on pictures of the bride and groom, providing a way to cope with tightening U.S. immigration laws that only allowed wives to come to America. Toyono gave birth to their first American son, Nanyu, a year later and four other children in the years to come. Since English was one of the few skills she had not acquired in Japan, her long tenure in the southern Nevada desert proved to be a very isolating experience.

Bill Tomiyasu worked some of the property owned by railroader Tom Sakai (in the area that is now Shadow Lane) for a few years as he brought his own Paradise Valley farm (surrounding what is now the Wayne Newton Ranch) under production. According to Nanyu Tomiyasu, the community supported and encouraged his father in every way possible. The local bank lent him $1,200 to acquire his original lease on 160 acres. Initially, perhaps, this was part of the "syndicate's" holdings, but Tomiyasu soon purchased his own land. Not surprisingly, he and other farmers encountered no resistance to "controlling" the local agricultural market as time unfolded.[19]

Tomiyasu took his calling seriously. He experimented in growing a wide variety of crops, carefully recording the effects of various planting times, irrigation techniques, row patterns, and similar details in his journals. By the 1920s, he was marketing sizable amounts of lettuce, celery, carrots, tomatoes, asparagus, melons, cantaloupes, potatoes, corn, millet, and alfalfa, not to mention a considerable amount of pork, beef, and fowl. He established partnerships and, according to his son, Tomiyasu's business supplied up to 50 percent of the local produce demand in the '20s and early '30s, before refrigerated trucking of vegetables from California cut the demand for many of his crops. The Tomiyasu "ranch," as locals called farms, also contributed to the construction of Boulder Dam, becoming a chief supplier of the commissary that fed thousands of employees. The family sold to area markets and restaurants, supplied the Union Pacific with the asparagus and other choice produce served in the Pullman dining cars, and shipped surplus crops to towns in southern Utah and northern Arizona.

Generous in offering planting advice to his neighbors and honest in his dealings, Bill Tomiyasu made many friends. The local newspapers periodically celebrated his accomplishments, as in 1930 when the editor of the *Las Vegas Review-Journal,* A. E. Cahlan, singled out Tomiyasu's cantaloupes as "the best in the whole region."[20] A more steadfast and influential friend was Eugene Ward, who owned a chain of local grocery stores. Ward eventually entered politics and served as the Clark County sheriff from 1938 through World War II.

The children of Clark County's Issei farmers enjoyed a high level of social integration and recognition as well. Although unending farm work limited opportunities for extracurricular activities, the local schools and teachers of this period were apparently quite good, inclusive, and supportive. Three of the Tomiyasu children would go on to attend the University of California at Berkeley; one son, Kiyo, became a renowned laser engineer and daughter Uwamie became one of the first Nisei research physicians after the war. Integration and acceptance were the rule in nearby Moapa Valley too, where the large Yamashita and Ishimoto families began farming in the early 1920s, after California passed its Second Alien Land Law. Jimmy Yamashita had even been elected student-body president of his high school just before the outbreak of World War II.[21] The Tomiyasu, Yamashita, Sakai, and Ishimoto families, along with a half dozen others dating back to the railroading and farming frontier, had made great strides against anti-Japanese sentiment in the decades leading up to the war.

The Crisis

Only forty-nine Japanese Americans lived in Clark County by 1940, of whom pioneer farm families of long standing accounted for the majority. Nevada did not become part of the evacuation zone that came to encompass western Washington and Oregon, all of California, and the southern parts of Arizona. Only a few groups living east of the exclusion zones suffered the effects of mass internment and mass relocation, such as the Japanese community in the copper-mining towns of Ruth and McGill near Ely, Nevada, and the Japanese railroading families of Clovis, New Mexico. Nevertheless, many Issei males in the interior region, particularly leaders of their communities, were arrested and incarcerated, and many families suffered harsh persecution, economic distress, and a variety of tough restrictions. Extreme racism and hysteria had spread across the region by early 1942, as the government began to plan and implement the mass relocation of Japanese Americans away from the West Coast. Federal officials also contemplated mass incarceration for the large Nikkei population of Hawaii and the few thousand who were scattered across the inland states, even though that ultimately did not happen. Across Nevada and other land-locked reaches of the Western Defense Command, in other words, Japanese Americans faced the serious threat and felt the sting of the war, contrary to the popular notion that only the Japanese of the West Coast truly suffered.[22] In the case of Las Vegas, however, local circumstances played a huge and positive role in shaping unusual outcomes.

One Las Vegas resident did fall victim to the complexity of events and actions that comprised the larger disaster. An uncle of the Tomiyasu children, Ikuguro "Fred" Nagamatsu, wrote some letters to the *Review-Journal* trying to defend Japan's military aggression in Asia and against the United States in the days and weeks following the declarations of war. A university graduate and intellectual, once mentioned by the newspaper in the 1930s for inventing an important water-well improvement, Nagamatsu was suddenly identified as the enemy. He was arrested by local authorities, turned over to Department of Justice operatives, spent some time in the Department of Justice internment camps, and eventually repatriated to Japan.[23]

But the Nagamatsu case was the exception to the rule. No other Japanese residents were arrested, and no intense public fear or unrest surfaced locally. Witnesses have explained that most Las Vegas residents knew each other well, and the Japanese farm families were much respected. It probably helped that no Japanese cultural institutions or activities had been evident over the years to raise suspicions. Moreover, produce retailer turned county sheriff Gene Ward worked diligently to protect his Japanese American friends from abuse, telling Nanyu Tomiyasu after the war that he was not about to let FBI agents "or anyone else come in here and disrupt all of your lives." Decades of tolerance and respect paid off in other ways as well, such as when the high-school students in the Moapa Valley voted to retain Jimmy Yamashita as their student-body president in 1942, after some parents raised objections to that peculiar situation. For their part, the Japanese Americans of Clark County did all they could to dispel any suspicions and prove their loyalty. Many Nisei sons joined the armed services, and the farmers redoubled their efforts to produce vegetables and meats to counter wartime food shortages.[24]

Nonetheless, some trouble did occur. A bit behind the pack, the *Review-Journal* had climbed aboard the "Jap-hunt" bandwagon by February 1942, printing a string of news stories and negative editorials that painted the Japanese in America, including those living in Las Vegas, as dangerous. For example, late that month managing editor A. E. Cahlan described an alleged feud between a local Japanese (possibly the "militant" Fred Nagamatsu) and a Mexican woman—the former supposedly arguing that Mexico did not have the backbone to stand up to America, like Japan. "The Japanese are still at large as are many in this vicinity," Cahlan warned, adding that many citizens "are finding it difficult to understand why ALL Japanese are not put somewhere under surveillance—where they can do NO damage." Other editorials and news articles told readers of FBI raids on the West Coast that were supposedly netting large stores of guns, explosives, maps, and signaling devices; how the "Nips" had leased land next to every important military installation along the coast; and how the "AMERICAN-BORN" Japanese were obviously a part of these "plans for conquest." The most fantastic local story concerned reports that "little brown men," operating out of caves on the Colorado River, had fired shots at Boy Scouts who were hiking in the area. This, of course, turned out to be a hoax, but Cahlan's paper kept up its campaign for several weeks.[25]

Other local and regional forces rocked the boat. The immediate prewar years and the war itself had brought some transformations that strained race relations in general and heightened civil-defense concerns. Las Vegas had been steadily growing and changing from a small railroad town into a tourism destination and part of the national defense network. Many newcomers brought prejudices with them, and some leaders of the new tourism industry began to advocate Jim Crow policies against blacks and other minorities to satisfy the segregationist mentality of tourists from California and the South. Furthermore, Clark County had also become the most significant defense area in Nevada by the outbreak of the war, given Boulder Dam, the recently established Army Air Corps gunnery school, later Nellis Air Force Base, and the new Basic Magnesium processing plant in Henderson. Las Vegas was courting a greater federal presence and garnering more attention from state officials, and none of this bode well for its politically vulnerable Japanese American residents.[26]

These changes may help to explain the emergence of a little-known local plot to "evacuate" Japanese Americans from southern Nevada. Records of the Clark County Defense Council (CCDC, part of a larger state and national civilian defense network) make no mention of any "Japanese problems" in the area until March 10, 1942. That evening, however, board members of the CCDC heard Executive Secretary I. R. Crandall state that the Chamber of Commerce had appealed to the state defense council for help in having the area declared a "military area for evacuation of all aliens." Crandall then read a letter he had recently sent to the state director of civilian defense asking: "Will you kindly contact Lieut. General John L. DeWitt [the officer in charge of the Western Defense Command] asking that this portion of Nevada be included in the military zone recently designated by him which will enforce an order for the evacuation of all Japanese aliens, American citizens of Japanese descent, German aliens and Italian aliens in that order." Three days later, Crandall announced the plan to a general meeting of the defense council, adding that the state director "felt certain immediate action would be taken." A letter in the collection from the director states that he "quite approve[d] of this [proposed] measure."[27]

The way these exclusion plans were introduced to the CCDC indicates that the plot was hatched by a small group, which may have included A. E. Cahlan, who served on the CCDC Executive Committee. Moreover, it was inspired by the highly publicized evacuation plans being drawn up on the West Coast, and it reflected the strong message Nevada was sending at the time that it did not want to become a "dumping ground" for "California Japs." Although it hardly constituted a major campaign, the CCDC's call for Japanese removal cannot be dismissed as a minor aberration or small threat. Anti-Japanese sentiment had certainly penetrated the minds of some powerful locals by that point, raising the real possibility of a disaster. But the plot probably came too late in the drama (and was too politely delivered, perhaps) to cause an expansion of the evacuation zones into southern Nevada.[28]

Local attitudes and experiences varied as the war progressed. Locals continued to treat their Japanese neighbors well, for the most part, but fear of "all those other Japs" remained strong. When farm interests in the Moapa Valley lobbied hard to import cheap Japanese labor from the relocation camps to help with the 1943 spring harvest, trouble ensued. Various groups, including the local defense councils and the American Legion, opposed this temporary influx of Japanese and demanded curfews, travel restrictions, and constant supervision by law-enforcement authorities. At least one Nisei still in school at the time reported an increase in insults and abuse on the part of some European American students and teachers. Furthermore, a good deal of confiscated "contraband" property, including guns as well as radios, flashlights, and other potential "signaling devices," turned over at the start of the war never made it back to the rightful owners. The most salient fact, however, is that the local Japanese American community weathered the crisis, avoiding most of the suspicion, the hostility, and the material and mental damages suffered by the vast majority of their kin. Local history—a long legacy of trust, friendship, respect, integration, hard work, and cooperation—figured large in these positive outcomes, and it set the stage for further advances in the postwar years.[29]

New Beginnings

For a quarter century following the war, the Japanese community of Las Vegas remained minute. Like their counterparts around the country, local Issei parents strongly encouraged their children of both sexes to attend college and pursue professional careers. Prior to 1957, when the first local institution of higher learning was established, this meant leaving southern Nevada, at least temporarily. Others eventually relocated away because miscegenation laws and customs, combined with the small population, made it difficult to find a suitable spouse. Few newcomers arrived until the 1970s. Nevertheless, these decades of transition were very significant to laying the groundwork for the Japanese population boom of recent years.

Some of the big-picture changes were national and international in scope. First, the war exposed the horrors of racism unleashed and advanced the civil-rights cause in general. As for the Japanese Americans who went peacefully to the camps and willingly to the battlefields, they had demonstrated particularly well their right to be called "loyal Americans." Japan and the United States, during and after the occupation period and the Korean conflict, became essential partners in the Cold War and in rebuilding the global economy. Furthermore, national and state leaders recognized mistakes in retrospect and in light of realities. In 1952, for instance, Nevada Senator Patrick McCarran, a longtime supporter of the Japanese farm families of his state, cosponsored legislation that finally granted citizenship to the Issei and reopened the door to immigration, albeit with a quota of only 185 per year. Late in that decade, Nevada's anti-Asian, antimiscegenation law fell when the famous labor organizer Harry Bridges and his fiancée, Noriko Sawada, got the courts to bless their Reno wedding wishes.[30]

Across the West and the nation, the Nisei-run Japanese American Citizens League (JACL) and other community groups renewed lobbying against alien land laws and similar restrictions, winning a string of victories in the postwar courts and legislatures of the West. Also, as Hawaii achieved statehood (1959) and anti-Asian racism subsided on the West Coast, Japanese Americans—including two U.S. senators—began to win elections to Congress. The various revolutions of the '60s brought more change, including key civil-rights and voting-rights laws that leveled the playing field for Asian Americans. One can count the bipartisan Civil Liberties Act of 1988, which granted redress to the victims of evacuation, as a clear sign of how far Japanese Americans had advanced and attitudes had changed in a few decades.[31]

Locally, the mélange changed both more and less than elsewhere. The seeds of a megaresort tourism industry were planted in the 1950s and grew steadily thereafter. The expansion of Nellis Air Force Base and the Nevada Test Site fueled economic development as well. These and other forces brought a few more Japanese American settlers to the area to pursue a range of occupations. Still, the number of old-timers and newcomers of Japanese descent remained tiny up through the early 1970s, and Las Vegas maintained a small-town feel that harkened back to earlier times.

In the postwar decades, as the regular supply of produce from California stabilized, the Japanese farming families of Las Vegas tended to switch to growing, marketing, and planting landscape vegetation. The oldest sons Henry Sakai and Nanyu Tomiyasu, who had inherited their fathers' horticultural operations, made this transition. Fast-growing trees and alkaline-resistant shrubs and grasses replaced vegetables as the chief contribution of the local Japanese gardeners to the shade-starved community. For decades, Tomiyasu also served as the primary landscape architect for the Las Vegas Country Club, the Sahara Hotel, and other resorts. An impressive tribute to the family came in 1974, when Yonema "Bill" Tomiyasu Elementary School, reputed to be the first elementary school on the U.S. mainland to be named after a Japanese American, opened its doors. The Tomiyasu family later worked with students to add a beautiful Japanese garden and bridge to the school grounds.[32]

Other long-established Japanese families started to play a larger role in the diversified economy. In 1967 Sam Nakanishi, the son of a railroader from the early days, and his family opened the Osaka Restaurant on West Sahara, paving the way for similar small businesses. As noted, most of the Nisei had moved away from Las Vegas, but some from the second and third generations, including architect George Enomoto, pursued successful professional careers in town. Wayne Tanaka, who came to Las Vegas in the early 1970s, made his mark as an education administrator, eventually earning the "Nevada Principal of the Year" honor and the Clark County School District's "Excellence in Education" award. Defense-related occupations brought other Nisei and Sansei to the Valley around this time, as did the blossoming tourism and gaming industries. Those newcomers who could speak the language of the Japanese tourists and conventioneers were particularly valuable additions to the community. Among them were Joe and Lillian Morizono, an Issei-Nisei couple from Los Angeles, who also settled in Las Vegas in the early 1970s. Both spoke Japanese well, so Joe pursued his dream of becoming a poker dealer and came to specialize in dealing to Japanese tourists, while Lillian gave up a career with Bank of America to work as an agent and translator for a Japanese travel company.[33]

Quite a few who came in the "second influx" were Issei women whose experiences were somewhat reminiscent of the "picture brides" of earlier days. Nanyu Tomiyasu did not marry until late in life, and his wife Setsuko, like his mother, came straight from Japan, following "arrangements" made on both sides of the ocean. Others, including Akiko Bline and Emiko Childers, came as the wives of American officers and servicemen stationed at, or retiring near, Nellis AFB. Both women married their husbands in Japan in the 1950s and have lived in Las Vegas since the early 1970s. Still, the Japanese American population remained very small. Physical dispersal and a legacy of integration, combined with the demands of working and raising families (complicated in some cases by the language barrier), apparently discouraged much group interaction into this period.[34]

The founding of the Japanese American Club in 1973 and the Las Vegas chapter of the JACL soon thereafter marked a major turning point. Established mainly by recent settlers from California and Hawaii, these groups fostered a sense of community and sponsored cultural activities so common in the vibrant subcultures they had left behind. In those years, it should also be noted, most Asians and people of color still felt unwelcome or uncomfortable in mainstream clubs. By the end of the decade, the two groups breached some philosophical differences and merged into one club. The new JACL chapter's membership peaked at around four hundred, a sure sign of just how much population growth had occurred in the 1970s alone. George Goto, a talented Nisei horticulturalist who relocated from Los Angeles and specialized in Japanese-style hotel landscaping, played an instrumental leadership role in the growth of these clubs and in increasing their visibility. Under his leadership, the Japanese Americans made significant contributions to the annual fundraising efforts of the local Public Broadcasting Service television station and assisted other charitable causes.[35]

Meanwhile, the "homebody" Issei wives and other women gradually started traditional dance and flower-arranging groups that functioned quietly and often separate from the Nisei-Sansei-led JACL. Another significant development of the seventies was the establishment of a Soka Gakkai Buddhist congregation in town, followed soon by a second, more traditional Nichiren-style worship group. (Today the Soka Gakkai boasts a temple and a membership of around 1,600 people, though most are not Japanese, while the other Buddhist group continues to be served by a traveling minister based in Phoenix.)[36] A local subculture was emerging—but a rather fractured one comprised of people with various cultural experiences and a limited sense of the whole. One of the more significant divides was between the long-established families and the newcomers, most of whom knew little about the history of the Japanese in Nevada and Las Vegas. Local educators Caryl Suzuki and Sue Fawn Chung did much to bridge these gaps in the mid-1990s by organizing a series of well-attended conferences and exhibits in Las Vegas that publicized and compared the local, state, and regional stories of the Japanese Americans.[37]

The Legacy Continues

Since the 1980s, the Asian American populations of Las Vegas and Nevada have grown tremendously, with the most dramatic increase coming over the last decade or so. The U.S. Census Bureau estimated that in 2006, 10,014 people in the Las Vegas metropolitan statistical area claimed Japanese ancestry, up from 2,883 in 1990. The Filipino population in 2006 was six times larger, and the Chinese outnumbered the Japanese by roughly 8,000 souls.[38] Nonetheless, the Japanese Americans living in Las Vegas today far outnumber those of all previous periods combined, and they continue to make an impact disproportionate to their numbers, which remain relatively small.

They are a diverse group. A sizable proportion are Nisei of retirement age who have elected to spend their golden years in Las Vegas, including Alyce Nakanishi Loui and a few other native sons and daughters who returned home after decades of living out of state. Most of these seniors and many other recent "transplants" moved here from California and Hawaii because of the favorable housing market, low tax rates, and the overall economic health of the city, as well as the "quality of life" they had witnessed or enjoyed during previous visits. Today, newcomers from Hawaii, the "Japanese Hawaiians" by their proud self-identification, are roughly equal in numbers to the "Japanese Americans"—those who hail mainly from the West Coast states. Meanwhile, the ranks of the "Japanese Nevadans" (families of old) have grown only slightly over the generations. And then there are the "new immigrants"—people from Japan perhaps living here temporarily and working for hotels and other companies, who may number in the low thousands, as well as over a quarter million Japanese tourists who visit annually. Many Japanese American residents of the Valley, particularly those born after the 1960s, are of mixed race and heritage, and some of the youngest are only a quarter Japanese. There is no residential concentration, and in large sections of the city one is far more likely to encounter Japanese tourists than Japanese Americans.[39] If this picture is blurry, the recent past is blessed with many signs that the positive legacy continues to grow.

As with most of the city's ethnic communities, megaresort tourism planted the cornerstone for the rapid growth of the Japanese population in recent years. The construction of the San Remo Hotel and Resort in the 1980s, funded by Japanese and Japanese American investors, symbolized a growing interest in the industry, and Japanese investment in today's hotel corporations remains substantial. Statistics, meanwhile, bear striking witness to the significance of the Japanese tourists. In 1998 they ranked as the largest category of non-North American foreign visitors to the United States (11 percent of the total) and accounted for 21 percent of all the expenditures by these visitors. About 350,000 Japanese visited Las Vegas in 2006. Since the 1980s, a strong yen has encouraged increases in leisure activities and travel by the Japanese, and Las Vegas has long been among their top three principal destinations. The city has fostered and gained a reputation as one of the gateways to the Grand Canyon and other western parks, the premier gambling Mecca, the convention capital of the Southwest, a great bargain, and a safe city for foreign visitors. Thousands more come to take or renew their wedding vows every year.[40]

An accounting of tourism dollars and visitor statistics hardly tells the whole story of recent change occurring on the economic and cultural fronts. Hundreds of people from Japan arrive every year to work in the gambling pits, specialty shops, and Japanese restaurants of the town. Japanese and Japanese American newspapers and magazines are helping to fuel interest in the city and reshape the community. The University of Nevada, Las Vegas, attracts others, and the campus rivals any hotel for the largest concentration of Japanese people at any given time.

Another active force behind recent developments is the Japan America Association of Southern Nevada, established in 1995. Creating local, regional, and international networks, it is dedicated to fostering social, cultural, educational, and economic exchange between the two countries. Individuals continue to make a profound impact as well, and Wayne Tanaka stands out among them. As the honorary consul general of Japan in Las Vegas, Tanaka played a significant role in the selection of the Southern Nevada Japanese Teachers Association to cosponsor (along with the Japanese consul general in San Francisco) the 150-year anniversary of the Japan-U.S. Student Exchange Program in 2004.[41] For such a relatively small community located so far from the major Japanese American population centers, this was quite a coup.

Today, the local Japanese American community as a whole looks vastly different than it did in 1945—or in 1975 for that matter. Thousands of Japanese names appear in the white and yellow pages of the telephone directories. Japanese investments and tourist dollars continue to have an increasing impact on the city's economy. Japanese-style clubs and community groups also abound, teaching and preserving traditional dance, flower arranging, Taiko drumming, and martial arts and offering language training, religious instruction, and other types of Japanese cultural activities to all who show an interest.

These are just some of the signs that a unique chapter in the history of the Japanese Americans continues to play out in Las Vegas. Among "the peoples" profiled in this larger study, the Japanese have contributed one of the richest legacies, the significance of which has too often been neglected in the history of this fabled western boomtown. Theirs is a story that speaks volumes about racism and antiracism in bygone eras, the economic forces and rich cultural diversity that have shaped the present, and intriguing possibilities for the future.

Notes

In recounting the early history to 1945, Andrew Russell drew mainly from his earlier study, "A Fortunate Few: Japanese Americans in Southern Nevada, 1905 to 1945," *Nevada Historical Society Quarterly* 31, no. 1 (Spring 1988): 32–52. Fumiko Sasaki researched the postwar period and the modern contours of the community, and the two authors collaborated on the writing of the combined text. They are greatly indebted to Japanese Las Vegans Nanyu Tomiyasu and Wayne Tanaka and historian Sue Fawn Chung for generously sharing their knowledge and insights.

1. Numerous studies explore these challenges and reveal links between the Chinese and Japanese experiences, including: Sucheng Chan, *Asian Americans: An Interpretive History* (Boston: Twayne, 1991); Harry H. L. Katano and Roger Daniels, *Asian Americans: Emerging Minorities* (Englewood Cliffs, N.J.: Prentice-Hall, 1988); Roger Daniels, *Asian America: Chinese and Japanese in the United States since 1850* (Seattle: University of Washington Press, 1988); Gary Y. Okihiro, *Margins and Mainstreams: Asians in American History and Culture* (Seattle and London: University of Washington Press, 1994); Ronald Takaki, *Strangers from a Different Shore: A History of Asian Americans* (New York: Penguin Books, 1989).

2. Other noteworthy books that explore these topics include: Roger Daniels, *The Politics of Prejudice: The Anti-Japanese Movement in California and the Struggle for Japanese Exclusion* (Berkeley and Los Angeles: University of California Press, 1962); Yuji Ichioka, *The Issei: The World of the First Generation Japanese Immigrants, 1885–1924* (New York: Free Press, 1988), and Gary Y. Okihiro, *Cane Fires: The Anti-Japanese Movement in Hawaii, 1865–1945* (Philadelphia: Temple University Press, 1991).

3. See also Bill Hosokawa, *Nisei: The Quiet Americans* (New York: William Morrow, 1969); Harry H. L. Kitano and Roger Daniels, *Japanese Americans: The Evolution of a Subculture* (Englewood Cliffs, N.J.: Prentice-Hall, 1969); Stephen S. Fugita and David J. O'Brien, *Japanese American Ethnicity: The Persistence of Community* (Seattle:

University of Washington Press, 1991); Valerie J. Matsumoto, *Farming the Home Place: A Japanese American Community in California, 1919–1982* (Ithaca, N.Y.: Cornell University Press, 1993); David K. Yoo, *Growing Up Nisei: Race, Generation, and Culture among Japanese Americans of California* (Urbana and Chicago: University of Illinois Press, 2000).

4. See, Andrew B. Russell, "Friends, Neighbors, Foes and Invaders: Conflicting Images and Experiences of Japanese Americans in Wartime Nevada" (master's thesis, University of Nevada, Las Vegas, 1996); Elmer E. Rusco, *Good Times Coming? Black Nevadans in the Nineteenth Century* (Westport, Conn.: Greenwood Press, 1975); Russell R. Elliott, *History of Nevada* (Lincoln: University of Nebraska Press, 1973); Dudley O. McGovney, "The Anti-Japanese Land Laws of California and Ten Other States," *California Law Review* 35 (1947): 7–54; Lance Mulkey, "Nevada's Odd Response to the 'Yellow Peril': Asians and the Western Ineligible Alien Land Laws" (master's thesis, University of Nevada, Las Vegas, 2004).

5. Wilbur Shepperson, *Restless Strangers: Nevada's Immigrants and Their Interpreters* (Reno: University of Nevada Press, 1970), 131, 136–37; Elliott, *History of Nevada*, 233–50; Phillip I. Earl, "Nevada's Miscegenation Laws and the Marriage of Mr. & Mrs. Harry Bridges," *Nevada Historical Society Quarterly* 37, no.1 (Spring 1994): 1–17.

6. Russell, "Friends, Neighbors, Foes and Invaders," examines how these dynamics played out, particularly in Churchill, White Pine, and Clark Counties.

7. *Las Vegas Age,* June 23, 1906; Russell, "A Fortunate Few"; Phillip I. Earl, "Shots Fired in Caliente During 1906 Racial Conflict," *Nevada State Journal,* April 10, 1983.

8. *Las Vegas Age,* May 1, 1909.

9. *Las Vegas Age,* January 31, 1914.

10. U.S. Department of Commerce, Bureau of the Census, *Fifteenth Census of the United States, 1930: Population* 2, no. 4 (Washington, D.C.: Government Printing Office, 1932); Census Manuscripts transcribed by Patricia A. Scott, ftp://us-census.org/pub/usgenweb/census/nv/clark/1920/ (accessed March 10, 2007). For larger estimates, see Nanyu Tomiyasu, interview by Mark French, Las Vegas, Nevada, April 12, 1977, University of Nevada, Las Vegas, Lied Library, Special Collections. Given that anti-Japanese sentiment always concerned the railroads, it was not uncommon for companies to "hide" Japanese workers and families from census takers by temporarily relocating them when counts were conducted, and this could help account for the discrepancies.

11. See Harry A. Millis, *The Japanese Problem in the United States: An Investigation for the Commission on Relations with Japan Appointed by the Federal Council of the Churches of Christ in America* (New York: MacMillan, 1915), 35.

12. Russell, "A Fortunate Few"; Sam Nakanishi, interview by Andrew Russell, Las Vegas, Nevada, August 6, 1987. Sam's father worked for the railroad. His family lived for a time in company housing, but they left Las Vegas when Sam was eight, so his recollections of those experiences were limited.

13. *Las Vegas Review-Journal,* December 24, 25, 1930.

14. *Las Vegas Review,* July 14, 1922.

15. Russell, "A Fortunate Few"; Phillip I. Earl and Guy Louis Rocha, "The National Railroad Strike of 1922 and the Decline of Organized Labor in Nevada," *Journal of the West* 25 (April 1986): 44–51; *Las Vegas Review,* March 30, 1923.

16. Nanyu Tomiyasu, interview by Andrew Russell, March 22, 1987.

17. Andrew B. Russell, "American Dreams Derailed: Japanese Railroad and Mine Communities of the Interior West" (Ph.D. diss., Arizona State University, 2003), explores the causes and devastating impact of the mass firings.

18. See Russell, "A Fortunate Few," for fuller discussion of lackluster attempts at farming.

19. Russell, "A Fortunate Few," which drew mainly from Nanyu Tomiyasu, interview by Andrew Russell, March 22, 1987.

20. *Las Vegas Review-Journal,* June 28, 1930. This article focused on an operation Tomiyasu and a partner, Fred Haganuma, had begun in Searchlight, Nevada.

21. See "A Fortunate Few" for fuller discussion of these signs of success, inclusiveness, and generally good Japanese-Anglo race relations in the prewar period. However, this should be weighed against the reports of discrimination against Chinese Americans, African Americans, Native Americans, and others, profiled in Simich and Wright's previous book and elsewhere in the literature.

22. A vast amount of literature deals with the causes and consequences of the forced evacuation, and the collective works of historian Roger Daniels, such as his highly accessible *Prisoners Without Trial: Japanese Americans in World War II* (New York: Hill and Wang, 1993), are a good starting point to learn about this epic event. A guide to the smaller but growing body of literature that deals with Japanese Americans of the interior and their wartime experiences can be found in Russell's thesis and dissertation.

23. Russell, "A Fortunate Few"; Nanyu Tomiyasu, interview by Andrew Russell, March 22, 1987; informal conversations between Nanyu Tomiyasu and Andrew Russell, 1995.

24. Russell, "A Fortunate Few."

25. Ibid. For the specific reports referenced, see: *Las Vegas Review-Journal,* February 26, 1942, March 4, 16, 19, 1942.

26. These big-picture changes are addressed in Eugene P. Moehring, *Resort City in the Sunbelt: Las Vegas, 1930–1970* (Reno and Las Vegas: University of Nevada Press, 1989), particularly chapter 6: "Civil Rights in a Resort City." Russell, "Friends, Neighbors, Foes and Invaders," documents increasing anti-Japanese sentiment on the part of Nevada's governor and in the Carson-Reno area during the early months of the war.

27. This "plot" came to light while Russell was researching for his thesis in the *Records of the State Council of Defense* at the Nevada State Archives, Carson City, specifically: Minutes of Executive Council Meeting, March 10, 1942; Minutes of (General) Meeting, March 13, 1942, Box 7, MCCDM Notebook; Shamberger to Cradall, March 9, 1942, Box 10, "Clark County" File.

28. Russell, "Friends, Neighbors, Foes and Invaders." For the destruction that played out in the expanding evacuation zone throughout March and April, see the wider literature.

29. Russell, "Friends, Neighbors, Foes and Invaders"; "A Fortunate Few"; Russell's conversations with Nisei George Enomoto, who reported great difficulty in the public schools.

30. The big-picture changes are covered in some of the broader works on Asian American history cited above. Connections between McCarran and the Japanese farmers are noted in some of Russell's writings, but how that may have influenced the "Japanese-friendly" McCarran-Walters Act is open for further study. Earl, "Nevada's Miscegenation Laws," documents the significance of the Bridges case.

31. For more on the redress movement and related postwar changes, see: Mitchell T. Maki, Harry H. L. Katano, and S. Megan Bethhold, *Achieving the Impossible Dream: How Japanese Americans Obtained Redress* (Urbana and Chicago: University of Illinois Press, 1999); Leslie Hatamiya, *Righting a Wrong: Japanese Americans and the Passage of the Civil Liberties Act of 1988* (Stanford, Calif.: Stanford University Press, 1993); Yasuko Takezawa, *Breaking the Silence: Redress and Japanese American Ethnicity* (Ithaca, N.Y.: Cornell University Press, 1995).

32. Authors' conversations with long-time residents Nanyu Tomiyasu, Wayne Tanaka, and Sue Fawn Chung.

33. Ibid.; Lillian Morizono, interview by Fumiko Sasaki, Las Vegas, Nevada, April 1, 2007.

34. Setsuko Tomiyasu, interview by Fumiko Sasaki, Las Vegas, Nevada, April 10, 2007; Akiko Bline and Emiko Childers, interview by Fumiko Sasaki, Las Vegas, Nevada, April 15, 2007.

35. In the 1980s, Goto was also very active in representing the interests of the JACL members of Las Vegas who sought redress compensation under the Civil Liberties Act. Morizono, interview; Tomiyasu, interview by Fumiko Sasaki; conversations with Sue Fawn Chung.

36. Hiroko Fry, interview by Fumiko Sasaki, Las Vegas, Nevada, April 8, 2007. Fry, who remains an active member of the church, is also a "war bride" who came to Las Vegas in the 1970s.

37. Suzuki, Chung, and Russell also put together a modest-sized community oral history project and developed a traveling photo-textual exhibit on Japanese American women ("Nevada's Strength and Diversity") in conjunction with the symposium.

38. U.S. Census Bureau, American Community Survey, "Table B02006, Asian Alone by Selected Groups, 2006," http://factfinder.census.gov/ (accessed July 16, 2008). See also http://mumford.albany.edu/census/AsianPop/AsianPopData/4120cc.htm (accessed September 3, 2007).

39. This rough profile of the present community contours and reasons for coming to (or back to) Las Vegas is based on Sasaki's interviews and conversations with various residents, particularly Wayne Tanaka, Alyce Nakanishi Loui, Mel Ozeki, Colin Izumo, Belwayne Arakai, Ben Hasegawa, and Yasu Sugimoto. See also Laurence

Downes, "Hawaiians Find an Unlikely Eden in Las Vegas," *New York Times,* October 27, 2002.

40. Edwin McDowell, "For Japanese Tourists, It's First Stop Las Vegas," *New York Times,* October 25, 1998. The 2006 tourist numbers were provided to Sasaki by the Las Vegas office of the Japan Travel Bureau.

41. Curriculum Vita of Wayne Tanaka and conversations with the authors. See also Yukie Karasawa, "Minami Nevada Ni Nezasu Nihongo Benron (The Japanese Speeches Rooted in Southern Nevada)"; "Dai Sankai Nihongo Benron Taikai Okonau (The Third Japanese Speech Contest Celebrated)," *Nichi Bei Times,* December 9, 2006.

CHAPTER 4

The Cubans

WILLIAM CLAYSON

Few Cubans in Las Vegas would agree that any good came out of Fidel Castro's 1959 revolution. One might argue, however, that Las Vegas gained from the communist takeover of Cuba. If not for Fidel, much of the capital that built the Strip might have blown with the tropical wind to Havana along with the entertainment and the high rollers. In the mid-twentieth century, a cruise or flight across the Florida Straits was nearly as easy as a drive across the Mojave Desert. The island provided many more enticements than the creosote and dry wind of the Las Vegas Valley. Cuba offered everything early Las Vegas had to sell, but hoteliers in Havana had no need to build artificial beaches.

Las Vegas also benefited greatly from the people who fled the Castro revolution—Cuban immigration has had a greater impact there than on any city outside of Florida. The U.S. Census Bureau reported that 10,959 people of Cuban ancestry called Las Vegas home in 2006. Local leaders in the Latino community estimate that the figure may be closer to 25,000. While either estimate represents a small minority of the overall population and only a thin slice of the city's burgeoning Latino population, Las Vegas hosts the eighth largest Cuban American community in the country and has the highest number of Cubans per capita west of the Mississippi.[1]

The reason for the Cuban presence in Las Vegas is obvious. When Castro closed Havana's casinos after the revolution, he inadvertently provided Las Vegas a trained and ready workforce of baccarat dealers, singers, cooks, and maitre d's. Experience in the tourism industry and connections with early casino operators gave Cubans a natural advantage over other immigrants. Cubans also possessed business acumen and a work ethic that drove some into the highest levels of management in megaresort corporations. Good paying casino jobs and a relatively large number of Cubans fostered a vibrant social network, which the first generation of immigrants and their second and third generation Cuban American families maintain into the twenty-first century.

The casino economy provided definite advantages to Cuban exiles who made their way to Las Vegas after Castro's takeover, but more recent arrivals from Cuba have much in common with other Latino immigrants. New Cuban immigrants, especially those who came during the 1980 Mariel boatlift and since the economic crisis in Cuba following the 1991 collapse of the Soviet Union, found less economic opportunity than their predecessors. Other than favored status in terms of immigration policy, the Cuban immigrants who continue to flow into the city have no discernible economic or social advantages over other Latin American immigrants. In short, two Cuban American communities exist in Las Vegas. One came out of the revolution, helped build the Las Vegas Strip, and gained affluence and prominence in the city as it grew. The other group, those who have come from the island in the past quarter century or so, struggles to earn a living within the massive Latino working class of the metropolis that Las Vegas has become.[2]

A handful of Cuban immigrants had arrived in Las Vegas prior to Castro's 1959 revolution. The Sands and the Stardust casinos had imported experienced dealers to work baccarat and roulette tables as early as 1952. Jacinto Campillo, a comic dancer and band leader, immigrated to the United States and played at Thomas Hull's El Rancho Vegas, the first hotel-casino on the Strip, in the early 1950s. Famous Cuban band leaders such as Xavier Cugat and Desi Arnaz headlined Las Vegas stages throughout the fifties.[3]

Yet Cubans had little motivation to come to Las Vegas to deal cards or entertain in the casino business prior to 1959. Gambling and tourism had been a significant sector of the Cuban economy since the 1920s. The expansion of the U.S. economy during and after World War II also boosted the Cuban economy, as Havana became a tourist mecca for newly affluent Americans. The corrupt regime of strongman Fulgencio Batista fostered the gambling business as a way to bring in much needed revenues. Batista had close ties with American organized crime figures like Meyer Lansky and Charlie Luciano, who provided capital to operate multimillion-dollar casino venues such as the Hotel Nacional, the Sans Souci, and the Capri. Nothing in Las Vegas at the time compared to the Nacional—a palatial resort with old-world Moorish architecture, luxury suites, and airy archways overlooking Havana's old harbor. The connections to the Mafia at these resorts were no secret, but Lansky and other bosses ensured clean games to keep the customers coming. In exchange for maintaining the Mafia's monopoly on the gambling business in Havana, the racketeers paid Batista 20 percent of the take, along with licensing fees and untold thousands in bribes. Then on New Year's Eve 1959, Castro's supporters flooded the streets of Havana and stormed the casinos in a Cuban version of Bastille Day. The mobs looted bars, overturned baccarat tables, and smashed slot machines, shouting, "¡Viva Fidel!"[4]

When Castro nationalized the properties and abolished gambling later that year, Las Vegas beckoned experienced casino operators. The Las Vegas Cuban population boomed from less than 250 to about 1,700 by the end of the sixties, including about 300 Cuban American children born in the city. This represented a substantial presence in a town of only about 80,000 people.[5]

The generation of Cubans that came to Las Vegas in the 1960s was composed, for the most part, of middle- and upper-class transplants from Havana. This generation, often referred to as the *exilio,* or the exile, fled Cuba to escape communism. They had lived a different life than the majority of Cubans, who had remained trapped in the same rural poverty that had stifled their ancestors for centuries. The tourist economy that Batista and the mobsters built had created a cosmopolitan capital not far removed from the economy of the United States. Havana had literacy and mortality rates and transportation and communications infrastructures comparable to those of American cities. Most importantly for those who moved to Las Vegas, it had wealth in American dollars. Many of those who came to the city arrived with money, skills to earn solid incomes, or family connections to get work. Further, the Cubans were largely spared the discrimination that Mexican immigrants or native Mexican American people suffered from throughout the American Southwest.[6]

Cold War immigration policy provided advantages to Cubans over other Latino groups. After 1966, federal policy essentially allowed any Cuban a chance to become a legal resident one year after arriving in the United States or its territorial waters. The Clinton administration revised this policy in 1995, allowing in only those Cubans who made it to shore. This so-called "wet feet, dry feet" policy required immigration authorities or the Coast Guard to return refugees to Cuba or a third country if captured in U.S. waters. Despite the new restrictions, Cubans maintain an advantage over other immigrant groups from Latin America. Thanks to the simple fact that Cuba is a communist dictatorship, the Florida Straits remain the only major hurdle that Cubans must negotiate to become legal residents of the United States. Some Cubans faced bureaucratic obstacles in trying to enter the United States legally through third countries, but no Cuban need attempt to survive within the economy as an undocumented immigrant.

The statistics show the advantages the exiles had as immigrants to Las Vegas. By 1980 the annual median income for Cuban households in the city reached nearly $16,000. While this was about $2,000 less than the median for the city as a whole, it exceeded the average income of Mexican Americans by nearly $3,500. Las Vegas Cubans also had higher incomes than those in Florida.[7]

Beyond their experience in gambling and tourism, Cubans were also an asset to Las Vegas casinos because they possessed what the late historian Hal Rothman called a "certain cachet," meaning that they brought with them the tropical flair and sense of class of the Havana of legend. In 1960s Las Vegas, having some bona fide Cubans in the casinos added to the city's credibility as an exotic tourist destination. The Cubans also fit into the scene early Las Vegas cultivated—hip but not subversive to the Cold War mainstream, like the Rat Pack. When Jay Sarno opened Cleopatra's Barge in Caesars Palace in 1970, for example, he hired Jacinto Campillo as a band leader to open the stage. Campillo moved his extended family to Las Vegas and remains in the city to this day.[8]

The exilio generation built a thriving social network in the sixties and seventies. The Cuban community lacked a geographic center—there has never been a Little Havana in Las Vegas—but Cuban families did cluster in certain parts of town. The largest concentrations lived in the suburbs that surround Maryland Parkway, east of the strip near St. Anne's Catholic Church and Gorman High School. Families also maintained close ties with other Cubans through employment, restaurants, and El Círculo Cubano, a social club established by Agustín Menéndez in 1970. El Círculo sought to create a social environment of "a distinctly Cuban atmosphere . . . to further and maintain the culture and traditions of our Cuba of yesterday [*Cuba de ayer*]."[9] This desire to maintain Cuba de ayer informed much of the sense of community among the exilio in Las Vegas. El Círculo members came together for dances and domino tournaments, but also to talk business and politics. Cuban immigrants from the exile generation emphasize business success and political involvement as fundamental aspects of life.

The first generation of Cubans to come to Las Vegas assumed leadership roles in the local community. Although El Círculo no longer exists, Cubans formed the core leadership in the development of the Latin Chamber of Commerce of Nevada, the most influential Latino organization in the city. Under the direction of architect Arturo Cambeiro and then-governor Mike O'Callaghan, the Latin Chamber was incorporated as a nonprofit organization in 1976. In 1978 the organization hired Cuban-born Otto Mérida to serve full time as its executive director, a position he has held ever since. The Latin Chamber has grown from fifty members to thirteen hundred since its founding. The organization remains the primary advocacy group for Latino-owned businesses in the state. It provides scholarships, job training, and job contacts to local Latinos. Politically, the chamber has become the primary access route for candidates hoping to tap into the growing Latino community in Las Vegas. Mérida and other members of the Latin Chamber's leadership have often been appointed to local commissions and planning boards by governors and mayors through the years. Recently, the Latin Chamber has spawned a political organization called Hispanics in Politics (HIP), which has already proven influential. In 2007 HIP sponsored a town-hall meeting with New Mexico governor and then-presidential candidate Bill Richardson.[10]

The success story of the exile generation in Las Vegas resulted in part from the tight-knit nature of the community. Until the corporate boom in the gaming industry in the eighties and nineties, prospective workers typically secured employment in Las Vegas casinos through personal or family relationships. This trend was not unique to Cubans, but members of the exile managed casino floors or knew pit bosses who helped fellow islanders secure better paying jobs. Immigrant Liliam Lujan-Hickey, who came to Las Vegas in 1962, argued that the "only way" to get a job as a dealer in a casino was through connections in management. One measure of the strength of Cuban connections was the fact that Cuban immigrants in the sixties and seventies could succeed in the casino business without learning English. More than a third of all Cuban residents in Las Vegas in the seventies spoke no English at all, yet the incomes of Cubans rose throughout the decade. Mario Cuellar, for example, arrived in Las Vegas with his wife and two sons in 1970. He was in his late forties and had no marketable skills. He worked first as a busboy at the Stardust, then, through his uncle, secured a position dealing cards at the Las Vegas Club. He never learned English but worked as a dealer at various casinos for more than twenty years.[11]

Clearly though, having connections was not enough to succeed and advance in the economy. The success story of early Cuban immigrants in Las Vegas resulted as much from a willingness to make sacrifices and work hard as it did from connections. Just getting to the United States was often a harrowing experience. Las Vegas attorney Waldo de Castroverde spent twenty months in a Cuban prison after being captured by Fidel's troops at the Bay of Pigs in 1961. At just sixteen, Otto Mérida was separated from his parents as part of "Operation Peter Pan," a Johnson administration effort to relocate Cuban children in the United States. Nora Rodríguez's family spent two years in Spain wading through red tape until an aunt in Lake Tahoe agreed to sponsor them. Some took manual-labor jobs to support their families until they could get established in the United States. Louis Fabré, a Las Vegas businessman, recalls his father, a medical doctor in Cuba, sweeping streets in New Jersey while awaiting his license. Arturo Cambeiro, who had a degree in architecture from the University of Havana, worked for minimum wage while learning English in order to earn his architect's license in the United States.[12]

Along with a work ethic and willingness to sacrifice, Cubans of the exilio also have a characteristic commitment to achieving personal and family success. The ambition common to Cubans is not merely financial, but also creates a drive toward educational attainment and career advancement. This is not surprising, given that the people who fled the Castro regime included the educated upper strata of prerevolutionary Cuba, but many wealthy Cubans had to start from scratch when they reached the United States.

The Cuellar family exemplifies this nexus of hard work and ambition that created success for Cuban immigrants and their children in Las Vegas. Mario Cuellar dealt cards, and his wife, Serafina, worked for a local physician as a nurse's aide. Coming from such modest occupations, the Cuellars expected much more from their sons, Mario and Mauricio. The younger Mario received his army commission through the ROTC program at the University of Nevada, Las Vegas, and currently serves as a lieutenant colonel on active duty. Mauricio, a talented pitcher in high school, earned an athletic scholarship to a junior college in California, then returned to Las Vegas to enter the casino business. He started dealing cards in 1985, moved up to pit boss at the Pioneer Club, and then became the casino manager at the Gold Strike in Jean and general manager at the Railroad Pass Hotel in Henderson. In 2000, just fifteen years after entering the business, Mauricio opened the enormous Monte Carlo Hotel on the Strip as the casino manager.[13]

Cubans have also thrived outside the casino business. The architecture firm built by brothers Arturo and Domingo Cambeiro went from nothing to rank among the premiere architectural firms in the city. The firm designed the Thomas and Mack Center, the city's largest sports venue, on the UNLV campus in 1983. While Arturo Cambeiro died in 1990, Domingo continued to expand the firm and design many Las Vegas landmarks. These include the Clark County Government Center, the Showcase Retail and Entertainment Center on the Strip, the West Las Vegas Library, and the huge McCarran International Airport parking structure and baggage-claim area. The Clark County School District named an elementary school in honor of Arturo Cambeiro. Domingo Cambeiro does not have a school named for him yet, but his firm has been the principal architect for prototype designs of many recently constructed schools in the Las Vegas area.[14]

No individual better exemplifies Cuban success in Las Vegas than Tony Alamo, one of the most powerful figures in the casino industry by the 1990s. Alamo fled the Castro regime in 1961 and began his career in the casino business cleaning toilets at Harrahs casino in Reno. Alamo worked hard, never complained, always came to work on time, and worked as often as he possibly could. The managers at Harrahs rewarded him by moving him first into the coin room and then into dealing blackjack and craps. While dealing craps for Harrahs, Alamo became close friends with fellow dealer Michael Ensign, who would also become a mogul in the casino industry (his son John has served in the U.S. Senate for Nevada since 2000). Within little more than a decade, Alamo had moved into management with rival Circus Circus in Las Vegas. Alamo explained the secret of his success in an interview with author Pete Earley:

> If I went to work as a dishwasher in a restaurant, I would eventually end up managing that restaurant because I will do my job well. I will volunteer for extra work, for the toughest assignments. I will work overtime. I will work seven days a week. I will go to work before anyone else and I will go home after everyone else and I will do that year after year. This is the secret to success in life—working hard.[15]

His hard work paid off. After serving as the general manager of Circus Circus, Alamo was hired by Kirk Kerkorian to oversee the construction of the new MGM Grand, at the time the largest hotel in the world. Alamo then went to work for Gold Strike resorts with his old friend Michael Ensign to manage the development of the Monte Carlo. When Circus Circus bought the Monte Carlo, the company placed Alamo in charge of a $250 million renovation of the struggling Luxor Hotel and Casino. Finally, Alamo topped his long career managing the construction of the Mandalay Bay Hotel-Casino at a cost of nearly a billion dollars.

Responsibility came his way because the barons of the Strip knew that no one understood the casino business better than Tony Alamo. In designing casino floors, Alamo maximized space for slots and tables and designed attractions that minimized the time customers spent waiting in lines at buffets, bathrooms, or theme rides and not gambling. Slot-machine areas in most casinos are arranged according to "Tony Alamo's urinal theory." Alamo understood that most people prefer some personal space when they sit down at a slot machine, like men at urinals in public restrooms, so he added an extra eight inches between slots to draw more players. Few of the millions of tourists who visit Las Vegas each year realize that a Cuban refugee created much of their experience. For his contributions to the community, Alamo, like architect Arturo Cambeiro, has a local elementary school named for him. In 2003 the Board of Regents of the state higher education system gave him the "Distinguished Nevadan Award." Alamo also passed his work ethic on to his children, who have become prominent citizens in the community themselves. His son, Tony Jr., is a cardiologist and his daughter, Nancy, works for the school district as a psychologist.[16]

Cuban ambition goes beyond personal wealth or career success. Cubans also seem uniquely motivated to define and build a rich and full life. Oscar Barillas, for example, served Las Vegas as the city's only Spanish-speaking psychiatrist in the late 1970s and 1980s. He had also been a Golden Gloves boxer, a championship ballroom dancer, and a published poet. Barillas may have been influenced by a chance meeting and conversation he had with Ernest Hemingway on a Havana beach in 1954, but his zest for living life to its fullest is quintessentially Cuban. Another example is Dr. Carlos Campo, a professor of English at the College of Southern Nevada (CSN). Campo could have easily spent his career teaching introductory English courses to incoming freshmen but chose instead to earn his Ph.D. and publish. He is a recognized authority on Arthur Miller, served as the dean of Arts and Letters at the college, and served as the interim Vice President for Academic Affairs through the 2007–2008 academic year.[17]

Ambition and hard work are characteristic ideals of Cuban masculinity, but Cuban women also share these traits. Cuban women are often encouraged to become educated and pursue careers for other than economic reasons. Three generations of women from the Lujan family in Las Vegas help to illustrate this. Lilliam Lujan-Hickey came from Havana in the wake of the revolution. Her husband owned a gym in the city and had been the weight-lifting coach for the Cuban Olympic team. The family came to Las Vegas to find work in 1962. A year later, she was widowed with three children when her husband died of a heart attack. The family survived on the small salary she earned as a medical secretary, but she found time to volunteer with the Cuban Refugee Program under the Nevada State Welfare Department. She went to work full time for the Welfare Department in 1970, beginning as a secretary and moving her way up to become coordinator for employment and contract services. Hickey also served on the Latin Chamber of Commerce board of directors and on the Nevada State Board of Education. Not to be outdone by the men previously mentioned, Hickey also has an elementary school named in her honor. Her daughter, Lilliam Shell, earned her degree from UNLV and now serves as the regional operations director for Nevada Health Centers, Inc., a private company established to provide health care for underserved rural communities in the state. Lilliam Lujan's granddaughter, Alena Shell, worked as the executive secretary of the Southern Nevada American Civil Liberties Union (ACLU) and is currently attending the Boyd School of Law at UNLV.[18]

Incoming Cubans continued to work hard, but the advantages they enjoyed in the sixties and seventies began to dwindle as the city grew near the end of the century. The statistics show that Cuban immigrants in Las Vegas slipped economically as the century came to a close. Cubans remained below the average in annual income for non-Hispanic whites but fell behind other Latino groups as well. The median annual income of Cuban American households in Clark County, at $22,957 in 1990, was $4,000 less than the figure for Mexican American households. By 2000 Cuban American family income continued to lag slightly behind that of Mexican Americans.[19]

In the broadest sense, this decline has come to pass because the newer generation of immigrants came from a different Cuba and to a different Las Vegas than the exilio. When Castro closed the casinos, the number of tourists coming to Cuba declined to almost nothing. Skills in leisure management or hotel operations were irrelevant to the revolution until the collapse of the Soviet Union, when, without outside support, the Castro regime found the tourist trade a needed source of income. After the first wave, immigrants arrived in Las Vegas with fewer skills transferable to the local tourist economy. The latter immigrants also came, for the most part, with nothing but the assistance they received as refugees from the U.S. government and charities such as Catholic Community Services. The legal status of Cubans gave them some advantage over those who arrived from elsewhere in Latin America, especially undocumented immigrants, but Cubans had to compete for unskilled jobs with thousands of other newcomers.

The connections within the casino business that helped Cuban immigrants to get good paying jobs also reached their limits as the city expanded in the 1990s. The population of southern Nevada had grown exponentially, topping 1.4 million by 2000 and approaching 2 million by 2006. As gaming evolved into a corporate enterprise, workers found jobs through Culinary Workers, Local 226, or human-resources departments instead of informal social networks. Having connections still helps, but the process has by necessity become much less personal. When the Red Rock Resort opened in 2006, for example, more than 100,000 people applied for just 2,600 jobs. It would be difficult for a non-English-speaking Cuban immigrant to stand out against such competition, even if he or she had a relative or friend working in management. The Cubans who came to Las Vegas in the wake of the revolution came to what was essentially a small town, with a local economy run on personal connections. More recent arrivals came to an economy that grouped Cubans and other Latino immigrants together into a large pool of low-cost labor.[20]

The 1980 Mariel boatlift presented another obstacle to Cuban immigrants coming to Las Vegas. Mariel changed attitudes toward new Cuban émigrés. Between April and November, Castro opened Mariel harbor for emigration, offering an opportunity for anyone interested in leaving to do so. About 125,000 Cubans accepted the offer, including 86,000 in May alone. This influx inflated the Cuban population in the United States by 15 percent. The Immigration and Naturalization Service estimated that as many as 2,000 of the "Marielitos" ended up in Las Vegas, expanding the Cuban population in the city by nearly a third.[21] The large influx of mostly male, single immigrants accounts for much of the statistical economic decline of Las Vegas Cubans.

Since U.S. policy offered Cubans asylum as political refugees, the Coast Guard could not turn back the makeshift flotilla of crammed boats, even after it became known that Castro used the Mariel boatlift to empty his jails and mental hospitals. Some estimates placed the total number of released prisoners at 25,000, though it is clear that the Castro regime had jailed the majority of these for political violations or minor crimes. Castro also placed an estimated 1,200 violent criminals and an uncertain number of potentially violent mental patients on the flotilla, and the Cuban government provided no method for identifying the criminals. The vast majority of the Marielitos simply wanted out of Cuba to work or join relatives in the United States, but the prisoners placed on the flotilla sullied the image of the rest.[22]

The sensationalized media attention given to Castro's ploy made assimilation into American life much more difficult for the Marielitos. The U.S. public, including many Cuban Americans, did not embrace the Marielitos as refugees escaping a communist dictatorship. Instead, they became associated with the stereotyped image of Tony Montana, the psychotic Cuban drug dealer played by Al Pacino in *Scarface*.[23] In Las Vegas, the local press jumped on the story, running sensationalized accounts of the "Marielito banditos [sic]." In a series of articles in the *Las Vegas Sun*, reporter Alan Tobin emphasized "the brutality of the criminal element" among the Marielitos. In May of 1983, one headline in this series read, "When a Marielito Threatens Death, Death Usually Occurs." Another article in the series described the Santería cult. Santería is a blend of African mythology and Roman Catholicism practiced among Afro-Caribbean people, including black and mulatto Cubans. The *Las Vegas Sun* article depicted Santería as a sinister cult in which Marielitos worshipped a Yoruba cognate of Saint Barbara as a "warrior god."

A report in the *Las Vegas Review-Journal* claimed that the Marielitos accounted for twenty-one murders in Las Vegas between 1981 and 1983. The spike in violent crime led the Metropolitan Police to create a "Marielito Bandito" task force to track down and keep tabs on local Marielitos. Metro compiled a list of 540 hard-core criminals who, if "picked up for any reason," would be "immediately incarcerated in federal detention centers." There is no question that some of the Marielitos became involved in violent crime, but the killings detailed in the press were all "Marielitos killing Marielitos." Local Cuban leaders understood that the majority of Marielitos shared the aspirations of other immigrants, but they feared the criminal stigma of the boatlift would threaten "the American public's perception of Cubans."[24]

Nearly two decades after the boatlift, a notorious drug dealer named José Vigoa further denigrated the image of the Marielitos in Las Vegas. Vigoa was a promising young military officer in the Cuban army, trained as a commando in the Soviet Union. After combat tours in Afghanistan and Angola, Vigoa abandoned his military career to join the refugees at Mariel in 1980. He turned to crime soon after his arrival in Las Vegas, because the tourist economy seemed to offer only dead-end food service jobs. He became a minor kingpin in the narcotics trade in Las Vegas and served several incarcerations on charges related to drugs and violence. In 1998 he brought the *Scarface* legend to life by orchestrating a string of brazen casino robberies at five major strip resorts, killing two security guards and baffling the police. Now serving five consecutive life terms for robbery and murder in Ely State Prison, Vigoa regrets ever coming to the United States. "I had so many beautiful dreams when I came to America," he lamented in an interview with author John Huddy. "Now look at the mess I'm in. Justice?"[25]

Along with the stigma associated with criminals like Vigoa, the boatlift also changed the racial makeup of the Las Vegas Cuban community. Black and mulatto Cubans comprised about 40 percent of the Marielitos. For Afro-Cubans living in Las Vegas, the combination of being black and Latino created unexpected complications. One Afro-Cuban immigrant, Bernardo Ricardo, left Cuba with the Mariel boatlift after having spent thirteen years in one of Castro's prisons, allegedly because he had served as a soldier in Batista's army before the revolution. Ricardo found work as a kitchen helper at the Bourbon Street Casino and Caesars Palace but found it difficult to develop personal relationships with coworkers. He felt that other Latinos, especially the many Mexican immigrants who work in kitchens on the Las Vegas Strip, were disinclined to socialize with him because he is black. At the same time, he had difficulty communicating with black coworkers because, in his words, he "had a hard time learning 'black English.'"[26]

The status of Cuban women also changed after Mariel. The earlier cohort of Cuban exiles, particularly the affluent families, often encouraged women to get an education and launch careers in their own right. At the same time, mothers could often afford to remain in the home, and it was less common among married Cuban couples for women to work than is the case with other Latino groups in Las Vegas. Among more recent immigrant families, however, women often have little choice but to work in order to feed families and pay the rent. By 1990 nearly a third of Cuban families were headed by single women.[27] This is certainly a primary factor in the financial slide of Cuban families suggested by census reports.

Despite the economic and social obstacles faced by recent Cuban immigrants, there is wide agreement among them that no matter how difficult life in the United States gets, it is always better than life in Cuba. Under the Soviet umbrella, the Castro revolution had provided tangible benefits to the poor in Cuba. Infant mortality rates declined, literacy rates rose, and health care became more accessible. Urban poverty rates declined to just above 6 percent by 1985, a figure lower than that in the United States. Any advance, however, came at the cost of political and economic repression. To get away from such repression, it remained routine even in the best times of the Castro regime for Cuban immigrants to risk their lives to get to the United States.

Following the collapse of the USSR, living conditions on the island worsened. Unemployment, malnourishment, and shortages of medicine returned Cuba to Third World status. Between 1989 and 1993, the Cuban economy lost 35 percent of gross domestic product. Through the 1990s, the Cuban diet did not meet basic nutritional standards established by the United Nations. In Havana, for example, government food rationing provided less than half the caloric needs of adults. The end of Soviet sponsorship of the Cuban economy, then, further compelled migration. Fidel Castro had opened the door for the Marielitos in 1980, but, due to the failures of his economy, he was unable to keep it shut in the 1990s.[28]

Even Cubans who had relatively privileged positions in Cuba have made their way to Las Vegas, some moving from professional occupations to low-paying manual labor jobs. Sergio Fernández, for example, was a veterinarian in Cuba but found work in Las Vegas as a custodian at the Reed Whipple Cultural Center. María García, who had been the head librarian at the Center for International Music in Havana, came to Las Vegas at fifty-five years of age and found work as a maid at the Imperial Palace. Despite the status and prestige these individuals lost, each was grateful for the economic and personal liberties life in the United States has provided them. Conveniences that Las Vegans consider necessities remained beyond the reach of Cubans still on the island. The abundance of food brought tears to the eyes of García when she first visited a supermarket in Las Vegas. Ricardo pointed to his automobile to explain this feeling, saying, "I have a car . . . I never had a car in my country!"[29] Some of the later immigrants have also replicated the wealth and prestige of the earlier exiles. Sergio Pérez, for example, having left Havana in 1991, now owns two of the most popular Cuban restaurants in Las Vegas.[30]

One recent high-profile case suggests that even Castro's Cuba can produce valuable talent for the Las Vegas tourist industry. In 2004 performers from a Cuban dance show called the "Havana Night Club" applied to the U.S. government for visas to perform in Las Vegas. Strip icons Siegfried and Roy urged the troupe to play Las Vegas after seeing their show in Europe. The Cuban government denied the troupe at first, as did the U.S. State Department. Nicole Durr, the show's director, had to prove to immigration officials that "Havana Night Club" performed independently of the Castro regime. Once the U.S. government agreed to grant the visas, the Cuban government acquiesced, with the understanding that once the troupe performed in Las Vegas, they would not be allowed to perform in Cuba again. "Havana Night Club" played at the Wayne Newton Showroom at the Stardust from August until November of 2004. When the run was about to end, some fifty members of the troupe applied for asylum at the Foley Federal Building in Las Vegas before their visas expired. The cast members' defection garnered international attention, and the United States gave them permanent asylum in July 2005.[31] The case became even more controversial when federal authorities denied travel visas to a group of Cuban scholars wishing to attend the international Latin American Studies Association Convention in Las Vegas that same year. A critic alleged that U.S. visa policy toward Cuba seems biased toward performers, advising scholars to "show the officials in D.C. that they can dance and show some flesh. Chanting 'Babalu' might help."[32]

Regardless of motivation, coming of age within the Castro regime influenced the values of those who left Cuba to escape the material deprivation of the island. Mérida explained that the difference between the generation that fled Cuba in the wake of the revolution and more recent Cuban immigrants is primarily a difference in perspective. For the exilio, Castro was a brutal communist dictator and a thief who stole property, nationalized private businesses, and stripped honest Cuban families of their livelihoods. For those who have come since the Mariel boatlift, the Castro regime is primarily an economic failure. They continue to leave Cuba as economic immigrants, not political refugees. Despite the favored status given Cuban immigrants by federal policy, Cubans come to the United States today for the same reasons that impel other Latin American immigrants—work and better living conditions.[33]

One illustration of this difference in perspective is willingness to accept government assistance. Cuban immigrants who escaped from Castro in the 1960s and their now-adult children tend to have a conservative opinion toward welfare systems. Even if they needed assistance, which few ever have, most would consider it a profound humiliation to fill out forms and wait in line for government handouts. Those who left Cuba as adults reared in the revolution seem more accustomed to taking advantage of whatever assistance the federal or state government is willing to offer.[34]

Willingness to visit Cuba also helps to illustrate the divide between the exilio and more recent immigrants. The older generation of Cuban exiles, for the most part, is fervently opposed to visiting Cuba until the Castro regime is dismantled. Since they would spend money while visiting the island, the exilio members argue that some of that income will fall into the hands of the communists, a concession they refuse to make even if it means never seeing family members again. "I cannot go back," Waldo de Castroverde explained, "but maybe in the future. I take my [blood pressure] pills every day. If I die before [Fidel Castro] does, I'll be very upset with the man upstairs."[35]

More recent immigrants do not share such concerns, and many visit Cuba routinely, bringing money into the economy on visits to friends and family. Visitors can obtain permission from the U.S. Treasury and State Departments to visit family on an annual basis. It is also common to travel to Cuba via a third country, such as Mexico or Canada. The journey can be arduous and expensive. Nora Rodríguez described the costs travel agents charged her parents to get into Cuba through a third country as "just robbery." Despite such troubles, the Cuban government encourages immigrants to return. Travel agencies offer guidance over the Internet about how to get around federal restrictions. To encourage travel from the United States, the Castro regime has gone to the extreme of making it illegal for Cuban customs officials to stamp American passports.[36]

There is a growing concern among many Cubans of both generations that the continuation of the U.S. economic embargo on Cuba has done little to loosen the communist grip on power but has caused immeasurable harm to the Cuban population. For some, traveling to Cuba to visit family is a mission of mercy. Children are undernourished and otherwise healthy adults have failing eyesight due to vitamin deficiencies. Unlike the heyday of the Soviet era, when the Cuban health-care infrastructure rivaled or exceeded that of the United States, Cubans today have little access to current drugs or recent medical technologies. For these reasons, some Cubans go back despite concerns that some of their spending money might end up in the coffers of the Castro regime. Further, visiting remains the only reliable way to communicate with people on the island, as the revolution in information technology that has transformed the world in the past decade has left Cuba behind, and few Cubans have access to the Internet.

Some of the old-timers have returned to Cuba despite their hatred of the Castro regime. At age seventy-five, Lilliam Lujan-Hickey returned in 2007 to visit her sick brother. She regretted the trip, because it dirtied her fond memories of the island. "The country is destroyed," she explained, "the people are so poor. There's not enough food, no toys for the kids. It was very sad, very emotional for me."[37]

Assimilation over generations presents yet another difference between Cubans from the exile generation and more recent arrivals. The second and third generation Cuban American descendants of the exilio have assimilated into mainstream American culture in much the same way as European or Asian immigrant groups. They take pride in their Cuban heritage but speak English at home and do not emphasize ethnicity in their social or political lives. Although Alena Shell considered her upbringing "more Cuban than anything else," she admitted to having few Cuban or Latino friends in high school or at UNLV.[38] Las Vegas businessman Louis Fabré, as another example, is proud of his Cuban roots and speaks fluent Spanish but thinks of himself primarily as an American and has an accent that is more reminiscent of New Jersey, where he grew up, than his native Havana. Fabré, who moved to Las Vegas in 1998 from Southern California, better exemplifies the recent trend in the transplantation of Californians to Las Vegas than the experience of a Cuban immigrant.[39] Recent immigrants, on the other hand, are more likely to speak Spanish at home, and few develop social networks outside of the Spanish-speaking community. The 2000 census estimated that 8,426 of 10,959 Cubans living in Las Vegas spoke Spanish as their primary language at home, a dramatic increase from 1980 figures.[40]

Historically, the exiles tended to reject labels like "Latino" or "Hispanic" and have been criticized for presuming a degree of superiority over immigrants from elsewhere in Latin America. They also rejected the activism that had characterized Latino politics in the United States in the 1960s and 1970s. While the Chicano youth were hanging posters of Che Guevara and shouting "¡Viva la raza!" the Cubans became fiercely patriotic about their new homeland. Lilliam Lujan Hickey, for example, considers herself "more American than apple pie and Chevrolet."[41] Cubans had little need to launch an identity crusade like the Chicano movement, because they ultimately had little to protest. Few Cubans faced discrimination or oppression. UNLV Anthropologist M. L. Miranda explained the divide between Cubans and the Chicanos: "Cubans had never been victims of racial and ethnic oppression. They were proud to be Cuban and did not feel in the least inferior to anyone else; on the contrary, they saw themselves as superior."[42] It would not be unusual for a Cuban to take offense at being called a Mexican. Yet few Cubans in Las Vegas insist on politically correct labels like Cuban American or Cubano/a. Mario Cuellar expressed this sentiment well: "I'm an American by choice and I decided to become a citizen of the United States and I think it's the greatest country in the world, but if they ask me what I am—I say I'm Cuban. I understand the mentality of the Cuban-American, but when someone asks, I say I'm Cuban."[43] Nora Rodríguez, an English instructor at CSN, argued further that few Cuban women wish to be called "Cubana," and some might even be offended by "Latina."[44]

Despite the prevalence of Cuban pride, it has become more common for the children and grandchildren of the exiles, especially those who attend UNLV or other colleges, to identify socially and politically with other Latinos. Because the Cuban population remains tiny in comparison, Cuban youth often join social circles with Mexican American young people.[45] Some of the youth have also abandoned the strict loyalty to the Republican Party that has traditionally characterized Cuban American politics.

The best known Cuban American Democrat in Nevada is Dario Herrera, who won election to the Clark County Commission in 1998 at just twenty-five years of age. Herrera became the chairman of the Commission in 2000. The state Democratic Party groomed him to run for Nevada's third congressional seat. Herrera made headlines when Bill Clinton invited him for a round of golf. But his plans were derailed when a nasty bribery scandal came to light involving Herrera and the owner of a chain of strip bars. Herrera's indictment and sentencing to three years in federal prison ranks as the greatest recent political disappointment of the Latino community in Las Vegas, but his affiliation with the Democratic Party had already separated him from many Cuban leaders.[46] Since Herrera's downfall, a new Cuban star has risen within the ranks of the state Democratic Party. Moisés Denis, born and raised in Las Vegas to Cuban-born parents, represents the 28th district in the State Assembly. Denis, according to one local reporter, had become one of "the darlings of the Democratic presidential candidates" as they prepared for Nevada's party caucus for the 2008 campaign. Despite being only a sophomore member of the state legislature, every major Democratic candidate called Denis to ask for his endorsement and presence at campaign rallies.[47]

Losing ethnic identity in the process of assimilation is a bigger source of concern for Cubans in Las Vegas than politics. Liliam (Lujan) Shell travels to Miami to "feel Cuban again."[48] Others focus on teaching their children Spanish or observing Cuban traditions such as exchanging Christmas gifts on December 24. Keeping the sacraments of the Roman Catholic Church also helps some to maintain their ethnic identity.

Cubans in Las Vegas remain predominately Roman Catholic, but, as with any other ethnic group, there is some degree of religious diversity. In the late sixties and early seventies, much of the local Cuban community attended St. Anne's Catholic Church on Maryland Parkway, neighboring

Bishop Gorman High School. With the extensive suburbanization of Las Vegas over recent decades, there is no religious center for the Cuban community. Cubans attend parishes all over the Valley, and some are exploring new religions. assemblyman Moisés Denis, for example, is a bishop in the Church of Jesus Christ of Latter-day Saints. Many are nominally Catholic but do not attend church services regularly. Whether they attend regularly or not, Roman Catholicism remains central to Cuban culture. Parents who are not regular parishioners often observe the sacraments by having their children baptized and requiring them to go through confirmation. Like many other ethnic groups with Catholic cultural moorings, Cubans often prefer elaborate church weddings. The Catholic Church also remains significant to the Cuban population in Las Vegas because Catholic Charities of Southern Nevada has been the primary source of migration assistance for Cubans coming into the area for decades.[49]

Cubans in Las Vegas have many outlets beyond politics and religion to help maintain their ethnic identity. If one so desired, it would be possible to eat at a different Cuban restaurant in southern Nevada every night of the week. The epicenter of Cuban cuisine in Las Vegas is the Florida Café Bar and Grill in the lobby of the Howard Johnson's on the Strip near Downtown. The cuisine at the Florida Café was imported straight from Cuba by owner and chef Sergio Pérez, who opened the restaurant in 1992. The atmosphere is thick with the feel of old Havana and south Florida. The walls and ceiling are bedecked with tropical decor and painted murals of island scenes. The Florida Café is likely the only place north of Miami where one can eat *masas de puerco* with a cold beer on a barstool shaped like a tall mambo drum. The Florida Café has become the point of entry into the local Cuban community for newcomers to the city. The troupe from "Havana Night Club" became regulars at the Florida Café not long after their well-publicized defection.[50]

Pérez also owns the Havana Grill on the south end of town. On a drive further down the Strip from the Florida Café, one will find a simpler atmosphere in Rincón Criollo, a café in a storefront with the type of sidewalk access that is a relic in the car-centered economy of the American West. An unusual blend of Cuban and Mexican cuisine can be found at Mamacitas, on East Fremont Street in the less touristy section of Downtown. Las Vegas has even exported its brand of island cuisine to the heart of Cuban America in south Florida at the Las Vegas Cuban Cuisine restaurant in Ft. Lauderdale.[51]

It seems likely that Cubans will continue to play a leading role in Las Vegas in coming decades. One certainty about the future of Las Vegas is that more and more conversations will be in Spanish. While undocumented immigration from Latin America makes demographic estimations difficult, it is reasonable to envision a majority Latino population in Las Vegas before midcentury.[52] With such growth, the bilingual exilio members remain well placed in their political and economic leadership in the city. Thanks to the hard work, sacrifice, and success of their parents, second- and third-generation Cuban Americans also have a bright future in Las Vegas. More recent arrivals are also likely to advance in the economy. Unlike many of their Mexican counterparts, new Cuban émigrés have no need to fear the possibility of draconian immigration crackdowns. Their legal status allows for Social Security cards, checking accounts, mortgages, and all the other benefits denied those who subsist in the cash-for-labor economy.

Recent improvements in the Cuban economy may slow the flow of immigration from the island. While Cubans continue to endure real hardship, living conditions have begun to improve thanks to the opening of new sectors of the economy. The government has steered the economy away from agriculture toward a service economy fueled by the two million tourists that visit the island each year. An influx of U.S. dollars from Cuban families in the United States—nearly a billion dollars per year—has also provided a boost to the economy. By the turn of the twenty-first century, nearly half of all money in circulation in Cuba was U.S. dollars. Since the financial crisis triggered by the collapse of the Soviet Union, the Castro regime has decriminalized the dollar and relaxed restrictions on retail trade. New retail markets, mostly in the form of modest street vending, have allowed for increased food consumption. Some estimates indicate that life expectancy in Cuba is equal to that of the United States and that infant mortality rates on the island are lower. Cuba has also just begun to tap natural-gas reserves and is poised to become a major regional producer. Another hope for a rebound in the Cuban economy is offered by Hugo Chávez. The Venezuelan president's reverence for Castro and the support provided by his vast oil wealth, along with his vitriolic opposition to U.S. policy in Latin America, has breathed some new life into the Cuban revolution.[53]

With regard to the historic relationship between Cuba and Las Vegas, it is ironic that tourism is playing a major role in the gradual recovery of the Cuban economy. While the Castro regime has made no overtures about legalizing casino gambling, the regime has come full circle and has begun to rebuild the tourism-based economy the mafiosos started in the 1950s. While Americans still face restrictions, Cuba has become a choice destination for tourists all over the world. The crowds on Havana's beaches resemble the crowds on the Las Vegas Strip. They will still earn more and live better in Las

Vegas, but the difficulties of the journey and the improvements in the Cuban economy may encourage would-be émigrés to forsake a move to the desert to take tourism-related jobs in Havana.[54]

It is probably faulty reasoning to assume that the resignation and inevitable demise of Fidel Castro pose a central question about the future of the Cuban community in Las Vegas. Fidel's brother, Raúl, who assumed power in February of 2008, is unlikely to make any dramatic changes in the island's government. There will likely be some loosening of the economy akin to what Vietnam and China have accomplished within the bounds of continued communist dictatorship. Perhaps some future American president may have the courage as well to reach out and reestablish diplomatic ties with Cuba. Raúl's relative unpopularity with the Cuban people may also compel him to seek out a deal with Washington.[55] Otto Mérida expressed some hope of "a transition to a more democratic form of government, one with more respect for human rights, more free enterprise. But whatever changes, it will be very gradually." Part of the problem, Waldo de Castroverde argued, is that "Cuban youth don't care about freedom. . . . They have never lived under freedom, they don't know what freedom is."[56]

While many older exiles still intend, nearly a half-century later, to return to Cuba to reclaim property lost to the revolution, wide agreement exists among Las Vegas Cubans that too much time has passed to rebuild Cuba de ayer. Even in the unlikely event that some future Cuban regime would abandon the revolution altogether, property once owned by members of the exilio is occupied by other families who may not be willing to hand it over based on deeds from the fifties. The pleasant villas in which the exiles raised their children prior to the revolution are either no longer standing or crumbling. Perhaps, in the words of Otto Mérida, the best path to take will be "*borrón y cuenta nueva*"—to wipe the slate clean and start anew.[57]

Notes

1. David Ovalle and Elaine de Valle, "Defectors Welcomed Cuban-style in Las Vegas," *The Miami Herald,* November 18, 2004. Found at http://canf.org/2004/ 11n/noticias de cuba/2004 nov 18; U.S. Census Bureau, "American Factfinder," http://factfinder.census.gov; Otto Merída, interview by author, September 12, 2006.

2. William Clayson, "Cubans in Las Vegas," *Nevada Historical Society Quarterly* 38, no. 1 (Spring 1995): 1–18.

3. Carlos Campo, interview by author, February 15, 2007.

4. "Cuba's Capones: Top Dogs in Batista's Casinos," Cuban Information Archives, Document 0190, http://www.cuban-exile.com/doc_176–200/doc/0190.html.

5. John Scarne, *Scarne's Complete Guide to Gambling* (New York: Simon and Schuster, 1961), 414; Hal K. Rothman, *Neon Metropolis: How Las Vegas Started the 21st Century* (New York: Routledge, 2003), 180.

6. David Rieff, *The Exile: Cuba in the Heart of Miami* (New York: Simon and Schuster, 1993), 14; Rothman, *Neon Metropolis,* 180.

7. U.S. Department of Commerce, Bureau of the Census, *1980 Census of Population and Housing: Detailed Characteristics, Nevada* (Washington, D.C.: Government Printing Office, 1983), table 195.

8. Rothman, *Neon Metropolis,* 180; Campo, interview.

9. ¿Qué es el Círculo Cubano?" *Boletito Informativo: El Círculo Cubano de Las Vegas,* vol. 3, year 1 (December 1970), 3.

10. Las Vegas Latin Chamber of Commerce Web site, "Our History," http://www.lvlcc.com/our_history.html.

11. Lilliam Shell, interview by author, October 4, 1993; Otto Mérida, interview by author, September 28, 1993; Clayson, "Cubans in Las Vegas," 7.

12. Lynnette Curtis, "Looking Back at Cuba: Expatriates Expect Homeland to Change Little After Castro," *Las Vegas Review-Journal,* March 2, 2008; Nora Rodríguez, interview by author, February 25, 2007; Louis Fabré, interview by author, January 23, 2007; Malvin Miranda and Tom Rodríguez, *Hispanic Profiles in Nevada History: 1829–1991* (Las Vegas: Latin Chamber of Commerce of Nevada, 1991), 49; Clayson, "Cubans in Las Vegas," 7; http://www.dccarchitects.com/firm.htm.

13. Nugget Gaming corporate Web site, http://nuggetgaming.com/about-us/cuellar.html.

14. Miranda and Rodríguez, *Hispanic Profiles in Nevada History,* 49; Clayson, "Cubans in Las Vegas," 7; http://www.dccarchitects.com/firm.htm.

15. Pete Earley, *Super Casino: Inside the "New" Las Vegas* (New York: Bantam, 2000), 224–25.

16. Ibid.; Mérida, interview, 2006; "Regents Review," University and Community College System of Nevada newsletter, vol. 6, issue 6 (May 2003).

17. Ed Koch, "Oscar Barillas, 83, dies in Las Vegas," *Las Vegas Sun,* May 10, 2006, 2; Campo, interview.

18. Lilliam Shell, interview by author, October 30, 2006; Miranda and Rodríguez, *Hispanic Profiles in Nevada History,* 65–69.

19. U.S. Department of Commerce, Bureau of the Census, *1990 Census of Housing: Detailed Housing Characteristics, Nevada* (Washington, D.C.: Government Printing Office, 1990), table 77; U.S. Census Bureau, "American Factfinder," http://factfinder.census.gov.

20. Howard Stutz, "Help Wanted, a Lot of It," *Las Vegas Review-Journal,* February 19, 2003, article online at http://www.hotel-online.com/News/2007_Feb_19/k.LVC.1171995211.html.

21. Alan Tobin, "LV Marielitos Can Seek Resident Status," *Las Vegas Sun,* November 30, 1984, B1 (the Immigration and Naturalization Service is now the U.S. Citizenship and Immigration Service).

22. Clayson, "Cubans in Las Vegas," 9.

23. Thomas Boswell and James Curtis, *The Cuban American Experience: Culture, Images, and Perspectives* (Totowa, N.J.: Rowman and Allanheld, 1983), 51–57; "What Happened to the Marielitos?" *The New York Times,* November 25, 1987, B6.

24. Alan Tobin, "When a Marielito Threatens Death, Death Usually Occurs," *Las Vegas Sun,* May 16, 1983, 11; Alan Tobin, "Law Abiding Cubans Worry About Tarnished Image," *Las Vegas Sun,* May 15, 1983, 1; "Metro to Crack Down on 'Marielito Banditos,'" *Las Vegas Review-Journal,* June 10, 1983, 1.

25. John Huddy, *Storming Las Vegas: How a Cuban-Born, Soviet Trained Commando Took Down the Strip to the Tune of Five World-Class Hotels, Three Armored Cars, and Millions of Dollars* (New York: Ballantine, 2008), 354.

26. Bernardo Ricardo, interview by author, September 29, 1993.

27. Mérida, interview, 2006; *1990 Census of Housing: Detailed Housing Characteristics, Nevada,* table 105.

28. Jorge I. Domínguez, "The Cuban Economy at the Start of the Twenty First Century: An Introductory Analysis," in *The Cuban Economy at the Start of the Twenty-First Century,* ed. Jorge I. Domínguez et al. (Cambridge: Harvard University Press, 2004), 4–5.

29. *1990 Census of Housing: Detailed Housing Characteristics, Nevada,* table 105; Sergio Fernández, interview by author (with interpreter Sergio Fernández Jr.), September 22, 1993; María García, interview by author (with interpreter Sergio Fernández Jr.) September 22, 1993.

30. David Ovalle and Elaine de Valle, "Defectors Welcomed Cuban Style in Las Vegas," *Miami Herald,* November 18, 2004, http://canf.org/2004/11n/noticias-de-cuba/2004-nov-18.

31. David Ovalle, "Havana Night Club Peformers Granted Asylum by US," *Havana Journal,* July 22, 2005, http://havanajournal.com.

32. Nelson P. Valdes, "Habana Night vs. Latin American Scholars in Las Vegas," *CounterPunch,* October 2004, http://www.cubavsbloqueo.cu/Default.aspx?tabid=509.

33. Mérida, interview, 2006.

34. Rodríguez, interview.

35. Curtis, "Looking Back at Cuba," 3.

36. Mérida, interview, 2006; U.S. State Department, U.S. Interest Sections, Havana, Cuba, http://havana.usinterestsection.gov/entry_requirement.html; http://www.cubatravelusa.com/.

37. Fabré, interview; Brian Latell, *After Fidel: Raul Castro and the Future of Cuba's Revolution* (New York: Palgrave, 2005), 261; Lilliam Shell, interview, 2006; Curtis, "Looking Back at Cuba," 2.

38. Alena Shell, interview by author, February 2, 2007.

39. Fabré, interview.

40. Persons reported speaking "a language other than English at home." U.S. Census Bureau, "American Factfinder," http://factfinder.census.gov.

41. Curtis, "Looking Back at Cuba," 2.

42. M. L. Miranda, *A History of Hispanics in Southern Nevada* (Reno: University of Nevada, Press, 1997), 149.

43. Clayson, "Cubans in Las Vegas," 1.

44. Rodríguez, interview.

45. Alena Shell, interview.

46. Rothman, *Neon Metropolis,* 177; Merida, interview, 2006.

47. Erin Neff, "The Start of Something Big," *Las Vegas Review-Journal,* April 19, 2007.

48. Lilliam Shell, interview, 2006.

49. Rodríguez, interview; Campo, interview; Alena Shell, interview.

50. Ovalle and de Valle, "Defectors welcomed Cuban-Style in Las Vegas," 1.

51. SouthFlorida.com, www.southflordia.com/events/22530,0,4114685,reviews.venue.

52. United States Census Bureau, American Factfinder, factfinder.census.gov, the Census Bureau estimates that 27.2 percent of the 2006 population of Clark County is "Hispanic or Latino of any race." This represents 482,899 individuals. The estimate, of course, does not include undocumented immigrants.

53. Domínguez, "The Cuban Economy," 2–6; Omar Villanueva, "The Cuban Economy Today and Its Future Challenges," in Jorge I. Domínguez et al., *Cuban Economy,* 85; Anthony DePalma, "'Sicko,' Castro, and the '120 Years Club,'" *The New York Times,* May 27, 2007, section 4, p. 3.

54. Villanueva, "The Cuban Economy Today," 69–71.

55. Latell, *After Fidel,* 222, 248.

56. Curtis, "Looking Back at Cuba," 2.

57. Otto Mérida, interview, 2006.

CHAPTER 5

The Scandinavians

JONATHAN R. STRAND & MELANIE C. YOUNG

The term "Scandinavian" refers to peoples emanating from the northern European, or Nordic, countries of Denmark, Finland, Iceland, Norway, and Sweden. Owing to Viking explorations from AD 700 to 1000 and to later Swedish, Norwegian, and Danish explorers, there are also significant Scandinavian populations throughout Europe, notably in the Faeroe Islands and in several Baltic countries, including Estonia. There are many differences among the Scandinavians based on their country of origin. Indeed, many rivalries have existed among Scandinavians of different nationalities. We use "Scandinavian" in the broadest sense to refer to the people who trace their roots to one or more of the Nordic countries.

The story of Scandinavians in Las Vegas unfolds largely in the twentieth century. In many ways, an account of Scandinavians in the city is textbook transnationalism. Social critic Randolph Bourne describes transnationalism as a process by which immigrants "became more and more objectively American," but also "more and more German or Scandinavian or Bohemian or Polish." Bourne suggests that "assimilation . . . instead of washing out the memories of Europe, made them more and more intensely real."[1] Scandinavians maintain an ardent recognition of their national identities and continue to practice customs and celebrate holidays they or their progenitors observed in their home societies. In particular, there are very active Norwegian and Swedish civic groups that carry on important traditions. The evidence we have gathered suggests that these groups express conspicuous transnationalism while simultaneously assimilating and acculturating to American society. The entire footprint of Scandinavians in Las Vegas is small compared to that of numerous other ethnic groups, but the richness of traditions and sincerity of practice by local Scandinavians means the footprint is quite deep.

It is noteworthy that Scandinavians have maintained connections with their homelands through not only community organizations, but also various print and media resources. Given the advances in communications and technology, these resources allow immigrants alternative modes to maintain ties to the homeland. Local Norwegians, for example, can subscribe to newspapers that discuss Norwegian happenings, heritage, and community, including the *Norwegian American Weekly* (formerly the *Western Viking*) and the *Norway Times* (*Nordisk Tidende*). Indeed, one interviewee from the Sons of Norway had been a subscriber to both publications for years and shared the content of past issues. Readers receive accounts in English and Norwegian of events in both nations. Moreover, the *Nordisk Tidende* is a notable publication, since it predated the establishment of major American-based Norwegian organizations such as the Sons of Norway. The publication was started by a Norwegian immigrant, Emil Nielsen, in 1891 and is now available via the Internet.[2] Numerous Swedish publications are available via the Internet as well, including the *Svenska Dagbladet, Dagens Nyheter, Goteborgspoten,* and *Sydvenska Dagbladet.* Swedish American newspapers include the *Nordstjernan,* the *Swedish Press,* and *Vestkusten.*[3] Daily Swedish-language radio programming is available throughout the United States via the Internet, Sirius satellite, and shortwave, as well as various local AM/FM stations throughout the nation.[4] Scandinavians in Las Vegas exhibit mature transnationalism, and in doing so they link themselves geographically and temporally to their forbearers' rich traditions and cultures.

Vikings Land in the United States and Nevada

It is now accepted that Norwegian Vikings visited North America centuries before Christopher Columbus reached the Caribbean. The Viking footprint in North America, however, was small, ephemeral, and limited to parts of Newfoundland. The next notable migration of Scandinavians to North America occurred in the 1630s. The few dozen Swedes and Finns who established New Sweden along the banks of the Delaware River were quickly acculturated into larger English and Dutch settlements.[5] Most historians agree that there is little relationship between the colonial settlements and later mass migrations.[6]

In the nineteenth century, owing in large part to economic conditions in Norway and Sweden, the number of people migrating to the United States from Scandinavia increased greatly. In the 1820s and 1830s Norwegians settled in New York and later moved to Illinois. In 1845 a settlement in Iowa named New Sweden marked the first large wave of Swedish immigrants, many of whom settled in Chicago. By the middle of the nineteenth century, Scandinavians were concentrated in territories that would become the states of Illinois, Minnesota, and Wisconsin.[7] These midwestern states offered immigrants ample opportunities, especially after the 1862 Homestead Act, which made farmland readily available and cheap. In addition to the economic pull factors, the Midwest offered landscapes not completely dissimilar to those back home. Swedes, Danes, Finns, and Norwegians became successful American farmers, craftspeople, and professionals. Part of their success was no doubt due to the fact that they "blended easily into the mainstream of white America."[8] While immigrants from Scandinavia mainly settled in the Midwest, a number of them ended up in the West, including Nevada. Some of these immigrants traveled to the United States on fishing and whaling ships that arrived in the Pacific Northwest and California.

Push factors also contributed to emigration from Scandinavian countries. Economic cycles in Sweden, Norway, and Denmark resulted in several waves of emigration. In Sweden there were notable crop failures in the mid-1860s that occurred at the same time as a boom in population growth.[9] Many of the economic and agricultural downturns in Scandinavian countries corresponded with boom periods in the United States and thus encouraged migration.[10] A second push factor is a familiar one in American history: religious intolerance. Many early immigrants from Scandinavia were seeking the opportunity to pursue their own religious practices without interference from government or running afoul of local mores. For example, one of the first postcolonial waves of Swedes—the Janssonists—arrived in 1846 and established a community in Bishop Hill, Illinois, in order to practice a form of Lutheranism contrary to the Lutheran Church of Sweden. Later, several groups of Scandinavians who converted to Mormonism in Sweden, Norway, Iceland, and elsewhere settled in Utah.[11] Other notable push factors, such as class differences and fear of military conscription, probably played less of a role.

An oft-cited factor in immigration to the United States was the role of the media (newspapers) and pop culture (novels) in Scandinavian countries. While newspaper editors were often critical of people who left, and many even "denounced the exodus and branded all emigrants as traitors," the popular excitement from the often extraordinary news of life in America—technological advances, rapid accumulation of wealth, and political freedoms—left "no doubt that the viewpoints expressed on the editorial pages carried very little weight."[12] Notable yarns about life in the New World were disseminated through personal letters home. These letters acted to increase positive perceptions of the United States, not only reaching immediate family, but also acting to "influence a whole village. In some instances they were read from the pulpit on Sunday mornings."[13]

Scandinavians also read books about America written by immigrants. *A Pioneer in Northwest America, 1841–1858,* written by Gustaf Unonius and published in 1862, consists of a collection of personal letters touting the social and economic opportunities of the New World. Perhaps the most influential contemporary work about life in the United States was the 1837 *A True Account of America for the Information and Help of Peasant and Commoner*, by Norwegian immigrant Ole Rynning. The book offered a guide to survival and success in America. Widely distributed throughout Scandinavian nations and referred to as the "America Book," Rynning's portrait was a commercial success—its first three editions in multiple Scandinavian languages sold out within a year.[14]

Following Nevada's entry into the Union in 1864, the number of foreign-born residents increased steadily due to the general westward migration and to tales of riches to be found at the Comstock Lode. Nevada gained greater recognition in Scandinavia from Evelyn Teal's fictional account of the life of John A. (Snowshoe) Thompson in Nevada during the Comstock Lode bonanza, which describes Thompson as a "delightfully stubborn, squarehead Norwegian."[15] According to census data, the apogee of foreign-born Nevadans of Scandinavian descent occurred around 1910, when Swedish-born immigrants peaked at 708 and the Danes followed with 616.[16] Available occupation statistics suggest that during the late 1800s a great number of Scandinavian-born immigrants were employed in Nevada as miners, farmers, or laborers. By 1920 many were unemployed, presumably because the state's primary industry was oversaturated with workers who had become redundant as the mining industry faltered.

Since 1920, the number of Danes, Finns, Norwegians, and Swedes immigrating to Nevada has steadily decreased. While economic pull factors within the Scandinavian nations may partially explain the lower number of emigrants, the limited number is likely also associated with the changes in U.S. immigration policies as well as disruptions caused by the World Wars. In the post–World War II era, migration has continued to decline.

According to the 2000 census, Nevadans of Norwegian and Swedish ancestry far outnumber those claiming Danish, Finnish, Icelandic, or general Scandinavian descent. As a percentage of Nevada's population, individuals claiming at least one of these ancestries totaled less than 6 percent. Throughout the state, self-identified Norwegians numbered 38,353 and Swedes 36,105, together constituting approximately 4 percent of the Nevada population. A total of 19,400 residents claimed Danish Ancestry, representing less than 1 percent of the state's population. General Scandinavian ancestry, claimed by 4,694 Nevada residents; Finnish heritage, selected by 4,056 residents; and Icelander ancestry, chosen by 706 residents, accounted for approximately half of 1 percent of the state's population. Not surprisingly, Swedish and Norwegian cultural heritage and traditions are more prominent in the Las Vegas community than those of the Danes, Finns, or Icelanders.

Scandinavians in Las Vegas

Throughout the twentieth century, the Las Vegas Valley has experienced its share of famous—and infamous—Scandinavians. Some Scandinavians were prominent in politics. For instance, the late James Seastrand served over twenty years on the North Las Vegas city council and sixteen years as the city's mayor, during which time the city's population more than doubled. Another prominent Las Vegan was Raymond J. Barnes, an organist of international note who was active in the International Guild of Organists and was instrumental in the installation of a large organ in UNLV's Beam Music Center. Barnes also played the organ for over thirty years at the Trinity United Methodist Church and, until his death in 2006, was the organist for the Las Vegas Reformation Lutheran Church. Arguably the most infamous Las Vegan of Scandinavian descent was Deil Gustafson. Gustafson was a midwesterner who in 1971 bought the Tropicana Hotel. The one-armed Gustafson reportedly worked with nefarious members of organized crime and in 1979 was essentially forced by gaming regulators to sell the Tropicana because of his purported criminal ties. His legal troubles from the sale of the Tropicana led to a conviction for bankruptcy fraud in 1995. He later turned against his former partners in the Tropicana deal and testified against them, although jury members found him a less than convincing witness.

One of the most prominent longtime Nevada residents of Scandinavian descent still residing in the Las Vegas Valley is Lonnie Hammargren, who served as lieutenant governor from 1995 to 1999.[17] While serving, Hammargren chaired the Nevada Economic Development Commission as well as the Nevada Tourism Commission. He also served on numerous boards, including the state Boards of Education and Transportation. For a time, Hammargren chaired the Clark County Republican Party. Later, he was elected to a six-year term on the Nevada Board of Regents, the body governing Nevada's higher-education system. Hammargren also figures prominently in the community as a result of his professional accomplishments. A board-certified neurosurgeon, Hammargren was the first to establish a practice in Las Vegas in 1971.[18]

Throughout the years, Hammargren has drawn public and media attention not only as a talented physician and respected elected official, but also as an eccentric. His Las Vegas residence—actually three conjoined homes located in the southeast part of the Valley—has been featured on cable television's Home and Garden network.[19] His home showcases many Nevada artifacts and memorabilia, including numerous hotel and casino signs, a car owned by Redd Foxx, a Brontosaurus skeleton, and a staircase once belonging to Liberace. He hopes to establish it as a museum named the Hammargren Home of Nevada History.[20]

Hammargren's activities recently drew local media attention again when, in an unorthodox gathering in late March of 2007, he held a funeral for himself at the local Community Lutheran Church, followed by a traditional New Orleans funeral march to his home. The event culminated in his descent to an Egyptian sarcophagus beneath his home. "He noted that in Las Vegas, it is legal to be buried in your own yard."[21] A Minnesota newspaper even published the funeral announcement as an invitation to all Hammargrens still living in Minnesota to attend. In short, Lonnie Hammargren continues to enrich the colorful history of Nevada and to command media attention for both professional accomplishments and personal antics.

While Nevada's Scandinavian population includes active politicians, entrepreneurs and artists have also left their print on the state, but with less news coverage and fanfare. For instance, Olaf Stanton is president of Characters Unlimited, a company that manufactures lifelike mechanical human replicas.[22] His animated figures are on display throughout the world and viewable in Las Vegas at such venues as Antiquities International, located at the Forum Shops inside Caesars Palace, the Clark County Museum, and the Auto Collections at the Imperial Palace.[22]

Another notable figure was Norwegian-born, naturalized American artist and sculptor Oskar J. W. Hansen. Hansen designed and built the monument of dedication on the Nevada side of Hoover Dam, the plaque commemorating the men who died during the dam's construction, and the bas-relief series on both the Nevada and Arizona elevator towers.[23] Though it is unclear whether he is a relative of Oskar, businessman Bert Hansen currently owns the High Scaler Cafe, located at the entrance to Hoover Dam. He was also integral to the building of the high-scaler bronze monument located in front of the cafe.

Many contemporary local Scandinavians settled in Las Vegas for retirement, while Nellis Air Force Base reportedly drew others. Still others cite job opportunities as the driving force for moving to the Valley. Educational opportunities also serve as a draw: for instance, in recent years several Swedish student-athletes have attended UNLV as members of the swimming team.[24] Based on our interviews, our impression is that Scandinavians move to Las Vegas for the same wide variety of reasons that draw most ethnic groups.

The Ties That Bind: Scandinavian Organizations in Las Vegas

Unlike a few older American cities with established Scandinavian neighborhoods, such as Chicago with its Andersonville, Las Vegas has no Scandinavian district. There is no exclusively Scandinavian restaurant or market.[25] Nor are Las Vegas Scandinavians bound by religious identity, as some ethnic groups are. While the majority of those who profess a faith are Lutheran, as they are in their home countries, Las Vegas Scandinavians are also Mormon, Catholic, and members of other denominations. We found little evidence that Scandinavians favor any one of the Valley's dozen or so Lutheran churches or that the churches serve as focal points for the Scandinavian community or reinforce ethnic identity. In fact, a local resident remarked that the Swedish Vasa club brought members to the church, not vice versa.

The institutions that bring together those Scandinavians who choose to express their ethnic identity are the civic groups. These groups are dominated by Swedes and Norwegians, but some also attract Finns, Danes, and Icelanders to their ranks.[26] In fact, several non-Scandinavians have joined these groups, some of whom have lived and worked in a Nordic country, while others are simply interested in the culture, language, and heritage of Scandinavian countries. Las Vegas is home to an honorary consulate for the government of Sweden and is visited each year by thousands of Scandinavians, some of whom attend meetings and events held by local community groups.[27] The Las Vegas Scandinavian community, therefore, is an eclectic mix of first, second, and third generations as well as expatriates who want to interact with others who share similar interests in all things Scandinavian.

Sons of Norway

The Sons of Norway is an international fraternal benefit society established in Minneapolis in 1895.[28] Originally open only to men, the organization admitted women beginning in 1912, although individual lodges were slow to follow. This secular organization seeks to preserve Norwegian heritage and disseminate information about Norwegian culture, which it does in part through the national monthly magazine, *The Viking*. The Sons of Norway also sponsors various charitable causes, including scholarships. One of the original purposes of the Sons of Norway was to provide health and life insurance to Norwegian immigrants and their descendants in the United States; in 2006 the total value of the outstanding life-insurance policies issued by the Sons of Norway was over half a billion dollars.[29] There are over 69,000 members in the order's 400 lodges, with most members and lodges located in the United States. Lodges elect representatives to district conventions, which in turn elect district representatives to an annual international convention.[30]

There are two lodges in Clark County. The older and larger is lodge 6–152, the Vegas Viking Lodge.[31] The smaller yet very active lodge 6–165 is found in Henderson and has a name as colorful as that of its larger neighbor, the Desert Troll Lodge. Its membership base is in Henderson and Boulder City. Nevada lodges are part of the Sixth District of the Sons of Norway, which also encompasses Arizona, California, Colorado, and Utah.

The Vegas Viking Lodge was established in 1992 with some 110 charter members. Currently it has approximately 140 members, of whom 35 to 50 regularly attend meetings.[32] Most members are second- and third-generation Norwegians. In 2001 the Vegas Viking was honored as both the Sixth District and the International Sons of Norway "lodge of the year." Throughout the year, the lodge sponsors a variety of events largely to raise money for paying its national dues, covering operating costs, and funding competitive scholarships. The lodge publishes a newsletter, *The Vegas Viking News,* several times a year. It announces important events, lodge news, tidbits of interesting news, correspondence from current and past members, and recipes for Norwegian dishes. Parts of the newsletter are published in Norwegian, including news items reprinted from other sources. One example of a reprinted news item is a story on Norwegian ethnographer Thor Heyerdahl, whose theory that Polynesian islands were populated by peoples from South America was recently challenged by DNA evidence.[33] The same issue also included a discussion of the Sons of Norway shield. The March 2007 newsletter included an item on seventy-six ways to eat *lefse* (a Norwegian potato pastry) and jokes such as "How does a Viking communicate?"[34] The newsletter is central to binding the local Norwegian community and linking it to both the national organization and the home country.

The Vegas Viking Lodge is very active throughout the year, holding meetings monthly except during the summer.[35] Lodge meetings begin with members singing the national anthems of the United States, Canada, and Norway, the latter sung in Norwegian. Each February since 1999 the lodge has held a lutefisk dinner, in recent years attended by as many as four hundred people.[36] To raise money for its scholarships, the lodge usually holds a garage sale or silent auction and luncheon on or around St. Patrick's Day. On the seventeenth of May it celebrates Syttende Mai, marking Norwegian independence, by attending the Desert Troll Lodge's picnic.[37] As part of this celebration, the lodge marches with Norwegian flags and its replica Viking longboat, the *Ormen Korte.* In recent years the Vegas Viking has included its longboat in the Las Vegas Helldorado Days parades.[38] The local lodge holds a dinner for Leif Erikson Day in October. In November the Vegas Viking organizes a bazaar, where Scandinavian items such as jewelry, clothing, calendars, rosemalings (a decorative flower-painting technique native to Norway), as well as baked goods are sold. Holidays in December are also important for lodge members, including Saint Lucia Day (December 13) and, of course, Christmas. The lodge's fundraising efforts support a variety of charitable causes, most importantly the lodge's annual scholarships for local Norwegian American students—a total of $1,500 in 2006 and $2,500 in 2007. The scholarships are based on recipients' "ancestry, financial need, academic performance, extracurricular activities," and the location of their universities.[39] In addition to the scholarships, the lodge donates money to several charities.

The Desert Troll Lodge, with around sixty members, was created in March of 2003 to accommodate members concentrated in the southeast end of the Valley and Boulder City. Siri Poehls pursued the establishment of the second local lodge and served as its first president.[40] Like its sister lodge, the Desert Troll holds monthly meetings and publishes a newsletter, which includes information on upcoming events, news from Norway in English and Norwegian, reports on lodge accomplishments, recipes, and a kids' page with drawings, word activities, and Norwegian stories. While some Desert Troll Lodge events are coordinated with Vegas Viking activities, others are sponsored exclusively by Lodge 6–165. In 2007 the lodge brought Norwegian pianist Knut Erik Jensen for a concert at the Community Lutheran Church. Members also acted as host families for the Aal Tour America performers group that visited Las Vegas from Norway in 2007, which involved housing approximately eighty children. The lodge sponsored a luncheon with the group, and the touring children performed at the Community Lutheran Church, giving a multimedia performance promoting Christianity.

The Desert Troll Lodge is very welcoming to people who have no known Scandinavian progenitors. Frances Pallesen, current vice president of the Desert Troll Lodge, stated in a publication, "[a]s far as I know, I don't have a speck of Scandinavian blood in me. . . . Through association with my husband and his family, both here in the United States and Norway, I have learned to love as my own, the Norwegians, their culture and history, and I have a deep commitment to help my husband share this wonderful culture with our son . . . and our two grandsons."[41]

The Desert Troll also engages in its own fund-raising and community activities. The lodge sponsors Juletrefest in December, a Christmas party usually held at the local Elks Lodge where traditional Norwegian culture, food, and practices are celebrated. In addition, a traditional Viking feast potluck is held in October. Participants are instructed on the type and acceptable preparation of food, encouraged to dress appropriately for the occasion, and treated to a presentation on the history of early Vikings and Leif Erikson's contributions to the discovery of America. Moreover, members are active contributors to the local community through their "Adopt a School" and "Adopt a Vet" programs. The organization collects labels from various food products to sponsor field trips for students from Robert E. Taylor Elementary School and provides social opportunities for residents of the Southern Nevada Veterans Home in Boulder City. Finally, the Desert Troll actively encourages participation in the Sons of Norway Cultural Skills Program. The program consists of fourteen cultural skills areas, and members are awarded pins for completion of tasks and milestone achievements. Specialized areas include traditional Norwegian cooking, Norwegian rosemaling, *hardanger* embroidery, and Norwegian language and cultural skills, among others. The lodge holds language classes the second and fourth Mondays of every month to assist local members in earning their language and cultural skills pin.

Vasa Order of America

The largest and oldest Swedish American fraternal organization in the United States is the Vasa Order of America established in 1896 in New Haven, Connecticut.[42] Its original mandate was to provide aid to Swedish immigrants when illness or death struck a family. Today the organization focuses on advancing understanding of Swedish traditions and culture, fosters awareness of important Scandinavians in American history, and offers scholarships.[43] The Vasa Order boasts over 22,000 members worldwide, spread across the United States, Canada, and Sweden and divided into nineteen districts with over three hundred lodges. The Las Vegas Valley is included in the Pacific Southwest District number 15, which is dominated by lodges in Southern California. A Grand Lodge oversees the entire organization.[44] The Vasa Order's flagship publication, the bimonthly *Vasa Star,* disseminates information on events and news from the nineteen districts and includes Swedish language lessons and stories about scholarship winners.[45] There is a well-maintained archive of Vasa Order materials, including newsletters and other documents, housed in a historic building in Bishop Hill, Illinois. The archive provides assistance with genealogical research and serves as a clearinghouse for information on the Vasa Order of America.

In Las Vegas, the Vasa Order of America lodge #715, the Valhalla Lodge, was established in 1975. It has hosted the regional Vasa Order meetings in 1979, 1981, and 1994. The Valhalla Lodge has over fifty members, of whom about thirty attend meetings regularly. Members include second- and third-generation Swedes along with several immigrants from Sweden. A few members are non-Scandinavians who are interested in Sweden, some of whom have lived and worked in that country. Meetings are held monthly except for a hiatus during the summer. Swedish tourists often attend meetings.[46] The Valhalla Lodge publishes a newsletter about once a month that announces events, carries news of lodge members, and disseminates information about Swedish cultural traditions. The December 2006 newsletter, for example, included a description, authored by the lodge's cultural leader, of a now-defunct holiday called Mickelsmass.[47]

Valhalla Lodge celebrates several holidays throughout the year, the most prominent of which are Walpurgis in late April or early May, the Midsommer Fest in June, and Saint Lucia Day on December 13. Many members regularly travel to Scandinavia during Las Vegas's hot summer months. In September the lodge celebrates the return of members from summer vacation with a potluck dinner. In December the lodge celebrates what is perhaps the most important holiday, Saint Lucia Day, named after the Christian martyr, Saint Lucy of Syracuse. In addition to special events and lodge meetings, members regularly engage in informal social gatherings. In November 2005 the Valhalla Lodge celebrated its thirtieth anniversary with a dinner and party at Caesars Palace in Las Vegas. The "Jubilee Dinner," as it was called, attracted many longtime local members as well as visitors from other lodges. In sum, through its newsletter and by holding regular events, the Vasa Order's Valhalla Lodge provides the social space essential to maintaining and disseminating cultural knowledge of Sweden.

Swedish Women's Education Association

The Swedish Women's Education Association (SWEA) is perhaps the most exclusive of all Scandinavian organizations due to the fact that it conducts all its meetings entirely in the Swedish language.[48] SWEA was established in 1979 and now has over eight thousand members in eighty chapters in some forty countries. Primarily a social and professional networking organization, SWEA publishes an international newsletter twice a year. True to its educational mission, SWEA awards doctoral scholarships and in general promotes education about Swedish culture, literature, and language. In 2000 the USA-Canada western regional organization for SWEA met in Las Vegas.[49]

The Las Vegas chapter of SWEA was established in 1996 and presently has around thirty to thirty-five members.[50] The local chapter's newsletter highlights the activities of its members, many of whom are first-generation Swedes who work in Las Vegas, and offers stories from other chapters around the globe. Throughout the year meetings are held in members' homes and at local restaurants. Special events are held for important holidays, such as Saint

Lucia Day. Recent immigrants from Sweden are often helped by chapter members with housing, employment, and other needs. While this organization is relatively small and limited to Swedish speakers, it has a unique place in the local Swedish community.

Conclusion

Although a significant number of Las Vegans claim Scandinavian ancestry, residents and visitors alike detect little evidence of a Scandinavian presence in the Valley. Scandinavians lack the community institutions that many local ethnic groups have—markets, restaurants, exclusive churches, soccer teams, and, in a few cases, neighborhoods. The only manifestations of a Scandinavian presence are the civic ethnic organizations. But for the few who choose to manifest their Scandinavian roots and identity, the clubs offer the means to socialize with like-minded individuals, preserve and live culture and traditions, and maintain ties with the ancestral countries. In sum, the organizations provide the opportunity for those who are so inclined to remain Norwegian or Swedish—or Scandinavian—while also living in the American mainstream.

Notes

This research would not have been possible without the cheerful cooperation of members of the local Scandinavian community. We thank Evy Hannelius, Gwen Knighton, Carl-Uno Manros, Alice Salversen, Guri Gupton, Herb and Fran Pallesen, and Honorary Consul for Sweden Lena Walther. Lars Jenner, Archivist with the Vasa National Archives, provided very useful materials for this work. Kris Gorton assisted with translations from the Swedish of some key materials.

1. Randolph Bourne, "Trans-National America," *Atlantic Monthly* 118 (July 1916): 86–97. Citation here refers to Carl Resek, ed., *War and the Intellectuals: Collected Essays, 1915–1919* (New York: Harper and Row, 1964), 107. For a discussion of the transnationalist debate, see Eva Morawska, "Immigrants, Transnationalism, and Ethnicization: A Comparison of This Great Wave and the Last," in *E Pluribus Unum? Contemporary and Historical Perspectives on Immigrant Political Incorporation*, ed. Gary Gerstle and John Mollenkopf (New York: Russell Sage, 2001), 175–212.

2. http://www.norway-times.com/history.html.

3. All Internet newspaper sources are available via links on the Embassy of Sweden—Swedish Media Web page at: http://www.swedenabroad.com.

4. http://www.sr.se/cgi-bin/International/nyhetssidor/index.asp?nyheter=1&ProgramID=2054.

5. While assimilated into colonial society, they and their descendants did retain their religious affiliations with the Lutheran Church and as late as 1697 spoke Swedish. See Sten Carlsson, *Swedes in North America 1638–1988: Technical, Cultural, and Political Achievements* (Stockholm: Streiffert, 1988), 18.

6. For example, Carlsson describes emigration from Sweden during the 1700s as "highly inconsequential." See Sten Carlsson, "Chronology and Composition of Swedish Emigration to America," in *From Sweden to America: A History of the Migration,* ed. Harald Runblom and Hans Norman (Minneapolis: University of Minnesota Press, 1976), 114–48, 115.

7. Due to out-migration from these areas, a large Scandinavian presence also exists in North Dakota, South Dakota, Kansas, and Nebraska.

8. Jussi M. Hanhimaki, *Scandinavia and the United States: An Insecure Friendship* (New York: Twayne, 1997), 2.

9. Lars Ljungmark, "The Push- and Pull-Factors Behind the Swedish Emigration to America, Canada, and Australia," in *European Expansion and Migration: Essays on the Intercontinental Migration from Africa, Asia, and Europe,* ed. P. C. Emmer and M. Morner (New York: Berg, 1992), 79–103.

10. See the discussion regarding Iceland's demography in Helga Skuli Kjartansson, "Icelandic Emigration," in Emmer and Morner, *European Expansion and Migration,* 105–19, 112–13.

11. See William Mulder, *Homeward to Zion: The Mormon Migration from Scandinavia* (Minneapolis: University of Minnesota Press, 1957). Note that in 1955 writer Halldór Laxness from Iceland won the Nobel Prize in Literature for his novel *Paradise Reclaimed,* which tells the tale of an Icelander who converts to Mormonism in the late 1800s and eventually moves to Utah.

12. Lars Ljungmark, "The Push- and Pull-Factors Behind the Swedish Emigration to America, Canada, and Australia," in Emmer and Morner, *European Expansion and Migration,* 79–103, 90–91. In Sweden by the turn of the twentieth century, government officials as well as civic groups publicly lamented the negative effects of emigration on agriculture production, and by 1907 there was a national debate on the topic; see Ann-Sofie Kalvemark, "Swedish Emigration Policy in International Perspective," in Runblom and Norman, *From Sweden to America,* 94–113.

13. Scott, Franklin D., *The Peopling of America: Perspectives on Immigration* (Richmond, Va.: William Byrd Press, 1972), 25.

14. Dennis Wepman, *Immigration: An Eyewitness History From the Founding of Virginia to the Closing of Ellis Island* (New York: Facts on File, 2002), 107.

15. Wilbur S. Shepperson, *Restless Strangers: Nevada's Immigrants and Their Interpreters* (Reno: University of Nevada Press, 1970), 197.

16. Data from the Nevada State Data Center.

17. Hammargren's most recent attempt to reenter the political landscape occurred in 2006, when he vied for the Republican Party gubernatorial nomination but lost to would-be governor, Jim Gibbons.

18. Retrieved from: http://www.nevadadays.org/hhome/mediareleases.htm (accessed August 27, 2007).

19. Molly Ball, "Spotlight on Hammargren Home," *Las Vegas Review-Journal*, May 29, 2006, 3B.

20. "One Person's Treasures: Eclectic Collection Multiplies at Home of Las Vegan with Equally Eclectic Life," *Las Vegas Review-Journal*, July 16, 2007. Retrieved September 17, 2007, from http://www.lvrj.com/news/8526012.html.

21. Mary Helen Swanson, "Man Will Attend His Own Funeral," *The Post Review*: East Central Minnesota, March 30, 2007. Retrieved September 17, 2007, from http://ecmpostreview.com/2007/march/30mwaof.html.

22. Jennifer Robison, "Ernie, Zoltar and Uncle Sam Among Characters on Company's Roster," *Las Vegas Review-Journal*, December 17, 2006, 3J.

23. Bureau of Reclamation Web site, http://www.usbr.gov/lc/hooverdam/History/essays/artwork.html.

24. See the profile in Shane Bevell, "How Swede It Is: Team's Reputation Draws Six Swimmers from the Land of the Midnight Sun," UNLV *Magazine* (Spring 2007): 6–7.

25. A short-lived marketplace called Scandinavian Styles owned by Hans Ahren recently closed. As reported in the *Las Vegas Sun*, the store was a focal point for the various communities. See Kristen Peterson, "Scandi-Land: Unique Boutique Becoming Focal Point for All Things Scandinavian," *Las Vegas Sun*, September 9, 2004, www.lasvegassun.com/sunbin/stories/text/2004/sep/09/517481621.html> (accessed August 5 2007). There are Scandinavian design centers and furniture stores, however, in Las Vegas.

26. Las Vegas lacks chapters of several important organizations, such as the Danish Brotherhood, the Danish Sisterhood, and the Finlandia Foundation. The Danish Brotherhood does seem to have a lodge in Big Bear, California, but our attempts to contact it failed. There are Finlandia Foundation chapters in California, but in our communication with their members they were unable to help us locate local Finns. We also were unable to locate a Las Vegas chapter of the Icelandic American Association. The nearest chapter appears to be in Southern California.

27. The Honorary Swedish Consulate in Las Vegas deals with about one case per week of a Swedish citizen needing help with some aspect of travel to Las Vegas or immigration status in the United States.

28. Part of this section is drawn from Dina Titus and Thomas C. Wright, "The Ethnic Diversity of Las Vegas," in *The Peoples of Las Vegas: One City, Many Faces*, ed. Jerry L. Simich and Thomas C. Wright (Reno and Las Vegas: University of Nevada Press, 2005), 18–36.

29. http://www.sofn.com/about_us/showPage.jsp?document=index.html (accessed August 16, 2007).

30. See the comments by Magne Smedvid in *The Scandinavian Presence in North America*, ed. Erik J. Friis (New York: Harper's, 1973), 77–82.

112 The Scandinavians

31. A third lodge in Nevada is located in Reno: the Hvite Fjell (lodge 6–151). Reno is also home to lodge #29 of the Daughters of Norway. The lodge is named after Olympic Gold medal skater Sonja Henie. Interestingly, Carson City is also home to a Daughters of Norway lodge, which was established in 2001 as the Queen Maud (lodge #42).

32. Readers interested in this lodge's activities should consult www.vegasviking.com.

33. The story was reprinted from www.aftenposten.no and appeared on page 7 of the July 2007 *Las Vegas Viking News*.

34. Both items found on page 6 of the March 2007 *Vegas Viking News*; the punch line for the joke is "by Norse code."

35. The Sons of Norway by-laws require at least eight meetings a year. The Vegas Vikings meet ten or more times a year.

36. Lutefisk is fish (usually cod) prepared with lye prior to cooking. Fortunately for attendees of the annual dinner, alternative items are offered.

37. Syttende Mai is often called "Constitution Day." In recent years the Vegas Viking Lodge has held its picnic in early May and encouraged its members to attend the picnic held by the Desert Troll Lodge in Henderson on May 17.

38. A photo of the replica boat with the 2007 scholarship awards winners and members of the Vegas Vikings onboard was featured in the August 2007 Sons of Norway publication *The Viking*.

39. *Vegas Viking News,* May 2007, 3.

40. John Santana, "Sons of Norway Lodge Officially Launched," *Boulder City News,* March 6, 2003.

41. Frances Pallesen, *Desert Troll Stories* (Henderson, Nev.: Herb and Fran Pallesen, 2005), xiii.

42. Vasa refers to the House of Vasa and is associated with the Swedish royal family. Readers interested in the Vasa Order of America should visit its Web site: www.vasaorder.org.

43. See the comments by Bertil G. Winstrom in Friis, *Scandinavian Presence,* 86–89.

44. There is one other lodge in Nevada: lodge 711 in district 12 is located in Reno and holds meetings in Sparks. The Reno lodge was established in 1974, one year prior to the Las Vegas lodge.

45. Another news magazine many Swedes subscribe to is the monthly publication the *Swedish Press,* which has articles in English and Swedish and tends to emphasize key holidays, food, and travel.

46. See the lodge note from the July/August *Vasa Star,* page 16.

47. See Ruthie Byers, "Mickelsmass: Archangel Mickael's Day, More Important Than Christmas?" Valhalla Lodge 715 newsletter, December 2006, 3. Mickelsmass was a harvest festival that marked the change from fall to winter.

48. This fact prompted one interviewee to exclaim that even though she speaks fluent Swedish, she refused to join a club that was so exclusionary.

49. See "Swedish Women Get a Touch of Home in Vegas," *Las Vegas Sun* online, September 20, 2000: http://www.lasvegassun.com/sunbin/stories/sun/2000/sep/23/510810351.html (accessed August 24, 2007).

50. Readers interested in joining can visit http://www.chapters-swea.org/lasvegas.

CHAPTER 6

The Muslims

ASLAM ABDULLAH

At a gathering of Muslims in the oldest of Las Vegas's five mosques on a pleasant April night in 2007, a young doctor transplanted from Egypt talked about the challenges of bringing together Muslims who, despite their common belief in Islam, came from various ethnic and philosophical backgrounds. "What we have in this city is enormous diversity within the Muslim community, and what we need now is a forum where Muslims can meet to discuss the challenges of adjusting to it."[1]

The doctor sought a means of reconciling the needs of the growing multiethnic Muslim community within the ever-expanding city of Las Vegas. In his audience were people from twenty-three diverse ethnic backgrounds, including several sub-Saharan African groups, Caucasians, Hispanics, Indians, Pakistanis, Lebanese, Egyptians, Jordanians, Palestinians, Iraqis, Somalians, Bangladeshis, Burmese, Algerians, and Moroccans. The group also included Muslims who had helped to found the Masjid As-Sabur mosque in 1986. At that time, the mosque primarily served the African American members of the Nation of Islam, a group founded in 1930s Detroit by Elijah Mohammad.[2] In the twenty-plus years since the founding of Masjid As-Sabur, Muslims from different backgrounds have come together under Islam to practice their beliefs and to find solutions to common social and political problems.[3] Such alliances have provided important avenues of support for Muslims in Las Vegas, a city that is home to people from every Muslim group that has immigrated to the United States in the last fifty years.

The Muslim presence in Las Vegas is quite visible. It is no longer unusual to see a Muslim woman in a scarf in shopping malls or to see bearded Muslim businessmen from different ethnic backgrounds offering their goods and services around the Valley. There are over ten restaurants serving special religiously permitted food, *halal,* including the Mediterranean Café at Maryland Parkway and Tropicana Avenue and Origin India at Harmon Avenue and Paradise Road. These and other halal restaurants serve not only Las Vegas residents, but also the large number of Muslim tourists who visit the city to observe its glamour without participating in its gambling. In addition, a wide range of other businesses specialize in food products specific to countries with large Muslim populations, including Ethiopia, Lebanon, Iran, Morocco, Pakistan, India, African, Bosnia, and Malaysia.

The written and spoken languages of the Muslim immigrant population have become commonplace in Las Vegas. Throughout the Valley, signs in English, Bengali, Arabic, and Persian advertise Islamic goods. And the Clark County judicial system, which provides interpreters for non-English-speaking residents appearing in court, has certified interpreters for languages commonly associated with Muslim immigrants, including Punjabi, Urdu, Hindi, Amharic/Ethiopian, Persian, Bengali, and others.[4]

History of Muslims in the United States and in Las Vegas

Muslims were among the first explorers to reach North and South America. Though some believe that Muslims made contact with indigenous Americans before Columbus, their findings are based on ethnographic and linguistic similarities between people of the West African coast and peoples of the Gulf of Mexico region and remain controversial.[5] There is little controversy, however, that Moriscos, Spaniards of Muslim faith forced by King Ferdinand and Queen Isabella in 1502 to convert to Christianity or be expelled, were among those who accompanied Spanish conquistadores. Muslims were also among slaves working plantations for the British, Dutch, Spanish, and Portuguese. At one time, the British outlawed the importing of bondsmen from areas with large Muslim populations.[6] According to Dr. Sulayman Nyang of Howard University, among the prohibited were the "Jalofs, Biafras, Mandingos, Hausas, and Fullahs. Prior to the ban, an estimated 25,000 Mandingos, 45,000 Fullah, 15,000 Hausa, and 5,000 Muslims from other communities had been brought to British colonies between 1726 and 1806."[7] According to Sylviane A. Diouf, about 10 percent of the African slaves came from Muslim backgrounds, but little is known about them.[8] According to one authority, "There is no evidence of any African Muslim slave family that survived slavery and maintained Islam as a way of life."[9]

Muslim immigrants began arriving in the United States in significant numbers in the early twentieth century. Some settled in Dearborn, Michigan, while others, particularly peasants from Punjab, India, settled in farming areas such as Sacramento, California. It was not until the 1950s that professionals became a presence among the Muslim immigrant population. Physicians, engineers, scientists, and teachers settled in America after completing their studies. Many of these Muslims settled and built mosques in the

Midwest, including places such as Detroit and Ann Arbor, Michigan; Gary, Indiana; and Cedar Rapids, Iowa. Along with professionals, visiting scholars and missionary groups from the Middle East and South Asia began arriving in the United States. They formed their own organizations, including the Muslim Student Association, which led to the formation of the Islamic Society of North America.[10] During the mid-twentieth century, Muslims also began settling in Las Vegas.

From its founding in 1905, Las Vegas was a diverse community of European Americans, African Americans, Mexicans, Chinese, Japanese, Native Americans, and others, and with the passage of a century it has become a microcosm of the world's population, including the range of Muslim ethnicities. The rapid economic growth of Las Vegas created a demand for labor and opportunities for entrepreneurs and professionals in various walks of life. This, coupled with the unprecedented increase in immigration to the United States from the 1970s to the present and the emergence of Las Vegas as a resort destination and business center, has lured Muslims from all over the United States and abroad. They have moved to the city to gain better jobs and cheaper living costs and to start their own practices and businesses. The spiritual director of Jamia Masjid, Nevada's largest mosque, estimated that in 2006 Las Vegas had at least 4,600 Muslim households, most with three, four, or more members.[11] The year-round convention industry also attracts Muslims from all over the world, many of whom visit the local mosques and often seek partners within the local community to promote their businesses. According to Muhammad Taha, imam (resident religious leader) of the Islamic Information Center at Tropicana Avenue near Maryland Parkway, Muslims from seventeen nationalities who had come to attend various conventions visited that mosque in 2006.[12]

Some of the first Muslims in Las Vegas were African American families who were members of the Nation of Islam. The Nation of Islam was founded in Detroit by Elijah Poole, who took the name Elijah Muhammad and established Temples of Islam as well as several schools, called Universities of Islam. Following Elijah Muhammad's death in 1964, Louis Farrakhan, his son-in-law, assumed leadership of the Nation of Islam. In 1977 an internal struggle between Louis Farrakhan and Elijah Muhammad's son, W. D. Muhammad, split the Nation of Islam.[13]

The first Nation of Islam Temple in Las Vegas was opened in the early 1960s on D Street in the historically black Westside.[14] It was during the national leadership of W. D. Muhammad that the African American Muslim community of Las Vegas also split. Those who identified with Minister Farrakhan remained loyal to the Temple, while others, who had responded to the call of W. D. Muhammad, established their own places of worship. They began worshiping at homes and, in the late 1980s, built a mosque known as Masjid As-Sabur, whose initial construction costs came from a donation by former world heavyweight boxing champion Mike Tyson. The Las Vegas African American Muslim community is now independent and runs its affairs without outside religious interference.

Las Vegas Muslim Ethnicities and Populations

Estimates of Las Vegas's Muslim population, as well as that of the United States, are based on media reports and guesswork on the part of Muslim leadership and as a result are quite varied. Imam Fateen Saifullah, leader of the Masjid As-Sabur, puts the number of African American Muslims at between one and two thousand,[15] while Mujahid Ramadan, a prominent social activist and a pioneer of organized Muslim work among African Americans in Las Vegas, estimates five thousand.[16] Estimates of the national Muslim population range from three to six million. According to an informed source, the U.S. Muslim population is approximately one third African American, one third Indian and Pakistani, 12 percent Arab, 5 percent sub-Saharan African, 4 percent Iranian, 3 percent Albanian, 2 percent Turkish, 2 percent Southeast Asian, and 2 percent white American, while smaller groups round out the demographic. The ten states with the highest concentration of Muslims are California, New York, Illinois, New Jersey, Indiana, Michigan, Virginia, Texas, Ohio, and Maryland.[17] As of 2000, there were over 1,200 mosques and 168 Islamic schools in the country.[18]

In a 2004 five-part series on Las Vegas's Muslims, Peter King of the *Los Angeles Times* offered an estimate of southern Nevada's Muslim population. "There are about 10,000 Muslims in Las Vegas, and they come from all over. In the mosques on any Friday, one can find well-to-do doctors from the Indian subcontinent, barrel-chested circus tumblers from Tangier, cabdrivers from Compton, war widows from Kabul."[19] Muslim community leaders estimate today's Las Vegas Muslim population at 18,000.[20]

Interviews with members of several ethnic groups and a closer look at the census data reveal that the actual number of Muslims in Las Vegas may exceed 18,000. According to the 2000 census, Clark County was then home to some 124,885 African Americans and 6,183 Arabs,[21] while the 2006 Census Bureau estimates found 167,144 African Americans and a slightly reduced Arab population of 5,682.[22] Estimates of the local African American Muslim population range widely, from 1,000 to 5,000.[23] Among Arabs, the 2000 census lists 2,857 as Lebanese, 967 as Syrian, and 772 as Egyptian, with smaller numbers of Palestinians, Jordanians, Moroccans, Iraqis, Yemenis, Kurds, Algerians, Saudi Arabians, Tunisians, Kuwaitis, Libyans, and others.[24] Of these 7,108 Arabs, it is estimated that some 3,600, or around half, are Muslims.[25] Iranian Muslims claim over 5,000 in the Valley, while Afghanis put their population at around 2,000. The Bangladeshis estimate 500, Albanians and Bosnians around 700 each, Somalis around 800, the Turks some 500, Southeast Asians (including Malaysians, Indonesians, Filipinos, the Singaporeans, and Chinese) around 300 each, Ethiopians and Eritreans approximately 400 each, Hispanics some 300, and Caucasians around 100.[26] By far the largest group is from Pakistan, whose population in Las Vegas is around 6,000.[27]

Who were the first immigrant Muslims to settle in Las Vegas? This is an interesting question in the community. Peter King writes that

> the first Muslims to settle in Las Vegas, according to mosque lore, were three acrobats from Morocco who came to perform on the Strip in the early 1960s. One of them remains a mosque regular, but he shyly declines when asked to cast light on a popular, perhaps apocryphal, side plot to this pioneer story. The three acrobats, the story goes, were offered a chance in those days to purchase property beyond what were then the far limits of the Strip. They declined, convinced that $5,000 was too much to pay for what they considered an unpromising piece of real estate—the very same ground where Caesars Palace now stands. No wonder the man might not want to talk about it.[28]

African American community leaders, however, suggest that they were the earliest Muslims in Las Vegas.[29]

Each ethnic community arrived in Las Vegas under different circumstances. The people of Indian, Pakistani, and Bangladeshi origin trace their presence in the city to the small student community that came to UNLV in the early 1960s to pursue higher education. Many of them decided to settle after completing their educations. The Iranians trace their origin in Las Vegas to the Iranian student population in the mid-1970s and to subsequent migration due to the change of political regime in Iran. The Afghans trace their history to their exodus after the occupation of their country by the former Soviet Union between 1979 and 1989. The Bosnians arrived during the Balkan war in the mid-1990s. The Somalis, Ethiopians, and Eritreans came during the period of political instability in their countries in 1980s and 1990s. The migration of several Muslim communities has been facilitated by liberalized U.S. immigration policies.

Profiles of Some Muslim Communities

The Iranians' organization, the Persian Association, often sponsors cultural and religious activities for the community. Two of the most common festivals of the Iranian community are the celebration of the Iranian New Year, known as Naw Roz, and the commemoration of the martyrdom of the grandson of Prophet Muhammad, which are held either at individuals' homes or at the Jamia Masjid, which most Iranians attend. The Iranian community consists mainly of businesspeople and professionals, some of whom send their children to Islamic schools organized on Sundays in the city's mosques. First-generation Iranians still use the Persian language to express their religious and ethnic identity and usually speak Persian at home. However, the younger generation seems to be most conversant in English and has little or no knowledge of the Persian language. The community is served by four Persian restaurants. Acknowledging the contributions of the Iranian community, the Las Vegas City Council declared March 31, 2007, as Persian Day.[30]

The Afghan community started immigrating to Las Vegas on a substantial scale after the 1979 Soviet occupation of Afghanistan, although a few Afghan students had settled in Las Vegas in the early 1970s. The Afghan community conducts its religious affairs in Arabic, Persian, or Pashto, the most widely spoken of Afghanistan's many languages. Afghans conduct Friday congregational prayers in Pashto but join the Jamia Masjid for all other religious needs. Most Afghans work in small businesses, while a few are professionals. The Afghan community has an informal association that brings the community members together on special cultural or ethnic occasions.[31]

Pakistanis comprise the largest Muslim community in Las Vegas. A high proportion of its population is engaged in professions such as engineering, medicine, and teaching. Others work in hotel-casinos, the transportation industry, and small businesses. Pakistanis are actively involved in politics and have their own network of organizations and associations. The Pakistani American Association is a major entity that celebrates the national day of Pakistan and other Pakistani festivals. The community also has a branch of the Association of Pakistani Physicians in North America that regularly organizes fundraisers for individuals and political parties contesting elections. It also runs a free health clinic in one of the local mosques. Additionally, it organizes fundraising events for literacy in Pakistan. Recently, it organized a major fundraising event for the victims of the 2006 Pakistan earthquake. Most people of Pakistani origin attend Jamia Masjid for religious services.[32]

The Bangladeshi Muslim community is fairly new, having begun settling in Las Vegas in the mid-1990s. The community has an independent Bengali

Association that organizes the celebration of Bangladesh Independence Day and other cultural functions. For their religious needs, Bangladeshis gather in a Westside mosque known as Hasibullah, named after the Bangladeshi founder and donor of the property. The small community consists of professionals in the fields of medicine and engineering, professors, and a few business owners.[33]

The Arab community consists of people who trace their ancestry to some thirty-three ethnic groups, with the Lebanese being the largest in Las Vegas. Professionals and businesspeople predominate among the Arabs. They attend all of the five local mosques, but their largest gathering takes place in a full-time Islamic school built by a wealthy Egyptian physician. Named after the father of the founder, Omar Haykal Islamic Academy offers congregational prayers every Friday. The community has a number of organizations such as the American Arab anti-Discrimination Committee, the Palestinian Solidarity Association, the Christian Muslim Association, and The Awdah, an organization dedicated to the return of Palestinian refugees to their homeland. Within the broader Arab community, each ethnic group has its independent network of relationships that reaches beyond Las Vegas.[34]

When Somalia was undergoing civil war in the mid-1990s, a large number of its citizens entered the United States as refugees. The great majority of them moved to Minnesota, North Dakota, and neighboring states, while some found their way to Las Vegas. They generally congregate in two mosques, the Islamic Information Center, located close to UNLV, and the Jamia Masjid, on the east side of town. They have their own organization and usually assemble at their homes to celebrate cultural events.[35]

The Bosnians migrated to Las Vegas in the mid-1990s, when the Balkan region was experiencing political crisis and war during the breakup of Yugoslavia. Many of them own or work in small businesses. Their relationship with other Muslim communities of the Valley is still in its embryonic stage.[36]

Muslim Organizations

Currently, six major religious institutions serve the Muslim community. Five serve orthodox Muslim communities, while the sixth is affiliated with the Nation of Islam. Most have experienced expansion in the last five years.

The city's oldest place of Muslim worship belongs to the Nation of Islam. Located in the historic Westside, it is in very poor condition and has a small membership. However, its members are dedicated to their mission; every Friday they can be seen selling their newspapers on major Las Vegas streets.

Jamia Masjid, the Islamic Society of Nevada, is the largest Muslim place of worship. It attracts more than three thousand congregants to special events such as the feast following the conclusion of the month of fasting, known as Ramadan. The Jamia Masjid had its origin at UNLV in 1976 when a group of students started organizing Friday congregational prayers on campus. As the number of congregants increased, the organizers found other venues, including the homes of some Muslim professionals who had recently moved to the city. In response to the growth of the Muslim population, a wealthy Muslim physician donated a property for religious activities, including the five daily prayers, special events during the month of fasting, and Sunday school for children. As the observant population continued to grow, construction began in 1993 on the Jamia Masjid mosque at Nellis Boulevard and Desert Inn Road. Construction was completed in 1994, but the burgeoning congregation soon outstripped the available space. In 1996 the mosque added facilities for Sunday school and in 2002 embarked on yet another expansion project. Today the mosque offers religious services for an estimated five hundred people on a weekly basis.

The Jamia Masjid has become the focal point of several social and community-related events. It organizes an annual national conference on the Quran, the Muslim religious scripture, which features prominent national speakers and scholars. The mosque also organizes regular events during Muslim festivals. Ramadan, the ninth month of the Islamic lunar calendar, is a special month that regularly brings about two hundred Muslims to the mosque on a daily basis. During this period, the community fasts and breaks the fast together, prays together, and demonstrates a unity that goes beyond ethnicity. The month of Ramadan concludes with special prayers and the festival known as Eid, held at the Jamia Masjid. The Eid prayers and Friday prayers are preceded by sermons, which focus on current affairs. Much of the Jamia Masjid's expenses are funded through donations.[37]

Masjid As-Saboor mosque was built in 1977 by former members of the Nation of Islam on the basis of the donation the community received, as noted above, from former heavyweight champion Mike Tyson. The mosque has undertaken a number of social projects, such as feeding the homeless, offering free health clinics, and providing schooling for poor and needy families. Recently, the mosque teamed up with a Los Angeles-based Muslim philanthropic organization to initiate a number of new social-service projects. The mosque offers five daily prayers in addition to Friday congregational prayers. It also makes arrangements for special nightly prayers during the month of fasting, in addition to offering Eid congregational prayers. The mosque is run on donations offered by its members.

In 1995 a philanthropist from Bangladesh purchased a property on the west side of town and opened it for prayers. The Hasibullah mosque, which was named after him, now attracts some fifty predominantly Bangladeshi congregants every Friday whose donations underwrite mosque operations. It also offers regular nightly prayers during Ramadan.

The Islamic Information Center was started in 2002 as a resource center on Islam, primarily for UNLV students. The center was first located near UNLV and moved closer in 2004 when it bought a property on Maryland Parkway south of Tropicana Avenue. The center attracted congregants and offered regular prayers but stopped offering Friday congregational prayers after several objections from neighbors. However, it offers the regular five daily prayers and special nightly prayers during the month of Ramadan. Regular congregants support the mosque financially. The center recently bought a two-acre property near McCarran International Airport to build a mosque and an Islamic center. The construction of the mosque that will be known as Masjid Noor (Light) on the new property began in April 2008. "We are developing plans and raising funds," explained Khaliq Baig, the mosque's main organizer.[38]

With the exception of the Nation of Islam, the Muslim Student Association, established in 1976 by UNLV students, is perhaps the oldest Muslim organization in Las Vegas. Its activities have depended on the level of activism of Muslim students. Today it has some thirty to forty members, organizes seminars and lecture series on Islam and Muslim peoples, and offers prayer facilities to campus Muslims. A former president of the group, Nur Kausar, who was born in Pakistan and came to Las Vegas when she was four years old, indicated that the association allowed her to meet Muslims from beyond her homeland, including other Asians, Arabs, black Muslims, and converts.[39]

Omar Haykal Islamic Academy started as a full-time school in 2001. It now has some seventy students and goes through the eighth grade. It follows the state curriculum besides teaching children a few courses on Islamic ethics and Arabic language. Recently, the academy opened its doors to the general Muslim public for Friday congregational prayers and special prayers during Ramadan. The academy also organizes Eid prayers, mostly attended by people of mixed ancestry. It is supported financially by a wealthy physician for whose father it is named.

The Islamic Shura Council (ISC) is a newly formed consultative body of Muslim organizations in Las Vegas. While leaders of the various organizations had previously consulted informally on issues of common interest, the formation of the ISC has given new impetus to unity. Consisting of the five major centers and mosques as well a representative of the Muslim Student Association, the council is still in its infancy and in the process of evolution, having been established in the second week of March, 2007. It plans to help Muslims coordinate and exchange information about their activities.

Ethnicity, Occupations, and Politics

Mosques and the Islamic centers are the only places where Muslims of various ethnic groups interact on a regular basis. Supplementing these formal places of religious teaching are religious and social activities conducted by the ethnic communities to serve their religious needs and affirm their ethnic and national identities. While English is the lingua franca in most of the formal Islamic centers, in other settings the ethnic communities use their mother tongues to provide religious instruction and conduct their celebrations. The ethnic communities tend to marry internally, sometimes in arranged marriages, although marriages among people of different ethnicities are not uncommon. Some Las Vegas Muslims subscribe to cable and satellite programs broadcast in Arabic, Urdu, Bengali, Persian, and several African languages, a practice that reinforces ethnic and national cultures while allowing the individuals and families to live transnationally to some extent. Despite the proliferation of Muslim ethnicities and their related activities, by bringing the diverse groups together, the mosques and Islamic centers reinforce a common Islamic identity among Las Vegas's Muslims.

Shias and Sunnis, the two main branches of Islam, exist within their own religious domains, yet interaction during important religious festivals is quite common. Shias believe that religious leadership must be restored to the descendants of the family of the Prophet through the lineage of his daughter Fatima. Sunnis, on the other hand, believe that the leader should be selected through a process of consensus among Muslims. Shias normally observe their holy days that fall in the first month of the Islamic lunar calendar either in their homes or in rented halls. Iranian Shias usually observe days of religious significance in the Jamia Masjid.

A large number of Muslims are physicians, engineers, and university and college professors; these professionals are the financial backbone of the various religious projects in the city. Others are cab drivers, unskilled workers, small business owners, and hotel-casino employees.

Las Vegas culture presents challenges to all Muslims. Some have become part of the gambling city, while others live completely apart from the casino culture. Many Muslims might take a visiting relative to one of the stage shows or a dinner buffet, and that is generally the limit of their engagement with casino-type entertainment. But reality is different for hotel-casino workers, many of whom live with guilt associated with their employment.

They often find themselves in a dilemma, for they are fully cognizant of the fact that their faith prohibits them from indulging in gambling, alcohol, or pork-related businesses. Some feel that the lack of alternate jobs offering equivalent wages and benefits leaves them no choice but to work in these prohibited areas, and among casino workers some compensate by increasing the amount of charity they offer. Those who have business dealings with alcohol or pork usually find a creative way to avoid breaking the religious laws. Some donate the profits earned in alcohol or pork to their charities, while others distribute them as a bonus to their employees.[40]

Las Vegas Muslims collectively have relatively few votes, but in the past several elections they have exercised their votes as a bloc. Many believe that the Muslim community's votes gave U.S. Senate majority leader Harry Reid his narrow reelection victory in 1998. Several Muslims from the African American community have stood for election to the Las Vegas City Council, and an immigrant Muslim from Bangladesh recently contested the Democratic primary for the 29th assembly district. Mosques have organized voter registration drives and invited candidates to address their congregants. Elected officials, including members of the Nevada congressional delegation, have visited the Jamia Masjid several times during the last five years. Muslims have also organized several fund-raising events for congressional and local candidates. On several occasions, national Muslim political organizations have solicited the help of the local community to lobby on Muslim issues.

Impact of the September 11 Events

Since September 2001, the Islamic community has come under a bright spotlight. "Everyone now wants to know who we are and what do we do," said Dr. Bashir Chowdhry, chairman of the board of trustees of the Islamic Society of Nevada.[41] September 11, 2001, made the community the subject of many newspaper articles and FBI investigations. The community was a suspect as well as a partner in the search for elusive terrorists. Many community members were visited by law-enforcement agencies; some were deported, and some were detained. Several newspaper stories suggested that a few of the nineteen hijackers had visited the city. But law-enforcement agencies have not found any link between the hijackers and the local Muslim community. "We are as much a victim of the 9/11 tragedy as the whole nation is," explained Dr. Chowdhry.[42] Diba Hadi, an executive with a private social-services agency, said: "Sept. 11, of course, touched everybody and all lives. Yes, we were questioned. We were harassed, on and off. We were pulled over. But it happens, you know. Unfortunately, I think that before Sept. 11 people were much more receptive to the Muslim community. And it is very unfortunate that that has changed."[43] "The first few months after 9/11 were the toughest time for the community. We were seen with suspicion and our loyalty to the country was questioned," remembers Dr. Khalid Khan, president of the Islamic Society of Nevada.[44]

In the immediate aftermath of the attacks, there were a number of relatively small-bore incidents involving Las Vegas Muslims, or people mistaken for Muslims. Police officials told reporters that they had responded to about fifteen hate crimes, some verbal, others physical, in the first week after September 11. Punches were thrown at an Arab-looking tourist on the Strip. A teenage girl was taunted at a soccer game and pelted with ice cubes. "Go back to Afghanistan!" her tormentors shouted. The girl was from India—a Hindu, not a Muslim.[45]

Within hours of the September 11 strikes, a young man described by witnesses as looking like a skinhead marched onto the campus of a private Islamic grade school, brandishing cans of spray paint. The handsome, tan-and-green facility had opened, with some fanfare, only the day before. The intruder was hustled away by authorities but vowed to return and "reclaim the neighborhood."[46]

A few of these encounters were reported in the Las Vegas newspapers; others were passed along through mosque grapevines. As the government began to take a skeptical look at Muslim immigrants and visitors, the mosques buzzed with stories of detentions and deportations. Several Muslims, for example, volunteered the story of how one family's hajj party, celebrating their pilgrimage to Mecca, was crashed by a cadre of FBI agents. Recalled Ismael Banks, a taxi driver: "Every weekend we'd hear about something . . . 'They came and they took so and so. We haven't seen so and so in a month.' It went unreported, but a lot of these people, we still don't know what happened to them. It's a here today, gone tomorrow type of thing."[47]

No hard data are available, but it is believed that a number of immigrant families returned to their native countries after September 11, fearing what a war on terrorism might portend for Muslims in general and Middle Easterners in particular. I personally know at least five families that decided to return to their country of origin after September 11, 2001. I also know of a young man who was harassed by immigration authorities even though he was a legal resident. "In the end he had to leave the country," said Akbar Moten, an old-time resident of Las Vegas.[48] Many of those who stayed have made adjustments in their everyday lives, seeking to avoid notice or forestall confrontation. Many shied away from the mosque, or altered or even dropped obviously Islamic names. "Frank" for "Farooq," "Mo" for "Muhammad,"

"Ben" for "Basit," and "Shaw" for "Shah" are common alterations one can notice in some people's business cards.

Dr. Khalid Khan recalls, "We were nervous but determined to fight the stereotyping of the community."[49] Indeed, the response began immediately. On the first Sunday after September 11, the Muslim community organized an open house for Las Vegans at Jamia Masjid; the event attracted some five hundred people, including the mayor of Las Vegas and members of the U.S. Congress. Community leaders used the opportunity to inform the visitors of their faith and activities. They condemned terrorism and vowed to work tirelessly to ensure that Las Vegas Muslims would be vigilant. The community also sent its representatives to various media outlets, local non-Muslim places of worship, and schools to talk about the efforts of Muslims to condemn terrorism and violence in general. Since then the community has organized several forums condemning groups that promote violence in the name of Islam. One such forum, "Islam and Non-Violence," was reported in the local press; the Voice of America picked up the story and lauded the efforts of the local community in combating terrorism.[50] Between September 2001 and September 2007, the city's leading newspapers, the *Las Vegas Review-Journal* and the *Las Vegas Sun,* published over twenty-five articles and news items on Islam and local Muslims, profiling the Muslim community and giving details of its activities.

Through September 2007, FBI officials and other law-enforcement agents had visited the Jamia Masjid on five separate occasions to develop better ties with the Muslim community.[51] Over the years, relations with the FBI have become cordial. In April 2008, a Jamia Masjid representative was invited to participate in an FBI regional conference attended by Muslims, Sikhs, and other minorities as well as FBI agents.[52] The presence of a Muslim at the FBI Citizens' Academy along with other prominent members of the Las Vegas community in June 2008 speaks to the mutual trust the Muslim community and the FBI have established over the years.

In 2004 the Muslim community joined the local interfaith council, and in 2008 it formally became part of the Community Interfaith Council. Prominent Muslim leaders such as Dr. Bashir Chowdhry, Dr. Ikram Khan, and Dr. Aslam Abdullah have participated in a number of interfaith forums since then. During the 2004 Asian tsunami disaster, the Muslim community organized the first interfaith prayer for the victims of the disaster and held a fund-raising event for relief to Indonesia, Thailand, Bangladesh, India, and Sri Lanka. These efforts were applauded by local officials, and Nevada Governor Kenny Guinn declared April 30, 2004, "Muslim Family-Value Day."

Conclusion

Islam arrived in Las Vegas in the 1960s, with the establishment of the small Nation of Islam community. Muslim immigration to Nevada began in the 1960s, with the arrival of the three acrobats from Morocco and Muslim students at UNLV, followed by professionals seeking employment in medicine, engineering, and university and college teaching. The first Friday congregational prayer took place in 1976 at UNLV. Soon, the level of such activities increased and the notion of a Muslim community comprising various ethnic groups started to crystallize. The first mosque catering to immigrants opened in 1977, and since then the city has seen a substantial increase in the Muslim population. It now has five mosques and a full-time Islamic school, besides having a Muslim Student Association at UNLV and various other organizations.

The emerging Islamic identity has not replaced loyalties to ethnic groups. There is a clear distinction between Muslim and ethnic events and identities. People still tend to socialize and marry within their own ethnic communities, and they affirm their ethnic identity by observing their traditional ethnic celebrations. Yet all Muslims relate to each other on religious matters using English as their lingua franca. The mosques and Islamic centers are the places where their Islamic identity is clearly manifested and affirmed. The coming together of Muslims of various ethnicities is giving rise to an Islamic identity that is influenced by American pluralism, democracy, and freedom. People tend to speak in these terms when talking about Islam, and they see a parallel between the universal aspects of their faith and American society. The older generations of Muslims have a strong sense of identity with their homelands, while the younger generation seems to identify with Islam but less with their ancestral homelands. The older generation still cheers the cricket or soccer teams of their countries, while the younger generation is more interested in basketball, baseball, or football. The presence of dozens of Islamic ethnic groups in Las Vegas has created challenges for Muslims. The emergence of a multiethnic Islamic identity, integration of the new with the old generation, and assimilation into the broader society without losing their religious identity are a few of these ongoing challenges.

Notes

1. The meeting took place on April 27, 2007.
2. Masjid As-Sabur is located in downtown Las Vegas and was founded in 1986. Joan Whitely, "The Long Shadow of 9/11: Seeking Acceptance," *Las Vegas*

Review-Journal, September 3, 2006. A brief history of the Nation of Islam can be found at http://www.noi.org/history_of_noi.htm.

3. See Andrea Kannapell, "From Different Paths, Muslims Seek Common Ground," *The New York Times,* November 23, 1997, NJ6; Andrea Elliott, "Between Black and Immigrant Muslims, an Uneasy Alliance," *The New York Times,* March 11, 2007, 1. For general information about Muslims in the United States, see *Muslim Life in America,* Office of International Information Programs, United States State Department, online at http://usinfo.state.gov/products/pubs/muslimlife.htm.

4. According to Reza Sulaimani, who is a court interpreter of Persian.

5. See Ivan van Sertima, *They Came Before Columbus* (New York: Random House, 1976); Abdullah Hakim Quick, *Deeper Roots* (London: Ta-Ha, 1996); Amatullah Rahman and Ajile Aisha, "A History of Islam Among African Americans," http://groups.msn.com/IslamicSouls/historyinislam.msnw?action=get_message&mview=0&ID_Message=5832&LastModified=4675574532860832815.

6. For more on the African diaspora, see John Thornton, *Africa and Africans in the Making of the Atlantic World, 1400–1800,* 2nd ed. (Cambridge: Cambridge University Press, 1998); Janet J. Ewald, "Crossers of the Sea: Slaves, Freedmen, and Other Migrants in the Northwestern Indian Ocean, c. 1750–1914," *American Historical Review* 105, no. 1 (2000): 69–91; Edward A. Alpers, "Sailing Into the Past," *SAMAR* 13 (Winter/Spring 2000). See also http://leb.net/lexington/bhist.htm; http://www.islamfortoday.com/historyusa1.htm. See also Elisabeth Siddiqui, essay at http://groups.msn.com/IslamicSouls/historyinislam.msnw?action=get_message&mview=0&ID_Message=5832&LastModified=4675574532860832815.

7. Sulayman Nyang, "Islam and the African American Experience," *Islam Horizons* 18 (Islamic Society of North America): 39.

8. Sylviane A. Diouf, "Literacy: A Distinction and a Danger," *Forgotten Roots* (Hayward, Calif.: Zaytuna Institute, 2000); see also Sylviane A. Diouf, *Servants of Allah: African Muslims Enslaved in the Americas* (New York: New York University Press, 1998).

9. Austin D. Allen, "There are Good Men in America, but All Are Very Ignorant of Africa and Its Muslims," *Forgotten Roots,* 3; Sulayman Nyang, *Islam in the United States of America* (Chicago: ABC International Group, 1933), 13.

10. For details about the ISNA and its emergence, see http://www.isna.net/.

11. He estimated that 29 percent of them were South Asian (Pakistani, Indian, Bangladeshi, Sri Lankan); 17 percent African Americans; 15 percent Iranians; 13 percent Afghani; 11 percent Arab; 7 percent Turkish; 4 percent Bosnian; and 4 percent African (Somalian, Eritrean, Ethiopian). Aslam Abdullah, cited in Joan Whitely, "The Long Shadow of 9/11: Seeking Acceptance," *Las Vegas Review-Journal,* September 3, 2006.

12. Muhammad Taha, interview by author, December 11, 2006.

13. Bilal was the first black to accept Islam when Prophet Muhammad introduced Islam in the seventh century. Most Africans Americans at one time described themselves as Bilalians. A study of Warith Deen Muhammad and his ties to Orthodox

Islam is found in Zafar Ishaq Ansari, "W. D. Muhammad: The Making of a 'Black Muslim Leader' (1933–1961)," *American Journal of Islamic Social Sciences* 2, no. 2.

14. Mujahid Ramadan, a local African American leader, interview by author, April 13, 2007.

15. Imam Fateen Saifullah, religious leader of Masjid As Sabur, interview by author, April 20, 2007. (Masjid is Arabic for Mosque.)

16. Mujahid Ramadan, interview.

17. http://groups.msn.com/IslamicSouls/historyinislam.msnw.

18. "The Mosques in America: A National Portrait" by CAIR, http://amp.ghazali.net/html/mosques_in_us.html.

19. Peter King, "Islam in Las Vegas," *Los Angeles Times,* August 7, 2004.

20. Various community leaders, including Muhammad Azam, a Muslim student leader; Dr. Bashir Chowdhry; Dr. Suhail Anjum; and Dr. Ikram Khan, interviews by author, April 2007.

21. For African Americans, U.S. Census Bureau, *American Community Survey,* "acs Demographic and Housing Estimates—Clark County, Nevada, 2000"; for Arabs, see "Table qt-p13: Ancestry 2000-Clark County, Nevada," both at http://factfinder.census.gov/(accessed July 16, 2008).

22. U.S. Census Bureau, *American Community Survey,* "Table b04001, First Ancestry Reported—Clark County, Nevada, 2006," http://factfinder.census.gov/ (accessed July 15, 2006).

23. Imam Fateen Saifullah, interview; Mujahid Ramadan, interview.

24. U.S. Census Data 2000, http://www.census.gov/prod/2003pubs/c2kbr-23.pdf.

25. Abdul Aziz Eddeabarh, a prominent Muslim of Morrocan descent who lived in Las Vegas from 1995 to 2005, interview by author, March 23, 2007.

26. Various ethnic community leaders, Muhammad Azam, a Muslim student leader; Dr. Bashir Chowdhry; Dr. Suhail Anjum; and Dr. Ikram Khan, interviews by author, April 2007.

27. The 2000 census figures are much lower. For example, the statewide population of Pakistanis is 392, with Clark County estimated at fewer than 100; Iranians statewide is 2,587, with 2,124 in Clark County; Lebanese, 2,897 statewide, with 2,453 in Clark County; Syrians, 997 statewide, with 777 in Clark County; and Egyptians, 772 statewide, with 642 in Clark County. By 2006 the census estimated Clark County's population of Arabs to be 5,682; of Egyptians, 475; of Lebanese, 2,881; of Syrians, 164. U.S. Census Bureau, *American Community Survey,* "Table B04001, First Ancestry Reported—Clark County, Nevada" 2006, http: factfinder.census.gov/ (accessed July 15, 2008). Such discrepancies are common. The census tends to undercount immigrants, while immigrant communities tend to overestimate their own numbers.

28. Peter King, "Islam in Las Vegas," *Los Angeles Times,* August 6, 2005.

29. Mujahid Ramadan, interview.

30. Reza Sulaimani, a prominent Muslim community member of Iranian descent, interview by author, April 20, 2007.

31. Najibullah Naqshbandi, a prominent Afghan Muslim community member, interview by author, April 23, 2007.

32. Khan and Chowdhry, interviews; Dr. Suhail Anjum and other prominent Pakistani American leaders, interviews by author, April 11–27, 2007.

33. Muhammad Khan and Raees Ahmed, prominent members of the Bangladeshi community, interviews by author, April 11–27, 2007.

34. Several prominent members of the Arab community, including Jenina Kadri, interviews by author, April 11–27, 2007.

35. Several prominent members of the Somali community, including Nasir Abdullahi Saed and Sadia Osman, interviews by author, April 11–27, 2007.

36. Several prominent members of the Bosnian community, including Ismail Sulaimanovic, interviews by author, April 11–27, 2007.

37. Khalid Khan, president of the Islamic Society of Nevada, interview by author, April 11–27, 2007.

38. Khaliq Baig, main organizer of Masjid Noor, the planned new mosque, interview by author, April 27, 2007.

39. Eric Leake, "Join the Club," *UNLV Magazine,* Spring 2007.

40. Peter King, *Los Angeles Times,* http://www.latimes.com/news/nationworld/nation/la-na-vegas1aug01.story posted at http://www.groupsrv.com/religion/about62713.html.

41. Dr. Bashir Chowdhry is the chairman of the board of trustees of the Islamic Society of Nevada. His comments are based on interview by author, March 15, 2007.

42. Chowdhry, interview, March 15, 2007.

43. Peter King, "Islam in Las Vegas," *Los Angeles Times,* August 5, 2004.

44. Khalid Khan, interview by author, January 19, 2007.

45. King, "Islam in Las Vegas."

46. Ibid., August 6, 2004.

47. Ibid., August 7, 2004.

48. Akbar Moten, a member of the Islamic Society of Nevada, interview by author, January 17, 2007.

49. Khan interview, April 11, 2007.

50. The lecture series "Islam and Non-Violence" took place on August 13, 14, 15, 2005, at the Jamia Masjid.

51. Khan interview, April 11, 2007.

52. The author of the article participated in the conference that discussed Muslim-FBI relations.

Sons of a federal judge, the five Foley brothers all became attorneys and prominent political leaders in their own right. *Standing, from left,* Thomas and Roger. *Sitting, from left,* George, John, and Joe. Courtesy Mary Lou Foley

Three southern Nevadans—Stephen and Rachel Snyder, flanking Hannah Courser—hauled out the shamrocks for a local tradition, the forty-third annual Sons of Erin St. Patrick's Day parade, an event that brings together the Irish and those who would like to be. Courtesy *Henderson Home News,* photograph by Richard Brian

Early Germans observe their first artesian well on their Paradise Valley property in 1909. *Left to right,* Edward von Tobel Sr.; his wife, Maria; and Jake and William Beckley. Courtesy Special Collections, University of Nevada, Las Vegas

Vagabonds German Karneval Club. Courtesy Vagabonds Club

Yonema "Bill" Tomiyasu, in California, 1908–10. Courtesy Special Collections, University of Nevada, Las Vegas

Japanese American Club at the International Festival, ca. mid-1980s. Courtesy Sue Fawn Chung

The Lujan family gathers for a birthday party with friends in 1964. In the early sixties, Cuban exiles in Las Vegas formed a tight-knit community. Courtesy Lilliam Lujan-Shell

Cuban Lujan family at the Desert Inn, 1967. Courtesy Lilliam Lujan-Shell

The Sons of Norway at the Las Vegas Centennial Helldorado Days parade in 2005. The participants, beginning with the woman wearing the black folk dress on the far left and continuing clockwise: Henny Morse, Amanda Fehr, Heidi Fehr, Elin Fehr, Karen Holien, Fran Pallesen, Roy Kristiansen, Micky Kristiansen, Arlys Huebner, Alexis Manning, and Lucas Bang. Courtesy Erik R. Pappa

"Hammargren Hammers in Lieutenant Governor Primary Race." Dr. Lonnie Hammargren, of Swedish ancestry, won the following general election and served in that position from 1995 to 1999. Courtesy Dr. Lonnie Hammargren

Students with their teacher at one of the many Sunday Islamic schools in Las Vegas, 2008. For Muslim families, religious education is an important part of their lives. Courtesy Islamic Society of Nevada

Above, left: Kirk Kerkorian, of Armenian ancestry, in front of the International (now Las Vegas Hilton) Hotel, 1969. Courtesy Special Collections, University of Nevada, Las Vegas

Above, right: UNLV's Jerry Tarkanian, of Armenian ancestry, chews on his towel during a Rebels basketball game in 1985. Courtesy Special Collections, University of Nevada, Las Vegas

Members of the Argentine Association of Las Vegas prepare to participate in the Día de las Américas parade in downtown Las Vegas. Photograph by Griselda Mezzotero

A gaucho stands on a float prepared by the Argentine Association of Las Vegas for the Día de las Américas parade. Photograph by Griselda Mezzotero

The Korean Kim sisters in the casino. *Left to right,* mother, Sue, Min, Ai Ja. Courtesy Special Collections, University of Nevada, Las Vegas

Sue Kim and the Kim Brothers, August 24, 1988, "Roaring '20s Revue" at the Holiday Casino. Courtesy Special Collections, University of Nevada, Las Vegas

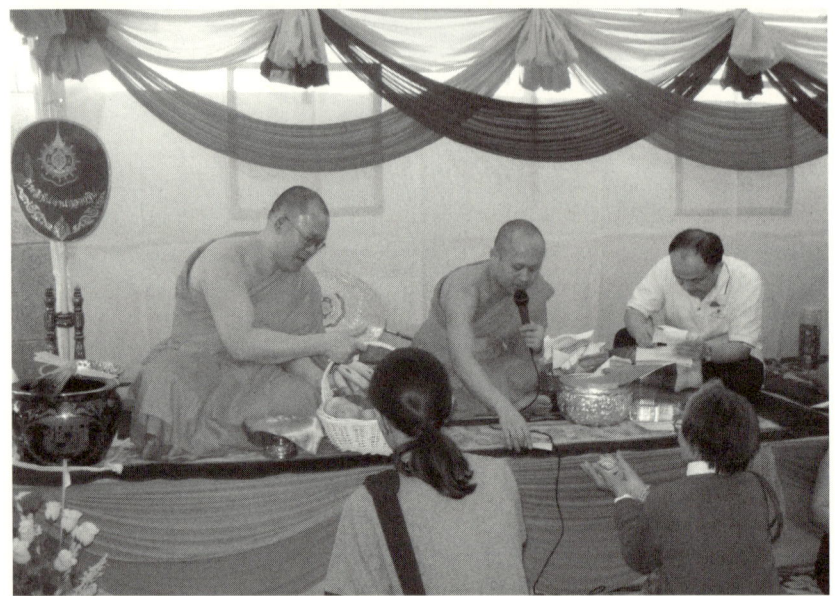

A layperson offers food to two Buddhist monks during the Thai Kathin festival in Las Vegas in 2007. Photograph by Jiemin Bao

Thai women making merit at a Las Vegas Buddhist temple in 2004. Photograph by Jiemin Bao

Fasil and Elizabeth at the Ethiopian Millennium Celebration. Courtesy Michelle Kuenzi

Members of the EMAN leadership with Michelle Kuenzi (*second left on first row*) and Congresswoman Dina Titus (*second right on first row*) at the Ethiopian Millennium Celebration. Courtesy Michelle Kuenzi

Huelga de Dolores celebration, April 1, 2008, Guatemalan Unity Committee (COMUGUA), Rafael Rivera Community Center, Las Vegas. Courtesy Israel Fuentes

A moment during a February 3, 2008, event protesting the FARC guerrillas, one of three armies outside the state tangled in a decades-old conflict. The protest, against the guerrilla practice of kidnapping, was held at Oiga, Mire, Vea, a Las Vegas restaurant. The event was held in concert with others worldwide (most of which occurred February 4) by an estimated 13 million people. Courtesy Andrea Jímenez

CHAPTER 7

The Armenians

MICHELLE TUSAN

When Las Vegas started as a small railroad town in 1905, Armenians showed little interest in pioneering this new southwestern frontier. They had traditionally been farmers, craftsmen, and merchants in their ancestral home in the eastern Mediterranean, and Las Vegas's vast desert, with few natural resources and limited connection to larger regional trade networks, did not look promising as a site to forge a "new Armenia."

Other regions in the West held more promise. The fertile San Joaquin Valley in central California offered the ideal combination of cheap land and an already thriving Armenian community that attracted new immigrants willing to make the long journey from eastern Anatolia to the western United States. The establishment of Fresno as what people of the time called an "Armenian colony" during the early twentieth century followed the classic immigrant story of chain migration. I remember my grandmother telling the story of a letter that her parents received from a former fellow villager from the town of Moush who had settled in Fresno in the 1890s. "It is just like home," he declared, "come and join me in America." He had apparently written many such letters, since Fresno soon became a town filled with "Moushetsies" and Armenians from other villages seeking to make a new start. For his efforts he was rewarded with the unofficial title of "King of the Moushetsies," a moniker that he used to garner privileges befitting a founding father.[1] This story repeated itself countless times in the centers where Armenians settled, including New York, Michigan, and Massachusetts as well as California.[2]

The Armenian Diaspora

Armenians in the United States form part of a broader diaspora that has dispersed Armenians across the Middle East, Russia, western Europe, and the Americas. Armenia's ancient civilization developed at the historically important crossroads of the Black Sea, Euphrates River Valley, and upper Tigris River. The location of this highly sophisticated civilization, noted for its artistic and literary achievement, at the center of crucial eastern trade routes guaranteed that this relatively small group of people would constantly have to fend off threats from invaders. In the sixteenth century, Armenia was conquered by the Ottoman Turks, whose control lasted until the collapse of the Ottoman Empire itself at the end of World War I. As Ottoman subjects, Armenians represented a Christian minority among a Muslim majority. This earned them status as second-class citizens and eventually led to the almost total destruction of the Armenians at the hands of their Ottoman rulers during World War I.[3]

Relations with and persecution by the Ottoman Turks deeply marked the Armenian character and history and led to the diaspora. Most of the early Armenian settlers in the United States were fleeing the pogroms perpetrated by the Ottoman Turks that ravaged every Armenian settlement in eastern Turkey in 1895 and resulted in the deaths of over 100,000 people.[4] Often with little more than a warning from a sympathetic Turkish neighbor, Armenians fled these massacres in droves and left for the Middle East, western Europe, and the Americas. Another wave of immigration, after the United States eased immigration restrictions for those coming from the region following World War I, resulted from even more dire circumstances. In 1915 a systematic genocide of the Armenian peoples living under Ottoman rule, carried out at the orders of the sultan, killed an estimated 1.5 million people out of a population of around 2 million.[5] By 1924, when restrictive legislation virtually halted Armenian and other non-western European immigration, almost 100,000 Armenians in total had settled in the United States.[6]

Armenian immigration to the United States in more recent years has resulted from instability in the Middle East and the former Soviet Union. Immigration from these regions was made possible after the quota restrictions instituted in 1924 were eased in 1965. Armenian immigrants came to the United States in increasing numbers in the wake of the 1975 civil war in Lebanon and again following the 1979 Islamic Revolution in Iran. As many as 160,000 Armenians came to the United States during this period.[7] During the late 1980s and early 1990s, Armenian immigration came largely from areas formerly controlled by the Soviet Union, including the Republic of Armenia and Russia. Today it is estimated that around 800,000 people of Armenian descent live in the United States. A large number of these immigrants, both "new" and "old," are concentrated in the West. Los Angeles often has been called the second largest "Armenian" city in the world, behind Yerevan, the capital of modern-day Armenia.[8]

Armenians in the United States and Las Vegas

In the United States, Armenians have been free to recreate a life for themselves that follows many traditional patterns of the "old country." During the late nineteenth century, families from neighboring villages in Armenia settled close to one another in the United States. They built churches, traded with one another, and encouraged their children to marry other Armenians. As outsiders who had faced the worst side of prejudice in their homeland, they recognized from the beginning the importance of making a place for themselves in the communities in which they settled. The early arrivals dealt with this challenge in two ways. First, they maintained close ties within their own communities. Second, they worked to build institutions that would provide economic, social, and political opportunities that offered them prestige within the larger communities in which they settled. This pattern continues to characterize Armenian American life throughout the United States. In the West, this has meant finding new ways to strengthen bonds within and between the more recent and older communities that make up the Armenian diaspora.

For people living in the Las Vegas Valley at the turn of the twentieth century, however, Armenians were not neighbors, friends, and colleagues, but news. An examination of the *Las Vegas Age*, the first newspaper published in the Valley, shows the extent to which Armenians figured in the world of early Las Vegas. Between 1905 and 1925, the paper included a range of news items on Armenia and Armenians dealing with war, genocide, immigration, and Armenian culture. A 1905 story told of Armenian orphans presenting an American flag that they had sewn by hand to the U.S. government.[9] Reports of the "Armenian colony in Fresno" and customs such as how Armenian women made butter by suspending churns from ropes and shaking it from side to side also received attention.[10]

The main way early Las Vegans learned about Armenians, however, was through stories of genocide and war. Sympathetic accounts of villages inhabited by "wealthy" Armenian "merchants and traders" that were subsequently destroyed by competing ethnic groups living in the region—namely Russians, Kurds, and Turks—appeared regularly.[11] Other stories outlined domestic and cultural problems within Turkey as they related to the treatment of Armenians and other ethnic Christian minorities.[12] After World War I, attention turned to relief work in the region. In 1920 the *Age* reported that Herbert Hoover deemed the humanitarian crisis in the Near East "the most desperate in the world,"[13] and subsequent stories called for increased relief work among the Armenians.[14] Ads from the Near East Relief

Society and retailer JC Penney asked Las Vegans to give money to fund humanitarian work.[15]

Such stories demonstrate a relatively positive view of Armenians. Early Las Vegans apparently took a sympathetic line on the issue of Armenian immigration to the United States.[16] When the first Armenian families settled in southern Nevada around 1911, reports surfaced of citizens reaching out to ease their transition to American life.[17] By 1924 Las Vegas Armenians were enrolled as members of the class of 521 students at the state's only university in Reno.[18] This followed a larger nationwide pattern, in which Armenian college students were said to outnumber other immigrant groups in proportion to their numbers during this time.[19] Sympathy for Armenians only went so far, however. When the president raised the specter of military intervention, writers in the *Age* demurred: "Sympathy with Armenia and willingness to give freely to mitigate Armenian suffering are one thing. To send thousands of American young men there to do garrison and police duty for many years to come, at the expense of billions to the Treasury, as proposed by the President, that is quite another thing."[20]

The Armenian Community Today

Las Vegas's Armenian population grew slowly. In 1978 the Armenian American Cultural Society was founded as one of the first Armenian community institutions in Las Vegas.[21] As emigration from the Middle East and the former Soviet Union accelerated from the mid-1970s on, Las Vegas's Armenian population began to grow, especially during the boom years of the 1980s and 1990s. Jobs, entrepreneurial opportunities, and Las Vegas's emergence as a retirement center, meanwhile, attracted Armenian Americans from their original settlements in California and the East. These multiple points of origin have created a diversity among Las Vegas Armenians that is reflected in the religious, cultural, and political institutions they have formed in the Valley.

While the 2000 U.S. census found 2,276 people in Clark County who claimed Armenian ancestry and estimated 3,078 for 2006, local Armenians estimate their number at between 10,000 and 20,000.[22] The Las Vegas Armenian community is new in comparison with those established in the late nineteenth century. Thus—unlike Fresno, California; Watertown, Massachusetts; or Detroit, Michigan—Las Vegas has not seen the development of neighborhoods dominated by Armenian immigrants. New arrivals seem just as likely to settle in Henderson as in Summerlin or North Las Vegas, their choices based on personal preferences, financial means, and professional needs of individuals and their families. This pattern (or lack thereof) is indicated by the absence of concentration of businesses, churches, and schools catering to Armenian residents. Although there are three local Armenian churches, all located in the northwest, one finds Armenian bakeries and markets dispersed throughout the Valley.

This pattern of settlement has meant that for Armenian Americans, Las Vegas has developed as a diaspora within a diaspora. Like other Las Vegans, many Armenians continue to maintain strong ties to the places from which they came, whether in the United States, the Middle East, Russia, or Armenia itself. This sense of rootedness or what some historians call a "translocal" identity is powerful even among Armenian Americans whose families have been in the United States for multiple generations. For example, one family that I spoke with indicated that although they have lived in Las Vegas for over eleven years, they still maintain ties to the institutions where they grew up. When it came time to baptize their children, they chose churches where their children's grandparents resided in Michigan and Toronto.[23] My husband and I made a similar decision with our own son and, later, our daughter.

One reason for this loyalty to "hometowns" is the relative newness of Armenian institutions in Las Vegas. While the Armenian American Cultural Society dates from 1978, the first Armenian church in Las Vegas was established only in 1992.[24] In recent years, an Armenian Protestant church and a second Orthodox denomination have been added.

As southern Nevada's Armenian population grows, Las Vegas may develop as a top destination for Armenians from both the United States and abroad.[25] In fact, this has already begun to happen among the most recent Armenian immigrants to the United States. For those arriving primarily from Russia and Armenia during the last ten to fifteen years, a sense of cohesiveness in their community has developed quickly. This group has built its own institutions, separate from those established by Armenians who immigrated to the United States much earlier from the Middle East and "Western Armenia," the region now part of eastern Turkey. For example, of the two Orthodox churches in Las Vegas, the more established congregation caters primarily to recent immigrants from Russia and Armenia.

Part of the reason for this development certainly has to do with their shared experience as new immigrants to the United States. Issues such as visas, residency requirements, and citizenship questions play an important role in bringing this group together. In many immigration cases, members of this community must seek translators who speak either Russian or Eastern Armenian, a dialect that is distinct from the language spoken by the older group of immigrants from eastern Anatolia. Community involvement has proved important in other ways. When two Armenian sisters, Emma and

Mariam Sarkisian, were threatened with deportation in 2005, the community banded together to draw attention to their plight. Senator Harry Reid intervened on behalf of the women, who had immigrated legally to the United States with their father from the Soviet Union in 1991. The Nevada senator worked with then-secretary of Homeland Security Tom Ridge to allow them to avoid deportation to the Republic of Armenia while they straightened out their residency status.[26]

Despite distinctions between "old" and "new" Armenian Americans, there are signs that the larger Armenian community is thriving as more Armenians from both groups settle in Las Vegas for both personal and professional reasons. As one woman I interviewed put it: "the community is becoming more constant."[27] There is a project afoot for an Armenian Yellow Pages, an endeavor that would have been hard to imagine ten years ago. As religious, political, and cultural community institutions multiply and strengthen, the ties among Armenians who consider Las Vegas home continue to grow.

Religious Life

Armenians are very proud of their Christian heritage. In fact, the kingdom of Armenia became the first state to adopt Christianity as its official religion in CE 301. The establishment of the Apostolic Church followed, and it continues as the main Armenian confession. One hundred years later, an Armenian alphabet based on phonetic principles was developed; this allowed for a vernacular translation of the Bible, thus consolidating Christianity's hold among the Armenians.[28]

The history of Armenians' relations with the Ottoman Turks has resulted in further strengthening the connection of modern-day Armenians to their Christian past. Many Armenians still consider themselves members of the Armenian Apostolic Church, an institution that claims connection with the apostles of the early Christian Church. Although political divisions among Armenians during the early twentieth century resulted in the split of the Apostolic Church into two branches, the confessions remain intimately tied by adherence to the same religious doctrine. The troubled past of this "first Christian nation" shaped Armenian history in another important way. The constant threat of invasion and the later domination by Ottoman Turkey meant that Armenians, in the words of one historian, "assumed a role somewhat akin to that of the Jews in predominantly Christian Europe: they became bankers, skilled artisans, bureaucrats and businessmen."[29]

Today, Armenians living in Las Vegas have three churches to choose from: two Apostolic and one Protestant. An evangelical Bible study group meets separately each week. There are also Armenian Catholics living in the Valley, but at present they do not have their own congregation. The oldest local Armenian congregation, the Western Diocese Armenian Apostolic Church, dates from 1992 and holds services every Sunday. Its administrative and spiritual ties with the Apostolic Church based in Armenia have attracted a membership mainly among recent immigrants from Russia and Armenia.

The Western Prelacy Armenian Apostolic Church of Las Vegas was first established in 1998 but lost its momentum and later was restarted by the community. Its membership consists largely of people from the older Armenian American community who have come to Las Vegas from other parts of the United States. This church holds services on the second Sunday of each month on West Sahara Avenue.[30]

The Armenian Evangelical Church of Las Vegas, founded in 2004, has an established presence in the Valley and meets every Sunday on North Torrey Pines. Its members are drawn from the community of Armenians whose families adopted Protestantism as a result of the proselytizing efforts of missionaries who first arrived in eastern Anatolia in the late nineteenth century.

All of these churches are still in the early stages of developing an influential presence in the Las Vegas Valley. Lacking their own buildings, they rent space from other churches. The Western Prelacy church meets at the Lakes Lutheran Church and the Armenian Evangelical church at Christ Lutheran Church on Sunday afternoons. This limitation, however, has not stopped them from engaging in a host of traditional church activities, including weekly Bible studies, choir practice, ladies' and mens' auxiliary organizations, and regular cultural events. Each congregation has a growing list of active members. The Western Prelacy church has an estimated attendance of between fifty and seventy people at its monthly service, though total membership is larger.[31] The priest of the Western Diocese church reports similar numbers at its weekly services, estimating that around sixty members attend regularly.[32] At the Armenian Evangelical church, membership hovers at around one hundred members, with fifty regularly attending church each week.[33]

In many ways, the churches provide the focal point for both religious and cultural life. At the second anniversary celebration of the Western Prelacy church, the intersection of religion and culture was on display. The dinner reception was held at the Tarkanian Basketball Academy. The program included greetings from the Western prelate, Archbishop Moushegh Mardirossian, information on the church, and appeals for donations, as well as a lineup of traditional and contemporary Armenian entertainment. The Hamazkayin Fresno Dance Ensemble performed four traditional Armenian dances in elaborate costume, and a well-known Las Vegas singer from Yerevan,

Armenia, performed two songs from her latest album. Children from Homenetmen, or the Armenian "scouts," presented the flags of the United States, Nevada and Armenia and led the audience in singing the national anthems of both countries.

The event drew support from all parts of the Armenian community, with priests from all three Armenian churches in attendance with their wives. Those present at the dinner ranged from teenagers to seniors, who gave readily of their time and money in support of the evening. Donations also came from church board members, the Armenian business community, and even two members of the well-known rock-music group, "System of a Down." A representative of the Los Angeles Council of Churches offered his greetings and wished church members the best in their efforts to grow and acquire their own church building. Among the approximately two hundred people in attendance was honored guest councilwoman Lois Tarkanian, along with her son Danny and his wife.

Cultural Institutions

The close connection between religious and cultural life in the Armenian community has resulted in the development of organizations that draw heavily upon those people already involved in church activities. The membership of the key Armenian cultural organizations in the Valley—Homenetmen, the Armenian Relief Society (ARS), Triple X Fraternity, the Armenian American Cultural Society of Las Vegas, and the UNLV Armenian Student Association (ASA)—overlaps to a large extent with that of churches. This certainly has partly to do with the relative newness and small size of the community, requiring it to rely on the same people to lead local Armenian organizations. However, it also demonstrates the importance that this community places on the church as a center not just for religious, but also for political, economic, and cultural activity.

Most of the people I interviewed for this chapter showed great enthusiasm for Homenetmen, primarily due to its focus on the community's youth. Also known as the Armenian General Scouting and Athletic Union or, in Armenian, "Hye Marmnamarzagan Enthanur Miutiun," the organization recruits Armenian American boys and girls ages five and up and is affiliated with the Boy Scouts and Girl Scouts of America. The Las Vegas "Artsakh" Chapter, started in 1997, has seventy-five members, who participate in both scouting and athletic activities, the latter including basketball, swimming, tennis, track and field, and Ping-Pong.[34] The organization's mission is "to prepare exemplary and law-abiding citizens by providing physical and health education, endowing the mind and soul with the finest spirit of sportsmanship, and developing an understanding of responsibility and honor as they strive for individual and collective excellence."[35] This worldwide youth organization, which began in 1918 and has over ninety chapters and twenty-five thousand members on five continents, works to connect Armenians to one another around the globe.[36] Each year, the Las Vegas chapter competes at the Navasartian Games in Los Angeles. Recently, five members from the Las Vegas chapter went to Armenia.

Not surprisingly, relief work has played a central role in bringing Armenians together wherever they settle. Their own troubled history of war, genocide, and displacement has led to the development of Armenian-centered aid institutions. In Las Vegas, church auxiliary organizations raise funds for relief efforts and for the support of philanthropic activities of their respective congregations. Outside of the church, the ARS women's aid organization fills an important role in the community. "ARS members," according to the organization's brochure, "exhibit the tenacity of the Armenian spirit to survive despite all odds and to channel energies towards others less fortunate than themselves, making a difference in their local communities."[37]

The ARS was founded in New York City as a humanitarian organization in 1910. Today it has eighteen thousand members, with affiliates in twenty-four countries that participate in a host of educational, social service, health, and disaster relief efforts. Their reach began to extend to Armenia following the devastating 1988 earthquake, when they sponsored programs to help rebuild the country's infrastructure. The Las Vegas "Shoushi Chapter," founded in 1994, has an active presence in the larger community, most notably donating to local charities, sponsoring events such as the annual Mother's Day Picnic, and running a Saturday school for Armenian students where language and culture are taught.[38]

Other Armenian cultural institutions in Las Vegas, though relatively young when compared with their counterparts in places such as Los Angeles and Fresno, have grown and thrived in recent years. The Armenian American Cultural Society of Las Vegas, founded in 1978, has a seven-member board of directors, sponsors scholarships, and publishes a monthly newsletter, *Las Vegas Hyes*.[39] Armenian men's societies, including the California-based "Triple X Fraternity," have also found a home in Las Vegas, though not for the reasons the slightly odd name might incline one to think. Founded in Fresno by a group of Armenian men who found themselves excluded from other men's societies on account of their ethnicity, the organization sponsors philanthropic activities and offers a space for men and their families to socialize with other Armenians. The Las Vegas Triple X chapter is the only one outside of California.[40]

The number of Armenian students attending UNLV has grown along with the larger Armenian community, which resulted in the founding of the Armenian Student Association (ASA), an organization that has had a regular presence on campus for several years. This relatively active organization currently has a dedicated core membership and is one of the few venues where "old," or Western, and "new," or Eastern, Armenians come together for a common purpose.[41] Activities include raising money and collecting supplies for philanthropic projects in Armenia, genocide remembrance and education, and social activities. Every April 24 the organization hosts a program on the UNLV campus in commemoration of the Armenian Genocide.

Businesses

The number of businesses that cater to the Armenian community has grown in recent years to include bakeries, pastry shops, and grocery stores. Delicious pastries from Ararat Bakery, located on West Sahara, include traditional Armenian desserts and new American favorites. Mike's Bakery, on Maryland Parkway, sells traditional "Armenian pizzas," called *lajmajoon,* along with other savory treats. Also on Maryland Parkway, LA Price Mediterranean Market sells grocery items found in every Armenian kitchen. Armenian-run businesses such as Vegas Pita, run by Mr. and Mrs. Ruben Grigorian, supply the Valley with specialty Near Eastern breads.

Nevertheless, many still feel the need to travel to regions with more established Armenian shops to find specialty items unavailable in Las Vegas. Los Angeles is a favorite destination for many Armenians, who buy bread and even meat in well-known shops to supply their kitchens. Whenever she visits, my mother brings me baked goods from two of the famous bakeries across from the Apostolic Church in Fresno, and my father keeps me supplied with Akmak Crackers straight from the bakery in our hometown of Sanger. Some are willing to go even further to acquire their favorite Armenian products, which always taste better when they come from "home." Whenever Koko Darakjian's in-laws visit from Michigan, for example, they are instructed to bring a suitcase full of pastries from their favorite bakery. "No one makes baklava like they do," he exclaimed. Whole lamb, an essential ingredient in Armenian cooking, is still hard to find in Las Vegas. One couple traveled to a farm sixty miles from Las Vegas to buy a lamb to feed their guests.

The relative newness and small size of the Armenian community in Las Vegas have meant that Armenian businesses must cater to both Armenian and non-Armenian clientele. When I asked a clerk at the now closed Armenian-run Aladdin Market on East Tropicana Avenue if it was an Armenian market years ago, he declared, "We are a market for everybody." (His father then proceeded to help me to my car with my groceries and chat with me in Armenian.) Unlike more established Armenian communities, Las Vegas has no restaurants that exclusively prepare Armenian food. Rather, they exist under the broader category of "Mediterranean" food. As in other communities, the best place to get an Armenian meal is at a church-sponsored event, where the finest cooks are only too happy to use their talents for a good cause.

Remembering the Genocide

Perhaps nothing brings Armenians together more than the issue of the Armenian Genocide, and in this the Las Vegas community is no exception. Differences between "new" and "old" Armenian Americans fade away when it comes to commemorating the first genocide of the twentieth century. As in other Armenian communities throughout the United States, April 24 is set aside as a day of remembrance for the 1.5 million Armenians who died at the hands of the Ottoman Turks in 1915. Candlelight vigils, educational events, and political activities make up the host of events that mark this important day for the community.

Part of the reason for this coming together has to do with the problematic status of the Armenian Genocide itself in the American political consciousness. Although Nevada and several other states have joined the European Union in making declarations recognizing the Genocide, the U.S. government has never officially recognized the event. In 2005 then-Nevada governor Kenny Guinn issued a proclamation calling the 1915 genocide a "crime against humanity" and a "systematic and deliberate massacre of the Armenian people."[42] Recently, France passed a law making it a crime to deny that the Armenian Genocide happened.

Political considerations in this country, including perceptions of Turkey's status as a strategic ally in the Middle East, have blocked the passage of congressional resolutions on this issue for decades. House Speaker Nancy Pelosi supported an Armenian Genocide Resolution in 2007 that ultimately failed for these very reasons. Though some U.S. presidents, most recently including Ronald Reagan, have recognized the genocide, the policy of the State Department has followed the official Turkish line, which denies that the Armenian Genocide ever happened. The Turkish government has also spent a great deal of money lobbying Congress against a resolution. Recognition of the genocide, many critics claim, would force Turkey to pay reparations and reconcile land claims of descendants of those killed.

Commemoration activities in Las Vegas have taken on a higher profile in recent years. Articles in the *Las Vegas Sun* and, to a lesser extent, the *Las Vegas Review-Journal* have brought the issue home to Las Vegans in a new way.[43] Not since the humanitarian movements of the early twentieth century have the local media focused so much on Armenia and Armenians. This reflects a broader trend in which the Armenian Genocide has reentered public discourse as a "live" and highly contested issue, leading some to argue that genocide denial is coming to an end.

Recent high-profile court cases in Turkey over the question of what happened to the two million Armenians living in the Ottoman Empire during World War I have drawn attention to the issue.[44] This time it is native Turks, including Nobel Laureate Orhan Pamuk, along with other Turkish authors who have come to question their government's stance, have raised the issue. This position, however, is not accepted by all in Turkey, particularly Turkish nationalists. After the 2007 murder of Turkish Armenian journalist Hrant Dink in Istanbul, the Turkish nationalist who gunned him down exclaimed that Pamuk "should be careful." On the other side, Dink's murder prompted a march by several thousand persons who chanted, "We are all Hrant; we are all Armenians."[45]

Armenian Americans believe that much work remains to be done on the local level. As keynote speaker Raffi Hamparian of the 2006 Armenian Genocide commemoration in Las Vegas put it, the "cause for genocide recognition is in good hands because it is in your hands."[46] This community activism is reflected in the dissatisfaction that some feel with local media coverage of Armenian events. As a woman at the same event remarked, "Why did the *Review-Journal* not cover this event today?" She was particularly frustrated in light of the fact that the paper dedicated a whole section to remembering the Jewish Holocaust, an event that is also marked on April 24.

Other members of the Las Vegas political community, however, did recognize the importance of the event for Armenians. The commemoration drew comments from Las Vegas mayor Oscar Goodman and support from other politicians listed in the program, including John Ensign, Shelley Berkley, and Jon Porter. On April 20, 2008, an event commemorating the 93rd anniversary of the Armenian Genocide was held on the UNLV campus, featuring Armen Liloyan, the Republic of Armenia's consul general in Los Angeles, as the keynote speaker. Today, plans are in the works for a memorial to the Armenian Genocide at Floyd Lamb Park in Las Vegas.

Building Las Vegas While Forging Community

Las Vegas has seen the rise of a number of prominent Armenians who have helped to build and have promoted the status of the community here and abroad. The best known of this group include Kirk Kerkorian, Jerry Tarkanian, and Andre Agassi, whose father is of Armenian descent.[47] Both Kerkorian and Tarkanian continue to have a presence in both the Armenian and the larger Las Vegas communities.

Kirk Kerkorian, known as "the father of the megaresort,"[48] made his start in Las Vegas shuttling tourists to the small desert community from California in the 1940s on his Trans International Airlines. He used part of the profits from the enterprise to start a Las Vegas hotel, the International, which opened in 1969 as "the world's largest resort hotel."[49] His success as a developer continued as he bought up more land on the Strip and in 1973 completed his Hollywood-themed MGM Grand (today's Bally's) megaresort, a project made possible by his purchase of MGM studios. In early 2000, his company paid 6.4 billion dollars in a hostile takeover of Steve Wynn's Mirage Corporation.[50]

Born in Fresno in 1917 and moving with his family to Los Angeles during the Depression, Kerkorian has maintained strong ties to the Armenian diaspora from the beginning. Industry watchers noted his ethnicity early on. Journalist Susan Gould chose to introduce Kerkorian to her readers this way: "One of the most unpretentious phenomena around Las Vegas these days is the son of an Armenian fruit peddler named Kirk Kerkorian."[51] When his airline company started to grow in the 1960s, a significant number of California Armenians invested in his stock. Today, he uses part of his multibillion-dollar wealth to fund his charity, the Lincy Foundation, which has donated millions of dollars to Armenian causes in the United States and Armenia. In particular, he has focused on economic development in Armenia, pledging 200 million dollars to rebuilding infrastructure damaged by the 1988 earthquake.[52]

Jerry Tarkanian helped build Las Vegas in a different way. The famous and always controversial UNLV basketball coach led the Rebels to a National Collegiate Athletic Association (NCAA) championship, four Final Four appearances, and twelve NCAA postseason tournaments during his almost twenty-year tenure, earning him a permanent spot on almost all lists of the most influential Las Vegans.[53] This status, however, was earned at the expense of serious allegations made by the NCAA against Tarkanian's recruitment methods that dated back to the late 1970s. The long battle with the NCAA finally ended with the NCAA paying Tarkanian a $2.5 million-dollar settlement in 1998.[54]

One of the most winning coaches in the modern era was born in Ohio in 1930 and later attended Fresno State University on an athletic scholarship. He was part of a generation of Armenian Americans, like Kerkorian, who came of age during a formative period in the Armenian diaspora in the West. The Armenian Genocide cast a long shadow for Tarkanian, whose mother had fled Eastern Anatolia in 1915. For Armenians in Las Vegas, Fresno, and throughout the diaspora, Jerry Tarkanian would always be a hero. (I remember attending a lunch in honor of Tarkanian sponsored by Fresno State University basketball boosters at my church in Fresno during the late 1980s, when UNLV played the home team.) After resigning from UNLV amid mounting controversy in 1992, he was embraced by his alma-mater community, and Fresno's Armenians got their wish: an Armenian coach for their university.

The Tarkanian family continues to have a highly visible presence in the Las Vegas community. The basketball court at the UNLV's Thomas and Mack Center was named for Jerry Tarkanian, and Lois and Jerry Tarkanian Middle School was dedicated in April 2007 in Southern Highlands. Lois Tarkanian, Jerry's wife of fifty years, has served as a councilwoman for Ward 1 and remains interested in issues affecting the local Armenian community. As the first non-Armenian in her husband's family, she once remarked that she had "a lot to learn." Today she is engaged in the establishment of the Armenian Genocide Memorial, a project that she called "an imminent thing for the Armenian community."[55] Her son, Danny Tarkanian, has also entered public life in Las Vegas and is currently involved with the Tarkanian Basketball Academy.

Conclusion

For the city's Armenians, Las Vegas no longer represents an outpost in the desert, but is a place to put down roots, start businesses, and build community. The transnational and translocal connections that many still have with their families, whether in Armenia, Russia, the Middle East, other regions in the United States, or other locales, have served to strengthen rather than divide the local Armenian community. This connectedness has given many a sense of collective identity that continues to thrive in a region that still welcomes new arrivals. Many still adhere to the spirit of Pulitzer Prize-winning Armenian American author William Saroyan, who, having seen the horrors of genocide and war, came to understand ethnic identity in terms of community bonds rather than geography. As he wrote in 1935:

There is a small area of land in Asia Minor that is called Armenia but it is not so. It is not Armenia. It is a place. There are plains and mountains and rivers and lakes and cities in this place, and it is all fine, it is all no less fine than all the other places of the world, but it is not Armenia, since there is no Armenia. There are only Armenians, and these inhabit the earth, not Armenia, since there is not Armenia, gentlemen, there is no America and there is no England, and no France, and no Italy there is only the earth. . . . See if the race will not live again when two of them meet . . . a couple of Armenians talking in the world.[56]

Notes

1. Victoria Tusan, interview with author, 1990.

2. Robert Mirak, *Torn Between Two Lands: Armenians in America, 1890 to World War I* (Cambridge: Harvard University Press), 1983; Roger Daniels, *Coming to America: A History of Ethnicity and Immigration in American Life* (New York: Perennial), 2002, chap. 7; *North American Armenians* (New Haven: Human Relations Area Files, 1996); Charles Mahakian, *The History of the Armenians in California* (San Francisco: R and E Research, 1974).

3. Stephan Thernstrom, ed., *Harvard Encyclopedia of Ethnic Groups* (Cambridge: Harvard University Press, 1980), 136–37.

4. Thernstrom, *Harvard Encyclopedia,* 138.

5. David Bloxham, *The Great Game of Genocide: Imperialism, Nationalism, and the Destruction of the Ottoman Armenians* (Oxford: Oxford University Press, 2005); Melvin Ember, Carol R. Ember, and Ian Scoggard, eds., *Encyclopedia of Diasporas* (New York: Kluwar Acadmic/Plenum, 2004), 43; Merrill D. Peterson, *"Starving Armenians": America and the Armenian Genocide, 1915–1930 and After* (Charlottesville: University of Virginia Press), 2004.

6. Thernstrom, *Harvard Encyclopedia,* 136.

7. Alex Cohn, "Cultural Summary: North American Armenians" (New Haven: Human Relations Area Files, 1996), 4.

8. Ember, Ember, and Scoggard, *Encyclopedia of Diasporas,* vol. 1, 44.

9. "Armenian Orphans' Present," *Las Vegas Age,* October, 21, 1905.

10. "Laughs," *Las Vegas Age,* May 14, 1910; "Making Butter in Armenia," *Las Vegas Age,* April, 20, 1907.

11. "The Armenian Quarter of Shusha," *Las Vegas Age,* March, 17, 1906; "Solve Mystery of Priest's Murder," *Las Vegas Age,* July 6, 1907; "War Increases Violence," *Las Vegas Age,* June 23, 1906; "Leave Refugees to Face Famine," *Las Vegas Age,* June 12, 1909.

12. "Men Massacred, Women Abused," *Las Vegas Age,* May 15, 1909; "Over 1,000 Shot in Turkish Riots," *Las Vegas Age,* April 24, 1909; "Turkey: A Remnant of

146   The Armenians

Powerful Nation," *Las Vegas Age,* December 23, 1911; "Turk is Likable—Yet Fiendishly Cruel," *Las Vegas Age,* March 16, 1912.

13. "Near East Situation," *Las Vegas Age,* January 24, 1920.

14. "Women War Workers, Eager to Serve, Go to Aid Armenians," *Las Vegas Age,* January 10, 1920; "Death Rate Drops when Relief Arrives," *Las Vegas Age,* January 24, 1920.

15. "Near East Relief," *Las Vegas Age,* January 24, 1920; "Will you Give?" *Las Vegas Age,* December 6, 1924.

16. "Telegraphic News," *Las Vegas Age,* May 14, 1910; "Telegraphic Brevities," *Las Vegas Age,* January 4, 1908.

17. "Overton Brevities," *Las Vegas Age,* October 21, 1911.

18. "University President to Visit High Schools," *Las Vegas Age,* March, 8, 1924.

19. Thernstrom, *Harvard Encyclopedia,* 142.

20. "Quite So" and "Quite a Difference," *Las Vegas Age,* June 5, 1920.

21. Founding members included William Derderian, Owen Khatoonian, and George Gogian. Andy Armenian, e-mail correspondence, April 25, 2008.

22. "Committed to Remember," *Las Vegas Sun,* April 23, 2005; U.S. Census Bureau, *American Community Survey,* "Table B04001, First Ancestry Reported-Nevada, 2006," http://factfinder.census.gov/ (accessed July 15, 2008).

23. Koko and Hourig Darakjian, interview by author, January 20, 2007.

24. I initially came to know about this church, Armenian Apostolic Church of Las Vegas Western Diocese, through an ad in the Yellow Pages when we first moved to Las Vegas in 2001. However, I had difficulty obtaining any specific information about services when I called the church itself.

25. The Darakjians, for example, expected their in-laws from Michigan to move to Las Vegas in Spring 2007. Others, like the Armenian family, whose first members settled here five years ago, have seen relatives who lived in other places in the United States and abroad join them in Las Vegas. Hera Armenian, interview by author, March 10, 2007.

26. "Freed from Immigration Custody," *Las Vegas Review-Journal,* January 29, 2005.

27. Hera Armenian, interview by author, March 6, 2007.

28. Ember, *Encyclopedia of Disaporas,* 36–37.

29. Ibid.

30. Andy Armenian, current Parish Council president for the Western Prelacy Armenian Apostolic Church of Las Vegas, provided information on the history of the church. Andy Armenian, e-mail correspondence, April 23, 2008.

31. A different visiting priest from California performs the service each month. Koko Darakjian, interview by author, January 20, 2007.

32. Very Reverend Father Asbed Balian, interview by author, March 10, 2007.

33. Pastor Dr. Kegham Tashjian, interview by author, March 10, 2007.

34. Homenetmen Las Vegas "Artsakh" Chapter information flyer, 2006.

35. "Homenetmen's Mission," organization brochure, Homenetmen Western United States, 2000.

36. Ibid.

37. Armenian Relief Society of Western USA, Inc., brochure.

38. The chapter currently has thirty-nine active members. Houry Darakjian, interview by author, January 20, 2007. The current ARS Shoushi Chapter president is Siroun Bedirian.

39. Armenian American Cultural Society of Las Vegas Membership and Donation Form for 2006.

40. My father belonged to the Fresno Chapter when I was growing up, and I remember attending their annual Christmas party at the lodge. Recently, members of the Las Vegas Chapter traveled to Fresno along with their families to attend the annual convention. Hera Armenian, interview by author, March 6, 2007.

41. Ibid.

42. As quoted by Ed Koch, "Committed to Remember," *Las Vegas Sun,* April 23, 2005.

43. Ibid.; Ed Koch, "Armenain Left a 'Lasting Legacy,'" *Las Vegas Sun,* April 22, 2006; "Why is it OK to Deny Armenian Genocide?," reprinted in the *Las Vegas Review-Journal* from the *Los Angeles Times,* March 16, 2006.

44. The high-profile trials in 2006 of Elif Shafak, Perihan Magden, and Orhan Pamuk for "insulting Turkishness" by discussing the Armenian Genocide, under Article 301 in the Turkish code, drew worldwide attention to the Turkish attitude of silencing critics on this issue. *Guardian Unlimited,* online, August 3, 2006.

45. "Armenian Editor Is Slain in Turkey," *New York Times,* January 20, 2007.

46. 91st Armenian Genocide Commemoration, April 23, 2006, sponsored by the Armenian-American Cultural Society of Las Vegas.

47. Though Andre Agassi is currently not actively involved with the Armenian community in Las Vegas, his father, Mike, strongly identified the family with his Armenian past in his memoir, where he describes his immigration from Tehran to the United States during the 1950s. The family name had been "Agassian" before the telltale "ian" that indicated one was of Armenian descent was dropped "as a skin saving measure during a time when Turks frequently used Armenians for target practice." Mike Agassi, *The Agassi Story* (Toronto: ECW Press, 2004), 12. My grandfather did the same thing for a different reason. He dropped our "ian" to stave off prejudice against Armenians by potential customers and suppliers for his raisin-packing business, Tusan Packing, during the 1950s in California's Central Valley.

48. A. D. Hopkins and K. J. Evans, eds., *The First 100: Portraits of the Men and Women Who Shaped Las Vegas* (Las Vegas: Huntington Press, 1999), 178.

49. Eugene Moehring, *Resort City in the Sunbelt: Las Vegas, 1930-1970* (Reno: University of Nevada Press, 1995), 120–21.

50. Hal Rothman, *Neon Metropolis: How Las Vegas Started the Twenty-First Century* (New York: Routledge, 2002), 22, 28.

51. Susan Gould, "Kirk Kerkorian," *Signature* (September 1969): 31.

52. Berge Bulbulian, *The Fresno Armenians: History of a Diaspora Community* (Fresno: Press at California State University, Fresno, n.d.), 189–90.

53. Hopkins and Evans, *The First 100*, 242–44; Richard O. Davies, ed. *The Maverick Spirit: Building the New Nevada* (Reno: University of Nevada Press, 1999), 249.

54. Davis, *Maverick Spirit*, 269; Don Yaeger, *Shark Attack: Jerry Tarkanian and His Battle with the NCAA and UNLV* (New York: Harper Collins, 1992).

55. Plans were underway to have the site ready in 2009. Lois Tarkanian, remarks given at the Western Prelacy Church Dinner Reception, March 10, 2007.

56. William Saroyan, "The Armenian and the Armenian," *Inhale and Exhale* (New York: Random House, 1936).

CHAPTER 8

The Argentines

GUILLERMO MONKMAN

Argentina is a country of immigrants. Located in the southern portion of South America, Argentina is about one-third the size of the United States and has approximately thirty-nine million inhabitants. The official language is Spanish, and the country's capital is Buenos Aires. Beginning with the arrival of the Spanish in the mid-1500s, waves of mostly European immigrants made their homes in Argentina. As in the United States, the indigenous population was relatively small in number and was mostly wiped out by disease and war. Only in the northern regions of the country was there a large enough indigenous presence to produce a considerable mestizo (mixed Spanish and Indian) population.[1]

Close to 90 percent of Argentina's population is made up of descendants of immigrants from Italy and Spain, most of whom arrived in the late 1800s and early 1900s. Argentina has also received immigrants from most other European countries, including England, Scotland, Wales, Poland, Hungary, Ukraine, Russia, Croatia, Armenia, Germany, France, and Switzerland. It is commonly said that if you are a European American, you have cousins in Argentina. More recently, immigration to Argentina has originated in Syria, Lebanon, Japan, Korea, and post-Soviet eastern Europe. Argentina has also been a magnet for immigrants from neighboring South American countries. The country is predominantly Catholic, but there is also a substantial Jewish presence, mostly in the city of Buenos Aires.[2]

Immigrants went to Argentina for many of the same reasons for which they came to the United States. Some went seeking economic opportunities denied them in their own countries. Others went escaping war, conscription, religious persecution, or political oppression. During certain periods, the Argentine government paid the passage for tens of thousands of European immigrants and, because initially land was plentiful, provided some of them with inexpensive, yet excellent, farmland. These immigrants greatly contributed to transforming Argentina into one of the world's largest agricultural exporters. By the early 1900s, the Argentine economy was ranked among the most successful and fastest growing in the world, attracting large numbers of

European factory workers and merchants to several industrial cities throughout the country. It is estimated that between 1870 and 1930, over seven million immigrants made their way to Argentina. Immigration declined in the 1930s because of the worldwide economic depression, but it increased again during the Spanish civil war (1936–39) and after World War II.[3]

Argentina became a republic following independence from Spain in 1816, but democracy was quite limited until the 1910s. The landed oligarchy ran most levels of government in an authoritarian yet paternalistic manner. In spite of this, Argentina was attractive to immigrants because it was mostly an open and tolerant society. Though officially a Catholic country, religious freedom was the norm. Ethnic and racial discrimination was minimal, but European immigrants who tried to spread anarchist or communist ideas among the Argentine working class were persecuted.

Beginning in 1930, the military became a key player in Argentine politics. As an ally of the upper class, and on other occasions to "save the country" from disorder or the perceived threat of communism, the armed forces have orchestrated several overthrows of democratically elected governments. From 1930 to 1983, military officers, or civilians backed by the military, ran the Argentine government over 60 percent of the time. During these five decades, the persecution and killing of tens of thousands of Argentines for political reasons became a common occurrence, especially during the 1955–56, 1966–73, and above all during the 1976–83 period, known as the "dirty war." Since 1983, democracy has been restored in Argentina, and the military has been almost completely discredited in the eyes of the vast majority of the population.[4]

While the Argentine economy flourished in the early decades of the twentieth century, it began to slow in the 1950s and to decline beginning in the 1970s. From the 1980s on, severe economic crises gripped the country every few years, occasionally leading to hyperinflation and high unemployment. In spite of this, immigrants continued to arrive in Argentina. Unlike immigrants to Argentina in the early 1800s and early 1900s, these immigrants were primarily from poorer countries in eastern Europe and Asia. Furthermore, since the 1950s, Argentina has attracted hundreds of thousands of immigrants from several neighboring countries. Many of them became rural workers in the areas bordering Chile, Bolivia, and Paraguay. Others flocked to urban centers throughout Argentina, especially Buenos Aires, and became industrial workers and service-sector employees. The city of Buenos Aires has also attracted many professionals, artists, scientists, and technicians from countries in the region. Recent studies have shown that over 1.5 million people, or about 5 percent of Argentina's population, are foreign born; of these, about 900,000 are from neighboring countries.[5]

Argentine Emigration

As is the case with any country that has received considerable immigration, Argentina has seen its share of immigrants return to their places of origin or move on to other countries. Argentina also receives tens of thousands of seasonal migrants from neighboring countries every year. Occasionally, when the economy suffers a severe downturn, a significant number of recent immigrants return to their native countries. Over time, some native-born Argentines themselves have chosen to emigrate to other parts of the world for a myriad of reasons. However, it was not until the 1960s that considerable numbers of Argentines began leaving the country in search of a better life abroad.

Beginning with the 1930 overthrow of an elected government and with each subsequent military coup, thousands of Argentines periodically left the country to avoid discrimination, persecution, or even execution. Often, these political émigrés returned when a new government took power, but many of them remained in their newly adopted countries. Mostly for ideological reasons, many of those persecuted or removed from their jobs were university professors, teachers, and other intellectuals, who were eagerly welcomed in the countries where they sought refuge.

Many more were professionals, especially doctors, scientists, engineers, and technicians—products of Argentina's excellent system of education—who began leaving and continue to leave because of limited opportunities at home and greater economic rewards abroad. In addition to this, many developed countries have selective immigration policies, which particularly target young, skilled immigrants and their families. This combination of push and pull forces has been, and continues to be, a dominant feature of skilled emigration from Argentina. This "brain drain," which has severely affected the country's economic development, has been thoroughly documented by several Argentine organizations over the past half-century. On occasion, democratically elected governments have tried to implement "repatriation" programs, providing incentives for these exiled professionals to return, but with little success.[6]

From 1960 to 1970, an estimated 185,000 Argentines emigrated, and the number rose to over 200,000 in the following decade. Most of those leaving during this time were professionals and highly skilled workers, and their destinations were mainly western Europe, the United States, Mexico, and Venezuela. Emigration escalated during the last military dictatorship (1976–83); over 300,000 Argentines chose or were forced to leave the country for political reasons during this highly repressive period. While a few thousand of those political exiles returned after the fall of the dictatorship, most remained abroad.[7]

During the 1990s, severe and recurring economic crises in Argentina, coupled with strong demand for workers in developed countries, resulted in major increases in emigration. Favorable visa policies in Spain, Italy, Israel, and the United States also encouraged hundreds of thousands of Argentines to leave their country. Because Argentine immigrants had the reputation of being highly educated and/or skilled, these and other countries welcomed them with open arms. Also, because of the great distance between Argentina and Europe or the United States and the high cost of passage, the average Argentine immigrant was neither poor nor in need of social services in the host country. Therefore, it was almost unheard of for Argentines to enter or remain illegally in other countries or be deported in significant numbers from European nations or the United States. Beginning in the 2000s, this situation changed dramatically.[8]

In December 2001, the Argentine economy literally disintegrated. The country defaulted on its foreign debt payments, the value of the currency fell by two-thirds, unemployment reached 22 percent (officially), and over 50 percent of the population fell below the poverty line.[9] Moreover, the government compounded the crisis by taking over people's bank accounts in U.S. dollars and returned them in the country's currency, at the low official exchange rate. This maneuver cost thousands of Argentines their life savings and almost destroyed the banking industry. As a result of all this, hundreds of thousands of people took to the streets in protest. After police killed dozens of protesters, the president resigned and hastily transferred power to a new administration, launching a brief period of political instability.

The 2001 economic meltdown greatly increased the number of Argentines leaving the country. While exact numbers are impossible to gather, most estimates point to over 260,000 new émigrés between late 2001 and mid-2003. Although the number of emigrants has decreased since the economy stabilized in 2003, tens of thousands continue to leave every year.[10] Many of them are "invited" by family and friends who have begun to do well in their host countries; others simply have "given up" on Argentina altogether. Many went to Spain and Italy, claiming citizenship because of ancestral ties. Although the European Union has pressured these two countries to adopt more restrictive immigration policies, they continue to welcome the Argentine émigrés. To a large extent, Argentines are still seen as "preferred" immigrants because many of them are highly skilled and, with similar cultures and languages, assimilate easily. Nevertheless, among the waves of Argentines leaving for Europe and the United states since 2001 are a growing number of unskilled and uneducated, who become illegal immigrants after their tourist visas expire. Therefore, it is not surprising that host countries have begun to limit Argentine immigration and regularly deport scores of those residing illegally.

Argentine Immigration to the United States

In 2004 the Argentine consul in New York estimated that there were 1 to 1.5 million Argentines residing outside Argentina, of whom 300,000 to 600,000 were in the United States legally or illegally.[11] This estimate is much larger than the 100,864 recorded in the 2000 census who were found to be living in the United States.[12]

Prior to 1970, the U.S. census lumped immigrants from Argentina together with "other Hispanics." Despite the absence of historical data, there are reasons to believe that tens of thousands of Argentines had come to the United States before that date. As a result of the 1965 Immigration Act, and because of deteriorating political and economic conditions in Argentina, a significant number of professionals and skilled workers began leaving for the United States. Estimates of Argentines residing in the United States, inaccurate as they may be, put the numbers at about 12,000 in 1963 and as high as 75,000 by 1969.[13]

The Argentine population in the United States increased significantly during the extremely repressive military dictatorship of 1976–83, when the government detained, tortured, killed, and disappeared thousands of citizens.[14] In 1977 President Jimmy Carter began to openly criticize the military government's human-rights abuses and offered special visas for Argentines escaping political repression. During the late 1970s and early 1980s, between 20,000 and 40,000 Argentines made their way to the United States.[15] According to census data, there were 92,331 people from Argentina residing in the United States in 1990. Once again, unofficial numbers are much higher, as some Argentines were already staying illegally in the country.[16]

Argentina is a highly urbanized country; greater Buenos Aires alone accounts for some 11 million people, nearly a third of the country's population. Therefore, it is not surprising that the majority of Argentines coming to the United States are from Buenos Aires and other urban areas and that they have tended to settle in large U.S. cities. In the 1980s and 1990s, nearly a quarter of Argentines in the United States resided in the New York metropolitan area. Los Angeles, Chicago, and Miami also have quite large Argentine communities. Over 60 percent of Argentines living in the United

States are found in New York, California, and Florida.[17] While most earlier immigrants from Argentina had been highly educated and skilled, beginning in the 1970s lower middle– and working-class Argentines felt the need to leave because of political repression and economic difficulties. Since the end of the last military government in 1983, economics has been the primary push factor driving emigration. It is not unusual to hear stories of people selling everything they own, and even borrowing money, to make their way to the United States. Many of these immigrants have found employment in restaurants, supermarkets, retail stores, and the tourism industry.

The 1990s saw a steady number of Argentines leaving for the United States. The U.S. census recorded an increase of about 38,000 during that decade, for a total of 131,018 in 2000. The U.S. government facilitated the influx when it instituted a visa-waiver program for Argentina in the mid-1990s in response to the improving Argentine economy. This meant that Argentines traveling to the United States could enter the country and stay up to ninety days without going through the cumbersome process of applying for a visa. While this made it easier for Argentine tourists to visit the United States, the visa-waiver program also allowed for a dramatic increase in illegal immigration. In 2001, for instance, the economic meltdown propelled additional thousands of Argentines northward, many of whom entered legally but overstayed their ninety days. In response, the U.S. government cancelled the visa-waiver program in early 2002, citing the economic crisis and "the increase in the number of Argentine nationals attempting to use the program to live and work illegally in the United States."[18]

The official number of Argentines residing in the United States will not be known until after the 2010 census. Even then, as is the case with other Latin American immigrant groups, Argentines will be undercounted, especially among the growing number of illegal residents. As noted above, some estimate that there are between 300,000 and 600,000 Argentines in the United States. Even the lower number would mean more than a doubling of the total since the 2000 census. Anecdotal evidence from Miami, the principal port of entry for Argentines, sheds light on the accelerated growth of their population. While officially there were 20,000 to 25,000 Argentines in Miami in the early 2000s, Miami and Buenos Aires newspapers put the numbers at around 180,000, close to 75 percent of them undocumented. A significant slowdown in the Miami tourist industry and competition from other Latin American immigrants has made it difficult for many Argentines to find work there. Reflecting the changing nature of Argentine immigrants, churches in the Miami area are providing shelter and food to hundreds of Argentine families. Permanent Argentine residents in Miami have created a number of Web sites to assist recent arrivals; they tell many stories of the perils and suffering of countless Argentine illegals in the area.[19]

While Florida, California, and New York continue to attract the greatest number of Argentine immigrants, a growing number of immigrants are now settling in Nevada, Texas, Arizona, Illinois, and New Jersey, as well as Washington, D.C. There are Argentine associations and clubs in many states and localities, some made up of a few dozen members, while others attract hundreds of people to their social and cultural events. Argentine restaurants and markets, soccer clubs, and tango schools are growing in number in many parts of the country.

Argentines in Las Vegas

As is the case with other immigrant groups, the number of Argentines in the Las Vegas metropolitan area cannot be determined with any certainty. The 2000 census counted 1,309 people of Argentine ancestry in the Las Vegas Valley, while the Lewis Mumford Center estimated 2,435.[20] The census estimate for 2006 is 1,866.[21] The number, however, is likely to be much greater. Especially following the 2001 economic collapse, the number of Argentine arrivals—both legal and illegal—increased dramatically. Leaders of the late Argentine Association of Las Vegas as well as Argentine businessmen estimate that the number of Argentine immigrants in the area is well over 4,000. The number might also be higher because the children of Argentine immigrants who marry outside their national group may or may not be counted as Argentines.

Until the early 2000s, the vast majority of Argentines taking residency in Las Vegas were transplants from other U.S. cities. Many came from the Los Angeles metropolitan area, which has attracted significant Argentine immigrants since the 1950s and where people of Argentine ancestry may number 30,000 or more.[22] Even today, Los Angeles continues to be a gateway for many Argentines moving to Las Vegas. Others have relocated from New York, New Jersey, Houston, and Miami. However, as the number of Argentines in Las Vegas has increased, so has the incidence of direct migration from the home country. Many of these recent arrivals are family members or friends of established Argentine immigrants who have found relative success in the Las Vegas Valley.

Among the first Argentines arriving in Las Vegas in the late 1950s and early 1960s were several musicians and entertainers who found work in the casino industry. David Sailon, a Las Vegas resident since 1958, remembers how a small number of Argentine musicians struggled, and succeeded, in finding steady work in casino orchestras and lounges. Sailon went on to form a musical group, "The Magic Violins," with several other Argentine musicians, the group performing in many Las Vegas venues throughout the 1960s. Another member of the musical group, Oscar Carrescia, established a music shop and became a well-known violin teacher. Carrescia is also the founder and director of the Las Vegas Youth Camerata Orchestra, a much-acclaimed group that has received the Nevada Governor's Arts Award.[23]

During the 1960s, dozens of Argentines trickled into Las Vegas, mostly from the Los Angeles area, attracted by the still slow but steady growth of the casino industry. Anecdotal evidence points to a population of about 100 Argentine residents in the Las Vegas area during that decade. Many of them worked together; most of them knew each other; and they often gathered socially in each other's homes, especially for an *asado* (Argentine barbecue). During the 1970s, the Argentine population remained small, perhaps reaching 300, and most continued to work in hotels, casinos, and restaurants, while a small number of professionals and businessmen also began to settle in Las Vegas. Beginning in the 1970s, several casinos incorporated into their variety shows a gaucho act, which brought a new generation of Argentine entertainers to Las Vegas. It was during this time that the first Argentine restaurant, El Gaucho, opened its doors.

Though smaller in scale, the growth in the Valley's Argentine population has followed a pattern similar to that of Hispanics in general. The number of Hispanics in Clark County doubled in the 1980s and more than tripled in the 1990s. The 2000 census counted 302,143 Hispanics in the Las Vegas metropolitan area, accounting for 22 percent of the population. The Argentine economy deteriorated during the 1980s, pushing many people to emigrate to Europe and the United States. At the same time, economic growth in the Las Vegas Valley became a magnet for Argentines in places such as Los Angeles and Miami. This pattern accelerated in the 1990s. Several new hotels and casinos were built, adding tens of thousands of jobs in the construction and service industries. By 2000 Argentines in Las Vegas exceeded 2,000. Not surprisingly, as many as four Argentine restaurants and markets opened their doors and traditionally Mexican and pan-Hispanic food stores began carrying Argentine products.

In recent years, the Argentine population in the United States has doubled. The growth of Las Vegas's Argentine population mirrors or exceeds this pattern, with an estimated 4,000 to 5,000 Argentines residing in the Las Vegas Valley according to local community leaders. Some of this increase has resulted from illegal immigrants moving into the area in recent years. This is a new phenomenon explained by several factors. In the 1990s, some of the tens of thousands who took advantage of the visa-waiver program made their way to Las Vegas. The national economy also played a role. Following the 2001–2003 economic downturn, competition from other immigrant groups made cities such as Miami and Los Angeles less attractive than Las Vegas for Argentine immigrants. Despite enduring some economic troubles of its own during this time, Las Vegas became a magnet for immigrants and migrants alike. As those illegal immigrants became settled, they helped other undocumented Argentines to make their way to the Valley.

Argentine illegal immigrants tell similar stories about arriving and settling in Las Vegas. Eduardo's story is typical. Unlike undocumented Mexicans and Central Americans, he did not enter the United States by land but arrived as a tourist at an international airport. He came to Las Vegas before the visa-waiver program expired in early 2002, then simply stayed beyond the ninety-day limit, obtained a forged residency card, and—with the help of a relative—got a job. After a couple of years of hard work for very low wages, Eduardo improved his English skills and gained more lucrative employment. He was then able to help his girlfriend come to Las Vegas, and she is following the same steps he did.

Like many other Argentine illegal immigrants, Eduardo and Isabel were closely following the congressional debate over a new immigration bill, which they hoped would result in some form of amnesty. In the meantime, they must deal with more mundane issues faced by others in their situation, such as the difficulty in buying health and automobile insurance and the inability to go back to Argentina to visit family and friends. While entering the United States as a tourist has become more difficult in recent years for other than well-to-do Argentines, some continue to come as tourists and overstay their visas. Because of the presence of a growing number of well-established Argentines who can help and plenty of employment opportunities, Las Vegas continues to attract illegal Argentine immigrants. Furthermore, while the U.S. Immigration and Customs Enforcement (formerly part of the Immigration and Naturalization Service [INS]) has increased its crackdown on illegal immigrants in places such as Miami and Los Angeles, Las Vegas is widely considered a relatively safe place for undocumented immigrants.

Is There an Argentine Community in Las Vegas?

Before the expansion of Las Vegas's Argentine population in the 1990s, Argentines typically socialized in small groups and assimilated rapidly. Community activities were limited for the most part to small numbers of Argentines meeting in restaurants or in their homes. In the 1970s, several Argentine families rented homes near each other and interacted regularly. Historically, however, Argentines in Las Vegas did not settle in predominantly Hispanic neighborhoods, as other Latin American groups have done. In general, Argentine immigrants were likely to speak some English, have higher incomes, and become homeowners more rapidly than some Hispanic immigrant groups. To a large extent, this has resulted in Argentine immigrants' more easily integrating into the broad European American community and spreading throughout the Las Vegas Valley. Recent arrivals, however, many of them illegal and with little or no English language or professional skills, often move into predominantly Hispanic neighborhoods, where the cost of housing is lower.[24]

Many of the Argentines who moved to Las Vegas in the 1960s and 1970s came from the Los Angeles metropolitan area, where they had established an organization to connect the community, sponsor social and cultural events, and help arriving compatriots in their transition to a new country. The Argentine Association of Los Angeles has recently celebrated its fortieth anniversary, but attempts to replicate this type of organization in Las Vegas have failed repeatedly. During the 1980s, a group of Argentines joined with a handful of Uruguayans—their neighbors from the similar but much smaller country across the Río de la Plata, the river separating the two countries—to form the Club Rioplatense. The goal was simply to create a way for Argentines and Uruguayans in Las Vegas to connect and interact with each other. The club attracted a few dozen people, organized a few social events, but faded away after only a few months. In the early 1990s, an attempt was made to create a purely Argentine organization, the Club Argentino, but it also failed to last beyond the early enthusiasm of its founders.[25]

The most successful local Argentine organization to date was established in the early 2000s when several committed individuals founded the Asociación Argentina de Las Vegas (Argentine Association of Las Vegas), a club designed to bring Argentines together and to represent them in the broader Las Vegas community. The association organized picnics, dinners, dances, and cultural events and sought to help recent arrivals connect with local Argentines. The association also participated in Clark County's International Food and Folklife Festival and other ethnic-themed celebrations. While the Argentine Association never had more than a hundred dues-paying members, several events it organized drew large crowds. Nevertheless, this organization met the fate of its predecessors after a couple of years. Today, the only remnant of the association is its Web site, which serves as a bulletin board and "meeting place" for several hundreds of Argentine residents of the Las Vegas Valley and beyond.[26]

Opinions differ among Argentines as to why the community has not been able to establish a lasting organization as other ethnic groups in Las Vegas have done. Some point to the fact that Argentines, in comparison with some other immigrant groups, have more easily integrated into American society and thus have not felt a need for a separate ethnic-based organization to connect and represent them. Because most Argentines have European-like features and blend easily with European Americans, Argentines have not experienced the degree of discrimination and segregation that has brought people of other Hispanic groups together to achieve and defend their civil rights. While Argentines are likely to discuss a return to their home country, most are active participants in the mainstream social, economic, and political life of the United States. Those who have attained U.S. citizenship are likely to vote in American elections and less likely to vote in Argentine elections, even if they retain their original citizenship. Some Argentines feel that they are more individualistic than other Hispanics and prefer to meet in small groups rather than large gatherings. Others think that Argentines are often mistrusting of each other and thus are unlikely to work cooperatively with compatriots they do not know well. In the end, whatever the reasons may be, the Argentine community in Las Vegas has not had the capacity or the motivation to create a lasting organization.

Soccer, *fútbol,* is a passion most Argentines take with them wherever they immigrate.[27] As the Hispanic community began to grow in Las Vegas, several adult soccer leagues were founded throughout the Valley. Teams were often formed by immigrants from the same country or, in the case of Mexicans, the same region of origin. Argentines began forming soccer teams in the 1970s and have actively participated in local tournaments since then.[28]

The Argentine national team normally does very well in the quadrennial World Cup soccer competition organized by the Fedération Internationale de Football Association (FIFA). It has won the world's most prestigious sporting title twice (1978 and 1986) and often reaches the quarter or semifinal rounds. Along with Brazil, Argentina is one of the Western Hemisphere's soccer powers. Thus, Argentines living abroad, including those in Las Vegas, express their nationalism, reaffirm their culture, and live transnationally by following their national team on television.

Until the 1990s, most games involving the Argentine national team were available only on pay-per-view. These games were often shown in Hispanic restaurants, which became social gathering places for dozens of Argentines. Beginning in the mid-1990s, as satellite television expanded the sports menu, an Argentine restaurant began to regularly show not only international matches, but also games of the Argentine major soccer league, allowing the expatriates to relive their team allegiances from home. Once again, this resulted in regularly scheduled gatherings for many Argentine immigrants. While initially uniting Las Vegas's Argentines, however, progress in telecommunications more recently has contributed to dispersing them. Cable and satellite television services have made several Spanish-language television stations, including some from Argentina, available in people's homes. Therefore, an Argentine immigrant today can watch virtually every soccer game from home live, in the comfort of his living room. While a few Argentines may occasionally get together to watch some of these games, gatherings of dozens of Argentines to socialize during a fútbol game have all but disappeared.

Even when well integrated into U.S. culture, immigrants are also interested in news from home, both in the public sphere and in the realm of family and friends. For many years, social gatherings among Argentines were the best way to keep up with news from "back home." Now, because of Spanish-language newspapers published in Las Vegas and Los Angeles, cable and satellite television, and particularly the Internet, it is easier for Argentines in Las Vegas to stay up to date on news from home. But, as with soccer, staying informed is now an individual rather than a collective process and thus does not contribute to community building.

Argentines have a passion for food, inherited mainly from the Spanish and Italian immigrants who settled the country. Argentina is most famous for its beef, pastas, and wines. However, the food itself is not the chief reason why Argentines gather at the dinner table; they are famous for the *sobremesa*, which involves long-lasting conversations, wine, and coffee after the meal is over. From early on, Argentines in Las Vegas have met at each others' homes to prepare and consume traditional Argentine dishes.

Before the 1990s, Las Vegas Argentines were generally unable to enjoy traditional Argentine cuisine in local restaurants and, except for a limited quantity of Argentine groceries on the shelves of Hispanic markets, were forced to travel to Los Angeles to find groceries from home in abundance. Of the handful of Argentine restaurants and markets that opened around 2000, only one remains in business. For over ten years, the Rincón de Buenos Aires restaurant and market, on Spring Mountain Road, has been providing Argentine immigrants, and the community at large, with Argentine-style food and a wide variety of groceries from Argentina and other parts of South America. The Rincón has been a gathering place for Argentine immigrants and visitors. People often came together there to watch soccer games or listen to live performances by Argentine musicians. Furthermore, the Rincón's owners often worked with the Argentine Association of Las Vegas, hosting dinners and fund-raising events and providing supplies for picnics and food festivals. The presence of the Rincón market has ended the need to travel to Los Angeles for Argentine foods.

Most Argentine immigrants, even those who came to Las Vegas decades ago, have relatives in Argentina. While monetary remittances to family have been a common practice among many Hispanic groups, this is a relatively new phenomenon among Argentine immigrants. The severe and repeated economic crises since the early 1980s have made economic assistance from relatives abroad a lifesaver for many in Argentina. Still, the amount of money sent to Argentina by émigrés is rather small compared with that sent by Mexicans, Salvadorans, Colombians, or other Latin Americans. Nonetheless, according to the National Migration Directorate in Buenos Aires, Argentines living abroad remitted 724 million dollars in 2004, triple the 2001 figure.[29]

Conclusion

Conversations with many Argentines in Las Vegas and my personal history as a fifteen-year resident have led me to the conclusion that it is difficult to talk about one single Argentine community in the Valley. As is the case with other immigrant groups, the length of one's residence is a major determinant of attitudes and behaviors. The longer they have been in Las Vegas, the more likely Argentines will be integrated into American society or even "Americanized." On the other hand, most of those who have come in recent years still retain strong ties to Argentina and may even consider returning there in the near future. When they do socialize with their compatriots, those with longer histories in Las Vegas tend to interact with other long-term Argentine residents, while many of the more recent arrivals, including the hundreds of illegal immigrants, form their own subgroups. The failure to create an enduring ethnic-based organization can be seen as evidence of a lack of a sense of community among most Argentines in Las Vegas. Nevertheless, as their presence in the Valley continues to grow, there is little doubt that new attempts will be made to strengthen ties among Las Vegas's Argentines.

Notes

1. For an in-depth look at Argentine history and politics, I recommend the following books: David Rock, *Argentina 1516–1987: From Spanish Colony to Alfonsin* (Berkeley University of California Press, 1987); Daniel K. Lewis, *The History of Argentina* (Westport, Conn.: Greenwood Press, 2001); Gary Wynia, *Argentina, Illusions and Realities* (New York: Holmes and Meier, 1986).

2. Julio Rodríguez, "Argentinean Americans," http://www.everyculture.com/A-Br/Argentinean-Americans.html.

3. María Saenz Quesada, *La Argentina: Historia del país y de su gente* (Buenos Aires: Editorial Sudamericana, 2001), 388.

4. For more on the role of the military in Argentine politics and particularly on the "dirty war" of 1976–83, see Thomas C. Wright, *State Terrorism in Latin America: Chile, Argentina, and International Human Rights* (Lanham, Md.: Rowan and Littlefield, 2007).

5. Maia Jachimowicz, "Argentina: A New Era of Migration and Migration Policy," http://www.migrationinformation.org, February 2006.

6. In "Argentina: Como somos—los argentinos en el exterior," http://www.surdelsur.com/somos.

7. Jachimowicz, "Argentina: A New Era."

8. Migration Policy Institute, "Argentina's Woes Spur Emigration," http://www.migrationinformation.org, July 2003.

9. It is often difficult to know how reliable statistics on employment and poverty in Argentina really are. Most of the media and opposition political parties regularly criticize the Argentine government for underestimating or even manipulating negative socioeconomic indicators. Furthermore, it is important to point out that in Argentina, apart from unemployment, there is usually a significant degree of underemployment present as well, which is close to impossible to measure accurately.

10. Beatriz Busaniche, "Emigrados," Centro de Teletrabajo y Teleformación de la Facultad de Ciencias Sociales de la Universidad de Buenos Aires, http://caminandoutopias.org.ar.

11. Jorge Arguello, *Despacho Abierto*, "El invitado del mes: Hector Timerman—consul argentino en E.E.E.U.U.," http://despachoabierto.com.ar, 2004.

12. U.S. Census Bureau, "Table QT–P9 Hispanic or Latino by Type: 2000," http://factfinder.census.gov/servlet/QTTable? bm=y&-state=qt&-context=qt&-qr name=DEC 2000 sf1 U QTP9&-ds name=DEC 2000 SF1 U&-CONTEXT=qt&-tree id=4001&-redoLog=false&all geo types_N&- caller=geoselect-geo id=01000US&-geo id=38000US4120&-geo id=NESP&-sea (accessed July 18, 2008).

13. Julio Rodríguez, "Argentinean Americans," and "Argentine Immigration," http://www.umich.edu.

14. Exact numbers of those killed by the government during the 1976–83 military dictatorship are still not agreed upon today. While most of those "disappeared" by the government were murdered by security forces in one way or another, others went into exile and some were killed by political organizations. Furthermore, several hundreds of those killed by the military or police were members of guerrilla groups openly fighting against the government. Argentine human-rights organizations have accused the military government of "disappearing" about 30,000 people between 1976 and 1983. Nevertheless, the National Commission on Disappeared Persons (1984) documented that 8,960 people were kidnapped and murdered by the military government. Another 900 people were kidnapped and later released by the

government. Furthermore, 1,898 people were killed by security forces in military-type engagements. Finally, about 900 people were assassinated by right-wing paramilitary forces allied with the government. Taking into consideration that many people did not report relatives as disappeared or murdered, the overall number of people disappeared during the 1976–83 military dictatorship is estimated by reliable sources at between 15,000 and 20,000. See Saenz Quesada, "La Argentina," 661. The disappeared were abducted and taken to secret detention centers, where they were tortured and most were killed. Since the victims were never registered at public jails, they disappeared. For the most part, their bodies have never been recovered.

15. DHS Immigration figures show 29,897 immigrants from Argentina arrived between 1971 and 1980 and 27,327 arrived between 1981 and 1990. http://dhs.gov/ximgtn/statistics/publications/YrBk00Im.shtm, "Table Two" (accessed July 17, 2008).

16. "La otra cara, los que se fueron," http://www.oni.escuelas.edu.ar.

17. Jachimowicz, "Argentina: A New Era"; Rodriguez, "Argentinean Americans."

18. In *Migration News—Latin America,* March 2002, http://www.migration.ucdavis.edu.

19. Guillermo dos Santos Coelho, "Internet, una balsa virtual para los argentinis ilegales en Miami," 4/18/2002; Silvia Heguy, "La crisis de miles de argentinos que viven como ilegales en Miami," 4/10/2002 (both articles from www.clarín.com); Naomi Klein, "Miami or Bust," 10/27/2003 (in www.guardian.co.uk).

20. Lewis Mumford Center, State University of New York at Albany, at http://mumford.albany.edu/census/HispanicPop/HspPopData/4120msa.htm.

21. U.S. Census Bureau, *American Community Survey,* "Table B03001, Hispanic or Latino by Specific Origin, Las Vegas–Paradise, NV Metro Area, 2006," http://factfinder.census.gov/(accessed July 15, 2008).

22. The Lewis Mumford Center estimated the Argentine population in the Los Angeles metropolitan area to be 20,689 shortly after the 2000 census. Taking into consideration the large influx of Argentines into the United States in recent years, it can be estimated that this number has grown considerably.

23. Ron Sailon and Oscar Carrescia, longtime Argentine Las Vegas residents, interviews by author, March 2007.

24. Information gathered during interviews with Argentine residents in Las Vegas. Several individuals interviewed asked that their names not be used, either because they were illegally in the United States or because they did not want to speak on the record about friends who are illegal residents.

25. Osvaldo Montano, Argentine restaurant manager/owner in Las Vegas for over three decades, interview by author, April 2007.

26. Rubén Nervegna, former president of the Argentine Association of Las Vegas, interview by author, February 2007.

27. For more on the social and cultural importance of soccer in Argentine society, see Pablo Alabarces, *Fútbol y patria: El fútbol y las narrativas de la nación argentina* (Buenos Aires: Prometeo, 2002).

28. For more on soccer and the Hispanic community in Las Vegas, see Thomas C. Wright and Jesse Dino Moody, "The Salvadorans," in *The Peoples of Las Vegas: One City, Many Faces,* ed. Jerry L. Simich and Thomas C. Wright (Reno and Las Vegas: University of Nevada Press, 2005), 247–67.

29. Jachimowicz, "Argentina: A New Era."

CHAPTER 9

The Koreans

KATHLEEN JA SOOK BERGQUIST

Korea was an independent kingdom through most of its history. Japan occupied the country after the Russo-Japanese War in 1905 and formally annexed it in 1910. Following World War II, Korea was split between the Soviet-backed north (the Democratic People's Republic of Korea) and the Western-allied south (the Republic of Korea). The north invaded the south in 1950, launching the Korean War (1950–53) and beginning a continuing U.S. military presence in South Korea. Today, the communist north has some 23 million people and the capitalist south nearly 50 million.

The earliest known significant emigration from Korea began in the mid-1800s, when peasants immigrated to Russia and China seeking relief from famine, poverty, and oppression.[1] But it was the Japanese annexation of Korea in 1910 that precipitated emigration on a large scale, both to the region and throughout the world. Deprived of their property and opportunities for employment in Korea, early émigrés went to Japan seeking work. Involuntary migration became prevalent in the late 1930s, when laborers were forced to work in Japan's mines and factories and some 200,000 young Korean "comfort women" were forced to serve Japanese troops in World War II. Between Korea's liberation in 1945 and the start of the Korean War, 1.8 million of the approximately 2.4 million Koreans (Zainichi Koreans) who had immigrated to Japan were able to return.[2]

In 1997 the South Korean government established the Overseas Korean Foundation (OKF), a nonprofit organization under the auspices of the Ministry of Foreign Affairs and Trade. It was created in response to the ever-increasing numbers of Koreans in the diaspora and a desire to "sustain and reinforce the cohesiveness of Korean societies overseas."[3] The OKF and the Institute for International Economics reported in 2003 that approximately 6 million people of Korean origin reside outside of Korea. Eighty-five percent of the "Overseas Koreans" (*Chaewoe tongpo*) reside in Russia (540,000), Japan (640,000), China (1.9 million), and the United States (2.1 million). The OKF purports to be the "home" to all Koreans residing outside of Korea; its goals are maintaining national identity, broadening the Hanminjok (Korean people) network as a virtual community, and establishing business networks.[4] The South Korean government, then, deliberately fosters transnationalism among the diaspora.

From the Land of the Morning Calm to the Land of Opportunity

Immigration from Korea to the United States, from the early 1900s to the present, has been shaped in part by shifting U.S. immigration policies. Korea was the last northeast Asian country to establish diplomatic ties with the United States, and it was not until ratification of the Korean-American Treaty of Amity and Commerce in 1882 that the doors opened for Koreans to immigrate.[5] Thereafter, migration from Korea came in three major waves. The first (1903–24) began in 1903 with the landing of the SS *Gaelic* at Honolulu Harbor carrying 120 men, women, and children.[6] Approximately 7,000 laborers—mostly low-skilled, unaccompanied men with little education—soon followed, with modest desires to work hard and send money back to their families.[7] They nurtured strong emotional ties and dreams of returning to Korea, enduring grueling hours for meager wages.[8] As was the case with immigrants from Japan, China, and the Philippines, the earliest Koreans labored in the sugarcane fields of Hawaii and the orchards of California.

Anti-Japanese sentiment on the mainland resulted in the "Gentlemen's Agreement" of 1907, effectively halting immigration from Japan, and three years later, from its new Korean colony. Although the goal was to stop the importation of Japanese and Korean labor, the agreement did allow those already in the United States to petition to bring parents, spouses, and children to be admitted. The family exception led to the migration between 1910 to 1924 of over 1,000 "picture brides," who were introduced and matched to their husbands through letters and photographs. Subsequently, both the Immigration Act of 1917, which established a "barred zone" to exclude most Asians, and the 1924 Asian Exclusion Act, which eliminated legal Asian immigration, including the petitioning of wives and children, led to a three-decade hiatus in Korean immigration.[9]

The Korean War (1950–53) and the continuing presence of the U.S. military in South Korea spurred the second wave, which lasted until 1965. This and the subsequent wave almost exclusively involved persons from South Korea, as North Korea sealed its borders and prohibited emigration. During this period, more women and children came to U.S. shores. Wives of American soldiers were able to immigrate due to the 1946 War Brides Act; and, following the Korean War, orphaned children were able to be adopted internationally.[10] More than 1,500,000 U.S. troops served during the Korean War. After the war, the number of troops declined, with deployments of between 50,000 and 60,000 during the 1960s and about 40,000 in 2004.[11] Together, military spouses and orphaned children accounted for 77 percent of the migration to the United States following the outbreak of the Korean War through 1965, the wives constituting 40 percent and children 37 percent.[12] The remaining immigrants during the second wave included professional workers and an estimated 6,000 students, many of whom came to the United States to complete their education, which had been interrupted by the war, and who would return to Korea to contribute to its rebuilding.[13]

Harry and Bertha Holt, farmers from Oregon, adopted eight Amerasian children from Korea in 1955 in response to the plight of war orphans. The Holts were instrumental in generating interest in Korean adoption. They brought the needs of Korean orphans into the consciousness of middle America through national media attention and established Holt International Children's Services, which became the largest Korean adoption agency in the United States. Since then, an estimated 100,000 to 150,000 Korean children have been adopted into American homes, constituting the largest international adoption phenomenon in the world.[14]

The 1965 Immigration and Nationality Act (INA) eliminated "national origin" as the basis for immigration policy and paved the way for the third wave (1965–present), the largest migration of Koreans to the United States. The INA created a seven-point system that included occupational and family-based preferences to attract educated and skilled workers and facilitate family reunification. Two-thirds of the current U.S. Korean population arrived after 1970 or were born in the United States.[15]

The explosive growth of the South Korean economy in the 1970s fueled a different pattern of migration, in which individuals left home for reasons other than mere subsistence. Unlike the earlier poorer, low-skilled immigrants, the post-INA arrivals were typically young, college educated, urban, and middle class. However, as with their predecessors, the newer immigrants sought greater opportunities, including access to highly valued U.S. graduate education. While they also maintained significant familial ties to Korea, in part because of greater personal resources, technologies of communication, and ease of mobility, the newer arrivals were more likely to be truly immigrants rather than sojourners. This is reflected in the high rate of naturalization: more than one-half (50.08 percent) of foreign-born Koreans in the United States are naturalized U.S. citizens, compared to 25.5 percent and 22.24 percent for foreign-born Japanese and Mexicans, respectively. Nonetheless, despite graduate degrees and professional training, lack of

English-language proficiency posed barriers for many, leading them into entrepreneurial ventures such as family-owned grocery stores, dry cleaners, and restaurants. Korean immigration to the United States has slowed from more than 30,000 per year at its peak in the 1970s to approximately 15,000 per year today, reflecting increased prosperity and opportunities available in Korea.[16]

The year 2003 marked the centennial of Korean immigration to the United States. The following year, the Census Bureau estimated that there were 1,251,092 people of Korean descent living in the United States.[17] As with other Asian ethnic groups, Koreans established enclaves (Koreatowns) in large cities such as San Francisco, Los Angeles, New York, Seattle, and Chicago. The earliest Koreatown was established in San Francisco in the early 1900s as immigrants entered the mainland from Hawaii.[18] For many, these enclaves provide opportunities for mutual aid, ties to Korean culture and language, social networks, and access to business and commercial resources. They are welcome sanctuaries for new arrivals challenged by the demands of a different culture and language and with different systems to navigate. These communities also provide a buffer from external discrimination and xenophobia, especially for the newly arrived.[19] While playing a pivotal role for immigrant communities, these ethnic enclaves can impede integration.[20]

The 1960s brought significant changes in U.S. racial attitudes and policies. The civil-rights movement and legislation are the most visible manifestations of these developments, but the 1965 Immigration Act provided an opportunity for Asians to enter the United States after decades of restrictive policies.[21] The Voting Rights Act of 1965 eliminated the English-literacy tests to qualify to vote, removing barriers for nonnative speakers.[22] Antimiscegenation laws—which prohibited nonwhites, including Asians, from marrying whites—were found unconstitutional in 1967 following the landmark case, *Loving v. Virginia*. Affirmative Action helped Asian Americans to achieve greater access to education, employment, and housing.[23]

These developments allowed Asian Americans increasingly to leave the urban ethnic enclaves and enter the middle class; but while becoming more integrated into mainstream America, for the most part they retained ties to ethnic organizations and communities.[24] Koreans were no exception to this pattern. Eui-Young Yu, director of the Korean American Center's Census Information Center, reported that the 2000 census revealed a high degree of "scatterness" among Koreans, who are increasingly moving to the South and Southeast, often attracted by high-tech jobs.[25] High rates of entrepreneurship and small-business ownership have also contributed to the growing dispersion of Koreans. Nonetheless, the overwhelming majority of Koreans (96 percent) reside in large metropolitan areas and predominantly in the western states and the Northeast.[26]

Las Vegas Bound

The history of the Korean community in Las Vegas is as unique as Las Vegas itself. Among the earliest and most notable arrivals were a vegetable farmer, a family of entertainers, wives of U.S. military personnel stationed at Nellis Air Force Base, and an entrepreneur who became the industry magazine *Market Watch Leader*'s 2002 Retailer of the Year.

The fourth stop on the "Pioneer Trail," which was constructed in the city's centennial year of 2005 to celebrate the history of Las Vegas, is the Kim Produce Farm. In 1932 Frank Kim and his Hispanic wife, Juanita Sanchez, established a twenty-acre vegetable farm at what was then the northern city limits. Their son, Frank, graduated from Las Vegas High School in 1943 and served in the U.S. Navy during World War II. Afterward, he returned to Las Vegas to build his career. Kim was a "homebuilder, craftsman, landscape architect, pilot," and most significantly, a distinguished thirty-year veteran of the Las Vegas Metropolitan Police Department. Kim's legacy includes an elementary school named in his honor, where he is remembered as a man who "overcame prejudice by displaying a presence of dignity directed toward everyone he met."[27]

Other notable early arrivals were entertainers. The Kim Sisters, Sook-ja, Ai-ja, and Mia, came to Las Vegas in 1959.[28] Sent by their mother, the underage sisters traveled alone. The only English they knew were the lyrics to the Maguire Sisters' and Andrews Sisters' songs they had memorized. Sook-ja, the eldest, recalled the challenges of adjusting to a new culture and expressed deep cravings for the red pepper and garlic flavors of kimchee, the national dish of Korea.[29] "We didn't know what to make. Ai-ja got yellow *hwang-dal* [jaundice] . . . because we couldn't have kimchee. The food was a big battle. We could not get kimchee in those days. We could not make it, we could not buy it. So, we were literally sick about our food. We used to pick up the phone and cry to our mother. We needed kimchee."[30]

Upon arriving in Las Vegas, the sisters sang in the *China Doll Revue* twice weekly for four weeks at the Thunderbird Hotel. At the end of their contract they moved to the Stardust Hotel, where they performed six days a week for almost nine months. Impressed by their fresh young talent, Ed Sullivan invited them to perform on his national television show after seeing them at the Stardust. Their television appearances and a feature story in *Life Magazine* boosted their careers. The Kim Sisters became a permanent fixture on the Strip, headlining at the Stardust eight to nine months per year until 1974, while touring throughout the United States and Europe the rest of the year. They continued to perform together until 1991, including five years at the Las Vegas Hilton and eleven years at the Holiday Casino. The Kims, like most early Koreans in Las Vegas, used family-based immigration preferences to reunite their family in Las Vegas, sponsoring as many as forty-five relatives.[31]

The Korean War launched the second wave of Korean immigration to the United States, in which military brides figured prominently. The continuing presence of a large U.S. military contingent in South Korea has been responsible for an ongoing migration of military wives. Las Vegas has shared in the military-wives phenomenon through the presence of Nellis Air Force Base, which has operated as a training base for fighter pilots since the outbreak of the Korean War.[32] In Las Vegas, as in military towns throughout the United States, these women have often struggled with culture shock, isolation, and the difficulties of being far from family. In her study of Korean wives of American soldiers, Ji-Yeon Yuh concluded that limited English-language skills and a general unfamiliarity with American culture left many unable to adjust. Their isolation comes not only from cultural displacement, but often from stigmatizion by other Koreans who assume that they were camp-town prostitutes or that they married Americans just to escape poverty.[33] In an effort to support local air force wives, Chon Edwards, a community activist and Korean-born wife of a retired American embassy worker, founded the Las Vegas Korean American Women's Association (KAWA) in 1998.[34] Although the number of Nellis Air Force Base personnel who have Korean wives is unknown, the association remains active, providing a welcoming community for its members and cultural outreach to the greater Las Vegas community.[35]

Hae Un Lee chose to relocate his wife and three children to join relatives in Las Vegas in 1980. Although a bureaucrat in Seoul's Ministry of Health and Social Affairs, Lee arrived in the Valley with an entrepreneurial spirit. Like many new immigrants, he soon found that his lack of fluency in English presented barriers to employment, leading him eventually to conclude that he would have to create his own economic opportunities. The idea for Lee's Discount Liquor Stores was born out of observations that he was able to negotiate liquor purchases at a local grocery store without speaking English. Lee exemplifies the American immigrant dream of finding success through hard work and perseverance. He began with no knowledge of the retail liquor business, worked thirteen-hour days only to leave his store to bus tables at a local casino until 1 AM, took naps under his store counter, and was up in the predawn hours to print flyers. Today, he owns ten liquor stores throughout the Valley and beyond. Lee is a very visible member not only of the Korean community, but of the larger Asian and Las Vegas communities. He shares his success with others through Lee's Helping Hands, which donates thousands of dollars annually to local charities. Lee is active in local politics and has been described as a "formidable contact."[36]

Frank Kim Jr. and his father may have been the first Koreans in Las Vegas. When the Kim Sisters, the early military wives, and Hae Un Lee arrived, there was nothing but the skeletal beginnings of a Korean community. Lieutenant Benjamin Kim of the Metropolitan Police Department, who moved to Las Vegas in the early 1970s with his family, recalled that encountering other Koreans was rare and remembered the only Korean markets and restaurants as being in the Commercial Center.[37] Similarly, Hae Un Lee recalled that upon his arrival in 1980 there was only a handful of small Korean grocery stores and restaurants. This is in sharp contrast with the over thirty Korean restaurants that now feed the need for cultural connectedness that the early Kim Sisters so desperately craved.

Making a Home in the Desert

Las Vegas was identified as one of five "emerging communities" in a 2006 Asian American Justice Center report that examined the growth of Asian and Pacific Islander (API) populations in the United States.[38] In 2006 Clark County's API population was estimated at 134,067, or 7.6 percent of the county's total.[39] Koreans were the fifth largest Asian community in Clark County in 2006, after Filipinos, Chinese, Japanese, and Vietnamese. The census-counted Korean population nearly doubled between 1990 and 2000, from 3,376 to 6,618. Koreans comprised 0.4 percent of the Clark County population and 6 percent of the county's Asian population. The Korean population is expected to continue to grow through both migration and immigration. James Moon Jae Yu, chairman of the Las Vegas Asian Chamber of Commerce, attributed the increase in part to opportunities in the gaming industry, where many service positions do not require English-language proficiency.[40] Along with military wives, those who arrive through immediate relative- or family-based petitions, and those drawn to work in the service and entertainment industry, there are growing subgroups of 1.5th-generation (Korean Americans who immigrated to the U.S. as children) and 2nd-generation professionals and international university students. Pull factors to the Las Vegas area include affordable housing, proximity to the West Coast, and opportunities in hotel-casino, health-care, financial, and other industries.

Newer arrivals in the Las Vegas Valley are more likely than earlier Korean immigrants to hail from within the United States, most notably from

California. Writing prior to the recent volatility in the Las Vegas housing market, William Frey, a demographer with the Brookings Institute, cited the tight housing market in California as a cause for "spillover" residents moving to Las Vegas.[41] The attraction of Las Vegas as an affordable, livable city with boundless growth potential, opportunity, proximity to the West Coast, and easy access to the world through McCarran International Airport has made it a more viable place to build families and lives, rather than just a venue for vacations.

The infrastructure of Korean communities in the United States consists of a network of churches, civic associations, Korean-language newspapers, restaurants, small businesses, and, in some cases, either a formal or informal Koreatown. At the heart of the cultural life of the Las Vegas Korean community are the more than thirty churches that provide members places to congregate, to maintain social networks, and to foster ties to Korean language and traditions. The Presbyterian Church is the largest Christian denomination in Korea and in Korean American communities throughout the United States, including Las Vegas.[42] Local Korean churches also include Catholic, Methodist, Baptist, Assembly of God, and Salvation Army congregations. The seven or more Korean-language newspapers published in Las Vegas provide news from overseas and about the larger Las Vegas community.[43] The *Korean Central Daily* and LasVegasKorea.com represent a segment of the print and Internet-based media outlets in the Valley. The seemingly disproportionate number of churches and newspapers in the Korean community is in part a function of U.S. immigration policy, which provides for temporary work visas for religious workers and journalists.[44]

There are also a dozen or more civic and community organizations that reflect the community structure. Most metropolitan Korean American communities have a Korean association comprised primarily of first-generation members that provides cultural and educational links to the larger community. The Las Vegas Korean Association, with offices near downtown, publishes a resource directory for the Korean community that provides detailed listings of Korean-owned businesses and services, as well as information on immigration, English as a Second Language (ESL) classes, and other matters important to the community. There is an array of other special-interest and civic organizations, including the Korean Women's Association, the Korean Senior Citizens' League, the Korean Golf Association, the Nevada Korean Athlete Association, the Korean Soccer Association, the Korean Tennis Association, the Korean Chamber of Commerce, the Nevada Tae Kwon Do Association, and the Korean Church Association. Two formal organizations serve the social and welfare needs of the local Korean community: the Korean Family Counseling Center and the Korean Salvation Army.[45]

While, until recently, Las Vegas has had no formal Koreatown, the half-century-old Commercial Center, located at Sahara Avenue and State Street between Las Vegas Boulevard and Maryland Parkway, has long served as the unofficial Koreatown. The Commercial Center is home to several Korean as well as other Asian restaurants and markets that locals frequent. Over the years, the restaurants have served as community gathering places, including hosting the Korean Women's Association's monthly meetings.[46] More recently, the developers of Las Vegas's commercial Chinatown, established in 1995 along Spring Mountain Road west of the Strip, have encouraged pan-Asian investment, providing an alternative location for Korean-owned businesses, including a number of Korean barbecue restaurants and markets.

As of 2007, Las Vegas has a formal Koreatown Plaza at the northeast corner of Spring Mountain and Rainbow Boulevard, strategically positioned less than three miles west of Chinatown. According to James Yu, the 60,000-square-foot plaza under construction will include a Han Nam Korean supermarket, food court, and other retailers and businesses.[47] Despite the concentration in the Commercial Center, Chinatown, and the Koreatown in progress, Korean-owned businesses are not limited to ethnic enclaves. Indeed, many businesses, including neighborhood sushi restaurants located in strip malls throughout the Valley, are Korean owned.

Mirroring the growth of the Korean population is the increase in the number of professionals serving the community. There are over sixty Korean American realtors in the Las Vegas market and over thirty loan officers. There are currently three Korean-owned banks based in Los Angeles that have established loan offices in Las Vegas, including Wilshire State Bank. Manager Jinho Huh explained that Wilshire was attracted to the changing demographic of Las Vegas, which included an influx of Korean Americans from Hawaii and California seeking to do banking in Korean. The first Asian-owned bank in the Valley opened in May 2007, with staff purported to speak Chinese, Thai, Korean, Japanese, and Tagalog. The First Asian Bank's goal is to serve small Asian-owned businesses and "provide financial products for importing from or exporting to the Pacific." James Yu and Hae Un Lee represent the Korean community on the bank's board of directors.[48]

As the institutions of higher education in southern Nevada have grown, so has the enrollment of Korean and Korean American students. The University of Nevada, Las Vegas (UNLV) reported 3,797 Asian American students, including undergraduate, graduate, and professional students, in the fall semester of 2006, comprising 13.6 percent of the student population. In addition, UNLV reported 538 Korean international students in 2006, comprising approximately 45 percent of the Asian international students and almost 38 percent of all international students.[49] With over 250 Korean international students, the William F. Harrah College of Hotel Administration has the largest concentration of Korean students on campus and has established research and academic relationships with Kyung Hee and Yongsan Universities in Korea.[50] UNLV has a Korean Student Association, comprised primarily of international students, whose goal is to provide cultural education and outreach and "a sense of unity for both Korean and non-Korean students." Its function is similar to that of community-based Korean churches, offering a "safe haven" for students who are often culturally and linguistically isolated and "social comfort, identity development, and/or community advocacy."[51]

The College of Southern Nevada (CSN) reported 4,017 Asian American students in the fall semester of 2006, or nearly 11 percent of its student body. CSN also had 230 Korean international students, 36 percent of the international student body.[52] Reflecting the needs of Korean and other international students, both UNLV and CSN offer ESL classes. CSN also offers Korean-language classes in its Department of International Languages.[53]

Las Vegas's connection to Korea has become more formal and extends beyond the presence of the local Korean community. A sister-city relationship was developed with AnSan, South Korea, two decades ago.[54] According to Jim Doumas, deputy executive director of Sister Cities International, the affiliation began in 1987 during an economic-development mission to AnSan to promote foreign investment in Las Vegas.[55] AnSan Sister City Park, a fifteen-acre recreational area located in the northwest area of Las Vegas, commemorates that relationship. In 1994 student exchanges between the two cities started.[56] In 2006 Korean Air filled a void left by Japan Airlines when it discontinued service to McCarran International Airport. Korean Air became the only carrier with scheduled nonstop service between Asia and Las Vegas, offering three flights per week.[57] South Korean tourism increased 64.7 percent, from 68,000 visitors in 2004 to 112,000 in 2006. According to Terry Jicinsky, senior vice president of marketing, the Las Vegas Convention and Visitors Bureau hopes to raise the city's foreign visitation from 12 percent today to at least 15 percent by 2010. The bureau considers the flights from Seoul's Incheon International Airport integral to that goal.[58] And, of course, that connection increases the opportunities for Las Vegas's Koreans to live transnationally.

Korean Las Vegas Today

The Korean American community in Las Vegas is remarkable not only for its growth over its more than fifty-year history, but also for the way it reflects the uniqueness that is Las Vegas. New arrivals in the Valley will find a dynamic and thriving Korean community that is both similar to and different from those found in larger cities such as San Francisco, Los Angeles, and New York. For example, Las Vegas's Korean community is largely dispersed and exists without a historic residential and retail center; it maintains strong interethnic/pan-Asian affiliations within the larger Asian American community; and, finally, it is comparatively transient.

Eui-Young Yu's description of Koreans as being scattered rings true in Las Vegas. Without a historical ethnic space, Koreans are dispersed throughout the Valley. They have created communities of interest, rather than communities of locality, through churches and a variety of organizations and through restaurants, markets, newspapers, and other enterprises. At the same time, many Koreans are not connected to the larger Las Vegas Korean community, either by choice or owing to lack of opportunity. Self-selection may play a part: those inclined to venture to a city with a comparatively small Korean community and infrastructure may find such resources to be unnecessary. Furthermore, generational differences can create cultural barriers to participation. Many American-born or -raised Korean Americans do not speak Korean or lack fluency, which limits their ability and inclination to participate in the various associations comprised mainly of first-generation Koreans.

While dispersed, Koreans tend to reside largely in middle-class neighborhoods. On average, Korean families in Las Vegas are young, have three members, and are middle income. According to the 2000 census, the median age of Koreans in Clark County was thirty-eight years, with nearly 83 percent between eighteen and sixty-four years of age. Of the population twenty-five years or older, almost 82 percent had completed a high-school education, while almost one-quarter had completed a bachelors degree or higher. The median family income in 2000 for Korean families in Clark County was $48,953, compared to $51,227 for all Asians, and an overall median income of $50,485.[59]

Interethnic and pan-Asian alliances are common in civic organizations, commercial ventures, and personal relationships in Las Vegas. Koreans have joined and held positions on the boards of several pan-Asian organizations. For example, both the Asian Chamber of Commerce and the Organization for Chinese Americans (OCA) have had Korean Americans as presidents. Similarly, several Korean restaurants and businesses are located in and around Chinatown, and the new Koreatown Plaza is also situated near Chinatown.

Las Vegas is the most transient city in the United States: seven thousand to eight thousand people reportedly arrive in Las Vegas every month, while three thousand to four thousand leave. The 2000 census found that 63 percent of Nevadans had lived elsewhere five years earlier.[60] This transience is true as well for Las Vegas's Korean community, which tends to be less stable than its cohorts in other U.S. cities. The adage that "no one is from Las Vegas" applies most especially to Koreans in the Valley. The newer arrivals hailing from neighboring states have roots back home, sometimes parents, children, and extended family, making it easy and attractive to return. In 2000 slightly more than 77 percent of Koreans in Las Vegas were still foreign born.[61] Transience and a largely foreign-born population negatively impact the development of social capital, because community involvement is strongly correlated to a sense of connectedness with the community.[62] The existing churches and community organizations primarily serve the first generation; however, the measure of a sustainable ethnic community is its ability to also meet the needs of the younger generations. The relatively slow development of social and community resources within the Korean community that draw participation from the 1.5th and 2nd generations is an indicator of those tenuous roots.

Conclusion

Las Vegas's ties to Korea through tourism, immigration, and the technology that enables transnational living are significant. However, despite the fact that there is some Seoul being infused into Sin City, the size of the Las Vegas Korean community ranks only eighty-first among the one-hundred largest U.S. cities.[63] The Korean footprint in this desert home is still fresh, and because of the transient and diverse nature of the community, it struggles to deepen its imprint. Nonetheless, the early arrivals brought with them a pioneering spirit and a willingness to bet on Las Vegas, working days without end farming the arid land, entertaining and serving in the casinos, supporting military spouses, and nurturing small businesses. In typical Las Vegas style, the Korean community continues to reinvent itself and thrive in the energy and vibrancy of one of the fastest growing metropolitan areas in the nation.

Notes

1. B. B. Pak, *Rossiiskaya diplomatiya i Korea (1860–1888)* [Russian Diplomacy and Korea (1860–1888)] (Moscow-Irkutsk-St. Petersburg, 1998), 22.

2. Eika Tai, "Korean Japanese: A New Identity Option for Resident Koreans in Japan," *Critical Asian Studies* 36, no. 3 (2004): 355–82; Hee-gwan Chin, "Divided by Fate: the Integration of Overseas Koreans in Japan," *East Asian Review* 13, no. 2 (Summer 2001): 43–71.

3. "Overseas Koreans Foundation: Cohesiveness in Good Spirits," *News World*, July 2002, http://www.newsworld.co.kr/cont/0207/74.html.

4. C. Fred Bergsten and Inbom Choi, eds., "The Korean Diaspora in the World Economy," Special Report 15, January 2003, Peterson Institute for International Economics; Jeanyoung Lee Kyunghee, *Ethnic Korean Migration in Northeast Asia*, Kyunghee University, http://gsti.miis.edu/CEAS-PUB/200108Lee.pdf, p. 1; *Founding Background*, Overseas Korean Foundation, http://www.okf.or.kr/eng/introduction/okfFlotation.jsp.

5. Sarah J. Shin, *Developing in Two Languages: Korean Children in America* (Buffalo: Multilingual Matters, 2005), 42; see for example William B. Hauser, *History of Japan*, U.S. Commodore Matthew Perry forced Japan to abandon its seclusionist policy in 1854, leading to the Tokugawa shogun signing commercial treaties with the United States in 1858, http://www.euronet.nl/users/ftv/aikido/history.htm; Consulate General of the United States, Shanghai, *The History of the United States Consulate General in Shanghai*, treaty of "peace, amity, and commerce" between the United States and the Qing Dynasty in 1844, at http://shanghai.usconsulate.gov/consulate_history.html.

6. See *Korean American History*, Smithsonian Asian Pacific American Program, http://www.apa.si.edu/; Linda Sohn, "The Health and Health Status of Older Korean Americans at the 100-year Anniversary of Korean Immigration." *Journal of Cross-cultural Gerontology* 19 (2004): 204. The first group of immigrants consisted of fifty-six men, twenty-one women, and twenty-five children.

7. Shin, *Developing*; "Of the 7,226 immigrants to Hawaii during the years 1903–1905, 6,048 were male adults, 637 women, and 541 children," Lee Houchins and Chang-su Houchins, "The Korean Experience in America, 1903–1924," *Pacific Historical Review* 43 (1974): 554.

8. Shin, *Developing*, 42.

9. *Korean American History*, Smithsonian Asian Pacific American Program, http://www.apa.si.edu. See *Korean American History*, http://www.apa.si/edu; Shin, *Developing*, 43.

10. *Korean American History*, Smithsonian Asian Pacific American Program, http://www.apa.si.edu/; Korean adoption began officially in 1954 with the establishment of the Children Placement Services in Korea. Madelyn Freundlich and Joy Kim Lieberthal, *The Gathering of the First Generation of Adult Korean Adoptees: Adoptees' Perceptions of International Adoption* (New York: Evan B. Donaldson Adoption Institute, 2000), 2, http://www.adoptioninstitute.org/proed/korfindings.html.

11. Mee-Aeng Ko, *Coming to America: Korean Immigration to the United States*, (September 23, 2001), http://www.coe.missouri.edu/~makoeaa/Korea/Immigration.html; *Korean War Memorial*, http://www.ga.wa.gov/Visitor/korean/koreanwar.htm; Anthony Faiola and Bradley Graham, "U.S. Plans Major Cut Of Forces In Korea," *Washington Post Foreign Service*, June 8, 2004, http://www.washingtonpost.com/wp-dyn/articles/A22074–2004Jun7.html.

12. "Amerasians were children fathered by American servicemen and left behind by returning troops. In some cases they were abandoned." David M. Reimers, "The Legacy of the Korean War: The Korean-American Immigrant Experience," presentation at the Legacy of Korea: A 50th Anniversary Conference, October 25–27, 2001, sponsored by the Truman Presidential Museum and Library and the University of Missouri–Kansas City, http://www.trumanlibrary.org/korea/reimers.htm. Daniel Lee estimated that from 1950 to the mid-1990s, "some 90,000 Korean women have immigrated to America as wives of U.S. soldiers."

13. Shin, *Developing*, 43; see also *Korean American History*, Smithsonian Asian Pacific American Program, http://www.apa.si.edu/; *Coming to America: Korean Immigration to the United States*, http://www.coe.missouri.edu/~makoeaa/Korea/Immigration.html.

14. Adoption History Project, "International Adoption," http://darkwing.uoregon.edu/~adoption/topics/internationaladoption.htm; see also POV, "First Person Plural: Adoptions from South Korea," http://www.pbs.org/pov/pov2000/firstpersonplural/historical/skadoptions.html; see also Evan B. Donaldson Adoption Institute, "International Adoption Facts," at http://www.adoptioninstitute.org/FactOverview/international.html#22.

15. Shin, *Developing*, 41, 44. The total number of Korean immigrants arriving in the 1950s was 6,231; in the 1960s was 34,526; and, in the 1970s was 267,638.

16. Sam Chu Lin, "Scattered but Strong: Korean American Results from the 2000 Census." *Asian Week*, January 10–16, 2003; Shin, *Developing*, 44. According to Aruna Lee, "One out of three South Korean parents are willing to send their children abroad for the sake of a better education, according to a study by the Center for Korean Education Development in Seoul, published in the Korea Times of Los Angeles. In the past, parents would ask relatives living in the United States to adopt their children, but more parents are now seeking out Caucasian families who are strangers to them." "South Koreans buy into a U.S. education," *San Francisco Chronicle*, February 5, 2006. Lin, "Scattered"; Korean American Coalition, Center for Korean and Korean American Studies, CSLA, at http://www.calstatela.edu/centers/ckaks/census/PR_112202.pdf. Smithsonian Asian Pacific American Program, *Korean American History*, at http://www.apa.si.edu/.

17. U.S. Census Bureau, *American Community Survey*, "Table PCT027, Place of Birth for the Foreign Born Population, United States, 2003," at http://factfinder.census.gov/ (accessed July 16, 2008). By 2006 that figure declined to 1,023,956. U.S. Census Bureau, *American Community Survey*, "Table PCT027, Place of Birth for the Foreign Born Population, United States, 2006," at http://factfinder.census.gov/ (accessed July 16, 2008).

18. Korean American Museum, *Korean American History*, at www.kamuseum.org/community/history.

19. Ruben G. Rumbuat, "Acculturation, Discrimination, and Ethnic Identity among Children of Immigrants," 17, at http://www.ksg.harvard.edu/inequality/Seminar/Papers/Rumbaut1.pdf.

20. See for example Brian Trung Lain, "An Integrative Model for the Study of Psychological Distress in Vietnamese-American Adolescents," *North American Journal of Psychology* 7, no. 1 (2005): 89; Alejandro Portes and Ruben G. Rumbuat, "The Forging of a New America," Working Paper 01–01, 12, The Center for Migration and Development, Working Paper Series, Princeton University, http://maxweber.hunter.cuny.edu/eres/docs/eres/SOC217_PIMENTEL/portes1.pdf. Portes and Rumbuat argue for an acculturative versus assimilationist approach and note that "selective acculturation" as a "paced learning of the host culture along with retention of significant elements of the culture of origin" can lead to better psychosocial outcomes.

21. U.S. Department of State, "Repeal of the Chinese Exclusion Act 1943," http://www.state.gov/r/pa/ho/time/wwii/86552.htm.

22. U.S. Department of Justice–Voting Rights Act of 1965. U.S. Department of Justice, 2006, 3–20.

23. *Loving* v. *Virginia*, 388 U.S. 1, Lain, "Integrative Model"; John D. Skrentny, "Policy-elite Perceptions and Social Movement Success: Understanding Variations in Group Inclusion in *Affirmative Action*." *American Journal of Sociology* 111, no. 6 (May, 2006): 1762–1815.

24. See Lain, "Integrative Model"; Skrentny, "Policy-elite Perceptions."

25. Lain, "Integrative Model." "Scatterness" is a term coined by Eui-Young Yu, a sociology professor at Cal State, Los Angeles, and director of the Census Information Center for the Korean American Center.

26. U.S. Census Bureau, *The Korean Immigrant Population in the United States*, 26, http://www.census.gov/prod/2003pubs/c1o-03cic.pdf. The U.S. Census Bureau notes that Korean immigration since 1965 has been primarily from urban centers in Korea to urban centers in the United States. Another 44 percent of Korean/Korean Americans reside evenly in the Northeast (23 percent) and South (21 percent), and 12 percent reside in the South. California has the highest concentration, followed by New York, New Jersey, and Illinois.

27. "A Trail of History," *Las Vegas Review-Journal*, January 21, 2006, 1B; Frank Kim Elementary School, Clark County School District, "About Lt. Frank Kim," http://ccsd.net/schools/kim/ltfk/ltfk.html; "Over 30 Years on Force," *Las Vegas Review-Journal*, June 12, 1986. Until 1973, the unit was the Las Vegas Police Department; Frank Kim Elementary School, "About Lt. Frank Kim."

28. Myoungja Lee Kwon, "Interview with Sook-ja Kim on February 12, 1996–April 6, 1996," Las Vegas Women in Gaming and Entertainment Oral History Project, 1997, 66.

29. See Man-Jo Kim, Kyou-Tae Lee, and O-Young Lee, *The Kimchee Cookbook: Fiery Flavors and Cultural History of Korea's National Dish* (North Clarendon, Vt.: Periplus, 1999).

30. Kim, Lee, and Lee, *The Kimchee Cookbook*, 20.

31. See *Life Magazine*, February 22, 1960; Kwon, "An Interview with Sook-ja Kim."

32. Nellis Air Force Base, 99th Air Base Wing Public Affairs, "Fact Sheets, http://www.nellis.af.mil/library/factsheets/. Nellis Air Force Base began as the Las Vegas Army Air Field in 1941.

33. Christina Ko, "Korean-American Couples Face Language Barriers, Stereotypes, Culture Shock," *Stars and Stripes,* July 25, 2001.

34. Teri Weaver, "Korean Women Married to Foreigners Seek Anti-discrimination Law," *Stars and Stripes Pacific Edition,* October 21, 2005.

35. Personal communication, Airman and Family Readiness Center, Nellis Air Force Base; Jan Hogan, "Korean-Americans to Host Benefit," *ViewNews,* November 10, 2004.

36. Lisa B. Zimmerman, "Retailer of the Year: Hae Un Lee, CEO of Lee's Discount Liquor, Wins Big in Las Vegas," *Market Watch Leaders,* 2002, 44–48; Meredith May, "Mr. Lee: The Retailer Who Turned the Silver State into Platinum," *Patterson's Beverage Journal* (February–March 2007): 20–23; Hae Un Lee, interview by author, May 23, 2007; John G. Edwards, "Purchase of Bottle of Scotch led Korean Immigrant to Start Business," *Las Vegas Review-Journal,* July 16, 2007, 1D, 5D.

37. Benjamin Kim, interview by author, April 12, 2007.

38. Asian American Justice Center, "A Community of Contrasts: Asian Americans and Pacific Islanders in the United States," March 23, 2006, at http://65.36.162.215/dcm.asp?id=228; Lynette Curtis, "Las Vegas Listed as Emerging Community," *Las Vegas Review-Journal,* July 11, 2006, 1B.

39. U.S. Census Bureau, *American Community Survey,* "ACS Demographic and Housing Estimates, Las Vegas–Paradise, NV Metro Area, 2006," http://factfinder.census.gov/ (accessed July 16, 2008).

40. U.S. Census Bureau, *American Community Survey,* "ACS Demographic and Housing Estimates, Las Vegas–Paradise, NV Metro Area, 2006," http://factfinder.census.gov/ (accessed July 16, 2008); James Moon Jae Yu, interview by author, June 5, 2007.

41. "Valley Still the Fastest Growing Metropolitan Area in Nation," *Las Vegas Sun,* September 6, 2005.

42. Andrew E. Kim, "A History of Christianity in Korea: From its Troubled Beginning to its Contemporary Success," Korea Overseas Information Service, http://www.tparents.org/Library/Religion/Cta/Korean-Christianity.htm; *Presbyterian Heritage,* "Witness the Good News: Our Mission Heritage in Korea," May 19, 2002, http://www.history.pcusa.org/cong/heritage/2002/intro.html, "Early Christian influences in Korea in the 1800s included Catholic missionaries in China and evangelists from the Presbyterian Church in the United States of America (PCUSA) and the Foreign Missionary Society of the Methodist Episcopal Church in the United States."

43. Yu, interview.

44. Religious workers are classified as (R-1) and specialty occupations, including journalists (H1B). U.S. Department of State, Visa Types for Temporary Visitors, http://travel.state.gov/visa/temp/types/types_1286.html.

45. Lt. Benjamin Kim, Las Vegas Metropolitan Police Department, interview; Yu, interview.

46. Joe Schoenmann, "The Soho of Las Vegas," *Las Vegas Life,* March 2003, http://www.lvlife.com/2003/03/feature1.html; Jan Hogan, "Korean-Americans to Host Benefit," *View Neighborhood Newspapers, Summerlin,* November 10, 2004.

47. Yu and Lee, interviews by author.

48. David McKee, "Songs Bring Seoul to Las Vegas," *Las Vegas Business Press,* November 28, 2005; Yu, interview; Kevin Rademacher, "Lenders Continue National, Local Growth," *Business Las Vegas,* September 3, 2004, http://www.inbusinesslasvegas.com/2004/09/03/banking.html; John G. Edwards, "Asian Bank Approved," *Las Vegas Review-Journal,* April 7, 2007; John G. Edwards, "Group Plans Bank to Serve Asians," *Las Vegas Review-Journal,* July 14, 2006.

49. UNLV does not track U.S. citizens by ethnicity, only by race. UNLV, "Student Profile," *FactBook 2006,* 25, 32.

50. *Travel Daily News International Edition,* "Interview with Stuart Mann, William F. Harrah College of Hotel Administration, UNLV," *Daily Travel & Tourism Newsletter,* August 24, 2006, http://www.traveldailynews.com.

51. UNLV's Korean Student Association, http://www.unlvcsun.com/?mode=clubs.

52. Bearce, pers. comm.

53. See "International Languages Courses," College of Southern Nevada, http://www.csn.edu/pages/1399.asp.

54. See *Las Vegas Review-Journal,* "Starting Somewhere," April 23, 1997; Lisa Kim Bach, "Culture Connections: A Family Once Again Is Delighted to Welcome Students from Las Vegas' Sister City in South Korea," *Las Vegas Review-Journal,* April 21, 1998.

55. Jim Doumas, Deputy Executive Director of Sister Cities International, interview by author, February 2, 2007.

56. Bach, "Culture Connections"; Las Vegas Parks and Recreation, http://www.lasvegasnevada.gov/Find/parks_facilities.asp.

57. Elaine Sanchez, "Korean Air's First Las Vegas Flight Arrives Friday," news release, Clark County Office of Public Communications, September 21, 2006, http://www.co.clark.nv.us/public_communications/news_releases/060921_korea.htm.

58. Associated Press, "BC-NV–Korean Air Service" *Las Vegas Sun,* September 23, 2006.

59. U.S. Census Bureau, *Census 2000,* http://factfinder.census.gov.

60. Timothy Pratt, "Census Report: Nevada Most Transient State," *Las Vegas Sun,* September 24, 2003.

61. Dana Bykowski, "CitiesFirst™ Brings Resources for Improving Homeownership to Las Vegas," United States Conference of Mayors, November 17, 2003, http://www.usmayors.org/uscm/us mayor newspaper/documents/11 17 03/cities first.asp; Pratt, "Census Report"; U.S. Census Bureau, "Census 2000 Demographic Profile Highlights," http://factfinder.census.gov/.

62. See for example Robert Putnam, *Bowling Alone: The Collapse and Revival of American Community* (New York: Simon and Schuster, 2001).

63. U.S. Census Bureau, *Census 2000,* compiled by the Korean American Coalition–Census Information Center in cooperation with the Center for Korean-American and Korean Studies, Cal State University, Los Angeles, http://www.calstatela.edu/centers/ckaks/census/top_100_cities.pdf ranking is based on Korean population.

CHAPTER 10

The Thais

JIEMIN BAO

Thai Americans are among the fastest growing Asian populations in the United States, increasing 65 percent during the 1990s.[1] In 2000 California had the largest population of Thai Americans, with 46,868.[2] Although Nevada's Thai population was much smaller (4,220), it ranked eighth among the states.[3] Thai immigrants consist primarily of three major ethnic groups: Thai, Lao, and Chinese. In Thailand ethnic Thai have been regarded as superior to non-Thai, while ethnic Lao have been marginalized as "backward" and ethnic Chinese as "the other." However, immigration to the United States has disrupted these long-established ethnic hierarchies and boundaries. Thai immigrants have learned to set aside many intragroup differences, especially in the process of building Buddhist temples, which function as the religious, cultural, economic, and educational centers of Thai American communities.[4]

Thai Theravada Buddhist temples have been the most important institution for Thai Americans in Las Vegas, where monks and laypeople, men and women, young and old, Thai and non-Thai interact and socialize. Theravada Buddhism once was almost exclusively associated with Sri Lanka, Cambodia, Laos, Burma, and Thailand; Mahayana Buddhism with China, Japan, and, occasionally, Vietnam; and Tibetan Buddhism with Tibet. Transnational migration, globalization, and the tourist industry, however, have affected how and where Buddhism is practiced. Today, Theravada Buddhism and Thai culture are taking root in Las Vegas, thus confirming that culture is *not* some "bounded entity that occupies a specific physical territory," but rather that culture is "highly mobile."[5]

Thai temples provide a window through which to witness the ways Theravada Buddhism is being reterritorialized in Las Vegas.[6] Predominantly working-class immigrants have established and maintain six Thai Buddhist temples in the city.[7] The process of building a temple should be understood in relation to the immigrants' experiences in the United States and the Buddhist practices, gender ideologies, and networks that they brought with them from Thailand. I use (im)migrants and "transmigrants" interchangeably to convey the immigrants' mobility and transnational networking.[8]

The History of Thai Immigration to the United States and to Las Vegas

The first recorded Thai immigrants to the United States were Chang and Eng, the famous conjoined twins, who arrived in Boston on August 16, 1829. They were joined at the lower part of their chest by a strip of flesh "five to six inches long and eight inches in circumference."[9] In Siam (as Thailand was known before 1939), Chang and Eng were called the "Chinese Twins" because they had a Chinese immigrant father and a Chinese Siamese mother.[10] In the United States, however, the twins coined the term "Siamese Twins," emphasizing where they came from instead of their ethnicity. Chang and Eng became successful performers, American citizens, gentlemen farmers, and slaveholders. Their achievements can, in part, be attributed to their having arrived in the United States before many of the discriminatory laws aimed at Asian immigrants were implemented.

Following the twins, records of Thai immigration to the United States are sketchy until after World War II. According to Immigration Services records, from 1951 to 1960 just 458 Thais, mostly students, registered as immigrants.[11] The first Thai organization in the United States was established in the 1950s at the University of California, Berkeley. Many of these students were ethnic Chinese, whose ancestors had long been depicted as the "trading minority." Under the shadow of a Thai nationalist movement, some Chinese immigrants in Bangkok were harassed and a few even jailed on suspicion of being communist sympathizers. Sending their Thailand-born children to school in the United States was part of a family strategy to gain a foothold abroad. Ethnic Chinese with Thai nationality, then, were among the first Thai immigrants to come to the United States.

The early ethnic Lao immigrants from Thailand were primarily composed of two groups: missionary monks and women who married American servicemen stationed in Thailand or who came for rest and recreation during the Vietnam War. Ethnic Lao are called Thai Isan. Isan also refers to the northeast, Thailand's poorest region. From 1968 to 1977, 14,688 Thai women, most of them ethnic Lao, immigrated to the United States as wives of American servicemen; most came from peasant families and had only a primary-school education.[12] Ethnic Lao missionary monks, who began coming to the United States in the 1980s, make up a disproportionately high percentage of the total number of Thai monks in the United States, just as they do in Thailand. In Thai society, men are expected to enter a Buddhist monastic order as novices or monks at some point in their lives. The length of time a man ordains varies from days, weeks, or months to a lifetime. Middle-class Thai men, especially in the urban areas, tend to ordain for only a short time and then pursue their education or career as a means to gain upward socioeconomic mobility. Other men, especially in northeastern Thailand, ordain because their families are too poor to support them. The temple becomes their home and provides them with sustenance and an education. Some remain in the monkhood for life.

In response to the Immigration and Nationality Act of 1965 and a shortage of medical personnel, thousands of Thai nurses came to the United States. While the United States was relaxing its restrictions on immigration, Thailand was unable to absorb many of its own highly trained people into nonagricultural jobs despite a booming economy.[13] High inflation and low salaries in Thailand during the late 1960s and 1970s led many scientists and engineers, as well as nurses, to emigrate.[14] Since 1968, the year the Immigration and Nationality Act was fully implemented, increasing numbers of ethnic Thai, ethnic Lao, and ethnic Chinese have immigrated to the United States from Thailand, among them many students and white-collar professionals. Many students did not want to return to Thailand after graduating; some stayed in the United States and opened the first Thai restaurants, pioneers in an industry that continues to thrive to this day. Thus, a professional and entrepreneurial class has quietly but steadily emerged. By the 1980s, the Thai American population had become more broadly diversified by age, class, ethnicity, and occupation than ever before.

Ethnic Chinese, Lao, and Thai have immigrated to the United States at different times, carrying with them different histories, skills, ethnic identities, and cultural codes. Generally speaking, they are a young population; the median age was 31.8 in 2007.[15] The Thai population in the United States has increased from just 458 in 1960[16] to 150,283 in 2000,[17] after immigration accelerated in the 1970s and continued to increase in the 1980s and 1990s.[18] The statistics on Thais for the period 1960–80, however, include only immigrants. The 1980 Census was the first to provide data on Asian Americans, while Census 1990 and Census 2000 included Thais born in Thailand and those born in the United States who self-identified as Thai.

The initial Thai immigration to Nevada in the 1960s and 1970s followed a gendered pattern. There were a very small number of Thai men, mostly students, and a large number of Isan women, mostly wives of American servicemen stationed at Nellis Air Force Base. In the 1980s and 1990s, a number of Thais migrated from California and others states to Las Vegas for business opportunities, jobs, and affordable housing. They opened gift shops, real-estate offices, grocery stores, and restaurants. From the original Las Vegas Thai restaurant established in 1973, the number has grown to around fifty in

2007. The availability of casino jobs also attracted many newcomers. The Las Vegas metropolitan area contains more than 100 casinos, over 130,000 hotel rooms, and hundreds of restaurants. Johnny,[19] who came to Las Vegas in 1975 as a student, said, "One position in another state equals four positions here, because this is a 24 hour, seven days a week, town."[20]

One striking feature of Thais in Las Vegas is the continued gender imbalance. According to the U.S. Census Bureau, in 2000, 58.34 percent of Thai Americans were women (87,679) and 41.66 percent were men (62,604), but in Clark County 62.57 percent were women (2,352) and 37.43 percent were men (1,407).[21] Moreover, there were more working-class than middle-class Thai Americans in Las Vegas. The median household income for Thais in Clark County ($36,847) was 12.26 percent below the national average for all Americans ($41,994) and 6.79 percent below the median household income for Thais in the rest of the United States ($39,530).[22] The median age for Thais in the United States as a whole was thirty; for Thais in Clark County, thirty-four.[23] In terms of higher education, 23.39 percent of Thais nationwide had bachelor's degrees or higher, but for Thais in Clark County the rate was only 12.02 percent.[24] The availability of casino jobs not requiring higher education or advanced skills, relatively affordable housing, an older population, and women outnumbering men, combine to form a distinctive Las Vegas Thai American demographic profile.

According to census data, the Thai population in Nevada has steadily grown, from just 799 in 1980, to 1,823 in 1990, to 4,220 in 2000.[25] Clark County has the highest concentration of Thai Americans, with more than 89 percent of the state's total (3,759).[26] In my interviews, some Thais claimed that the actual Thai population in Las Vegas may be closer to 10,000 or even 15,000. Today a majority of Thais work in casinos and hotels as dealers, cashiers, masseurs, maids, and cooks. Others are teachers, construction workers, plumbers, carpenters, and salespersons. Only a small number of Thai immigrant men and women are entrepreneurs, engineers, architects, attorneys, medical personnel, accountants, managers, or state employees.

In the process of making Las Vegas their home, Thai immigrants not only established Buddhist temples, but also the Thai Cultural Art Association and the Muay Thai (kickboxing) Academy. The *Las Vegas News,* a Thai-language newspaper, comes out twice a month. (Several other Thai newspapers—*Thai News, Thai Vegas, Thai Vada Post, Bangkok News Las Vegas,* and *Thai Press*—came and went due to a lack of economic and human resources.) Although there is no Thaitown in Las Vegas, one can find Thai markets such as Bangkok Plaza and the Bangkok Market. Thai restaurants are present in all the main commercial areas. With the growing number of Thai immigrants and the second generation, community activities have increased. Thai Music and Dance Day is held in September, and Thailand Day is held in October to promote Thai culture. In November 2007, the first annual Thai Night was organized by the Thai Student Association at the University of Nevada, Las Vegas (UNLV), to raise money for children with physical impairments in Thailand.

Transplanting Buddhism in the Face of Conflicts, Disjunctions, and Meager Resources

Wat Thamma, the first Thai Theravada Buddhist temple in Nevada, was founded in Las Vegas in 1985. Regardless of their sect or ancestry, Buddhist practitioners were excited at the prospect of having a place to worship. Thais, Cambodians, Laotians, Burmese, Chinese, Sri Lankans, and Vietnamese transcended ethnic and cultural boundaries and pitched in to build the temple; those with financial resources donated money; those who had little money donated labor and time. Hundreds of people, in one way or another, participated in creating the temple from scratch. At that moment in history, the temple brought spatially and culturally separated people, even former enemies, together.

Twenty-two years after Wat Thamma was founded, ten additional Theravada Buddhist temples—including two Laotian, one Burmese, one Cambodian, one Sri Lankan, and five more Thai temples—have taken root in Las Vegas.[27] After accumulating sufficient capital, the immigrants and refugees established their own temple(s) based upon their country of origin. The Thai temples belong to two different schools of Buddhism: Mahanikai, or Great Society, which emphasizes Buddhist scriptures and/or meditation, and Thammayut, a dharma-adhering minority sect. Of the six Thai temples, five are Mahanikai and one is Thammayut. The splitting of congregations and formation of new temples indicate that diversity and divisions among Thais in Las Vegas have emerged.

Monks and practitioners in Las Vegas have different opinions about having six Thai Buddhist temples for a relatively small pool of participants. Some think it is good, saying it reflects the freedom they have in the United States to set up a new temple for any particular monk or group of monks that they wish to follow. (With over thirty thousand temples in Thailand, Thai law limits the number of temples that can be built per square kilometer.)[28] Some believe that it is "natural" for temple congregations to split: "It is just like bees who like to have separate hives." Others, however, wish that Las Vegas had one big temple where each monk could teach what he knows best with all the people joined together under one roof. One monk, Than Maha

Songkan, described the current situation at Wat Thamma: "A big body with small legs (*tuato kailek*) cannot stand up straight. It's like a tree with only a few leaves. It may dry up and die."[29] He stretched out his hand with the five fingers separated and said: "This has no power." Then he made a fist: "This has power."[30]

In the process of transplanting Buddhism, Thai temples, monks, and practitioners, all, in various ways, experience disjunctions created by migration and displacement. Operating a Thai temple in Las Vegas is very different from operating one in Thailand, where temples are supported by a much larger population, as over 95 percent of the inhabitants are Buddhist. Also, the government provides monks with free transportation and medical care. In Las Vegas, Buddhist monks are still a relatively rare sight, for only four to six live at each temple. In addition, all the temples are self-supporting and none charges a membership fee. The number fluctuates, but some Las Vegas temples may have as few as twenty or so regular members.

All temples in Las Vegas face the challenge of limited economic resources, for donations are the lifeblood that sustains them. For example, Wat Thamma received only $2,000 via donation boxes in the first seven months of 2006.[31] To attract more participants, the temples take turns organizing group activities. Wat Thamma follows the lunar calendar, holding rituals and celebrations on the same days they are held in Thailand. The Baby Temple, a nickname coined by the temple's abbot, holds events on Wednesdays, the most common day off for casino and service-industry workers. The Forest Temple schedules events on Sundays. Thus, for example, if one misses the celebration of Buddha's birthday at Wat Thamma, one can still join in the celebration at the Baby Temple or the Forest Temple. The temples have had to be flexible in their scramble for limited resources.

The Forest Temple is the only Thai temple in Las Vegas to receive financial support from the Thai government, which rewards it for having successfully propagated Buddhism overseas. This temple, more than any others I have visited, documents all activities by taking photographs, videotaping, and carefully documenting visitors. This record-keeping is tangible evidence that can be presented to the Thai state as proof of what the Forest Temple has accomplished in terms of transplanting Buddhism. Nevertheless, what the Thai state provides is far too little to cover the costs of maintaining a temple. To meet this challenge, the Forest Temple has developed various fund-raising strategies. In 1997 it set a goal of raising $100,000 to pay off its mortgage. The amount still owed was posted on a signboard in the parking lot, on the walls in the kitchen, and on a bulletin board in the multipurpose room. The mortgage was divided into $100 shares, and the names of individuals who had pledged $1,000 were listed on a chart showing how much each had paid to date. This put unspoken but clear pressure on those who did not donate or who did not pay up fast enough. This same strategy, slightly modified, was used to raise money to build a concrete wall around the temple property. When an individual gave enough money to pay for ten or twenty feet of construction, the donor's name was painted on that section of the wall. Thus, the wall became a visible record and a witness of participants' generosity or lack thereof. Economic capital, then, was successfully converted into symbolic capital.

Most money is raised at big celebrations such as Thai New Year and Buddhist Lent, when some temples bring in as much as $10,000 or even $30,000. Hundreds of people participate: Husbands, wives, children, and grandchildren all come together as a family outing and sometimes bring friends. Along with Buddhist rituals, there are Thai dance and musical performances by second-generation Thai Americans and immigrants; Thai DVDs, CDs, arts and crafts, T-shirts, and all manner of souvenirs for sale, as well as food stands selling a variety of regional Thai food and drinks. Most of the money collected at these festivals is donated to the temple.

"Women's Work" and the Propagation of Buddhism

Cultural notions such as "women's work" (*ngan khong phuying*)—nurturing, cooking, cleaning, and managing the family money—traveled with those Thais who immigrated to Las Vegas. According to Buddhist logic, individual status, such as being born male rather than female, is understood as a reflection of the merit, the positive karma, a person inherits from previous lives. Being male rather than female is considered a sign of having more merit, as the accumulation of (de)merit in one's previous lives exerts influence upon one's current life course. The Thai state reinforces such a belief by limiting the monkhood to men. Although it is a rite of passage for men to ordain temporarily in both Thailand and the United States, men are not expected to visit temples as frequently as women.[32] Most laymen offer alms only on special occasions such as birthdays or important Buddhist holidays.[33] Women, although prohibited from becoming monks, are expected to visit temples and support the monks. Offering alms and giving birth to a son who later ordains as a monk are the most common ways that women make merit. Thus, childbearing, motherhood, nurturing, and contributing daily necessities to monks are regarded as moral actions that lead to improving a woman's karma.[34] These gendered notions and practices have turned the women into the backbone of the temples in Las Vegas.

Gender-specific ways of "making merit" (*thambun*) influence the ways in which men and women engage with the temple. At all six temples, approximately 90 percent of the regular congregants are women, most ranging in age from their forties to their seventies. A recent study of Thai immigrants at a temple in Philadelphia found that two-thirds of the participants were women. Women were the caretakers who performed "women's work" such as cooking most of the meals and planning and preparing the festivals, and women increased their responsibilities by leading the chanting.[35]

At the Las Vegas temples, women do gendered work but also routinely conduct the chanting, whereas in Thailand, women only occasionally do so.[36] It is also women who do most of the preparations for big temple ceremonies. They do the shopping, decorate the site, prepare the food ahead of time, and dress up the children who perform. At the food court, usually the liveliest and most crowded part of any festival, most cooks are women, with four or five male cooks sprinkled in. At these events, men often set up tents and tables, direct cars into the parking lot, and serve as the cashiers or moderators. A few men are in charge of videotaping performances and emptying the trash cans.

According to monastic codes, monks should not prepare their own food but should rather have it prepared and offered to them as a way for laypeople to accumulate merit. In Thailand, monks go forth at dawn from their temples to receive alms from neighbors or villagers; the food is then divided into two meals, breakfast and lunch. (Monks are not supposed to eat solid food after midday.) In Las Vegas, however, monks' receiving alms on the street can easily be misunderstood, for many locals are not familiar with this practice. In response, the women sign up and take turns bringing food to the monks at each temple. Then they clear the tables, wash the dishes, and clean the kitchen.

In Las Vegas, Thai women are the primary financial supporters of the temples, although many do so on behalf of their family. Keo, a retired motel manager, invited a monk from Thailand who was known as a "moving meditation" master to visit Las Vegas. This led to the idea of establishing a meditation temple in the city. She donated her house together with 2.5 acres of land, thus laying the groundwork for the Forest Temple. Before immigrating, Keo never imagined that she would someday have the financial means to found a temple.[37]

Women with fewer resources than Keo may contribute to a temple's prosperity by knowing how to manage money. Wanna, a Chinese Thai woman in her sixties, thought it was wasteful to spend a large proportion of a temple's income on rent, so she persuaded her daughter to cosign a loan and buy a house that would be converted into a temple.[38] Now donations pay off the mortgage.

It is often regarded as a woman's "nature" to support the temple and nurture the monks, and generosity is viewed as a sign of being a good Buddhist, detached from material desires. Some women not only support their local temple, but also donate money to other temples in different locales. Somsamai, or "Mother Teresa" as some call her, is known for helping the poor and supporting Thai temples throughout the United States. As I was interviewing her, she showed me her checkbook. She had written out thirteen checks that month alone in amounts ranging from $30 to $60 to twelve different Thai Buddhist temples and an American charity. She told me that she donates less only when her property taxes or federal income taxes are due.[39] The amounts that she donates may not seem impressive, but she gives away much of her income.

These women brought Thai gender ideologies with them to the United States and continue conforming to them by supporting Buddhist institutions. The three women are not affluent; indeed, sometimes they live on meager means. After donating her house to found the Forest Temple, Keo has been living with friends. In 2002, just before turning sixty-five, she suffered a heart attack. With no health insurance, she ended up with over $400,000 in medical bills. Wanna still works as a cashier in a casino. "Mother Teresa," one of twelve children from a farming family, had been a single mother with three children before she married Kevin, a GI who was stationed in Thailand during the Vietnam War. After coming to Las Vegas with Kevin, she worked as a maid for twenty years at MGM and Bally's. In spite of limited income, all three are as committed to supporting temples as they are to supporting their own families.

It is not just working-class women who provide temples with financial support; rich immigrant businesswomen do too. Sophana, an entrepreneur who married a European American husband and owns a factory and over a hundred acres of land in Las Vegas, often donates to temples and individual monks. When one temple badly needed money, she provided a large no-interest loan. Every year she brings in monks from across the United States to hold a memorial service for her deceased parents and husband. On occasion, she and her siblings travel with family members to make merit at temples throughout the United States. Unlike working-class Thai women who drive to nearby states and stay with friends in order to attend temple events, Sophana can afford to fly and stay in a nice hotel. She and her extended family thus combine merit making to be good Buddhists and gain a better "rebirth" for the next life with tourism. Class differences are expressed in the various ways in which women perform "women's work."

In contrast to Las Vegas's tourism slogan, "What happens in Vegas, stays in Vegas," what happens at Thai Buddhist temples in Las Vegas travels to Thailand. In Bangkok in 2006, "Mother Teresa" was presented a gold-colored statue of a "Buddhist wheel" by Princess Maha Chakri Sirindhorn, an honor bestowed upon those who have dedicated their lives to propagating Buddhism. Thus, women's work on behalf of transplanting Buddhism to the United States has been acknowledged by Thai authorities.

Buddhist Temples: The Pillars of Thai Communities in Las Vegas

Thai temples in Las Vegas are grass-roots organizations that touch virtually every aspect of a practitioner's life. They are, first and foremost, religious centers—sites where monks and laypeople worship Buddha, practice meditation, conduct rituals, and make merit. Monks conduct rituals in a variety of locales, including homes, grocery stores, and restaurants; they give blessings on birthdays and anniversaries, at housewarmings, weddings, and grand openings, as well as at funerals and memorial services.

But a temple is more than a religious center. It also serves as a social and economic center. Practitioners come to the temple to seek advice from monks regarding family problems. Some newcomers visit to combat homesickness or isolation; some seek jobs through connections made there. People share economic, medical, and job information at the temple. On one occasion I observed Keo, the woman who donated her house to found the Forest Temple, trying to sell mangosteen, a health drink. Another woman brought cooked bird's nest soup to serve the monks and others as a way to promote her product. Real-estate, insurance, and travel agents also look for clients there.

A temple functions also as an educational center. Monks preach Buddhist ethics and extol Thai culture. Many Thai temples in the United States have revived a Thai tradition that no longer exists in urban Thailand, namely, running a civic school within a Buddhist temple. The purpose of these school programs is not just to pass on knowledge, but to cultivate "Thai-ness" (*khuam ben Thai*) and Thai identity among the second generation. At the temple's summer school, volunteer teachers come from Thailand to teach second-generation Thai Americans Thai language, dance, and music. These teachers live at the temple and are supervised by the monks and the Teaching Thai Language and Thai Culture Program at Chulalongkorn University, Thailand's premier university.

A temple also serves as a meditation center. At the Forest Temple, several prefabricated outdoor storage sheds are furnished with cushions, tiny desks, and sleeping mats and used for solitary meditation. A person may stay in a shed for one day, three days, or even fifteen days for a silent retreat. Practitioners are taught how to develop a "third" or "inner" eye in order to look inside themselves. Than Maha Anan, abbot of the Baby Temple, practices breathing meditation. Occasionally, European Americans come to learn meditation from him. He said, "They want me to teach them meditation but they think it is something they can learn in twenty minutes. They want instant relief. Meditation is not like taking two Tylenols for a headache. We are not like fast food. It's not like phoning in your order to the pizza place and going to pick it up. Meditation takes a lifetime to learn."[40]

A unique feature of Las Vegas is that Buddhism and the gambling industry, two vastly different regimes, converge to influence practitioners. The boundaries between Buddhist practices and gambling are constantly being crossed. Gambling addiction, I was repeatedly told, is the biggest problem that Thais as a group have encountered in Las Vegas. Anna came to Las Vegas in 1969 when her husband was stationed at Nellis Air Force Base. She visits Wat Thamma every week, and she also frequently gambles. She recalled playing blackjack at Binion's Horseshoe Casino for three days and two nights without stopping.[41] While gambling, Anna forgot about everything else, once even failing to remember to retrieve her pawned wedding ring. Her gambling addiction put enormous stress on her marriage and her family. Nonetheless, for her, winning was an outward sign of her inward goodness, while losing meant she needed to improve herself by making more merit at the temple. Like Anna, some practitioners come to the temple and ask Buddha to help them win a jackpot, promising to donate some of their winnings to the temple if their wish is granted.

The Buddhist temple has become an institution that provides help for gambling addiction, a distinctive feature of temples in Las Vegas. Than Maha Somchai, a monk who received a Ph.D. in India, pointed out to me that there is a link between "Sin City" and the fact that "people have too much desire."[42] He believed that the saturation of gambling culture promoted the temptation to get rich quick. Than Maha Anan, the abbot, said he cannot "command" people to stop, for "When you say 'stop' they will not stop. Their minds get caught up in the gambling."[43] The monks employ two main strategies to deal with pathological gambling. First, they advise people to do meditation and develop mindful "awareness" to try to detach from material desire. Second, the monks try the "damage control" method by asking people to put limits on the amount of money they gamble. Maha Somchai said, "We tell the people you have to limit your play. Don't lose all of your money. You have to control your mind. If you have ten dollars, use two dollars for your children, four dollars for living expenses, two dollars for society at large, and two dollars for your pleasure."[44]

Conclusion

Transplanting Buddhism to Las Vegas is a transnational process, with Thais engaging in complex negotiations with the United States, the country in which they dwell; Thailand, the country from which they came; and fellow Buddhist practitioners they encounter at the temple. Thai monks and practitioners, on the one hand, adapt to local work schedules and cultural practices and operate the temples according to county, state, and federal regulations. On the other hand, they continuously network with the Thai state to gain support and recognition. They constantly move between different systems and cultural codes to come up with innovative strategies for dealing with limited resources and displacement. The establishment of Buddhist temples, literally the reterritorialization of Buddhism, becomes part of their collective cultural struggle, even as the men and women engage in it along gender lines. Rather than becoming "Americanized," Thai Americans have enriched Las Vegas by introducing Thai culture and Thai food to American society, teaching meditation, and performing Thai music and dance for the general public. The transplantation of Buddhism does not constrain, but rather enables temples in Las Vegas to grow in diverse, creative, and innovative ways.

The Las Vegas case illustrates that Thai men and women, especially the working-class women who engage with gendered work at home, at the temples, and at the casinos, have accomplished more than they could ever have imagined before migrating to the United States. And while the process of transplanting Buddhism is both gendered and classed, the women, who are the glue holding the temple community together, have made significant contributions to the reterritorialization of Buddhism in "Sin City."

Notes

I would like to thank the monks and the Thai immigrants who generously shared their experiences with me and allowed me into their lives. I also want to thank Rayette Martin for her timely assistance in compiling the statistical data on Thai Americans.

1. U.S. Census Bureau, Census 2000, *We the People: Asians in the United States,* Special Reports (Washington, D.C.: Government Printing Office, December 2004), 1.

2. U.S. Census Bureau, Census 2000, Summary File 2 (SF 2) and Summary File 4 (SF 4), "Thai alone or in any combination." Census 2000 uses two categories for Thais: (1) "Thai alone" and (2) "Thai alone or in any combination." "Thai alone or in any combination" was not used until Census 2000. Percentages and statistics cited from Census 2000 data will be specified as calculated for "Thai alone" or "Thai alone or in any combination."

3. Rahpee Thongthiraj, "Unveiling the Face of Invisibility: Exploring the Thai American Experience," in *The New Face of Asian Pacific American Numbers, Diversity and Change in the 21st Century*, ed. Eric Lai and Dennis Arguelles (San Francisco: Asian Week with UCLA's Asian American Studies Center Press, 2003), 102–4.

4. Currently, no Thai temple in Nevada is exclusively supported or visited by only one ethnic group. Nevertheless, this does not mean that cliques based upon class, educational, and ethnic differences have disappeared, but rather that these differences are reconfigured and renegotiated in a new context.

5. Jonathan Inda and Renato Rosaldo, "Introduction: A World in Motion," in *The Anthropology of Globalization: A Reader*, ed. Jonathan Inda and Renato Rosaldo (Malden, Mass.: Blackwell, 2002), 11.

6. Inda and Rosaldo point out that "Deterritorialization always contains territorialization within itself. . . . the root of the word always to some extent undoes the action of the prefix, such that while the 'de' may pull culture apart from place, the 'territorialization' is always there to pull it back in one way or another. So there is no deterritorialization without some form of reterritorialization." See Inda and Rosaldo, "Introduction," 12.

7. The names and addresses of six Thai Buddhist temples in Las Vegas are: Wat Buddhaphavana, 2959 West Gowan Road, North Las Vegas, NV 89030; Wat Pa Buddhayanandharam, 5320 Kell Lane, Las Vegas, NV 89110; Wat Thai Las Vegas, 2920 McLeod Drive, Las Vegas, NV 89052; Wat Nevada Dhammaram, 1911 Spring Lake Road, Henderson, NV 89015; Bhodhiyana Meditation Center, Inc., 1221 North Mallard Street, Las Vegas, NV 89108; Wat Sri Jareon Dham, 5929 Duncan Drive, Las Vegas, NV 89108.

8. Linda Basch, Nina Glick Schiller, and Cristina Szanton-Blanc, *Nations Unbound: Transnational Projects, Postcolonial Predicaments, and Deterritorialized Nation-states* (Langhorne, Pa.: Gordon and Breach, 1994).

9. Irving Wallace and Amy Wallace, *The Two* (New York: Simon and Schuster, 1978), 14.

10. Wallace and Wallace, *The Two*, 15.

11. Jacqueline Desbarats, "Thai Migration to Los Angeles," *Geographical Review* 69, no. 3 (1979): 302–18, 305.

12. U.S. Department of Justice, Immigration and Naturalization, Annual Reports 1968–1977, table 6.

13. Andrew Mason, "Population and Economic Growth in East Asia," in *East-West Center Working Papers*, Population and Health Series (1980–), no. 88-25 (Honolulu: East-West Center, November 1999), 14.

14. Nantawan Boonprasat Lewis, "Thai," in *American Immigrant Cultures, Builders of a Nation*, vol. 2, ed. David Levinson and Melvin Ember (New York: Simon and Schuster and Prentice Hall International, 1997), 883–87, 883.

15. U.S. Census Bureau, 2005–2007 American Community Survey, "Thai alone or in any combination."

16. 1984 Statistical Yearbook of the Immigration and Naturalization Service, U.S. Department of Justice, Immigration and Naturalization Service, 4. U.S. Bureau of the Census.

17. U.S. Census Bureau, Census 2000, Summary File 2 (SF 2) and Summary File 4 (SF 4). "Thai alone or in any combination."

18. 1984 Statistical Yearbook of the Immigration and Naturalization Service, U.S. Department of Justice, Immigration and Naturalization Service, 4. U.S. Bureau of the Census, 1980 Census of Population, vol. 2, Subject reports, PC80-2-1E, Asian and Pacific Islander Population in the United States, published January 1988. U.S. Bureau of the Census, 1990 Census of Population, Asian and Pacific Islanders in the United States, issued August 1993, table 1: General characteristics of selected Asian and Pacific Islander groups by nativity, citizenship, and year of entry, 1990. U.S. Bureau of the Census, 2000 Census of Population and Housing, Summary File 2.

19. Temple names and personal names are pseudonyms except for those of well-known public figures, for example, Thailand's Princess Maha Chakri Sirindhorn.

20. The interview with Johnny was conducted by the author on July 7, 2006, at a restaurant in Las Vegas.

21. U.S. Census Bureau, Census 2000, Summary File 2 (SF 2) and Summary File 4 (SF 4), "Thai alone or in any combination."

22. Ibid.

23. Ibid.

24. Ibid.

25. Characteristics of the Population, Chapter D, Detailed Population Characteristics, Part 30, Volume 1: Nevada, PC80-1-D30, issued October 1983, Bureau of the Census; U.S. Census Bureau, 1990 Summary Tape File 1 (STF 1)—100-Percent data; U.S. Census Bureau, Census 2000, Summary File 2 (SF 2) and Summary File 4 (SF 4)], "Thai alone or in any combination."

26. U.S. Census Bureau, Census 2000, Summary File 2 (SF 2) and Summary File 4 (SF 4), "Thai alone or in any combination."

27. The Thai monks whom I interviewed identified this temple as "Burmese" because the abbot is Burmese. However, when I visited the temple, the abbot told me that most members are Thai. There are also Laotian, Chinese, European American, Hispanic, and Burmese congregants.

28. See "Temples" at http://www.thaibuddhist.com/temples.htm (accessed March 4, 2007).

29. "Than" is an honorific title. "Maha" is a title used when addressing a monk who has passed a level-three Pali exam.

30. Than Maha Songkam, interview by author, August 5, 2006, Las Vegas.

31. This figure was provided by one of the monks at the temple. Donation boxes are just one way to raise money. When monks conduct rituals or participate in community ceremonics, they often receive donations.

32. The men's lower attendance rate at Las Vegas temples may also be related to a smaller male than female population and to the fact that some men work the night shift or two jobs.

33. Thomas Kirsch, "Economy, Polity, and Religion in Thailand," in *Change and Persistence in Thai Society,* ed. G. William Skinner and Thomas Kirsch (Ithaca and London: Cornell University Press, 1975), 172–196, 184.

34. Barbara Watson Andaya, "Localising the Universal: Women, Motherhood and the Appeal of Early Theravada Buddhism," *Journal of Southeast Asian Studies* 33, no. 1 (February 2002): 7, 29; Charles Keyes, "Mother or Mistress but Never a Monk: Buddhist Notions of Female Gender in Rural Thailand," *American Ethnologist* 11, no. 2 (1984): 228–30; Thomas Kirsch, "Complexity in the Thai Religious System: An Interpretation," *Journal of Asian Studies* 36, no. 2 (February 1977): 251; Marjorie Muecke, "Make Money Not Babies: Changing Status Markers of Northern Thai Women," *Asian Survey* 24 (April 1984): 462; Andrea Whittaker, "Women and Capitalist Transformation in a Northeastern Thai Village," in *Genders and Sexualities in Modern Thailand,* ed. Peter Jackson and Nerida Cook (Chiang Mai: Silkworm, 1999), 47.

35. Wendy Cadge, *Heartwood: The First Generation of Theravada Buddhism in America* (Chicago: University of Chicago Press, 2005), 172–78; 180–83.

36. Gender-specific Thai terms are used to refer to a man or a woman who leads the chanting.

37. Interview by author, September 28, 2005, at a temple in Las Vegas.

38. Interview by author, September 11, 2004, at a temple in Las Vegas.

39. Interview by author, July 8, 2006, at a temple in Las Vegas.

40. Interview by author, July 1, 2006, at a temple in Las Vegas.

41. Interview by author, October 18, 2003, at a temple in Las Vegas.

42. Interview by author, July 30, 2006, at a temple in Las Vegas.

43. Interview by author, July 1, 2006, at a temple in Las Vegas.

44. Interview by author, July 30, 2006 at a temple in Las Vegas.

CHAPTER 11

The Ethiopians

MICHELLE KUENZI

Ethiopians have emerged as a rich, vibrant community in the Las Vegas Valley. Like many other local ethnic groups, the Ethiopian community is young. Still, one can see the imprints it is making on Las Vegas, perhaps most saliently in the form of cultural events and institutions and the many enticing Ethiopian restaurants found around the Valley. The community is vital and growing, and some of its leaders have visions of what they would like to see for their compatriots in the future.

Coming to Las Vegas

Ethiopia is the oldest African state and is widely admired for its rich, ancient culture. Indeed, the work of paleontologists and anthropologists has revealed that human beings originated in what is now Ethiopia, hence its appellation "cradle of humankind." Ethiopia is also the repository of cultural artifacts of significance to civilizations around the world. It is one of only two sub-Saharan African countries, along with Liberia, that the Europeans did not colonize, and, as such, it has been an emblem of African independence.[1] However, with a rank of 169 on the Human Development Index of the 177 countries for which data exist, Ethiopia is now one of the poorest countries in the world. Life expectancy is only 51.8 years, and annual per capita GDP at purchasing-power parity is only $1,055.[2] Perhaps it is not surprising that Ethiopians would seek in other countries a higher quality of life and better economic prospects than their native country affords.

Some scholars argue that it is not the "pull factors" of other countries that have caused Ethiopians to emigrate in large numbers. Instead, scholars such as Assefaw Bariagaber attribute the flow of people from Ethiopia to "push factors," the most important of which is political violence. Writing in 1997, Bariagaber observed, "the war in Eritrea, the conflict in the Ogaden, and the proliferation of armed opposition movements in the aftermath of the Ethiopian Revolution of 1974 made Ethiopia a zone of perpetual violence."[3] Such conditions help explain why Ethiopia has been "one of the most important refugee-generating countries of the world for the past 20 years."[4] Solomon Getahun agrees, observing that prior to the 1974 revolution and the events that followed, such as the "Red Terror," "almost no Ethiopian wanted to reside in the United States."[5] Indeed, between 1971 and 1980, only 1,307 Ethiopians with refugee status were admitted to the United States. In response to heightened governmental repression, the United States admitted 18,542 Ethiopian refugees between 1981 and 1990, while many others lacking refugee status arrived either with visas of different kinds or illegally.[6] It is hard to imagine that the terrible famines of the mid-1970s and mid-1980s and the extreme poverty in Ethiopia have not helped drive the emigration.

Estimates of the Ethiopian population in the United States vary significantly. According to the U.S. census, 86,918 people claimed Ethiopian ancestry in 2000. In contrast, Yewoubdar Beyene cites a 1999 joint report by the Ethiopian and Eritrean Catholic Apostolate that estimated the number of Ethiopians and Eritreans in the United States at 250,000 to 350,000.[7] He also notes that the Ethiopian government put the number at around 500,000, on the basis of 2003 Western Union remittance data.[8] Other estimates reach 1 million. The Ethiopian population is concentrated in Washington, D.C., Atlanta, Dallas, Los Angeles, and Seattle.

Based on my interviews, it seems that both push and pull factors played a role in bringing Ethiopians to the United States. The push factors include political persecution, the desire to avoid military service, the ethnically exclusive nature of the Ethiopian government that has been in power since 1991, and the lack of economic opportunities. The pull factors include job opportunities, better pay, and the ability to support one's family, both those in the United States and those left behind. Pull factors drawing Ethiopians specifically to southern Nevada, both from Africa and from other U.S. cities, include having a friend or family member in Las Vegas and seemingly bountiful employment opportunities. Economic motives are primary for many. As one interviewee observed, "In other places, the economy is down. There are low start-up costs for driving a taxi here, and you can earn $1,000 to $2,000 a week."[9]

Refugee resettlement has been responsible for the arrival of numerous immigrants directly from Ethiopia. Both Catholic Charities of Southern Nevada and the Ethiopian Community Development Council (ECDC), in conjunction with The ECDC African Community Center (ACC), have helped resettle Ethiopian refugees in Las Vegas.[10] Catholic Charities apparently began resettling Ethiopians in the early 1980s, but the organization had figures only for 1999 to 2007, during which time it resettled 333. ACC, which began resettling refugees in 2003, had aided 706 Africans to relocate in Las Vegas as of January 2007, of whom 64 are Ethiopian.[11] While refugee resettlement has been important in the establishment and growth of the Las Vegas Ethiopian community, direct immigration with other visa statuses and secondary migration from other U.S. cities have also been critical factors in the process.

Historical demographic data on the Las Vegas Ethiopian population are murky. One man I interviewed said that there were around 10 other Ethiopians when he came to Las Vegas in 1984. The U.S. Census Bureau did not count Ethiopians in 1990, but the same respondent estimates around 500 Ethiopians in that year. Up to that point, he recalls, he had to go to Los Angeles to experience Ethiopian culture and community, but with the ensuing explosion of Ethiopian immigration and migration to Las Vegas, that changed. While the Census Bureau counted 1,764 Ethiopians in 2006 and estimated 2,924 in 2006, local community members estimate the 2007 population at between 5,000 and 10,000.[12]

Employment, Living Conditions, and Remittances

Although Ethiopians occupy a variety of positions, working as accountants, engineers, administrators, and entrepreneurs of different sorts, they are highly represented in certain types of employment in Las Vegas. Men often work as taxi and limousine drivers and in casinos as dealers, porters, and kitchen, restaurant, and maintenance workers. I interviewed a woman taxi driver who estimated that there are between thirty and forty other female Ethiopian taxi drivers. More commonly, Ethiopian women have found work in the hotel-casinos as dealers, cocktail waitresses, and maids. Nursing reportedly attracts a number of women.[13]

Several scholars have commented on the downward mobility of Ethiopian immigrants in the advanced industrialized countries. Getahun laments the fact that the United States is now home to more Ethiopian professionals, including the medical doctors desperately needed at home, than Ethiopia.[14] What is most unfortunate, according to Getahun, is that highly skilled Ethiopians often work unskilled jobs in the United States. He notes that highly trained military officers "end up being taxi drivers and security guards; they represent the worst case of brain drain—brain hemorrhage."[15] Getahun notes that Ethiopians are one of the United States' most highly educated immigrant populations.[16]

Las Vegas Ethiopians confirm the downward mobility thesis. A highly educated and knowledgeable military officer is a taxi driver; he left Ethiopia because he found that the current government is ethnically exclusive in orientation and, since he is not a member of the favored ethnicity, he lacked opportunities for advancement. Another informant who was an assistant dean at an Ethiopian university drives a limousine and substitute teaches. Clearly, it is not easy for Ethiopian immigrants to find employment commensurate with their capabilities in Las Vegas. Still, in contrast to the findings of other studies, none of those interviewed expressed disappointment with his or her situation.[17] They aspired to improve their standing by pursuing education, but establishing a viable plan of action often proved elusive.

Along with other immigrants employed below their skill levels, Ethiopians suffer the consequences of low-paying jobs. One respondent expressed frustration that, other than people resettled as refugees, Ethiopian immigrants receive little help in learning English and adjusting to life in Las Vegas. Residential overcrowding is common. One man I interviewed shares a small apartment with two other men, a woman, and her child, forcing him to sleep on a couch in the living room—and many stories are worse. As with many immigrants, culture shock and, especially for individuals arriving without family, loneliness are part of the experience. According to some studies, new Ethiopian immigrants are at especially high risk for HIV/AIDS.[18]

Many of Las Vegas's Ethiopians send money home to support family members. Indeed, most of those I interviewed said they sent money either to support nuclear-family members or more distant relatives or both. One man said he sends money to fifteen people. A woman noted that AIDS has taken many in Ethiopia; she therefore supports a sister's two orphaned children and a widowed sister with three children. Some said that they did not know what their family members would do without their remittances.

In addition to aiding family members, some Las Vegas Ethiopians financially support their communities back home. For example, some local members of the Tigray ethnic group contribute to the Tigrai Development Association (TDA) for North America, an international association committed to building schools and developing infrastructure in the Tigray region of Ethiopia. Members of the local Tigrayan community also hold barbecues and dinners to raise money for such public-works projects; after collecting money for two years, they were able to finance a school where none had existed before. Such stories make clear that Las Vegas Ethiopians care deeply about the state of their country of origin.

As one informant noted, the expectations of people back home keep members of the Ethiopian community focused on working. These financial responsibilities mean that many hold more than one job, which can impinge on other goals, such as pursuing more education.[19] Despite that limitation, a couple of informants said that local Ethiopians are upwardly mobile, meaning that the socioeconomic status of the second generation is likely to surpass that of their parents.

Of course, many of these recent immigrants have faced substantial challenges. Several persevered under very difficult circumstances, having spent time in refugee camps in African countries that neighbor Ethiopia. A man who came to Las Vegas after two years in a refugee camp on the border of Somalia and Kenya found employment busing tables in a casino within two weeks. After working two jobs and putting himself through college, he was eventually able to start his own computer hookup business.

It is clear that the norms of mutual aid and cooperation have been crucial in helping newly arriving Ethiopians confront the myriad challenges before them. Many interviewees told of receiving help from other Ethiopians upon their arrival in Las Vegas and of helping immigrants arriving after them.[20] One refugee, for example, helped between thirty and forty fellow Ethiopians obtain work at the casino where he found his first job. Illustrating this solidarity, while I was interviewing a leader of the Tigrayan community, he received a call from a new immigrant working as a taxi driver who had not yet mastered Las Vegas geography. In response, this leader essentially played the role of a dispatch operator and helped the new taxi driver find his way around. It is not uncommon for Ethiopians to contribute money to a compatriot facing a financial problem such as a large medical bill.

Integration into Las Vegas

Some studies of Ethiopian diaspora communities report that their members have experienced discrimination and feelings of alienation from their surroundings. One researcher, for example, found that Ethiopian and Somali refugees in Toronto faced "social exclusion" and that "systems of institutional and everyday racism have created very formidable barriers for Ethiopians and Somalis as they integrate into their new country."[21] Indeed, 53 percent of the 115 Ethiopian and Somali respondents in the study attributed their difficulties in settling into their new environment to racial discrimination.[22] A scholar who interviewed 106 Ethiopians in the United Kingdom found that "More than a quarter (27 percent) felt they had experienced discrimination and racism when seeking employment."[23]

By contrast, everyone I interviewed felt that the Ethiopian community was well accepted and even appreciated in Las Vegas. They reported feeling comfortable in the broader community. One said, "You find Ethiopians everywhere, and everywhere they go, they are welcome." She added, "You have to live by the book. If you don't cross the line, you come on time, you can have a nice life here." Another interviewee enumerated the Ethiopian cultural characteristics that contribute to their success. He noted that Ethiopians tend to be quiet, hard-working, respectful of time and the law, and peaceful. This was a view echoed by others. One interviewee said that, in general, landlords like Ethiopians because they pay their rent on time, make little noise, and follow the rules. Several expressed the sentiment that Ethiopians quickly find jobs in Las Vegas, because employers have had positive experiences hiring their compatriots. Nearly all of the interviewees attributed the ease with which Ethiopians have integrated into Las Vegas life to the values of Ethiopian culture, which, in addition to the traits enumerated above, emphasizes respect for others.

What explains the difference in perception between Ethiopian immigrants in Las Vegas and elsewhere? Perhaps the relative abundance of jobs in Las Vegas that do not require English-language or technical skills is an important factor. In a study of Ethiopian refugees, I. Papadopoulos emphasized the importance of jobs, observing that "employment was reported to help them [Ethiopian refugees] to settle in the UK and to gain a sense of belonging and citizenship."[24] Although first-generation Ethiopians tend to be underemployed in Las Vegas, nearly all of those interviewed commented on the abundance of jobs. Another factor may be Las Vegas's rapid growth and increasing ethnic diversification. One could say that the city is still a fluid metropolis, leaving room for new groups to join it rather seamlessly. In addition, several interviewees cited that Catholic Charities and the ACC played an important role in the successful settlement and integration of Ethiopian refugees in Las Vegas.[25]

Despite feeling well integrated, the majority of my informants said that most of their friends were Ethiopian, while a few claimed friends of diverse backgrounds. The latter tended to have been in the United States longer and employed in professional occupations. A student I interviewed thought that there was little problem being accepted by the outside community, but that Ethiopians tended to feel most comfortable interacting with their own. A man working as a porter at a hotel-casino, who had been in the United States only two years, said that language posed a barrier to making friends outside his Ethiopian ethnic group. He noted that he had few opportunities to talk with people at work, in part because many of his coworkers were immigrants from around the globe for whom English proficiency was also a struggle. Since many Ethiopians have heavy financial responsibilities and spend much of their time working, they have little opportunity to meet people outside the workplace.

Ethnic and Political Divisions in the Ethiopian Community

How cohesive is the Ethiopian community? This question begs another question: How many Ethiopian communities are there in Las Vegas? The cohesiveness of Las Vegas's Ethiopian community is limited, in part, by ethnic divisions in Ethiopia itself.[26] Three groups constitute nearly three-quarters of the country's population: the Oromo (40 percent); the Ahmara (25 to 30 percent); and the Tigray (some 7 percent).[27]

Ethnicity has become the most salient organizing principle in political life in Ethiopia. Between 1930 and 1974, Ethiopia was governed by Emperor Haile Selassie, who was deposed by a Marxist-leaning military junta (the Derg) eventually headed by Mengistu Haile Mariam.[28] The Amhara were seen as the dominant ethnic group under both very dissimilar regimes. Under the Derg, ethnic militias, including the Tigrayan People's Liberation Front (TPLF) and the Oromo Liberation Front (OLF) emerged. Eventually, these and other antigovernment groups established the Ethiopian People's Revolutionary Democratic Front (EPRDF) and cooperated to expel the Derg from power in 1991.[29] A transitional government was established, and in 1995 parliamentary elections were held and a constitution was adopted. The constitution established ethnic federalism, in which regions defined on the basis of ethnicity are afforded a degree of autonomy and can even opt for secession. Nonetheless, the EPRDF government is commonly understood to be an instrument of the Tigray ethnic group, not a neutral arbiter. For its part, the political opposition is largely organized—and factionalized—along ethnic lines.[30]

The number of Ethiopian ethnicities represented in Las Vegas is unknown. However, the three noted above probably account for the great majority, and the fault lines in Ethiopia are visible locally. When asked about the level of cohesion in the local Ethiopian community, one woman said, "We don't get along at home, but we get along here." Most of those interviewed, however, acknowledged divisions. As one noted, "What happens back home, influences the community here," but he added that Ethiopians have a culture of forgiving and forgetting. Another man summed up the situation well, observing that the Ethiopian community is "not that cohesive, but it is also not that fragmented." Revealing the extension of ethnic and political tensions from home, he explained that there are some local members of the Tigrayan group who approve of everything the Ethiopian government does, while there are "Amhara who just want Amhara." He added, however, that many of Las Vegas's Ethiopians choose not to take sides in that struggle.

Ethiopian Associations and Mutual Aid

Ethnic and political divisions in the home country are evident in the principal Las Vegas Ethiopian–community civic organizations. The oldest, the nonprofit Ethiopian Mutual Association of Nevada (EMAN), was founded in 1988.[31] Catholic Community Services initially provided the facility at which twenty-five to thirty people gathered for monthly meetings. EMAN now counts over one hundred members and holds biweekly meetings in a facility that it owns. Its membership includes several Ethiopian ethnicities, although a majority are Amhara. EMAN emphasizes the value of inclusiveness; according to its brochure, it works to "promote cultural, social, educational and socio-economic development programs for Ethiopians and others in the city of Las Vegas and Clark County area." The organization provides services such as translation, job training, and placement and aspires to offer after-school programs such as tutoring and sports activities and to increase awareness about safe-sex education, gang and domestic violence, addictions, and contagious diseases. Since EMAN depends entirely on volunteers and members spend much of their time working, this is an ambitious agenda.

EMAN's president, Tilahun Tafete, envisions the emergence of a greater Ethiopia in Las Vegas in which Ethiopians would come together and "project out." He hopes to see an Ethiopian space emerge—an area of town where Ethiopian coffee shops and businesses would flourish, serving Ethiopians and the broader community alike, anchored by a conference center.

Another Ethiopian organization, the Tigrai Community Association of Las Vegas (TCA), was established in 1998. TCA has nine board members, though it does not yet have a building in which to meet and is not as institutionalized as EMAN. As one of its leaders noted, the TCA is an emerging organization.

Some among the EMAN leadership lament that members of the Tigray ethnic group have felt a need to establish a separate organization and believe that EMAN is capable of serving all those of Ethiopian ancestry in Las Vegas, regardless of ethnicity. They feel that TCA undermines unity and that its establishment was politically motivated, since they consider the Tigrayans to be supporters of the Ethiopian government, which many in EMAN at least quietly oppose. On the other hand, a TCA leader denied that political motives had inspired the founding of his organization. Rather, he emphasized cultural differences between the ethnic groups, including language, and argued that the language barrier prevents EMAN from effectively offering translation and job-training services to the Tigrayan group. Still, by pointing out that

EMAN's membership was mostly Amhara and thus could not claim to be an umbrella organization for all Las Vegas Ethiopians, his focus indicates ethnic, and not cultural, differences. And while he claims to be uninterested in politics in the home country, his mention of EMAN's opposition to the Ethiopian government makes it clear that ethnopolitical cleavages found at home are also present in Las Vegas.

In fact, some EMAN members are very concerned with the political situation in Ethiopia and are active in opposition parties, making the political struggle at home transnational. There is also a little unease among some EMAN members about permitting Tigrayans to listen in on their political discussions. Nonetheless, this appears to be a minority sentiment, and the EMAN leadership still aspires to incorporate all those of Ethiopian ancestry.

A third community organization, Oromo Community Group of Las Vegas, was established around ten years ago. According to one respondent, this organization has not been very active, although it promises to be so in the future. When asked why there was a need for a separate Oromo organization, my respondent echoed some of the points made by the TCA leadership: that language and culture, including music and wedding practices, differ across ethnic lines. These differences, my respondent noted, also apply to politics. According to him, the level of trust across ethnic groups is not very high, and therefore it can be hard for members of the different ethnic groups to work together.

Religious Diversity

Divisions within the Las Vegas Ethiopian community carry over to religion. There are Christians of Ethiopian Orthodox, traditional Protestant, and evangelical denominations, as well as Muslims. The evolution of the local religious institutions reflects the evolution of the Ethiopian community more generally. The St. Michael Ethiopian Orthodox Tewahedo Church in Las Vegas was established at the end of 1997 and incorporated in 1998. The congregation initially lacked space of its own and used the Greek Orthodox and Serbian Orthodox churches until it was able to buy its own property in 1999. Initially served by a priest from St. Mary Orthodox Church in Los Angeles, St. Michael's now has three priests, who hold services on Thursdays and Sundays. The congregation has approximately 100 members, primarily Amhara and Oromo, but around 150 come to pray, while 400 to 500 attend on days of celebration. This church is part of the Holy Synod in Exile, headquartered in Atlanta, which, reflecting the ethnopolitical divisions among Ethiopians, broke away from the established Orthodox Church in Ethiopia.

A second orthodox church, Hamere Noah Kidane Mehretwe St. Michael's, was established in December 2004. This denomination is run from Ethiopia by the official Orthodox Church with the approval of the Ethiopian government, a fact that underscores ethnic, political, and generational differences within the Las Vegas community. Rather than focus on those fracture lines, church leaders cite its more modern orientation and the youth programs it offers as the reasons for its founding. Services are conducted in both Amharic and Geez for the 236 member families.[32] After initially meeting at the Clark County Library, the congregation now rents space from Christ the King Catholic Church, which restricts worship to Wednesdays and Thursdays. Church leaders hope to purchase land soon.

The Ethiopian community is also served by an evangelical church, the Ethiopian Christian Fellowship Church, which was founded by some five people in 1999. Pastor Mequanent Alemu noted that the impetus for starting this church was to create a venue where Ethiopians could come together to worship and socialize. Indeed, the church has youth groups and has become an important venue for social interaction. Services are conducted in Amharic. The Ethiopian Christian Fellowship is a diverse church. It has a membership of 220 people, which is composed of Ethiopians of all ethnicities as well as some Eritreans. After four years of renting space, it bought its own facility in 2003.

In addition, Oromo speakers worship at the newly established Oromo Evangelical Church, founded in December of 2004.[33] Lacking its own facility, the Oromo Evangelical Church worships at the Lakes Lutheran Church of Las Vegas and awaits the arrival of its future pastor, Kefyarew Amante, from Australia. Presently, the membership consists of 50 to 60 adults and 12 children. Services are conducted in the Oromo language, and according to one of the founders, this church was established primarily to accommodate those Oromo who do not speak Amharic, the language of the three churches described above.[34] The Oromo Evangelical Church is affiliated with churches in Oromio, the Ethiopian region where Oromo are concentrated, and is a member of the United Oromo Evangelical Churches. The local church plans to host the 2009 conference of United Oromo Evangelical Churches, which promises to be a major event.

Approximately one-third of Ethiopians are Muslim, and they, too, are represented in the Las Vegas Ethiopian community. Ethiopian Muslims generally attend any of Las Vegas's five mosques, choosing their place of worship based on convenience or personal preference rather than ethnicity.

Social and Cultural Life

For a relatively young community, the Ethiopians have managed to establish a rich social and cultural life in Las Vegas. The transnational nature of Ethiopian social and cultural life is evident. The Ethio Café features the music of singers and bands from the home country and the larger Ethiopian communities around the United States. There are seven other Ethiopian restaurants in Las Vegas.[35] Most of the restaurants have satellite television services that offer Ethiopian stations. In addition to the restaurants, Ethiopian men often socialize at Starbucks, which one respondent said resembles a traditional Ethiopian teahouse. Women are not as likely to visit these venues; they more commonly socialize in private homes.[36]

Several Ethiopian stores and markets, such as Meskerem and Merkato, sell items of particular interest to local Ethiopians, such as *enjera,* the bread integral to most Ethiopian meals; Ethiopian spices; and phone cards. Chibo sells magazines from Ethiopia and from the Ethiopian community in Washington, D.C. Chibo is also a preferred site for sending remittances back to Ethiopia. As one respondent put it, one is "always thinking of home." Indeed, several respondents had returned to Ethiopia for visits. One respondent had returned to Ethiopia four times since coming to the United States in 1993.

Some events and celebrations are observed by the community as a whole. Not surprisingly, subcommunities such as the Tigray also have their own celebrations. As a Tigrayan leader noted, the Tigrayans differ culturally from other Ethiopian ethnic groups in terms of dance, music, dress, and hairstyles. It was, then, quite natural that they would have some cultural events of their own.

Events such as the Ethiopian Millennium Celebration attest to the Ethiopian community's desire both to maintain its culture and traditions and to play an important role in the larger Las Vegas community. Ethiopia follows the Coptic calendar, which is seven years behind the Gregorian calendar. Thus, September 12, 2007, was the day of the Ethiopian Millennium, and a grand celebration at the Palacio del Sol convention center marked this important date for the Las Vegas Ethiopian community. Approximately eight hundred people attended the dinner and festivities. The members of EMAN, the sponsoring organization, and the coordinating committee spent many hours preparing the event hall with a diverse display of Ethiopian culture and history. The evening started with an elaborate Ethiopian buffet meal, followed by speeches by the EMAN council, State Senate minority leader Dina Titus, and the author.[37] The mayor of Las Vegas officially recognized the celebration and sent a representative. Festivities continued well into the night, as those in attendance enjoyed various styles of Ethiopian music and dancing.

While the Millennium was a pan-Ethiopian celebration, even this very special occasion revealed ethnic divisions within the community. There was a separate Tigrayan event in addition to the primary celebration sponsored by EMAN. Some of the TCA leadership attended the EMAN-sponsored celebration as well as their own ethnic-centered one.

Conclusion

The Ethiopian community has flourished in Las Vegas, and every year it grows, both through reproduction and particularly through continuing immigration and domestic migration. It seems likely that this growth will continue. Since having a friend or family member in a location is a pull factor, Las Vegas is likely to become more of a destination of choice for those coming directly from Ethiopia. The push factors of poverty, lack of opportunities, political instability, and perceived ethnic exclusion in the Ethiopian government are unlikely to change significantly in the near future.

Las Vegas Ethiopians are divided by ethnicity, religion, politics, and membership in civic organizations. Recognizing the potential for counterproductive rifts within the Ethiopian community, the leaders of the two most active civic associations affirm their willingness and ability to work with their counterparts to unite around common interests and strengthen community-wide bonds. These leaders share a pride in the Ethiopian community and an enthusiasm about the role they envision it playing in Las Vegas. What seems to unite the two organizations is their leadership's desire to do good both for new immigrants from Ethiopia and for the Las Vegas community more generally. The leaders' propensity to reach out to others, offer help, and promote beneficial cultural and social exchange became evident during the course of my research. The person who put me in contact with the TCA leadership, for example, was a leader in EMAN who insisted that I meet people from all segments of the Ethiopian community. Similarly, the vice president of TCA then arranged interviews for me with members of the Oromo ethnicity to ensure that my set of respondents would be as representative of the Ethiopian community as possible. In these and other ways, the norms of fair play, solidarity, and cooperation appear strong among the community leaders, and the observation of one of my respondents rings true. The Ethiopian community is "not that cohesive, but it is also not that fragmented."

Notes

I am very grateful to all of those who allowed me to interview them and provided me with information. Tilahun Tafete and Aberham Teklu kindly supplied me with information about their respective associations and the Ethiopian community of Las Vegas more generally. George Ossavou and the excellent staff of ACC provided me with extremely helpful information on the institutions of the Ethiopian community and put me into contact with some of the leaders of the Ethiopian community. I extend my heartfelt thanks to them. All of the church leaders were very cooperative and forthcoming with information about their respective churches. I thank Pastor Mequanent Alemu and the parishioners at the Ethiopian Christian Fellowship Church for their warm reception of me when I visited the church. I also thank Ararat Mahderekal for taking me to her church. Sisay Hailu very kindly provided me with information about the Oromo Evangelical Church of Las Vegas. Don Mirjanian did a great job finding some of the demographic data used in this chapter. I am especially indebted to Getachew Gebreyes for responding to all of my e-mails and questions, putting me into contact with other community leaders, and even accompanying me to one of the Ethiopian churches. I am also grateful to Thomas Wright for putting me into contact with Getachew Gebreyes.

The observations in this chapter are based on the research I conducted from the summer of 2006 to the spring of 2008. During this time, I interviewed members of the Ethiopian community in Las Vegas from all walks of life, including community leaders; church leaders; students at the University of Nevada, Las Vegas; taxi drivers; hotel porters; an accountant; and a business owner. I conducted fourteen face-to-face individual interviews, several formal and informal group interviews, and several phone interviews. I also engaged in participant observation–style research. All of those I interviewed were born in Ethiopia. I do not list the names of all the people I interviewed, because I ensured some of my respondents of confidentiality so that they would feel comfortable expressing the full range of their thoughts and views.

1. Between 1936 and 1941, however, Ethiopia was occupied by Italy.
2. United Nations Development Program, "Human Development Report 2007/2008," statistics accessed at http://hdr.undp.org/en/media/hdr_20072008_tables.pdf.
3. Assefew Baraiagaber, "Political Violence and the Uprooted in the Horn of Africa: A Study of Refugee Flows From Ethiopia," *Journal of Black Studies* 28, no. 1 (1997): 26–42.
4. Ibid., 30.
5. Solomon Getahun, "Brain Drain and Its Impact on Ethiopia's Higher Learning Institutions: Medical Establishments and the Military Academies between 1970s and 2000," *Perspectives on Global Development and Technology* 5, no. 3 (2006): 257–75.
6. U.S. Department of Justice, Immigration and Naturalization Service, 1995 Statistical Yearbook of the Immigration and Naturalization Service.

7. Yewoubdar Beyene, "Potential HIV Risk Behaviors among Ethiopians and Eritreans in the Diaspora: A Bird's Eye View," *Northeast African Studies* 7, no. 2 (2000): 119–42.

8. Ibid., 124.

9. One woman I interviewed said that after being in Colorado, she asked which state was the hottest, and thus came to Las Vegas based on the weather. It is worth noting that most of the research for this chapter had been completed before the 2007 economic downturn.

10. A National Voluntary Organization, the ECDC has expanded significantly in scope and mission since it was established in 1983. The Department of State authorizes ECDC to resettle refugees in the United States. Headquartered in Arlington, Virginia, ECDC has offices in Washington, D.C.; Denver, Colorado; Las Vegas, Nevada; and Addis Ababa, Ethiopia. Abstracted from "The Ethiopian Development Council, Inc.: Who We Are" accessed at http://www.ecdcinternational.org/whoweare/default.asp.

11. The largest number of Ethiopian refugees resettled by ACC in any one year was thirty-seven in 2005.

12. U.S. Census Bureau, *American Community Survey*, "Table B04001, First Ancestry Reported—Las Vegas—Paradise, NV Metro Area, 2006," http://factfinder.census.gov/ (accessed July 15, 2008).

13. The observations I made based on my interviews are largely consistent with those of Yewoubdar Beyene, who cites a 1990 ECDC report. According to him: "Ethiopians and Eritreans are employed across the entire job spectrum, from working at low-paying 'dead end' jobs to holding esteemed positions in academia, medicine, and high-tech electronic and computer engineering companies. Most, however, work in a variety of service jobs, particularly in restaurants and hotels as parking lot attendants and taxi drivers." Beyene, "Potential HIV Risk Behaviors," 125.

14. Getahun, "Brain Drain," 257.

15. Ibid.

16. Ibid., 268.

17. For example, see Ransford Danso, "From 'There' to 'Here': An Investigation of the Initial Settlement Experiences of Ethiopian and Somali Refugees in Toronto," *GeoJournal* 55 (2001): 3–14.

18. For example, see Beyene, "Potential HIV Risk Behaviors."

19. A very bright engineering student at UNLV whom I interviewed must drive a taxi in order to support himself, meet his obligations, and put himself through school, although he finds driving a taxi very stressful. Nonetheless, he said that he was impressed with all of the opportunities he had found upon coming to the United States.

20. Mehari Redda was one of the first Ethiopians in the Las Vegas area, and, based on the interviews, it appears he did a great deal to help others in the Ethiopian community who came after him. Redda was the program director for ACC until fairly recently.

21. Danso, "From 'There' to 'Here.'"

22. Ibid., 7.

23. I. Papadopoulos., S. Lees, and A. Gebrehiwot, "Ethiopian Refugees in the U.K.: Migration, Adaption, and Settlement Experiences and their Relevance to Health," *Ethnicity and Health* 9, no. 1 (2004): 55–73.

24. Ibid., 63.

25. Because I did not select a large, random sample of Ethiopian Americans to interview, it is always possible that the views of those I interviewed are not representative of the wider community. Still, I conducted interviews with a diverse group of people, and the unanimity of the responses on this point lead me to believe that the opinions expressed are representative of the views of at least many in the Ethiopian community of Las Vegas.

26. With its approximately eighty ethnic groups, Ethiopia lacks a unified national identity. See Berhanu Mengistu and Elizabeth Vogel, "Bureaucratic Neutrality among Competing Bureaucratic Values in an Ethnic Federalism: The Case of Ethiopia," *Public Administration Review* 66, no. 2 (2006): 205-16.

27. U.S. Department of State, "Background Note: Ethiopia," accessed at http://www.state.gov/r/pa/ei/bgn/2859.htm.

28. While Ethiopia was occupied by Italy between 1936 and 1941, Emperor Haile Selassie was in exile.

29. S. Joireman, "Opposition Politics and Ethnicity in Ethiopia: We Will All Go Down Together," *Journal of Modern African Studies* 35, no. 1 (1997): 387–408.

30. See Joireman, "Opposition Politics."

31. The founders included Selomon Tadesse, Daniel Woldemariam, Mehari Redda, Gezahgne Teffera, Asefa Asega, and Gobena Shiferaw.

32. Geez is an ancient Ethiopian language of Semitic origin now used as the liturgical language in the Ethiopian church.

33. Among the founders of this church were Sisay Hailu, Tameru Tesso, Belay Gerba, Fufa Bache, and Sebie Deressa.

34. Apparently, many of the children of the first-generation Oromo immigrants do not speak Oromo and therefore attend the English services at the Lakes Lutheran Church.

35. I have counted eight restaurants in the Las Vegas area and have managed to sample the cuisine at nearly all of them. (A couple of my gracious interviewees treated me to lunch at an Ethiopian restaurant after our interview.) One of my colleagues has told me of another Ethiopian restaurant, which would mean that there are at least nine Ethiopian restaurants in the Las Vegas area.

36. Indeed, one young female respondent said that she did not go to Ethiopian restaurants in the Las Vegas area and thought those were places where mostly taxi drivers went.

37. I was very privileged to have an opportunity to participate in this lovely celebration. I am also grateful to the members of EMAN for the warm, generous hospitality they showed me and a number of UNLV professors who attended this event.

CHAPTER 12

The Guatemalans

JOHN P. TUMAN AND DAWN GEARHART

Over the course of the past twenty years, the Las Vegas metropolitan area has experienced important social changes. In particular, the region's population has become considerably more diverse. Although such change is due to many influences, growth in migration flows from Latin America has clearly played a significant role in reshaping Las Vegas's ethnic composition. Given that the majority of recent migrants from Latin American are from Mexico, previous research on migration from Latin America to Las Vegas has tended to focus on the Mexican community. By contrast, with the exception of some recent research on the Salvadoran community, there has been comparatively little research on migrants from Central American countries, including Guatemala.[1] In our attempt to address this gap in the literature, we focus on Guatemalan migrants from 1980 to the present.

Migration from Guatemala: Push and Pull Factors

Migration from Guatemala to the United States can be traced to a variety of influences that are related to "push" and "pull" factors. Push factors refer to economic and social conditions in the country of origin, Guatemala, that lead to migration; pull factors, by contrast, include conditions in the destination country, the United States, that are attractive to migrants.[2]

Since the 1960s, economic, social, and political trends in Guatemala have generated strong incentives for individuals to emigrate from their country. First, and perhaps most important, Guatemala's civil war (1962–96) created a large number of migrant refugees who fled violence and economic turmoil. The civil war stemmed from an agrarian land structure that perpetuated inequality and from conservative reaction to a reform project initiated by the government of President Juan José Arévalo (1945–50) and significantly expanded by President Jacobo Arbenz (1951–54). Following labor and social-welfare reforms adopted by the Arévalo administration, the Arbenz government implemented a far-reaching land reform in 1952. The reform provided land to many landless peasants, but it did so partly through redistribution of unused land held by the United Fruit Company (a U.S.–owned firm and the largest landowner in Guatemala in the 1950s) and of uncultivated lands held by elite families. As a consequence, the U.S. government and elements of the agrarian elite began to organize in order to roll back the reform.

By 1954 Arbenz had been overthrown by a clandestine program that was organized and funded by the U.S. Central Intelligence Agency (CIA).[3] In the aftermath, the land-reform program was reversed, while Guatemala's political regime made the transition back to authoritarian rule. Nevertheless, worsening inequality in the rural areas over the next two decades helped to generate a peasant revolutionary movement, concentrated mainly among *ladino* sharecroppers and led first by MR-13 and subsequently by the Rebel Armed Forces (FAR).[4] Buoyed by counterinsurgency military assistance provided by the United States, the Guatemalan military defeated these movements. An estimated eight thousand peasants were killed during the counterinsurgency campaign of 1965–68, while many more were displaced.[5]

Between 1975 and 1986, another peasant rebellion emerged among Mayan estate workers in the western highlands.[6] By 1982 rebel combatants had become unified under the leadership of the Guatemalan National Revolutionary Unity (URNG). The rebels gained support among other social classes and popular organizations in virtually every province, which provoked a strong reaction from Guatemala's economic elite, the military, and the U.S. government, particularly under the Reagan administration. The Guatemalan military implemented a large counterinsurgency campaign in the western highlands, which included the murder of combatants and civilians and the destruction of crops, forest resources, and villages. The impact was devastating: "From mid-1981 to 1983 alone, 440 villages were entirely wiped off the map and up to 150,000 civilians were killed or disappeared. There were over one million displaced persons, including a million internal refugees and up to 200,000 refugees in Mexico."[7] Many Guatemalans were forced into emigration (first to Mexico and later to the United States) as a survival strategy.

Although the cessation of conflict in the 1990s helped to bring a measure of stability to the countryside, other economic problems have continued to generate pressure for out-migration. Certainly, Guatemala's demographic structure has complicated conditions in the labor market, with attendant consequences for migration flows. Due to low levels of educational attainment among the rural population, the prevalence of poverty, and a lack of adequate family-planning services,[8] the total fertility rate in Guatemala remained high in recent decades, standing at an estimated 4.4 births per woman, on average, between 2000 and 2005.[9] The persistence of a relatively high fertility rate has resulted in a large concentration of young people in Guatemala's demographic structure; indeed, in 2001, 43 percent of the total population was under the age of fifteen. Consequently, the number of young people seeking employment has tended to exceed the supply of jobs in the formal sector of the economy. Recent market-oriented reforms and the growth of export-oriented garment production have done little to alleviate Guatemala's employment problem.[10]

Finally, in rural areas the persistence of a highly unequal distribution of land ownership has created barriers to opportunity and generated additional economic pressure for out-migration. Despite promises of land reform following the implementation of the 1996 peace accords, landholdings in Guatemala remain extremely concentrated. In 2004 large farms (of more than 110 acres)—which represented only 2 percent of all farms—controlled an estimated 56.5 percent of arable farming land in the country.[11] In this context, many rural families lack adequate access to land in order to generate income, creating incentives for some family members to migrate in search of wage work.

Although Guatemalans have been coming to the United States for many years now, migration flows were highest during the decade of the 1980s. Most Guatemalan migrants arrived in the United States via Mexico. During the counterinsurgency campaigns of the early 1980s, the Mexican government created resettlement zones in the Mexican states of Chiapas and the Yucatán for Guatemalans fleeing persecution. In 1984 alone, an estimated 10,000 Guatemalans took refuge in Mexico's official resettlement camps, while many thousands more were in unofficial sites throughout southern Mexico.[12] Over time, some Guatemalans who resettled in Mexico started to migrate to the United States.[13] In addition, Mexico's border with Guatemala is porous and, in some places, not well guarded by Mexican authorities.[14] For those seeking to reach the United States, the first step—crossing the border with Mexico—is not very difficult. Regardless of whether they arrived in Mexico through resettlement or individual migration, few Guatemalans in Mexico have had sufficient savings to travel immediately to the United States. Instead, once inside Mexico, many work in the informal sector of the economy and gradually head north toward the U.S.–Mexico border.[15] While migrants are waiting to cross into the United States, it is not uncommon for them to have their money stolen by the police or thieves. When they are ready to enter the United States, migrants often hire a guide (coyote) and cross with a small group that may be composed of Mexicans, Guatemalans, and other Central Americans.[16]

California and Florida, where agricultural work and other service-sector employment is plentiful, are favored destinations for Guatemalan immigrants.[17] By 2006 the numbers of Guatemalans residing in Florida and

California—as estimated by the U.S. Census Bureau—were 78,741 and 308,684, respectively, with the majority concentrated in the Miami and Los Angeles metropolitan areas.[18]

Over time, Guatemalans started to migrate to Nevada; some individuals probably arrived after working in Southern California. Data on migration flows to Nevada are not available, but the census figures on the "foreign born" population in Nevada allow us to make some inferences about migration trends. These figures suggest that in 1960, there were eight persons born in Guatemala residing in Nevada. Subsequently, between 1990 and 2000, the total number of Guatemalans living in Nevada increased from 907 to 5,443, a change of 502 percent.[19] Although there are no data on the ethnic and linguistic composition of the Guatemalan community in Nevada, civic leaders suggest that the community in Nevada, including the Las Vegas area, is composed of both ladinos and individuals of Maya descent.

Guatemalans' decisions to migrate to the Las Vegas Valley are related to several factors. In recent years, Las Vegas has seen growth in low-skilled, manual labor jobs in the hospitality, construction, and retail services sectors, which are well matched to the skill set of recent Guatemalan and Central American migrants.[20] Indeed, in 2000, of those Guatemalans twenty-five years of age or older residing in Las Vegas and North Las Vegas, only 19 percent and 40 percent, respectively, had finished high school.[21] It is thus unsurprising that in 2005, Latin American immigrants—including migrant workers from Guatemala—comprised 55 percent of the workforce in the construction industry, 21 percent of the combined wholesale and retail trade workforce, and 9 percent of the overall private service workforce in Clark County.[22] Although more refined data on the hospitality sector are not available, anecdotal reports suggest that there is a large concentration of Guatemalan and other Latin American workers in certain occupations in hospitality, including room cleaning and food service.

The wage and income gap between the Las Vegas metropolitan area and Guatemala also induces migrants to come to Las Vegas. The Culinary Union, Local 226, which has a large number of Latin American members, provides good wages and fringe benefits. Yet even when migrant workers in low-skilled jobs in construction, retail trade, and nonunionized hospitality are remunerated at (or slightly below) the legal minimum wage in the United States, the wage gap between average inflation-adjusted earnings in Las Vegas and Guatemala, as measured in constant U.S. dollars, can be fairly large. In 2007, for example, the value of the legal minimum wage in Guatemala was about $1 per hour.[23] A skilled sewing-machine operator working in Guatemala's garment export sector—where labor-rights violations are frequent—might have earned up to $1.18 per hour in 2007, one-fifth the legal minimum wage in the United States.[24] The U.S.–Guatemala wage gap is further reflected in estimates that point to large differences in individual income between Guatemala residents and Guatemalans in Las Vegas. The U.S. Census Bureau reported that in 2000, income per person (in constant 1999 dollars) among Guatemalans residing in Las Vegas and North Las Vegas was $10,429 and $15,291, respectively.[25] During the same period, the World Bank estimated that income per person for all of Guatemala was only $1,704.[26]

Another factor that has facilitated migration to Las Vegas has been a supply of housing stock that permits many migrants to share rooms and rent. Guatemalans and other immigrants have discovered apartment complexes where several people can share rent for a single-bedroom apartment and reduce monthly consumption costs. Given the amount one may be able to save from these arrangements, some workers are able to remit part of their earnings to family in Guatemala, using private companies that offer secure services for sending money back to many countries in Latin America.[27] Finally, over time immigrants have developed recruitment networks that have generated further migration of Guatemalans to the community.

The Contemporary Situation of Guatemalans in Las Vegas

The first Guatemalans probably arrived in Las Vegas in the early 1960s, but evidence points to considerable growth of the community since the decades of the 1980s and 1990s.[28] U.S. Census Bureau data indicate that between 2000 and 2005, the population of individuals of Guatemalan origin in Clark County grew from 3,042 to 5,515, an increase of 81 percent. By 2006 the population had reached 9,845.[29] Most of the Guatemalan population in Clark County is concentrated in Las Vegas, primarily in eastern parts of the city, with a smaller number in the city of North Las Vegas; fewer reside in Henderson and unincorporated Clark County.[30] By 2005, the most recent year for which complete data are available, Guatemalans were the fifth largest group among all Latinos and Latin Americans residing in the county, after Mexicans, Salvadorans, Puerto Ricans, and Cubans.[31] The census data, however, may represent an undercount of the true size of the Guatemalan population; for example, the government of Guatemala suggests that the number residing in the Las Vegas metropolitan area may be as high as 14,000 to 15,000.[32] At least one-fourth of Guatemalans in Las Vegas may lack the proper documents to work and reside in the United States legally, but their interests are partly represented by an honorary consulate's office in Las Vegas, which opened in 2004.[33]

As the community has grown, several tendencies have developed. Survey data on attitudes and social practices of the local Guatemalan population are not available, but the fragmentary evidence points to the following trends. First, growth in the Guatemalan population has created economic opportunities for some retail businesses that market Guatemalan foods and goods to local immigrants. Supermercado del Pueblo, a grocery chain, offers an assortment of processed foods and other products that are part of the Guatemalan diet. A local restaurant, Chapinmex, serves regional dishes from Guatemala and also provides space for meetings and parties.

Second, the activities of Guatemalan civic associations, Guatemalan-oriented businesses, and informal soccer games have all helped to create and maintain cohesion in the local population. Nevertheless, changes in religious affiliation have created divisions among some people in the community. The majority of Guatemalans are Catholic, but some practice a form of syncretism that blends Catholicism with rites that are Mayan in origin. This is plainly evident, for example, with Mayan dolls used by some in baptism ceremonies.[34] At the same time, there has been an increase in the number of Guatemalans attending non-main-line, evangelical churches in Las Vegas, such as Monte Horeb and the Centro Cristiano "Amigos de Israel."[35] Some evangelicals note that at times, they have felt that others in the community disapprove of their new religious affiliation—although this has not prevented Catholics and evangelicals from attending community celebrations together.[36]

In addition, Guatemalans as a group do not always feel integrated into the larger Hispanic community in the Las Vegas Valley.[37] As one civic leader commented, outsiders often view Guatemalans as part of the Latino community and not as a distinct group with a unique cultural identity. He expects that image to change with time. Another Guatemalan leader added: "Although I consider the Hispanic community a very large family joined together by history and language . . . when we say Hispanic, it's not all Mexicans. . . . The Guatemalan community has its own identity, and it's important to recognize the richness and wealth of each community."[38] Moreover, some Guatemalans observe that people from other Latin American countries—most notably, people from Mexico—may not treat Guatemalans with the respect they believe is due them.

Within the family structures of recent immigrants, there is evidence of both continuity and change. The census data suggest that marriage remains prevalent among the Guatemalan population in Las Vegas, with approximately three-fourths of men and women aged fifteen and older being married.[39] Although many work in the local economy, some Guatemalan immigrant women who are married or cohabiting may continue to have primary responsibility for cooking and house cleaning, as they did in the home country.[40] In addition, it has been suggested that domestic violence is a problem for some women.[41] The image of continuity in women's household roles should be balanced against other evidence that suggests their roles may be changing. Younger women of school age are being exposed to new ideas and values that may challenge the traditional division of labor in the immigrant household. Whether such education leads to mobility and changes in family relations remains to be seen. In addition, women are becoming more visible in community organizations. At present, for example, women occupy all four leadership positions—from president to legal advisor—in the principal civic association, El Comité de Unidad Guatemalteco de Nevada (COMUGUA), that represents Guatemalans in Las Vegas. While evidence of women in leadership positions tells us little about the pattern of gender relations in the household, such developments are suggestive of some advancement of women in the local immigrant population. Clearly, more systematic research needs to be completed in order to assess gender and family roles in Las Vegas Guatemalan households.

Finally, child-rearing practices among recent migrants appear to be very similar to those documented in ethnographic studies in Guatemala. If a child's godparents are present in the United States, they may continue to play an important role in baptism ceremonies and early socialization—although fragmentary evidence suggests that this practice is on the decline among migrants who have joined evangelical churches.[42] Beyond the extended family, mothers have primary responsibility for child care, regardless of the age of the child. Children are expected to enjoy themselves, but they must also be obedient and silent when their parents and other adults are gathered for meals or social events. As in other communities, however, as children acquire new values in schools, they sometimes assert their independence from parents, which may cause tension in the family. As one parent observed: "They [children born here] possess some of the morals and religious beliefs present in Guatemalan culture, but they also become more liberal."[43] One might expect that, as a consequence of their new hybrid values, first- and second-generation Guatemalan Americans might adopt child-rearing practices and family roles that are different from the ones experienced by their parents and grandparents.

Civic Associations, Civic Engagement, and Transnationalism

Formed in 2002, COMUGUA is the major civic association representing Guatemalans residing in the Las Vegas Valley. Like other immigrant associations in Las Vegas's Hispanic community, COMUGUA organizes cultural and social events while helping immigrants obtain important services from both the U.S. and Guatemalan governments. It has established regular meetings of the Guatemalan consulate (based in Los Angeles) in Las Vegas and has remained active in the national immigration debate.[44] Israel Fuentes, owner of an independent transmission shop in Las Vegas, served as the organization's first president from 2002 to 2005. Nancy Frago served as president from 2005 to 2007. The current president, Gayle Fuentes, is Israel Fuentes's daughter.[45]

As one step in preserving the cultural heritage of Guatemalans, COMUGUA operates a radio program, *La Hora Chapina,* on 1340 AM from 12 noon to 2 PM on Sundays.[46] The program features marimba music, news, and interviews. By most accounts, *La Hora Chapina* is very popular. In addition, for the past two years COMUGUA has organized the Huelga de Dolores, a Guatemalan day of celebration that dates back to the tyranny of Manuel Estrada Cabrera, dictator-president of Guatemala from 1898 to 1920. Held on April 1, during the week of Semana Santa (Holy Week), the Huelga has traditionally been viewed as a day when ordinary people can make fun of their government or politicians; as such, the celebration serves an important function in the Guatemalan political economy.[47] Guatemalans celebrating the event in Las Vegas have adapted it to include immigration politics as one of the themes satirized during the festivities. In 2007 between 250 and 300 people attended festivities that included a wide assortment of food, public lectures, and performances by a local comedian and a marimba band.[48]

In addition, COMUGUA has become involved in immigration politics. Although its leadership remained divided over the use of unconventional participation as a tactic to shape public policy, members of the organization nonetheless supported and participated in the 2006 immigration protests in Las Vegas. Over the past two years, COMUGUA leaders have also discussed immigration issues with organizations in Los Angeles, a city with a large Guatemalan community. Significantly, COMUGUA also became an affiliate of the National Alliance of Latin American and Caribbean Communities, an umbrella organization that is actively engaged in the national immigration debate. In 2006 former COMUGUA president Israel Fuentes traveled to Washington, D.C., where he met leaders of Latino organizations, organized by the National Alliance of Latin American and Caribbean Communities, and lobbied on behalf of immigration reform. Mr. Fuentes described this as a very positive experience, noting that "we [the leaders] were one" and that "it was a tremendous opportunity to try to shape immigration policies."[49]

Similar to other Las Vegas immigrant associations, COMUGUA is involved in transnational activities. In particular, the organization has secured financial support for public works and disaster relief for communities in Guatemala. For example, when the municipality of Santiago, Guatemala, was devastated by flooding and mud slides, the leadership of COMUGUA used its radio program to raise funds in order to purchase basic food supplies and provide other forms of disaster relief. Some members of the organization traveled back to Guatemala to distribute the supplies to hundreds of families. Presently, the organization is attempting to supply reading glasses for individuals in Guatemala who cannot afford them. COMUGUA has also coordinated activities with the consulate's office in Los Angeles and the honorary consulate's office in Las Vegas.[50] Since 2005, COMUGUA has hosted staff from the Guatemalan consulate to meet with local immigrants at the Rafael Rivera Community Center. The goal is to help Las Vegas's Guatemalans resolve administrative problems in the United States and any issues they may have in Guatemala. The consular meetings take place three times per year and are usually attended by 250 to 300 people, according to a COMUGUA estimate. All of these activities suggest that there is a significant transnational facet to the association's activities.

The transnationalism of the local community of Guatemalans goes well beyond the activities of its civic association. Individual labor remittances sent by Guatemalan workers in the United States—which amounted to some $3.6 billion in 2006—help to support family members and public-works projects back in Guatemala. Although Guatemala's electoral law does not permit absentee voting among Guatemalan citizens residing abroad, remittances have given migrants potential political influence over family members in Guatemala.[51] As Armando Sobenaris, a Guatemalan who works at the Monte Carlo Resort and Casino, observed: "The Guatemalans living in Las Vegas are in tune with what is happening back in their homeland.... Besides, for every Guatemalan in Las Vegas, you can multiply that times 4 to 8 voters he or she can influence back in Guatemala. The power of the remittances to influence how family members should vote cannot be underestimated."[52]

Israel Fuentes echoed the views expressed by Sobenaris. Indeed, Fuentes suggested that, given the increasing number of Guatemalans working in hospitality and other sectors, "it is no wonder why the Guatemalan community living in Nevada is becoming a stronger political force which will continue to garner attention from presidential candidates and the Guatemalan government."[53]

Guatemalan politicians are taking note of the potential influence of Guatemalan expatriates living in Las Vegas and other U.S. cities. A number of candidates in the 2007 presidential race contacted immigrant groups in the United States to let them know their positions on proposed U.S. immigration plans. Otto Pérez Molina, a former general who ran unsuccessfully for president as a candidate of the right-wing Patriot Party, visited Las Vegas in 2007 in the hopes of garnering support for his campaign back in Guatemala. By most accounts, Molina's campaign event was well attended. His visit was not the first time a Guatemalan presidential candidate had visited Las Vegas. When President Álvaro Colom, elected in 2007, was running for office in the 2003 elections, he campaigned in Las Vegas on a trip that included several major U.S. cities.[54] Like other candidates, Colom, a center leftist, spoke strongly in favor of immigration reform while he was in Las Vegas.

Conclusion

Our brief historical analysis of the Guatemalan community of Las Vegas suggests that during the civil war, state terror in the countryside led to massive dislocation and generated outflows of migrants from Guatemala to Mexico and later to the United States. Since the end of the civil war, poor economic conditions in Guatemala—which stem from demographic problems, a highly unequal distribution of land, and little growth in the formal sector of the economy—have created strong pressures for out-migration from Guatemala to the United States. At the same time, the relative abundance of low-skill jobs in construction, hospitality, and other service sectors in Las Vegas has made the metropolitan area attractive to many recent immigrants from Guatemala and other Central American countries. After Guatemalans arrive in Las Vegas, they tend to use civic associations and Guatemalan-oriented businesses as a way to maintain group cohesiveness.

While we have focused on the Las Vegas Guatemalan community, a broader analysis asks how various Guatemalan communities in the United States compare to one another. Among the many contrasts revealed through a brief comparative analysis, two differences stand out. Similar to the findings of this project, previous studies have noted that Guatemalans in Los Angeles and in south Florida have formed voluntary associations in order to address civic affairs in their communities.[55] Nevertheless, while Guatemalan civic associations in Los Angeles and Las Vegas have remained intact, some of the associations in south Florida dissolved only a few years after their formation. Similarly, members of COMUGUA and the Los Angeles Guatemalan associations have participated in immigration protests and have developed transnational projects; the associations in south Florida, by contrast, have had a narrow focus on service provision in the local community.[56] The sources of variation in levels of civic engagement, protest, and transnationalism among various Guatemalan communities in the United States are unclear, but the variation may be due to the stability of each immigrant community and the types of economic resources at its disposal. Most migrants in the south Florida Guatemalan community are employed in low-paid, seasonal agricultural jobs; unsurprisingly, out-migration from the community is frequent, which may tend to limit the capacity of local associations. By contrast, although Guatemalans in Las Vegas and Los Angeles may face precarious employment and poverty, they would appear to have more economic opportunities. Civic associations in Las Vegas and Los Angeles might have more capacity because they can draw on a membership base with more resources.

There are several lines of inquiry that might be usefully followed in future studies of Guatemalan immigrants. First, while we have documented a connection between immigrant involvement in COMUGUA and civic participation, it remains unclear whether Guatemalan civic associations such as COMUGUA are promoting a transition to U.S. citizenship among its members through voting or other forms of conventional participation. Certainly, the group's involvement in the 2006 immigration protests is suggestive that its members are interested in citizenship, but the linkages among civic membership, citizenship, and political participation are obscure and require more study. Second, we need to have a better understanding of the pathways through which immigrants experience mobility in the local market. For example, do successful small businesses operated by immigrants obtain financing from informal lenders within their community, or do they obtain loans from banks? To what extent has the Culinary Union, Local 226, helped immigrants to move up the occupational structure by providing job training to workers in the hospitality sector? Third, what would explain the variation in levels of participation, civic engagement, and transnationalism among various Guatemalan communities in the United States? In thinking about the best ways to approach such questions, we join other researchers in calling for more detailed, empirically rich studies that compare developments in the local Las Vegas community of immigrants to those in other Guatemalan communities in the United States.

Notes

1. For a highly informative study of the Salvadoran community of Las Vegas, see Thomas C. Wright and Jesse Dino Moody, "The Salvadorans," in *The Peoples of Las Vegas: One City, Many Faces,* ed. Jerry Simich and Thomas C. Wright (Reno and Las Vegas: University of Nevada Press, 2005) 247–67. See also John P. Tuman, "Latin American Migrants in the Las Vegas Valley: Civic Associations, Political Participation, and the Challenges Facing Migrants," Washington, D.C., Woodrow

Wilson International Center for Scholars, 2007, www.wilsoncenter.org/news/docs/background.%20paper-Las%20Vegas.doc (accessed March 18, 2008).

2. At the time of their departure from Guatemala, many Guatemalans view themselves as *international migrants* and hope to return to Guatemala after earning enough money in the United States. After arriving in the United States, however, some migrants change their minds and seek to become *immigrants*—even though some may lack the proper documentation for legal immigration. As such, the community in Las Vegas is composed of people who intend to stay in the United States permanently, people who would like to return to Guatemala, and others who consider both countries home. In addition, there is a subgroup of Guatemalans in Las Vegas that intends to stay permanently but engage in a migratory lifestyle within the United States. For these reasons, when discussing the factors that give rise to out-migration from Guatemala, we use the term *migrant*; when we discuss the Guatemalan community in Las Vegas, we tend to use the term *immigrant,* although one should keep in mind that the community includes both migrants and immigrants. Moreover, some immigrants view both the United States and Guatemala as their home countries.

3. For an overview, see Piero Gleijeses, *Shattered Hope: The Guatemalan Revolution and the U.S.* (Princeton: Princeton University Press, 1991); Susanne Jonas, "Guatemala," in *Politics of Latin America: The Power Game,* ed. Harry Vanden and Gary Prevost, 2nd ed. (Oxford: Oxford University Press, 2006), 266–95.

4. In Guatemala, the term *ladino* is used to describe people who have both European and indigenous (Maya, Xinca, or Garifuna) ancestors. Ladinos tend to be concentrated in the eastern provinces.

5. Jonas, "Guatemala," 272.

6. See Timothy P. Wickham-Crowley, "Winners, Losers, and Also-Rans: Toward a Comparative Sociology of Latin American Guerrilla Movements," in *Power and Popular Protest,* 2nd ed., ed. Susan Eckstein (Berkeley: University of California Press, 2001), 150–51. Wickham-Crowley notes that during this period, many Maya peasants had been displaced by Guatemalan military elites who were seizing land in order to engage in mining operations. After losing their lands, many peasants became estate laborers. Various revolutionary groups concentrated their organizing efforts on the Maya and estate workers.

7. Jonas, "Guatemala," 275. See also Beatriz Manz, *Refugees of a Hidden War: The Aftermath of Counterinsurgency in Guatemala* (Albany: State University Press of New York, 1988), 16–20; Nora Hamilton and Norma Stoltz Chinchilla, *Seeking Community in a Global City: Guatemalans and Salvadorans in Los Angeles* (Philadelphia: Temple University Press, 2001), 31–33.

8. Studies have documented that the modern contraceptive use prevalence rate in Guatemala is only 38 percent, the second-lowest prevalence rate in all of the Spanish-speaking countries of Latin America. The low prevalence rate has been attributed to the effects of the civil war, low levels of educational attainment, and resistance from a socially conservative national Catholic Church in the country. See Roberto Santiso-Galvez and Jane T. Bertrand, "The Delayed Contraceptive Revolution in

Guatemala," *Human Organization* 63, no. 1 (2004). On rural-urban differences in contraceptive-use prevalence, see also David P. Lindstrom and Elisa Muñoz-Franco, "Migration and the Diffusion of Modern Contraceptive Knowledge and Use in Rural Guatemala," *Studies in Family Planning* 36, no. 4 (2005): 277–88.

9. By comparison, the female fertility rates in Mexico, Honduras, El Salvador, Belize, and Nicaragua were 2.5, 3.7, 2.7, 3.2, and 3.7 respectively—all below the estimated rate in Guatemala. See United Nations Development Programme, *Human Development Report 2003* (New York: Oxford University Press, 2003), table 5, 250–52.

10. At the end of the civil war, policy makers introduced neoliberal, market-oriented reforms that involved a reduction in government social spending, privatization, and trade liberalization. The assumption was that new investment spurred by structural reform would create more jobs than the number of jobs eliminated by such reforms. As in many other countries, this assumption proved to be questionable, as employment and real wages fell. For example, the average annual change in real mean wages was -1.1 percent between 1985 and 1996. See United Nations Development Programme, *Guatemala: Los contrastes del desarrollo humano* (Guatemala: UNDP, 1998), 61. Since then, there has been little upward trajectory in real wages. For a general overview of research (that includes studies of Guatemala) on this period, see John P. Tuman, "Labor Markets and Economic Reform in Latin America: A Review of Recent Research," *Latin American Research Review* 35, no. 3 (2000): 173–87.

11. Francisco José Pérez, "Effects of Land Legalization in the Agrarian Dynamics of Indigenous Communities of Alta Verapaz, Guatemala," working paper, Center for International Studies, University of Ohio, 2005, 108. See also Instituto Nacional de Estadística (Guatemala) (INE), *Censos y encuestas,* http://www.ine.gob.gt/censos.html (accessed June 18, 2007).

12. Manz, *Refugees of a Hidden War,* 151–53.

13. Hamilton and Stoltz Chinchilla, *Seeking Community,* 33.

14. Gearhart's personal observation of Guatemalan-Mexican border crossing, where migrants could be observed crossing a river in plain view of authorities, 2006. To be sure, some Guatemalans enter the United States with an immigrant or nonimmigrant visa (e.g., visas for guest workers, tourists, businesspeople, students, and diplomats). Nevertheless, as noted, data provided by the Department of Homeland Security suggest that the vast majority of Guatemalans enter the United States without any legal authorization. For data and estimates, see U.S. Department of Homeland Security, *Yearbook of Immigration Statistics: 2007* (Washington, D.C.: U.S. Department of Homeland Security, Office of Immigration Statistics, 2008), tables 28, 32; Department of Homeland Security, Office of Immigration Statistics, "Estimates of the Unauthorized Immigrant Population Residing in the United States: January 2007," table 3, p. 4, www.dhs.gov/xlibrary/assets/statistics/publications/ois ill pe 2007.pdf (accessed July 26, 2009).

15. Anonymous (#1), interview by Dawn Gearhart, March 2007. See also Allan Burns, *Maya in Exile: Guatemalans in Florida* (Philadelphia: Temple University Press, 1993).

16. Guatemalan migrant, interview by Gearhart, Las Vegas, March 2007.

17. For examples, see Burns, *Maya in Exile*.

18. U.S. Census Bureau, American Community Survey, "Table B03100, Hispanic or Latino by Specific Origin—Florida and California," 2006, http://factfinder.census.gov/ (accessed July 15, 2008).

19. Calculated from various census data for the "foreign-born" population in Nevada, as compiled and reported in Nevada State Library and Archives, "Nevada Foreign Born Population, 1860–2000," http://dmla.clan.lib.nv.us/docs/nsla/sdc/stat.htm (accessed March 18, 2008). There are no data for the year 1980. In addition, although the census figures do not show any population of Guatemalan origin prior to 1960, this may reflect a lack of measurement of this population in the older census surveys.

20. See John P. Tuman, "Latin American Migrants in the Las Vegas Valley: Civic Associations, Political Participation, and the Challenges Facing Migrants," Washington, D.C., Woodrow Wilson International Center for Scholars, 2007, www.wilsoncenter.org/news/docs/background.%20paper-Las%20Vegas.doc (accessed March 18, 2008).

21. U.S. Census Bureau, "Census 2000 Demographic Profile Highlights, Guatemalans, Las Vegas and North Las Vegas," http://factfinder.census.gov/ (accessed February 22, 2008). These data do not allow one to differentiate between Guatemalans who arrived in the United States as adults and those who came as children; as a result, the educational attainment figures should be treated with caution. In addition, it is worth noting that when no adjustments are made for race or ethnicity, high-school graduation rates in the general population of both cities is much higher, standing at 78 and 66 percent, respectively, in Las Vegas and North Las Vegas in 2000. Finally, because fewer than 100 Guatemalans were residing in Henderson in 2000, the Census Bureau has removed all observations on Guatemalans in Henderson in order to protect individual privacy.

22. Calculated from migrant workforce data for each by sector, as reported in Progressive Leadership Alliance of Nevada, *The Demographic and Economic Facts about Hispanic Immigrants in Nevada*, Nevada: PLAN, 2007, table 6; labor-force data from U.S. Census Bureau, American Community Survey, "2005 Data Profiles—Clark County, Nevada—Income, Occupation, Work," http://factfinder.census.gov/ (accessed June 8, 2007). Anecdotal reports suggest that the migrant share of the workforce in some subsectors of the construction industry (e.g., new home construction) is higher than the overall figure of 55 percent, but this claim could not be verified because data for the number of migrants in each subsector were not available.

23. See *New York Times*, "Corrections," March 14, 2007, providing a correction to a previously published story about hourly minimum wages in Guatemala, http://query.nytimes.com/gst/fullpage.html?res=9C05E2D91131F937A25750C0A9619C8B63 (accessed March 20, 2008).

24. See National Labor Committee, "Daisy Fuentes Clothing Sewn in Guatemalan Sweatshop," Final Report, July, 2007, http://www.nlcnet.org/article.php?id=344

(accessed March 20, 2008). This report documents widespread allegations of labor rights abuse in the garment export sector. Additional reports suggest that United States embassy staff in Guatemala—who spoke on condition of anonymity—have verified problems in the garment sector and have found little or no improvement in compliance with national labor laws. See Peter S. Goodman, "Labor Rights in Guatemala Aided Little by Trade Deal," *Washington Post,* March 17, 2007, http://www.washingtonpost.com/wp-dyn/content/article/2007/03/15/AR2007031502452.html (accessed March 20, 2008).

25. Calculated from U.S. Census Bureau, "Census 2000 Demographic Profile Highlights, Guatemalans, Las Vegas and North Las Vegas," http://factfinder.census.gov/ (accessed February 22, 2008). See note 21 for an explanation of missing data for Guatemalan residents of Henderson.

26. See World Bank, "Country Brief: Guatemala," May 1999, http://WBLN0018.worldbank.org/External/lac/lac.nsf/412657d72e240425852567d6006b2721/43145249ae1fea1d852567d90070cbd9?OpenDocument (accessed March 20, 2008). The report found that in 1998, per capita income was $1,640, but a 4 percent increase for 1999 was forecast; the forecast was used for the estimated per capita income in 1999. The methodology employed by the World Bank may differ from estimation techniques used by the Census Bureau; for this reason, the comparison should be treated as a rough approximation. In addition, per capita income in Guatemala varies sharply across different regions; some areas of the country are well below the national mean for per capita income.

27. In 2006 Guatemalan migrants in the United States sent approximately $3.6 billion back to Guatemala. In some areas, the amount received was more than the amount one could earn in Guatemala (even when workers have completed secondary education). This points to the problem of stagnation in real wages and the persistence of the wage gap as a proximate cause of migration to the United States. See Juan Carlos Llorca, "Some Guatemalans Loaf in U.S. Cash Flow," *Las Vegas Sun,* May 29, 2007, 1.

28. In interviews carried out for this project, a civic leader noted that most Guatemalans arrived in Nevada in the early 1980s, with the majority concentrating in Las Vegas and Reno. Anonymous (#2), interview by Gearhart, Las Vegas, April 2007.

29. Data and calculations of relative change are taken from the U.S. Census Bureau, Census 2000, "Table QT-P9—Hispanic or Latino by Type, Clark County, 2000," and U.S. Census Bureau, American Community Survey, "Table B03001, Hispanic or Latino by Specific Origin—Clark County, 2005," http://factfinder.census.gov/ (accessed June 8, 2007). For 2006, see U.S. Census Bureau, *American Community Survey,* "Table B03001, Hispanic or Latino by Specific Origin—Clark County, Nevada, 2006," http://factfinder.census.gov/ (accessed July 15, 2008).

30. Calculated from U.S. Census Bureau, "Census 2000 Demographic Profile Highlights, Guatemalans, Las Vegas and North Las Vegas," http://factfinder.census.gov/ (accessed February 22, 2008).

31. U.S. Census Bureau, *American Community Survey,* "Table B03001, Hispanic or Latino by Specific Origin-Clark County, Nevada, 2006."

32. See the estimates discussed in Timothy Pratt, "More Guatemalans Move to the Valley." *Las Vegas Sun,* May 21, 2004, 8B. A community leader put the estimate at between 12,000 and 15,000 in 2007. Anonymous (#1), interview.

33. See Pratt, "More Guatemalans Move to Las Vegas."

34. Migrants who have joined Evangelical churches appear to have abandoned the syncretic rituals. Anonymous (#2), interview.

35. Many Central Americans attend the Centro Cristiano Amigos de Israel. Similar to other groups of recent migrants, Guatemalans who are upwardly mobile appear to be likely to join evangelical churches. The reasons for this pattern are not clear. Possibly, these churches offer a voluntarist explanation of social mobility that fits comfortably with migrants' own views of why they have prospered. It is also important to note that within Guatemala, as much as 40 percent of the population may belong to evangelical and pentecostal churches. For background, see Public Broadcasting Service, "Guatemala: A Rising Faith," Religion and Ethics Weekly, episode no. 836, May 6, 2005, available at http://www.pbs.org/wnet/religionandethics/week836/cover.html (accessed April 11, 2008). See also Susan D. Rose and Steve Brouwer, "The Export of Fundamentalist Americanism: U.S. Evangelical Education in Guatemala," *Latin American Perspectives* 17, no. 4 (1990), 42–56.

36. Anonymous (#2), interview, and Gearhart's observation of the Huelga de Dolores celebration in 2007, which included Guatemalans of differing faiths.

37. The degree to which Guatemalans feel integrated into the Latino community may vary. Some migrants speak Kanjobal Maya, an indigenous language, and identify themselves more as indigenous than as Latin American of Guatemalan origin. We lack reliable data on the degree of linguistic diversity in the local population; however, Guatemalans have been observed conversing in indigenous languages while dining in local restaurants.

38. Aldo Aguirre, as quoted in Pratt, "More Guatemalans Move to Las Vegas."

39. Of those Guatemalans age fifteen and older, 76 percent in Las Vegas were married; 77 percent in North Las Vegas were married. These estimates are not exact, because the denominator used for the calculations is the total Guatemalan population age eighteen and older, while the marriage figures are for population age fifteen and older. Calculated from U.S. Census Bureau, "Census 2000 Demographic Profile Highlights, Guatemalans, Las Vegas and North Las Vegas," http://factfinder.census.gov/ (accessed February 22, 2008).

40. As noted, this claim is based only on fragmentary evidence and observations of Guatemalans in Las Vegas and should be treated provisionally. It is, however, supported by anthropological studies in other parts of the United States. In his study of Maya migrants and migrants from other Caribbean and Central American countries, Burns notes, "Guatemalan and Haitian women have had to add their wage labor work to their already existing domestic work in child raising, cooking and home organization. . . . The average Guatemalan household contains between nine and fourteen members, half of whom are boarders not related to the owners of the house

or apartment. Women cook for the entire household and receive some compensation from non-relatives." Burns, *Maya in Exile,* 118–19.

41. The prevalence rate of domestic violence and murder of women in Guatemala is extremely high, prompting many investigations into the human rights situation in the country. For an overview, see Theresa Lawson, "Sending Countries and the Rights of Migrant Workers: The Case of Guatemala," *Harvard Human Rights Journal* 18 (Spring 2005): 233. Women's rights advocates have noted the existence of domestic violence against Guatemalan migrant women in Las Vegas, but, unfortunately, we lack reliable data on the prevalence rate. Importantly, it is unclear if the prevalence rate among Guatemalan migrants is statistically different from prevalence rates among other groups.

42. On this point, see Burns, *Maya in Exile,* 182–83. See also authors' field notes, April and May 2007.

43. Anonymous (#3), interview by Gearhart, Las Vegas, July 2007.

44. Anonymous (#1), interview.

45. Anonymous (#3), interview. This section was also based on information provided in El Comité de Unidad Guatemalteco de Nevada, "COMUGUA Informe," unpublished report, Las Vegas, March 2007, and El Comité de Unidad Guatemalteco de Nevada, "2nda Huelga de Delores de Nevada," unpublished report, Las Vegas, 2007.

46. This program was created prior to the founding of COMUGUA. La Hora Chapina has operated for over ten years and was initiated by one of the founders of COMUGUA.

47. See El Comité de Unidad Guatemalteco de Nevada, "2nda Huelga de Delores de Nevada," unpublished paper, Las Vegas, 2007. In an interview, one person commented that because of the political satire associated with this event, Guatemalans who celebrate the Huelga in Guatemala "know for a fact that they are risking their life in Guatemala, but in the United States this is not the case." See Anonymous (#3), interview.

48. Authors' estimates (taken from Gearhart, who attended the event), April 2007.

49. Follow-up remarks by Israel Fuentes, in roundtable discussions at the meeting, "Latin American Migrants in Las Vegas: Civic and Political Participation in a Binational Context," project organized by the Woodrow Wilson International Scholars and the Institute for Latin American Studies, UNLV, September 21, 2007. For a summary of the roundtable discussions at this meeting, see John P. Tuman, *Latin American Migrant Project: Civic and Political Participation in Las Vegas, Final Report,* Mexico Institute, Woodrow Wilson International Center for Scholars, March, 2008.

50. In recognition of the growing Guatemalan population in Las Vegas, the U.S. State Department recently recognized the offices of the honorary consul and vice consul in Las Vegas.

51. See Organization of American States, "Report of the Department for the Promotion of Democracy (DPD): The Human Rights of Migrants, Including Migrants

and their Families," Department for the Promotion of Democracy, OAS, Washington, D.C., 2006, http://www.oas.org/DIL/first_group_report_of_the_Dep_promotion_democr_eng.doc> (accessed March 22, 2008); *Congreso de la República de Guatemala, Reformas a la Ley Electoral y de Partidos Políticos,* Decreto número 10–2004, http://www.congreso.gob.gt/gt/leyes2.asp?year=2004 (accessed March 22, 2008).

52. As quoted in El Comité de Unidad Guatemalteco de Nevada, "Guatemalan Presidential Candidate to Visit Las Vegas," press release from COMUGUA, May 10, 2007, 1.

53. Ibid.

54. See Timothy Pratt, "Guatemalan Candidate Brings Campaign to Southern Nevada." *Las Vegas Sun,* July 8, 2002, 8A.

55. Burns, *Maya in Exile,* 60–61, in reference to the group called Kanjobal Association; Hamilton and Stoltz Chinchilla, *Seeking Community,* 123–24, 132–34.

56. Burns, *Maya in Exile,* 61–66, in reference to the Kanjobal Association and CORN-Maya in southern Florida; Hamilton and Stoltz Chinchilla, *Seeking Community,* 123–24, 132–34.

CHAPTER 13

The Colombians

TIMOTHY PRATT

When Juliana Rico and her twin sister, Lina, walked through the doors of the restaurant Oiga, Mire, Vea one Sunday afternoon in June 2007, it was a sign. The two college students from Bucaramanga were in trouble. They were in town on short-term visas and someone had stolen their passports and money. They looked to fellow Colombians for help. The sisters had heard that there was an association of Colombians in Las Vegas and that its board members would be at the restaurant that Sunday.

The Ricos' decision to seek help at the restaurant was a sign, then, of at least three things about the Las Vegas Valley's Colombian community. First, that it had grown large enough to sustain an association of compatriots organized enough to hold an activity like the one the Ricos were told about that day. The activity: local Colombians were casting ballots for the association's officers. Second, there was the restaurant itself. Six years earlier, it had become the Valley's first place to sample Colombian cooking; now it was the de facto meeting place for natives of the Andean country. The Valley's Colombian community had not attained the critical mass to sustain a restaurant in decades past. Finally, though, it was also a sign of the limits in size of the Valley's Colombian population, which several active members of the association estimated to be at 6,000 in 2007, somewhat larger than the 2006 census estimate of 4,061.[1] Unlike the much larger Mexican and Salvadoran communities, there are not yet enough Colombians in the Valley to anchor a consulate in Las Vegas. So in the end, the Rico sisters had to find their way to Los Angeles for the help they needed.

Still, before the year 2000, there was a much smaller association—a club, really—with a smaller range of activities and no such place to meet. There was also no place like Oiga, Mire, Vea for Colombians to dance Saturday nights.

Colombian Diaspora

As elsewhere in the United States, the number of Colombians in the Las Vegas Valley has increased at a dizzying pace in the last decade-plus, particularly in the second half of that span. Starting around 2000, press accounts began documenting a diaspora fleeing the South American country's internecine violence.[2] At the same time, there remains a dearth of research on Colombian immigrants and immigration and on related issues such as transnationalism and Colombians in the United States.[3]

As is true of most Latin American countries, poverty and lack of opportunity for education and for improving standards of living are core "push" factors driving emigration. But emigration from Colombia is fueled by more than these conditions, which are endemic to the developing world. For more than a decade, Colombia has had the dubious distinction of placing among top-ten lists worldwide in kidnapping, refugees, and homicide rates. The violence, which continues today, centers around two guerrilla armies—the Revolutionary Armed Forces of Colombia, or FARC, and the National Liberation Army, or ELN—and a paramilitary force that landowners assembled thirty years ago to defend themselves from the guerrillas. There are also criminals working for one or several of these groups.

These outside-the-law armies and assorted mercenaries have been at it for decades. In fact, a parallel conflict ripped the country apart in a period spanning from 1948 to 1966 known simply as *La violencia*. During those decades, violence between supporters of the liberal, conservative, and communist parties claimed the lives of at least 200,000 people, with at least as many losing their homes.

In the most recent incarnation of violence, however, the cocaine and, to a lesser degree, heroin trades have exponentially increased financing for weapons used by guerrillas and paramilitaries.[4] Likewise, the United States has increasingly financed Colombia's armed forces since the Clinton administration launched Plan Colombia in 2000.

Toward the end of the last decade, members of the country's upper middle and wealthy classes began fleeing this chaos. Of course, an unknown number were fleeing the seemingly intractable social and economic conditions that have contributed to Colombia's ongoing violence. Those conditions include corruption, leading to a lack of opportunities for those who are not among the favored upper classes. Many escaped to the neighboring countries of Venezuela, and, to a lesser degree, Ecuador, and others chose Spain. Many chose *el norte*—the United States.

By 2000 there were nearly a half million Colombians living in the United States, according to the Census Bureau. A good portion of these immigrants—nearly three of every ten—had settled in south Florida.[5] Seven years later, the number of Colombians in the United States was estimated at 1.1 million. Other recent studies place the number at twice that many.[6]

Colombians in Las Vegas

But Colombians also came to Las Vegas, many for the same reason as other immigrants—jobs.[7] In the 2000 census, Clark County's Colombian population was estimated at 1,558. By 2006 the census estimate had risen to 4,061.[8] In 2004 the local Colombian association's own census yielded the figure of 1,059.[9] But Humberto Restrepo, who coordinated the association's effort, estimates that less than a third of local Colombians participated. Though that census did not include questions about race, place of birth, or religion, Restrepo estimates that 50 percent of the Valley's Colombians come from Bogotá, the country's capital; 30 percent, from Medellín; and another 15 percent, from Cali. The latter two are cities of about two million each. Most Colombians in the Las Vegas Valley are mestizos, or of mixed race. Few black Colombians have settled in the area. Most are Roman Catholic.[10]

The Colombians who have come to live and work in southern Nevada have distinguished themselves from other Latin American immigrants in several ways. Many are well-educated professionals, for example. In the association's census, 46 percent of those surveyed had a technical or professional degree.[11] This has been noted of Colombian immigrants elsewhere. One south Florida survey showed that four of ten Colombians had a college education.[12] Similarly, 60 percent of those participating in the Las Vegas area's census said they spoke English "well" or "excellent."[13] In south Florida, seven of ten surveyed had at least a working knowledge of English.[14] As for the incomes of Colombians in the Valley, in the local survey, 37 percent of families reported earning more than $40,000 a year.[15] When it comes to immigration status, few have entered the United States by crossing the border without documents or via other illegal routes. The local survey reported that 81 percent were residents, citizens, or refugees.[16]

In the last five years, the Colombian Association of Las Vegas staged its first census and organized the first three visits to Las Vegas of the San Francisco–based Colombian consul. The association has also become involved in national issues of concern to Colombians, including the 2004 push to get congressional support for offering a special, temporary protected status to natives of the country who entered the United States after a certain date. (The so-called TPS status [Temporary Protected Status] has yet to be approved.)

In February 2008, local Colombians also took part in a plea for peace and against kidnapping that immigrants from the Andean country staged nationwide. These activities are signs of the transnational political lives many Colombians in the Valley lead, with one eye on affairs of their home country.

In the Las Vegas area, the Colombian diaspora has left an impact that belies its size. Professionals fleeing Colombia have made their presence felt in certain sectors of life in the Valley, such as Spanish-language media, health care, and engineering—a sign of their professional status that compares favorably with that of some other Latin American immigrants.

There are two major Spanish-language newspapers in the Valley: *El Tiempo* and *El Mundo*. *El Tiempo* is partially run by Hernando Amaya, the associate editor whose byline has accompanied many of the weekly's articles since 2002. A former communications director for the Colombian Army, Amaya came to the United States after one of the country's two guerrilla groups phoned him with death threats.

There are also two Spanish-language television news programs in the Valley, broadcast by Univisión and Telemundo. Univisión is more widely seen, and on most nights it draws higher ratings than even English-language news programs in the eighteen- to thirty-four-year-old demographic. Its director: Adriana Arévalo, who started her fast-paced career in her native Colombia covering kidnappings and murders. Then she reported from New York on the aftermath of September 11, 2001, to her compatriots. From there, Arévalo went to Miami, where she produced weekend episodes of *Primer Impacto*, the top-rated Spanish-language newsmagazine. Now she directs the flow of information to the Valley's 450,000-plus Hispanics, in the nation's second-fastest-growing Spanish-language television market.[17]

In health care, the research section of the Valley's only pediatric cardiology department is staffed by Colombians. Four of the Children's Heart Center's twelve doctors are also Colombian.

As for engineering, one recently arrived Colombian has designed the first new hotel tower in downtown Las Vegas in the last twenty years, while another is project manager at a company that handles one-fourth of the Valley's exterior work in residential construction.

Beginnings of a Club

Despite its recent growth, the local Colombian community was once so small that running into someone from the Andean country could take weeks.

Carmen Mahan remembers those days. Her family moved from Barranquilla to Miami in 1965. They were early victims of Colombia's violence, which has been raging for most of the last seven decades. A teenager, she did not know about all that, however. "I was busy thinking about where I was going tonight or who was going to call me," she recalls, her words still pushed along with a clipped Caribbean accent despite the passage of time. Years later, she learned that her family left their homeland because her older sister's husband, a major in the army, had been shot by assassins on the other side of the country's perennial political divide between liberals and conservatives.

By the time she understood why her family had come to the United States, Mahan was living in Las Vegas and married to a U.S. citizen.

Her husband got a job in 1974 at the MGM casino, and they have stayed in the Valley since. At that time, she recalls, "there were very few Colombians. If you ran into one, it was a surprise!" she exclaims, throwing up her hands with the animated conversational style typical of her homeland. By 1980 she had bought and was operating a hair salon. She was a business owner who spoke English most of the time.

Despite Mahan's deep assimilation, questions of identity surfaced in her own household. One afternoon, her son Kevin came home from school with a question. Actually, kids on the basketball court had asked him, "What are you?" So he asked his mother, "Am I Hispanic? Am I American?" Mahan replied, "You were born here and your Mom is Colombian. There's nothing you can do about that."

She tells this story in Spanish and English, both carried along by ocean winds in her voice. She looks back on raising her son, on the question, 'Who am I?' She remembers the pressure to assimilate. "I didn't realize at the time, 'You should talk to him in Spanish,'" she says. "I regret not teaching him. It was a different time," she offers.

Some years afterward, her son had left for college and Mahan was looking for a project. Something with meaning. A niece visited from Colombia. Someone asked her where she was from. Hearing her reply, the words cocaine and marijuana peeled off the person's lips. By that time, the movie *Scarface* and the television series *Miami Vice* had left most Americans with that sort of knee-jerk connection between Colombia and drugs. Mahan was tired of it. "Every time someone mentioned Colombia, it was the same reaction," she recalls. "I wanted to do something about that."

In June 1989, she and five compatriots formed the Colombian Club of Las Vegas. Mahan was president; the credo was, "The image of Colombia is the one you show." Shortly thereafter, the club's first party drew six hundred people. "That's when we find out there were so many Colombians," she says. One of the club's main functions at the time was to bring some level of respect to Colombians in the Valley, both from fellow Hispanics and from the community at large. "We wanted to be a part of the community," Mahan says. "The whole idea was that people notice Colombia." Clippings from the 1980s and 1990s, mostly in the Spanish-language press, show Mahan and

236   The Colombians

other club members at typical society-page events, accompanied by local Latin Chamber of Commerce officials and politicians.[18]

By the turn of the new decade, however, the crush of new immigrants from the Andean country brought the club to turn more of its attention to fellow Colombians. There were a number of compatriots arriving with political asylum cases, or work-related visas, or sometimes illegally. The club found itself seeking the Colombian consulate's services and lobbying for Temporary Protected Status, the same blanket relief offered Salvadorans after Hurricane Mitch or other countries after civil wars.[19]

By 2003 the club helped broker the San Francisco–based Colombian consul's first official visit. Before that, the community's small size and lesser needs meant that local Colombians had to make the trip to California. The club also carried out the local census. The group formalized its status in 2003, becoming a nonprofit association.

A Place to Meet

The consul's visit and other events drawing together members of the Valley's Colombian community have often been held at Oiga, Mire, Vea, the same cluttered depository of national symbols ranging from flags on a stick to malt-flavored sodas that the Rico sisters found one afternoon in June. Beyond symbols, the restaurant offers assorted ties to Colombia, including a phone line for calling home, a system for sending money orders, satellite channels offering the Andean country's beloved soccer games, and copies of a Los Angeles weekly featuring news of Colombian singers and TV stars. In this way, the restaurant has also become a transnational vehicle of sorts, unique in the Valley for Colombian immigrants.

Olmedo Hoyos owns the restaurant. Like the kitchen at a party, his restaurant has become the place where everyone meets. Ironically, the man behind the only symbol of stability for local Colombians is one of the few to enter the country *por el hueco* (through the hole), or crossing the Mexican border. This he did in 1981, after a childhood in Bogotá, the country's chaotic capital, that included his family's poaching a vacant lot in order to build a shanty when he was eight years old. Colombia's urban and rural poor have engaged in this practice for decades.

His youth also included working since shortly after learning to read, a school of hard knocks that started early. He sold cups of coffee. He sewed together scraps of leather into bags and jackets and sold them as well. He sold airline tickets. By the time he was eighteen, Hoyos decided to hop a plane to Mexico and cross the border.

After several attempts, he made it and established himself in the Los Angeles area. He worked with leather again, fixing shoes. When the chemicals started to bother him, a client who was starting up a natural foods supermarket called Mrs. Gooch's offered him a job at her store. He wound up staying there sixteen years, by which time he was manager of the cheese and wine department and a growing company called Whole Foods had bought the store. From there, Hoyos struck out on his own. He bought a Colombian restaurant with a partner in Van Nuys, California. A friend would come to the restaurant from Las Vegas. A few years of urging him to check it out and Hoyos finally came to look at locales. The rest, as they say, is history.

Hoyos's story has brought him to understand the immigrant experience from all sides, not only because of what he has endured, but also because he has seen members of the Colombian diaspora on a daily basis for so long. Oiga, Mire, Vea is now the place you'd go to if you wanted to borrow a traditional poncho from Medellín for a July 20 Colombian Independence Day party. Or just to make a Sunday morning feel more like home by buying a pack of *arepas,* or corn cakes, to go. "I'm the phone book for Colombians," he says, meaning this is where everyone winds up. He lists the requests that he has fielded: doctors, dentists, lost passports, abortions, apartments, jobs.[20]

But he also says that the restaurant is only an improvised solution, not a permanent one. Mahan agrees. After twenty years with the local Colombian club-cum-association, Mahan says some sort of cultural center is needed, and not having one is her only regret. "We need a place to teach our history, our culture," says Hoyos. "A place you can go to and look for a book."

Colombian Identity in Las Vegas

Of course, the issue they raise is, again, one of identity, the perennial question for all immigrants. How do we make a life in a new land while holding onto our own culture? This question acquires heightened meaning in the transnational experience common to immigrants of today, especially those with economic access to frequent travel and technologies such as computers.

To understand this issue, it is useful to speak with younger immigrants, the new Colombian Americans. Ana María Gutiérrez, for example. Gutiérrez spent her childhood among Bogotá's upper class, the daughter of a civil engineer. In Colombia that means going to private schools and the country club, with a maid and a chauffeur. In 2002 her father, Luis Alberto, began talking about the possibility of landing a job in Las Vegas. "Las Vegas?! Wowww . . . ," she remembers thinking. "All you heard about Las Vegas was casinos, parties."

By 2003 the Gutiérrez family was unpacking their bags in a Henderson gated community. Luis Alberto had obtained a work visa. Ana María became a student at Green Valley High School. There were days she did not go, often feeling out of place. "I stayed at home. I didn't know anyone," she says. She was shocked by a friend who had moved from Colombia to the United States four years earlier and had been transformed into an American teenager. She became depressed. Gutiérrez was used to music and dancing, a staple of Colombian social life. But all the girls she met wanted to go shopping in malls. When she went to parties, the liberal mores, including drug use, also struck her as strange.

But then she saw things she liked. Unlike Colombia's class-conscious society, she did not have to worry about what other people thought all the time. "Here, there's not so much, 'What is so-and-so going to say?' if you do something, or wear something," she says. And then there was the independence she saw in her friends. Now twenty-one and a first-year student at UNLV, she's the only one in her circle who still lives with her parents.

She looks forward to finding a job she likes and being able to buy her own things. She notes that in the United States, "What you're able to achieve it's because you've worked for it, not because you're pretty, or someone knows you." She straddles a line between two worlds, an experience common to all Colombians, to varying degrees, in their new lives in Las Vegas. For example, the "What are you?" question still makes her cringe. "You don't look Latin," they tell her, often possessed by the image of a Mexican immigrant, since over 70 percent of the Valley's Hispanic community has roots in Mexico. Gutiérrez is tall and slim, with sharp features, an image many people in the United States would never associate with Mexico. And she confronts the insult of seeing the name of her homeland spelled "Columbia."

Still, when she walks through the door of her house, she says, "It's like another world." She finds Luz Angela, her mother, watching *telenovelas,* the soap operas that border on obsession for Colombian families. This is possible, of course, thanks to modern satellite TV packages aimed at immigrants. Also, Gutiérrez finds her family cooking, instead of eating fast food. Her mother makes fried plantains and a special dipping sauce called *hogao*—a trick possible thanks to the ubiquity of Latino supermarkets in the Valley, development brought by earlier Mexican waves of immigration. And, like most Latino families, the Gutiérrezes eat together. Her boyfriend, from Las Vegas, sees all this as strange. He asks questions such as, "Why is everyone shouting? Why are they always laughing?" Gutiérrez wonders why he does not offer to drive her home when they are out together or feel stronger about dancing. "I feel like a lot of the things we fight about are cultural," she says.

Still, when she travels home for vacation—there are no direct flights to Colombia, but connections are available in Los Angeles and Miami—she discovers she is no longer fully Colombian. And she also is not completely *gringa*. Gutiérrez's experience is not unique. It was described by María Claudia Duque-Páramo in her graduate thesis at the University of South Florida on children born in Colombia and raised in the United States. "Acculturation does not mean full assimilation," she wrote, "but rather a blend . . . where a new culture, different from both home and host society, emerges."[21]

This is the state most Colombians in the Las Vegas Valley seem to reach, in the end. Many have had to flee violence or the fear of violence, bringing with them strong feelings for their land and culture as if another suitcase. Their formal education and the innate, cat-landing-on-four-feet sense of survival that Colombians possess have made it easier to start over. And the way Las Vegas often rewards those who work hard has suited many well.

The end result may best be captured by Gutiérrez's description of herself. "I'm happier feeling like I'm both," she concludes. "Not just one."

Notes

1. U.S. Census Bureau, American Community Survey, "Table B03001, Hispanic or Latino by Specific Origin—Clark County, Nevada, 2006," http://factfinder.census.gov/ (accessed July 15, 2008).

2. Myriam Berube, "Colombia: In the Crossfire," *Migration Policy Institute*, November 2005; Larry Rohter, "Driven by Fear, Colombians Leave in Droves," *New York Times*, March 5, 2000; Paul Brinkley-Rogers, "Colombian Exiles Face Uncertain U.S. Future," *Miami Herald*, June 6, 2001; T. Christian Miller, "Colombia's Fugitives from Woe," *Los Angeles Times*, March 31, 2001.

3. Arturo Ignacio Sánchez, "Colombian Immigration to Queens, New York: The Transnational Re-imagining of Urban Political Space" (Ph.D. diss., Columbia University, 2003).

4. Clifford Krauss, "War in Colombia Creates a Nation of Victims," *New York Times*, September 10, 2000. A good source for current information on Colombia is the online magazine colombiajournal.org.

5. "Colombian Population of the U.S. in Percentages of Total Colombian Population, by State," *The Latino Data Project*, Center for Latin American, Caribbean and Latino Studies Graduate Center, City University of New York, n.d.

6. Casey Woods, "U.S. Colombians seek more political clout," *Miami Herald*, September 23, 2007; *Migration Policy Institute*, November 2005.

7. Personal observation, based on interviews for this chapter and six years of reporting (in 2007) on the Las Vegas Valley's Hispanic community for the *Las Vegas Sun*.

8. U.S. Census Bureau, American Community Survey, "Table B03001."

9. Chart, "Gráficas del censo," *Colombian Association of Las Vegas,* 2004, courtesy Humberto Restrepo.

10. Humberto Restrepo, e-mail to author and interview by author, December 2007.

11. Chart, "Gráficas del censo."

12. "Study Reveals a Higher Level of Education Among Latin American Immigrants," *Hispanic PR Wire,* April 28, 2004.

13. Chart, "Gráficas del censo."

14. "Study Reveals a Higher Level of Education."

15. Chart, "Gráficas del censo."

16. Ibid.

17. Timothy Pratt, "New Voice Calls on Hispanics: TV News Director Seeks to Make Connection on How Events Affect Community," *Las Vegas Sun,* July 26, 2006.

18. Personal archives, Carmen Mahan.

19. Timothy Pratt, "Colombians Search for Safe Haven," *Las Vegas Sun,* April 5, 2003.

20. Alec Wilkinson describes the remarkably similar role that Orlando Tobón plays in the Colombian Community in Queens, New York. Alec Wilkinson, "The Patron: The Man to See in Little Colombia," *The New Yorker,* November 26, 2007, 88–103.

21. María Claudia Duque-Páramo, "Colombian Immigrant Children in the United States" (Ph.D. diss., Dept. of Anthropology, University of South Florida, 2004).

CONTRIBUTORS

ASLAM ABDULLAH is the director of the Islamic Society of Nevada in Las Vegas. He is also secretary general of the World Council of Muslims for Interfaith Relations, based in Chicago. Additionally, he is vice president of the Washington-based Muslim Council of America. He worked as vice president of the American Islamic College and editor-in-chief of the *Minaret Magazine,* published in Los Angeles. Currently, he is editor-in-chief of the independent *Muslim Observer,* an English-language weekly published in Detroit. He has authored eleven books, including *The American Muslim Identity* (2003), and over four hundred articles in newspapers and journals on Muslims and Islam.

JIEMIN BAO is associate professor of anthropology at the University of Nevada, Las Vegas. She is the author of *Marital Acts: Gender, Sexuality, and Identity among the Chinese Thai Diaspora* (2005).

KATHLEEN JA SOOK BERGQUIST is an associate professor in the School of Social Work at the University of Nevada, Las Vegas. She completed her master's degree in social work at Norfolk State University, her Ph.D. in counselor education at the College of William and Mary in Virginia, and her J.D. at the Boyd School of Law at the University of Nevada, Las Vegas. In her area of research, international adoption, she has coedited *Korean International Adoption: Fifty-Year History of Policy and Practice* (2007), and she is active as a community organizer in the local Las Vegas Asian American community.

WILLIAM CLAYSON is professor and lead faculty in history at the College of Southern Nevada. A specialist in recent U.S. political history, Clayson has published several articles on Lyndon Johnson's War on Poverty. He is the author of *Freedom is Not Enough: The War on Poverty and the Civil Rights Movement in Texas* (2010).

Contributors

DAWN GEARHART earned a J.D. from the William S. Boyd School of Law and a B.A. in Political Science (with a minor in Latin American Studies) from the University of Nevada, Las Vegas. She has studied and traveled in Latin America.

MICHAEL GREEN is a professor of history at the College of Southern Nevada. An author and editor of several books on the Civil War era and the history of Nevada and Las Vegas and a contributor to *The Peoples of Las Vegas: One City, Many Faces,* he edits the *Nevada Historical Society Quarterly* and the Wilbur S. Shepperson Series in Nevada History for the University of Nevada Press.

MICHELLE KUENZI is an assistant professor in the Department of Political Science at the University of Nevada, Las Vegas. She specializes in the area of African politics, her research focusing on political development in Africa. Much of her work in Africa has involved survey research, and she has directed two survey research projects in Senegal. She has published articles on public opinion and political behavior in Senegal and has also conducted research on party systems and the consolidation of democracy in Africa.

GUILLERMO MONKMAN is a professor of political science at the College of Southern Nevada. He received his M.A. from Virginia Tech University and his Ph.D. from the University of South Carolina. He teaches courses on American Politics, International Relations, and Latino Politics. A native of Argentina, he came to the United States in 1982 and moved to the Las Vegas Valley in 1992.

TIMOTHY PRATT is a reporter, translator, and poet who moved from Cali, Colombia, to the Las Vegas Valley in 2001. His work has appeared in *The New York Times, The Times of London, The Economist,* and dozens of other publications. For the last eight years, he has worked at the *Las Vegas Sun,* covering minority affairs, immigration, and social services.

ANDREW B. RUSSELL received his Ph.D. in history from Arizona State University and currently teaches at Central New Mexico Community College in Albuquerque. He has published several articles on Japanese Americans in the interior West and has aided in the development of exhibits and educational materials on the Japanese of Nevada, Arizona, and New Mexico.

FUMIKO SASAKI is an assistant professor at St. Edward's University in Austin, Texas. She teaches Asian politics and economy, international relations, comparative politics, and global studies.

JERRY L. SIMICH is emeritus associate professor of political science at the University of Nevada, Las Vegas. Among his recent publications are *General Index to Croatian Pioneers in California, 1849–1999*, with Adam S. Eterovich (2000), and *The Peoples of Las Vegas: One City, Many Faces*, edited with Thomas C. Wright (2005).

JONATHAN R. STRAND is an associate professor of political science at the University of Nevada, Las Vegas. His research has appeared in *World Development, Journal of East Asian Studies, International Interactions*, and elsewhere. He is the author of *Regional Development Banks: Lending with a Regional Flavor* (2010).

CAROLE COSGROVE TERRY is a doctoral candidate at the University of Nevada, Las Vegas, where she earned her M.A. in American Western History. Within her study of Germans' history in the West, her dissertation topic is Germans in urban California, 1850–1860. She has published several articles, and her prize-winning M.A. thesis is a discussion of Germans in Sacramento in the 1850s.

JOHN P. TUMAN is associate professor of political science and director of the Institute for Latin American Studies at the University of Nevada, Las Vegas. Recently, he received funding from the Woodrow Wilson International Center for Scholars to direct a study of civic engagement among Latin American migrants in the Las Vegas Valley. He is the author of *Reshaping the North American Automobile Industry: Restructuring, Corporatism and Union Democracy in Mexico* (2003). His articles have appeared in *Latin American Research Review, Political Research Quarterly, Social Science Quarterly, Industrial Relations Journal, Studies in Comparative International Development*, and several other journals.

MICHELLE TUSAN is an associate professor at the University of Nevada, Las Vegas, where she teaches European, British, and women's history. She is the author of *Women Making News: Gender and Journalism in Modern Britain* (2005) and "The Business of Relief Work," on Armenians in Constantinople, published in *Victorian Studies* (2009).

THOMAS C. WRIGHT is a distinguished professor of history at the University of Nevada, Las Vegas, specializing in Latin America. His recent books include *Latin America in the Era of the Cuban Revolution* (rev. ed., 2001), *The Peoples of Las Vegas: One City, Many Faces,* edited with Jerry L. Simich (2005), and *State Terrorism in Latin America: Chile, Argentina, and International Human Rights* (2007).

MELANIE C. YOUNG is an adjunct professor of political science at the University of Nevada, Las Vegas, specializing in American politics, Nevada politics, and popular culture. She has most recently presented research on music and politics during the Bush administration years at the 2009 American Popular Culture Association annual conference.

INDEX

Aal Tour America group, 106
Advent, 34
Affirmative Action, 168
Afghanis, 118, 119
African Americans, 53, 54; Muslims, 114, 115, 116–17, 118, 124, 128–29n13
African Community Center (ACC), The ECDC, 199, 203, 211nn11, 20
Afro-Cubans, 86
Agassi, Andre, 143, 147n47
Aladdin Hotel, 11, 16, 18
Alamo, Tony, 81–82
Albinus, Herb, 36
Albinus, Nicki, 36
Alemu, Mequanent, 207
Alpine Village restaurant, 42
Amante, Kefyarew, 207
Amaya, Hernando, 234
Amerasian children, 167, 178n12
American Historical Society of Germans from Russia, 39–40
Amhara Ethiopians, 204, 205, 206
Anan, Than Maha, 193
AnSan Sister City Park, 174
Arabs, 118, 120
Ararat Bakery, 140
Arbenz, Jacobo, 213, 214
Arden, Donn, 16
Arévalo, Adriana, 234
Arévalo, Juan José, 213
Argentine Association of Las Vegas, 155, 160
Argentines: community in Las Vegas, 157–61; emigration of, 151–53; history of Argentina and, 149–50, 152, 153, 154, 162n9, 162–63n14; illegal immigrants, 153–55, 156–57; immigrants to Las Vegas, 155–57; immigrants to U.S., 153–55, 163nn15, 22; restaurants and cuisine, 160–61; soccer and, 159–60
Arizona Club, 2
Armenian American Cultural Society of Las Vegas, 134, 135, 138, 139
Armenian Apostolic Church, 136, 137, 140
Armenian Evangelical Church of Las Vegas, 137
Armenian General Scouting and Athletic Union. *See* Homenetmen
Armenian Genocide Commemoration, 140, 141, 142
Armenian Genocide Memorial, 144, 148n55
Armenian Genocide Resolution, 141
Armenian Relief Society (ARS), 138, 139
Armenians: cultural institutions, 138–40; currently in Las Vegas, 134–44, 146n25; diaspora, 131–32; early settlers in Las Vegas, 133–34; first U.S. communities, 131, 132, 133; genocide, 132, 133–34, 140, 141–42, 144, 147n44; religious practice, 135, 136–38, 146n24; restaurants and markets, 140–41
Armenian Student Association (ASA), 138, 140
Arnaz, Desi, 77
Asian and Pacific Islander (API) population, 171
Asian Exclusion Act of 1924. *See* National Origins Act of 1924
Association of Pakistani Physicians, 119
Atlantic City, 8, 9, 11

Auld Dubliner Irish Pub, 18
Autobahn (German band), 36

Baby Temple, 188, 193
Baig, Khaliq, 122
Bailey, Margaret, 15
Bally's, 191
Bangladesh Independence Day, 120
Bangladeshis, 118, 119–20, 121–22, 124
Banks, Ismael, 125
Baptist Church, 58
Barbary Coast, 9, 16
Barden, Don, 17
Bariagaber, Assefaw, 198
Barillas, Oscar, 83
Barnes, Raymond J., 102
Basic Magnesium, 4, 6, 64
Batista, Fulgencio, 77, 78
Bavarian Brass Band, 35, 37
Bavarian Schuhplattlers, 34, 36, 43
Beatty, John, 15
Beckley, Jacob, 31, 32
Beckley, William, 31, 32
Bellagio, 43
Bells of Home (German-language radio show), 36
Bengali Association, 119–20
Beyene, Yewoubdar, 199
Binion, Lester "Benny," 10, 13
Binion's Horseshoe. *See* Horseshoe Casino
Bishop Gorman High School, 6, 9, 13, 79, 92
Bluebell Girls, 16
Bonanza Airlines, 15
Bosnians, 118, 120
Boulder Club, 8
Boulder Dam. *See* Hoover Dam
Bourbon Street Casino, 86
Bourne, Randolph, 98
boxing, 14, 83, 117, 121
Boyd, Bill, 9–10
Boyd, Sam, 9
Boyd Gaming, 9, 11
Boyer, Brendan, 16, 20
Boy Scouts and Girl Scouts of America, 138

Brencher, Willie, 35, 42, 50n34
Brendan's Irish Pub, 18
Briare, Bill, 7
Bridges, Harry, 66
Brizzoli, Greta, 42
Brookings Institute, 172
Brown, Dona, 19–20
Brunn, Sylvia, 37, 42
Bryan, Richard, 4, 20
Buchner, Walter, 35
Buddhism, 58; chanting, 190; different types/schools, 183, 187; gambling and, 193–94; meditation, 193; Soka Gakkai Buddhists, 68; temples in Las Vegas, 68, 183, 187–94, 195nn4, 7, 196n27, 197nn31–32; Thai monks, 184–85, 187–88, 189, 190, 192, 193–94; Thai women and, 189–92, 197n32. *See also* Thais
Buechler, Ralph, 44
Buol, Peter, 31

Cabrera, Manuel Estrada, 220
Caesar's Palace, 14, 79, 86, 103, 108, 118
Cafe Heidelberg, 36, 39, 41, 45
Cahlan, A. E., 12, 62, 63–64, 65
Cahlan, John, 12
Caliente (Nev.), 56, 60
California Casino, 9
Cambiero, Arturo, 79, 80, 81, 82
Cambiero, Domingo, 81
Campillo, Jacinto, 77, 79
Campo, Carlos, 83
Carrescia, Oscar, 156
Carroll, Dan, 18
Carter, Jimmy, 153
Cashman, James, 2
Castro, Fidel, 76, 77–78, 84–85, 87, 88, 89, 93, 94
Castro, Raúl, 94
Catholic Charities of Southern Nevada, 14, 20, 92, 199, 203
Catholic Church: Armenians and, 137; Colombians and, 233; Cubans and, 91–92; Ethiopians and, 199; Guatemalans and, 218; Irish and, 13–14
Catholic Community Services, 84, 205
Celtic Storm Dance Company, 17

Census Bureau. *See under* U.S. Census Bureau *headings*
Central Intelligence Agency (CIA), 214
Chang and Eng (conjoined twins), 184
Chapinmex, 218
Characters Unlimited, 103
Chávez, Hugo, 93
Chibo market, 208
Chicanos, 90
Children's Heart Center, 234
Chilean-American Association of Las Vegas, xvi
Chileans, xvi–xvii
Chinatown, 173, 175
Chinese: discrimination against, 53, 54; Koreans and, 173, 175; Las Vegas population, 69; Thais, 184
Chism Homes, 15
Chowdhry, Bashir, 124, 126
Christ Lutheran Church, 137
Christ the King Catholic Church, 207
Chung, Sue Fawn, 69
Church of Jesus Christ of Latter-day Saints, 92
Circus Circus, 82
Citizens Concerned About the Neutron Bomb, 14
Civil Liberties Act of 1988, 66, 74n35
Clark, William A., 1–2
Clark County Commission, 2, 91
Clark County Court Interpreters Office, xiv, 115, 128n4
Clark County Defense Council (CCDC), 64–65
Clark County Library, 207
Clark County Museum, 103
Clark County population, 2000–2006: Armenians, 134; Asian and Pacific Islander (API) population, 171; Colombians, 233; Cubans, 1990, 84; ethnicity statistics, xvii; Guatemalans, 216, 217, 226n22, 228n32; Hispanics, 93, 97n52, 156; Irish, 1; Koreans, 171, 175; Muslims, 117–18; Thais, 186. *See also under* U.S. Census Bureau *headings*
Clark County Republican Party, 102

Clark County School District: Cubans and, 81; English-language learners program, xv; ethnicity statistics, xiv; "Excellence in Education" award, 67; Language Fair, 39
Clinton, Bill, 78, 91, 232
Club Rioplatense, 158
Coast Casinos, 9
Coca-Cola bottling plant, 32
Cohen & Kelly's Irish Pub, 20
College of Southern Nevada (CSN), 16, 83, 91; Department of International Languages, 174; German clubs, 39, 44; Koreans and, 174
Colom, Álvaro, 222
Colombian Association of Las Vegas, 233
Colombian Club of Las Vegas, 235–36
Colombian Independence Day, 237
Colombians: current conditions in Colombia and, 232; currently in Las Vegas, 231, 233–39; immigration to Las Vegas, 233; immigration to U.S., 231–32; restaurants and, 231, 236, 237
Columbus, Christopher, 99, 115
Commercial Center, 171, 173
Community Interfaith Council, 126
Community Lutheran Church, 103, 106
Comstock Lode, 101
COMUGUA. *See* El Comité de Unidad Guatemalteco de Nevada (COMUGUA)
Corkhill, Charles "Corky," 2, 11, 15
Crandall, I. R., 64–65
Cuban Refugee Program, 83
Cubans: Afro-Cubans, 86; Cuba today and, 89–90, 93–94; currently in Las Vegas, 76, 86–94; exiles to Las Vegas after Castro revolution, 76, 77–78, 80–84; gaming industry in Las Vegas and, 76, 77, 79, 80, 81–82, 86, 87–88; Mariel boatlift immigrants, 77, 84–87; religious practice, 91–92; restaurants, 92; Spanish language and, 90, 93; visits back to Cuba by, 89–90; women, 86–87
Cuellar, Mario, 80, 81, 90–91
Cuellar, Mauricio, 81
Cugat, Xavier, 77

Culinary Union, Local 226, 8, 12, 84, 216, 223
Cunningham, Harold, 15
Cunningham, Lucille, 16

Dalitz, Moe, 11, 13, 17
Darakjian, Koko, 140
Darmstadt, Gerda, 41
Daughters of Erin, 20
Davis, Ashley, 21
Davis Dam, 11
de Castroverde, Waldo, 80, 89, 94
Delaney, Joe, 12, 20
Denis, Moisés, 91, 92
Desert Inn, 11, 43
Desert Troll Lodge, 105, 106–7
Deutsch American Society of Southern Nevada, 34, 35, 38, 40, 42
Dink, Hrant, 142
Diouf, Sylviane A., 115
Directorate for Chilean Communities Abroad, xvi–xvii
Doherty, Frank, 2
Dominican Order of Sisters, 15
Doumas, Jim, 174
Dummkopfs (band), 34, 35–36, 49n19
Dunes, 15, 43
Duque-Páramo, María Claudia, 239
Durr, Nicole, 88
Dwyer, Robert J., 13

Earley, Pete, 82
Easter, 33, 34, 42
Echelon Place, 10
Ecos de Chile folkloric group, xvi
Edwards, Chon, 170
Eid, 121, 122
El Círculo Cubano, 79
El Comité de Unidad Guatemalteco de Nevada (COMUGUA), 219–21, 222, 223
El Cortez, 8, 9
Eldorado Casino, Henderson, 9
El Gaucho restaurant, 156
Elliott, Russell, 55
El Mundo, 234
El Rancho Vegas, 2, 5, 77

El Tiempo, 234
Emerald Island Casino, 17
"Encounters of Chileans Abroad," xvi
Enomoto, George, 67
Ensign, John, 82, 142
Ensign, Michael, 82
Episcopal Church, 13
Erikson, Leif, 105, 106
Eritreans, 118, 199, 207
Ethio Café, 208
Ethiopian and Eritrean Catholic Apostolate, 199
Ethiopian Christian Fellowship Church, 207
Ethiopian Community Development Council (ECDC), 199, 211n10
Ethiopian Millennium Celebration, 208–9
Ethiopian Mutual Association of Nevada (EMAN), 205–6, 208, 209, 212n31
Ethiopian People's Revolutionary Democratic Front (EPRDF), 204
Ethiopians: currently in Las Vegas, 118, 200–202, 211nn13, 19, 20; different ethnicities of, 204, 205–6, 212n26; Ethiopian history and current conditions, 198–99, 201, 204, 210n1, 212n28; immigration to U.S. and Las Vegas, 198–200, 211n9; integration into Las Vegas, 202–3; languages, 207, 212nn32, 34; organizations of, 205–6; religious practice, 118, 206–7; restaurants and markets, 208, 212nn35–36; social and cultural life, 208–9
ethnic diversity, of Las Vegas, xi–xii, xiii–xv
ethnicity, components of, xvii
ethnic markets, xvi; for Argentines, 160–61; for Armenians, 140–41; for Ethiopians, 208, 212nn35–36; for Guatemalans, 218; for Thais, 186. *See also under* restaurants
exclusionism, 54–55

Fabré, Louis, 80, 90
Fadó Irish Pub, 18, 19
Farrakhan, Louis, 116

Fearon O'Connor School of Irish Dance, 21
Federal Bureau of Investigation (FBI), 124, 125, 126
Fernández, Sergio, 87
51s baseball team, 14–15
Filipinos, xixn14, 69
Fine, Jeffrey, 10
Finnegan's Pub, 18
First Asian Bank, 173
Fischbacher, Siegfried, 45–46
Fitzgeralds, 11, 17, 20
Flamingo Las Vegas Hotel and Casino, 8, 9, 17
Flatley, Michael, 11, 16
Florida Café Bar and Grill, 92
Foley, Roger Drummond, 5, 6
Foley, Roger T., 5
Forest Temple, 188–89, 190–91, 192, 193
Frago, Nancy, 220
Fremont Hotel and Casino, 8, 9
Fremont Street Experience, 7
Fresno (Calif.), 131, 133, 134, 139, 140, 143, 144, 147n40
Fresno State University, 144
Frey, William, 172
Frontier Club, 10
Fuentes, Gayle, 220
Fuentes, Israel, 220, 221

Gallagher, Tom, 11
Galloway, Fay, 15
gaming industry: Argentine entertainers and, 155–56; casinos in Cuba and, 76, 77–78, 84; Cubans and, 76, 77, 79, 80, 81–82, 86, 87–88; Irish and, 4, 5, 7–11; Muslims and, 118, 123–24, 127; Thais and, 186, 193–94. *See also individual casinos;* Strip, the
García, María, 87
Garside, Frank, 11–12
Gass, Octavius Decatur, 1
Gasteger, Stefan, 44
Gaughan, John D. "Jackie," 8–9
Gaughan, Michael, 9, 18
Gelber, Samuel, 32
Gemütlichkeit, 33

"Gentlemen's Agreement" of 1907 (immigration), 54, 166
German-American Mardi Gras Association, 35, 49n18
German-American Social Club of Nevada, 34, 35, 36, 37–38, 39, 40, 42, 43, 44
German brass bands, 34, 35–36
German Friendship Club, 38–39, 42
Germans: anti-German sentiment, 30–31; cultural activities, 33–37; currently in Las Vegas, 41–46, 47n6, 51n44; early settlers in Las Vegas, 31–33; immigration history, 29–31, 47n5; organizations of, 37–41; religious practice, 37; restaurants, 43–45, 50n40
Getahun, Solomon, 199, 200
Gold Coast casino, 9
Golden Nugget, 10, 16
Gold Strike, Jean, 81, 82
Goodman, Oscar, 142
Gorman, Thomas K., 13
Goto, George, 68, 74n35
Gould, Susan, 143
Greenspun, Barbara, 10–11, 12
Greenspun, Hank, 5, 12
Green Valley High School, 238
Green Valley Ranch Station, 17, 18
Grigorian, Ruben, 140
"G-Sting," 7
Guardian Angel Cathedral, 13
Guatemalan National Revolutionary Unity (URNG), 214
Guatemalans: children, 219; currently in Las Vegas, 217–22, 228nn32, 39; different groups of, 214, 224n4; fertility rate of, 214–15, 224–25n8, 225n9; Guatemalan history and, 213–15, 224n6, 225n10; honorary consulate in Las Vegas, 221, 229n50; and immigration laws, 220, 221–22, 223; immigration to Las Vegas, 216–17, 226n19, 227n28; immigration to U.S., 213–17, 224n2, 225n14; organizations of, 219–22; religious practice, 218, 228nn34–36; remittances to Guatemala, 217, 221, 227n27; women,

218–19, 228–29n40, 229n41; work in Guatemala and, 216–17, 226–27n24, 227n26
Guinn, Kenny, 4–5, 126, 141
Gustafson, Deil, 102
Gutiérrez, Ana María, 237–39
Gutiérrez, Luis Alberto, 237–38
Gutiérrez, Luz Angela, 238

Hacienda, 15
Hadi, Diba, 124
Hamazkayin Fresno Dance Ensemble, 137
Hamere Noah Kidane Mehretwe St. Michael's church, 207
Hammargren, Lonnie, 102–3, 110n17
Hamparian, Raffi, 142
Hansen, Bert, 103
Hansen, Oskar J. W., 103
Harmon, Harley A., 2, 32
Harrahs, 7, 8, 10, 17; in Reno, 81–82
Hart-Cellar Act of 1965. *See* Immigration and Nationality Act (INA) of 1965
Harvard Encyclopedia of American Ethnic Groups, xvii
Hasibullah mosque, 120, 121–22
Havana Grill, 92
"Havana Night Club," 88, 92
Hawaii, 63, 66, 69, 166, 168, 177n7
Hayes, Grace, 16
Heaney, Seamus, 16
Helldorado parade and rodeo, 2, 105
Hemingway, Ernest, 83
Herrera, Dario, 91
Heyerdahl, Thor, 105
High Scaler Cafe, Hoover Dam, 103
Hispanics: Argentines and, 153, 156, 158; Catholic Church and, 14; Clark County population, 93, 97n52, 156; Colombians and, 238; Cubans and, 90, 93; different groups of, xii; Guatemalans and, 217, 218, 228n37; Latin Chamber of Commerce of Nevada, 79–80, 83; in schools, xiv; television and newspapers for, 234
Hispanics in Politics (HIP), 80
HIV/AIDS, 201

Hofbräuhaus restaurant, 34, 35, 36, 38–39, 43–44, 45
Hohenstein, Ron, 20
Holiday Casino, 170
Holt International Children's Services, 167
Homenetmen, 138–39
Homestead Act of 1862, 99
Hoover, Herbert, 133
Hoover Dam, 2, 61, 64, 103
Horn, Roy, 45–46
Horseshoe Casino, 8, 10, 14, 193
Houssels, J. Kell, 8, 9, 10, 11
Howard Johnson's, 92
Hoyos, Olmedo, 236–37
Huddy, John, 86
Huelga de Dolores celebration, 220, 229n47
Huh, Jinho, 173
Hull, Thomas, 2, 77
Human Development Index, 198

immigration: Argentines, 153–55, 163nn15, 22; Armenians, 131, 132; Colombians, 231–32; Cubans, 76–78, 84–87; Ethiopians, 198–200, 211n9; "Gentlemen's Agreement" of 1907, 54, 166; German history of, 29–31, 47n5; Guatemalans, to U.S., 213–17, 224n2, 225n14; Guatemalans and immigration laws, 220, 221–22, 223; illegal immigrants, 153–55, 156–57, 215, 217, 225n14; integration and, 168, 179n20; Issei Japanese immigrants, 52–54, 59, 62, 66, 166; journalist and religious workers' visas, 172, 180n44; Koreans, 165–69, 177n7, 178nn12, 15, 16; recent trends in, xii–xiii, xiv, xv; restrictions on Japanese, 54, 59, 66; Scandinavians, 99–101, 110nn5, 7, 11, 12; Temporary Protected Status (TPS) for Colombians, 233, 236; Thais, 183, 184–87
Immigration Act of 1917, 166
Immigration Act of 1924. *See* National Origins Act of 1924

Immigration and Nationality Act (INA) of 1965, 31, 153, 167, 168, 185
Immigration and Nationality Act of 1952. *See* McCarran-Walter Act of 1952
Imperial Palace, 87, 103
Institute for International Economics, 165
International, the, 143
International Food and Folklife Festival, ix, 36, 38, 158
Iranians, 118, 119, 123
Ireland, Bill, 14
Irish: community involvement of, 14–16; early presence in Las Vegas, 1–3; entertainment, food, and drink, 16–19; gaming industry and, 4, 5, 7–11; media and, 11–12; organizations and, 19–21; politics and, 3–7; religion and, 13–14; sports and, 14–15, 17, 21
Irish American Club, 19, 21
Irish Pub Company, 17
Irish pubs, 17–19
Irish Show Band, 16, 20
Ishimoto family, 62
"Islam and Non-Violence" forum, 126
Islamic Information Center, 116, 120, 122
Islamic Shura Council (ISC), 122
Islamic Society of Nevada, 120, 124, 125
Islamic Society of North America, 116

Jack's Irish Pub, 18
James, Al, 2
Jamia Masjid mosque, 116, 119, 120–21, 123, 124, 126
Japan Airlines, 174
Japan America Association of Southern Nevada, 70
Japanese: anti-Japanese sentiment, 53–55, 65; current population in Las Vegas, 69–71; early settlers in Las Vegas, 55–62, 72n10, 73n21; early settlers in Nevada, 54–55; farm families, 60–62, 67; Issei immigrants, 52–54, 59, 62, 66, 166; naturalization and, 167; postwar decades, in Las Vegas, 66–69; railroad workers, 55–56, 57–60, 72n12; tourists to Las Vegas, 69–70; World War II and, 52, 62–65, 66, 73n22

Japanese American Citizens League (JACL), 66, 68, 74n35
Japanese American Club, 68
Japan-U.S. Student Exchange Program, 70
Jaye, Don, 20
JC Penney, 134
J. C. Wooloughan Irish Pub, 19
Jensen, Knut Erik, 106
Jicinsky, Terry, 174
John Paul II, Pope, 13
Johnson, Lyndon B., 80
Jones, Jan Laverty, 7
Joyce, James, 16
Joyce, Jim, 7
J. W. Marriott, 17, 19

Karneval, 33, 35, 37, 40, 42, 43
Karnevalgruppe Las Vegas Piepen, 40
Kausar, Nur, 122
Kavanaugh's Irish Pub and Grill, 18
Kelley, Michael, 12
Kelly, Margaret, 16
Kenny, Kevin, 3
Kerkorian, Kirk, 82, 143
Khan, Khalid, 125, 126
Kim, Benjamin, 171
Kim, Frank, 169
Kim, Frank, Jr., 169, 171
Kim Produce Farm, 169
Kim Sisters, 169–70, 171
King, Peter, 117, 118
Kinzel, Gerhard, 35, 36
KLAV radio, 36, 37
Knecht Ruprecht aus dem Walde (the servant from the wood), 33, 34
Korean Air, 174
Korean American Center, 168
Korean-American Treaty of Amity and Commerce (1882), 166
Korean Central Daily, 172
Korean Family Counseling Center, 172
Koreans: community emerging in Las Vegas, 171–74; currently in Las Vegas, 174–76; emigration of, 165–66; immigration to Las Vegas, 169–71; immigration to U.S., 165–69, 177n7,

178nn12, 15, 16; Korean history and, 165, 166, 177n5; organizations of, 172; orphaned children adoption program, 166–67, 177n10; religious practice, 172, 180n42; restaurants, 173
Korean Salvation Army, 172
Korean Student Association, 174
Korean War (1950–53), 165, 166–67, 170
Korean Women's Association, 172, 173
Koreatown Plaza, 173, 175
Koreatowns, 168, 172, 173
Kuerten, Klaus, 44, 45

Lackinger, Hans, 43
Lady Luck, 16
La Hora Chapina, 220, 229n46
Lake Las Vegas, 15, 18
Lakes Lutheran Church, 137, 207
Lally's pub, 17
Lampe, Suzette, 32
Langen, Jeanne, 21
Lappoehn, Else, 42
LA Price Mediterranean Market, 140
Last Frontier, 10, 16
Las Vegas, Nevada-Arizona Metropolitan Statistical Area (MSA), xvii
Las Vegas Age, 2, 11, 30, 56, 60, 133, 134
Las Vegas Asian Chamber of Commerce, 171, 175
Las Vegas Blackjacks, 21
Las Vegas Club, 8, 9, 10, 80
Las Vegas Convention and Visitors Authority, 11, 174
Las Vegas Country Club, 67
Las Vegas Events, 11
Las Vegas German Show, 37
Las Vegas Hilton, 170
Las Vegas Hyes, 139
LasVegasKorea.com, 172
Las Vegas Korean American Women's Association (KAWA), 170
Las Vegas Korean Association, 172
Las Vegas Metropolitan Police Department, 15, 20, 21, 85, 169, 171
Las Vegas News, 186
Las Vegas Ranch, 1

Las Vegas Reformation Lutheran Church, 102
Las Vegas Review, 11, 59
Las Vegas Review-Journal (R-J), 12, 33, 62, 63, 85, 126, 142
Las Vegas Schützen Club, 40
Las Vegas Slots Women's Rugby Club, 21
Las Vegas Sun, 4, 5, 12, 85, 126, 142
Las Vegas Youth Camerata Orchestra, 156
Latin American Studies Association Convention, 88
Latin Chamber of Commerce of Nevada, 79–80, 83
Lauer, Heinz, 43
Laxalt, Paul, 6
Lebanese, 120
Lee, Hae Un, 170–71, 173
Lee's Discount Liquor Stores, 170
Lee's Helping Hands, 171
Leif Erikson Day, 105
Lenten Desert Experience, 14
Lewis Mumford Center, 155, 163n22
Liberace, 16, 103
Liloyan, Armen, 142
Lincy Foundation, 143
List of Excluded Persons ("Black Book"), 5
Logan, Don, 14–15
Lois and Jerry Tarkanian Middle School, 144
Los Angeles Times, 117
Loving v. Virginia, 168
Lujan-Hickey, Liliam, 80, 83, 89–90
Luxor Hotel and Casino, 11, 82
Lynch, Rosemary, 14

Mackett, Mary, 40
"The Magic Violins," 156
Mahan, Carmen, 234–36
Mahanikai (Great Society), 187
Mahayana Buddhism, 183
Maifest, 35, 37, 38, 39, 45
Main Street Station, 9
Mamacitas restaurant, 92
Mandalay Bay Hotel-Casino, 82
Manning, Elfriede, 39, 44
Mardirossian, Moushegh, 137

Mariam, Mengistu Haile, 204
Market Watch Leader, 169
Masjid As-Sabur mosque, 114, 117, 121, 127–28n2
Masjid Noor mosque, 122
Matzdorf, Frank, 31
Matzdorf, Martha, 31
Maurer, Peter, 31
Mayans, 214, 218, 224n6
McAfee, Guy, 10
McCann, Dave, 12
McCarran, Pat, 3–4, 5, 12; Japanese and, 66, 74n30
McCarran International Airport, 3, 9, 81, 172, 174
McCarran-Walter Act of 1952, 31
McCarthy, Charles, 2
McCarthy, John, 15
McDoniel, Estes, 15
McFadden, Leo, 2
McFadden's Irish Pub, 18–19
McGovern, Leona, 2
McGrail's of Erin pub, 18
McGuire, Phyllis, 16
McIlvaine, Red, 12
McIntosh, J. O., 2
McMullan, Brian, 19
McMullan's Irish Pub, 19, 20
McNally Design Group USA, 17, 19
McNamee, Frank, Jr., 6
McNamee, Leo, 6
McShane, John, 14, 21
McWilliams, John T., 2
The Meadows, 31
Mediterranean Café, 114
Menéndez, Agustín, 79
Mérida, Otto, 79, 80, 88, 94
Mexicans, 53, 167, 218; clubs for, xvi, xixn14; *vs.* Cubans, 78, 84, 90, 93; in Las Vegas, 217, 231; transnationalism and, xvi
MGM Grand (hotel and casino), 6, 16, 82, 143, 191, 235
MGM Mirage, 9, 11
Mike's Bakery, 140
Miller, Bob, 4
Mint casino, 9, 10

Mirage Corporation, 143
Mirage Hotel and Casino, 45
Miranda, M. L., 90
miscegenation laws, 55, 66, 168
Moapa Valley, 63, 65
Moehring, Eugene, 15
Molina, Otto Pérez, 222
Molly Malone's pub, 18
Montana, Tony, 85
Monte Carlo Resort and Casino, 81, 82, 221
Morizono, Joe, 67
Morizono, Lillian, 67
Moroccans, 118, 127
Moten, Akbar, 125
Mount Charleston Lodge, 36
Mowbray, John, 6
MR-13 (of Guatemala), 214
Muay Thai (kickboxing) Academy, 186
Muhammad, Elijah, 114, 116
Muhammad, W. D., 116–17, 128–29n13
Mulroy, Patricia, 44–45
"Muslim Family-Value Day," 126
Muslims: Afghanis, 118, 119; Arabs, 118, 120; Bangladeshis, 118, 119–20, 121–22, 124; currently in Las Vegas, 114–15, 116–27; Ethiopians, 118, 207; ethnicities and populations, 114–15, 117–18, 128n11; history of, in U.S. and Las Vegas, 115–17; Iranians, 118, 119, 123; languages, 123; organizations of, 120–23; Pakistanis, 118, 119; restaurants, 114–15; September 11, impact on, 124–26; Shias and Sunnis, 123. *See also* African Americans
Muslim Student Association, 116, 122, 127

Nagamatsu, Ikuguro "Fred," 63
Nakanishi, Sam, 67, 72n12
NASCAR, 9
National Alliance of Latin American and Caribbean Communities, 220
National Collegiate Athletic Association (NCAA), 143–44
National Finals Rodeo, 11
National Liberation Army (ELN) in Colombia, 232

National Origins Act of 1924, 54, 55, 166
Nation of Islam, 114, 116, 120, 122, 127
Native Americans, xii, 53, 54
naturalization, xiv–xv, 167, 223
Navasartian Games, 139
Naw Roz, 119
Near East Relief Society, 133–34
Nellis Air Force Base, 4, 64, 67, 68, 103, 169, 170, 185, 193
Nevada American Civil Liberties Union (ACLU), 83
Nevada Arts Council, 20
Nevada Ballet Theatre, 8
Nevada Development Authority, 2
Nevada Economic Development Commission, 102
Nevada Gaming Commission, 6
Nevada Governor's Arts Award, 156
Nevada Health Centers, Inc., 83
Nevada Power Company, 32
Nevada Public Radio, 17
Nevada Public Service Commission, 32
Nevada Resort Association (NRA), 7
Nevada State Welfare Department, 83
Nevada Test Site, 4, 14, 15, 67
New Frontier, 45
newspapers: for Koreans, 172; Norwegian and Swedish, 99, 112n45; Spanish-language, 234; for Thais, 186
Newton, Wayne, 16
New York New York, 11, 16, 18
Nielsen, Emil, 99
Nine Fine Irishmen pub, 18, 19
91 Club, 10
Nordisk Tidende, 99
North Las Vegas Airport, 15
Norwegians, 98–99, 104–7, 112n45
Notre Dame alumni club, 21
Nyang, Sulayman, 115

O'Callaghan, Mike, 4, 79
Oceguera, John, 6
Oiga, Mire, Vea restaurant, 231, 236, 237
Oktoberfest, 33, 34, 37, 38, 39, 45, 49n17
O'Loughlin, Roisin, 14
Omar Haykal Islamic Academy, 120, 122

Opera House, 10
Organization for Chinese Americans (OCA), 175
Origin India, 114
Orleans casino, 9, 18
Oromo Community Group of Las Vegas, 206
Oromo Ethiopians, 204, 206, 207, 209, 212n34
Oromo Evangelical Church, 207, 212n33
Oromo Liberation Front (OLF), 204
Osaka Restaurant, 67
O'Shea's, 17
Osterbaum (Easter tree), 33, 42
Overseas Korean Foundation (OKF), 165

Pace e Bene Nonviolence Service, 14
Paddy's Pub, 16, 18
Page, Paul, 21
Pakistani American Association, 119
Pakistanis, 118, 119
Palace Station, 17, 18
Pallesen, Frances, 106
Pamuk, Orhan, 142
Papadopoulos, I., 203
Paradise Valley, 56, 61
Park Place Entertainment, 11
Pelosi, Nancy, 141
Pepe, Joseph, 14
Pérez, Sergio, 87, 92
Persian Association, 119. *See also* Iranians
Persian Day, 119
Petrasek, Irmgard, 42
Phillips, Barbara, 35, 40, 43
Pioneer Club, 81
Pioneer in Northwest America, 1841–1858, A (Unonius), 100
Pius XI, Pope, 13
Planet Hollywood, 18
Poehls, Siri, 106
police. *See* Las Vegas Metropolitan Police Department
Police and Fire Emerald Society, 21
political participation: Armenians and, 141–42; of Cubans, 80, 91; of Guatemalans, 220, 221–22, 223; of Irish, 3–7; of Scandinavians, 102–3

Poole, Elijah. *See* Muhammad, Elijah
population, of Las Vegas. *See* Clark County population, 2000–2006; *under* U.S. Census Bureau *headings*
Pot O' Gold Casino, 17
Praml International, 43, 44
Praxl, Franz, 35, 49n19
Presbyterian Church, 172
Price, Nelle, 6
Primer Impacto, 234
prostitution, 2
pupfish, 5
Putzi, Heidi, 44
Putzi, Rudi, 44

Quinn's pub, 18
Quorum Club, 7

radio, 17; German-language, 36–37, 38, 42, 44; for Guatemalans, 220, 229n46; Swedish-language, 99
Rafael Rivera Community Center, 221
Railroad Pass Hotel, 81
Ramadan, 121, 122
Ramadan, Mujahid, 117
Reagan, Ronald, 16, 141, 214
Rebel Armed Forces (FAR) of Guatemala, 214
Red Rock Resort, 84
Reed Whipple Cultural Center, 87
refugee resettlement, xiii; Cuban Mariel boatlift immigrants, 77, 84–87; Ethiopians, 198–200, 202, 211nn10, 11, 20; Guatemalans in Mexico, 214, 215
Reid, Harry, 124, 136
religious practice: Armenians, 135, 136–38, 146n24; Cubans, 91–92; Ethiopians, 118, 206–7; Germans, 37; Guatemalans, 218, 228nn34–36; Irish, 13–14; Koreans, 172, 180n42; Scandinavians, 100, 104, 110nn5, 11. *See also* Buddhism; Muslims
restaurants, xiii, xvi; Argentine, 160–61; Armenian, 140–41; Colombian, 231, 236, 237; Cuban, 92; Ethiopian, 208, 212nn35–36; German, 34, 35, 36, 38–39, 42, 43–45, 50n40; Korean, 173;

Muslim, 114–15; Thai, 185–86. *See also* ethnic markets; Irish pubs
Restrepo, Humberto, 233
Revolutionary Armed Forces of Colombia (FARC), 232
Reynolds Electrical and Engineering Company, 15
Ricardo, Bernardo, 86, 87
Richardson, Bill, 80
Rico, Juliana, 231, 236
Rico, Lina, 231, 236
Ridge, Tom, 136
Rincón Criollo, 92
Rincón de Buenos Aires restaurant and market, 160–61
Rio Las Vegas, 18–19
Riviera Hotel and Casino, 4
Robert E. Taylor Elementary School, 107
Rodríguez, Nora, 80, 89, 91
Roman Catholic Diocese of Las Vegas, 14. *See also* Catholic Church
Roosevelt, Theodore, 54
Roschel, Richard, 32
Rothman, Hal, 79
Rotweiß Club, 37, 40
Ruckle, Art, 36
Rynning, Ole, 101

Sahara Hotel, 9, 67
Saifullah, Imam Fateen, 117
Sailon, David, 155–56
St. Andrew Lutheran Church, 41
St. Anne's Catholic Church, 13, 79, 91
St. Anne's Elementary School, 6
St. Cyr, Lili, 5
St. Joan of Arc church, 13
Saint Lucia Day, 106, 108–9
St. Michael Ethiopian Orthodox Tewahedo Church, 206
St. Nicholas, 33, 34, 38
St. Patrick's Day, 17, 18, 19, 20–21, 22
Sakai, Henry, 67
Sakai, Tom, 59, 61
Salvadorans, 231, 236
Salvation Army, 58, 172
Sam's Town, 9
Sanchez, Juanita, 169

Sands, 77
San Pedro, Los Angeles and Salt Lake Railroad, 55–56, 57, 59
San Remo Hotel and Resort, 70
Santa Claus, 33
Santería cult, 85
Sarkisian, Emma, 135–36
Sarkisian, Mariam, 136
Sarno, Jay, 79
Saroyan, William, 144–45
Saunders, Larry, 30
Sawada, Noriko, 66
Sawyer, Grant, 5, 6
Scandinavians: early U.S. settlers, 99–101, 110nn5, 7, 11, 12; immigrants to Las Vegas, 101, 102–3; Norwegians, 98–99, 104–7, 112n45; organizations of, 103–4, 111nn25–26; overview of, in Las Vegas, 98–99; religious practice, 100, 104, 110nn5, 11; Swedes, 99, 104, 107–9, 111n27, 112n45; Swedish women, 108–9, 112n48
Scarface (movie), 85, 86, 235
"scatterness," 168, 175, 179n25
Schleidt, Frank, 37
Schmidt, Sharon, 32
Schneider, Helga, 42
Scott, Edward W., 30
Sean Patrick's Irish Pub, 18
Seastrand, James, 102
Selassie, Haile, 204, 212n28
September 11, 2001, 124–26
Sharon Lynn Academy of Irish Dance, 17
Sheehan, Jack, 12
Shell, Alena, 83, 90
Shell, Liliam, 83, 91
Shia and Sunni Muslims, 123
Showboat, 8, 9
Siefert, Tona Cashman, 2
Siegfried and Roy, 43, 45–46, 88
Silver Nugget, 10
Sin City Irish Rugby Club, 21
Sirindhorn, Princess Maha Chakri, 192
Sister Cities International, 174
Skinny Dugan's pub, 18, 20
Skyline Casino, 36
Smalley, James, 15
Smith, John L., 12
Smith, Joseph S., 32
Sobenaris, Armando, 221
soccer, 17, 159–60
Soka Gakkai Buddhists, 68
Somalis, 118, 120
Somchai, Than Maha, 193
Sommer, Sigrid, 33, 39, 44, 45
Songkan, Than Maha, 187–88, 196n29
Sons of Erin, 20, 21
Sons of Norway, 99, 104–7, 112n31, 34, 35, 38
Southern Nevada Japanese Teachers Association, 70
South Point casino, 9
sports: basketball, 14, 137, 143–44; boxing, 14, 83, 117, 121, 186; Irish and, 14–15, 17, 21; soccer, 17, 159–60
Squires, Charles P., 2, 56, 60
ss *Gaelic*, 166
Stanley, Christine, 36
Stanton, Olaf, 103
Starbucks, 208
Stardust Hotel, 9, 16, 36, 77, 80, 88, 169, 170
Stillpoint Spiritual Development Center, 14
Stone, Winifred "Winnie," 42
Strip, the: Armenians and, 143; Cubans and, 76, 77, 79, 80, 81–82, 86, 87–88; development, 1940s and '50s, 7–8; Irish and, 2, 11, 13, 16, 17, 18–19; Korean entertainers, 169–70; Moroccan entertainers, 118, 127
Sullivan, Ed, 169
Suncoast casino, 9
Sunset "Strip," 10
Supermercado del Pueblo, 218
Suzuki, Caryl, 69
Swain, Jonathan, 17
Swedes, 99, 104, 107–9, 111n27, 112nn45, 48
Swedish Women's Education Association (SWEA), 108–9, 112n48
Swiss Cafe, 45
Syburra, Helene, 42

"System of a Down" rock-music group, 138
Syttende Mai, 105, 112n37

Tafete, Tilahun, 205
Taha, Muhammad, 116
Tanaka, Wayne, 67, 70
Tarkanian, Danny, 138, 144
Tarkanian, Jerry, 14, 143, 143–44
Tarkanian, Lois, 138, 144
Tarkanian Basketball Academy, 137, 144
Teal, Evelyn, 101
Telemundo, 234
television: Channel 8, 12; for Hispanics, 234; Public Broadcasting Service, 68
Temporary Protected Status (TPS) for Colombians, 233, 236
Thai Cultural Art Association, 186
Thai Isan, 184, 185
Thailand Day, 187
Thais: gaming industry and, 186, 193–94; immigration to Las Vegas, 185–87; immigration to U.S., 183, 184–87; Lao ethnicity, 184, 185; restaurants, 185–86; schools within temples, 192; women, 189–92, 197n32. *See also* Buddhism
Thai Student Association, 187
Thammayut, 187
Theravada Buddhism: reterritorialization of, in Las Vegas, 183, 195n6; Thai Temples in Las Vegas for, 183, 187–94, 195nn4, 7
Three Angry Wives pub, 18
Thunderbird Hotel, 169
Tibetan Buddhism, 183
Tigrai Community Association of Las Vegas (TCA), 205, 206, 209
Tigrai Development Association (TDA) for North America, 201
Tigrayan Ethiopians, 201, 202, 204, 205, 206, 208, 209
Tigrayan People's Liberation Front (TPLF), 204
Titus, Dina, 7, 208
Tobin, Alan, 85
Tomiyasu, Nanyu, 61, 63, 67, 68
Tomiyasu, Yonema "Bill," 61–62

tourists: Japanese, 69–70; Muslims, 114–15
Trans International Airlines, 143
transnationalism, xv–xvii; Chileans and, xvi–xvii; Guatemalans and, 220–21; Koreans and, 166, 174, 176; Mexicans and, xvi; Scandinavians and, 98, 99; Thais and, 194
Trinity United Methodist Church, 102
Triple X Fraternity, 138, 139, 147n40
Tropicana Hotel, 8, 102
True Account of America for the Information and Help of Peasant and Commoner, A (Rynning), 101
Turkey, 132, 136, 141, 142, 147n44
Tyson, Mike, 117, 121

Underhill, Clarence, 32
Union Pacific Railroad, 6, 61; strike, 1922, 59–60
Union Plaza, 8, 9, 35, 40
United Fruit Company, 214
United Oromo Evangelical Churches, 207
United Service Organizations (USO), 13
U.S. Census Bureau, Las Vegas population:
—before 2000, xiii; Guatemalans, 216; Japanese, 57, 72n10; Koreans, 171; Scandinavians, 101; Thais, 186
—2000–2006, xii–xiii, xvii–xviii, 84, 175–76; American Community Survey, 2006, xvii–xviii; Argentines, 154, 155; Armenians, 134; Chinese, 69; Colombians, 231, 233; Cubans, 76, 90; Ethiopians, 118, 200; Filipinos, 69; Germans, 33, 51n44; Guatemalans, 216, 217, 226n21, 228n39; Irish, 1; Japanese, 69; Koreans, 171, 176; Muslims, 117–18; Scandinavians, 101; Thais, 186
U.S. Census Bureau, U.S. population:
—before 2000: Argentines, 153; Thais, 185
—2000–2006: Argentines, 153, 163n22; Colombians, 232; Ethiopians, 199; Guatemalans, 215–16, 227n26; Koreans, 168, 178n17, 179n26; Thais, 183, 185, 195n2
University of California, Berkeley, 184

University of Nevada, Las Vegas (UNLV), 90, 238; Armenians and, 138, 140, 142, 143–44; basketball, 14, 143–44; Beam Music Center, 102; Boyd School of Law, 10, 83; Foreign Language Department, 44; German clubs, 39, 41, 44; Irish and, 2–3, 4, 5, 9, 10, 11, 12, 14, 15–17, 20; Japanese students, 70; Korean students, 173–74; KUNV radio, 36; Muslims and, 118, 121, 122, 127; Newman Club, 2–3; ROTC program, 81; Sam Boyd Stadium, 10, 11; Scandinavians and, 102, 103; Thais and, 187; Thomas and Mack Center, 81, 144; William F. Harrah College of Hotel Administration, 174
Univisión, 234
Unonius, Gustaf, 100
Uruguayans, 158

Vagabonds Club, 35, 40, 43
Valhalla Lodge, 107–8
Vasa Order of America, 104, 107–8, 112nn42, 44
Vasa Star, 107
Vegas Pita, 140
Vegas Viking News, The, 105, 112n34
Vegas Viking Lodge, 104, 105–6
Vela, Dara, 36
Venetian Hotel and Casino, 16
Vigoa, José, 86
Viking, The, 104, 112n38
Vikings, 98, 99
Villanueva, Daniel C., 39, 50n29
Von Tobel, Edward, Sr., 30, 31–32
von Weiser, Wolfgang, 43
Voting Rights Act of 1965, 168

Walsh, Daniel, 13–14
War Brides Act of 1946, 166
Ward, Eugene, 62, 63
Wat Thamma temple, 187, 188, 193
Weihnachtsmann, Der (Father Christmas), 33, 42
Welch, Coleman "Coley," 14
Welch, John, 14
Wengert, Cyril S., 32
Wengert, Ella, 32
Wengert, Frank, 32
Wescher, Charles A., 32
Western Diocese Armenian Apostolic Church, 137
Western Prelacy Armenian Apostolic Church of Las Vegas, 137
Westlake, Winnie, 31, 47n7
Westside neighborhood, 2, 116, 120
The White House, 31
Whole Foods, 237
Wilshire State Bank, 173
Winterwood Ranch, 56
women: Cubans, 86–87; Guatemalans, 218–19, 228–29n40, 229n41; Irish, 21; Koreans, 170, 172, 173; Swedes, 108–9, 112n48; Thais, 189–92, 197n32
World Bank, 217, 227n26
World Cup soccer, 17, 159–60
World Series of Poker, 10
World War I, 30, 31, 33, 40, 132, 133, 142
World War II, 30, 165, 169; Japanese Americans and, 52, 62–65, 66, 73n22
Wynn, Steve, 10, 143

Yamashita, Jimmy, 62, 63
Yonema "Bill" Tomiyasu Elementary School, 67
Yu, Eui-Young, 168, 175
Yu, James Moon Jae, 171, 173
Yuh, Ji-Yeon, 170